Wellington's legacy
THE REFORM OF THE BRITISH ARMY
1830-54

For Emily and Olivia

Wellington's legacy
THE REFORM OF THE BRITISH ARMY
1830-54

HEW STRACHAN

MANCHESTER
UNIVERSITY PRESS

Copyright © Hew Francis Anthony Strachan 1984

Published by
Manchester University Press
Oxford Road, Manchester M13 9PL, U.K.
51 Washington Street, Dover, N.H. 03820, U.S.A.

British Library cataloguing in publication data
Strachan, Hew
  Wellington's legacy.
  1. Great Britain, *Army*—History
  I. Title
  355'.00941   UA649

ISBN 0-7190-0994-4

Library of Congress cataloguing in publication data
Strachan, Hew.
  Wellington's legacy.
  Bibliography: p. 272
  Includes index.
  1. Great Britain. Army—Organization—History.
2. Wellington, Arthur Wellesley, Duke of, 1769-1852.
I. Title.
UA649.S84   1984   355.3'0941   84-733

ISBN 0-7190-0994-4

UA
649
.S84
1984

Typeset by Graphicraft Typesetters Limited.
Printed in Great Britain
by Butler & Tanner Ltd, Frome and London

CANISIUS COLLEGE LIBRARY
BUFFALO, N.Y.

CONTENTS

	Preface	vii
	Introduction	1
1	The identity of the reformers	6
2	The soldier's life	50
	1 Recruits and recruiting	51
	2 Life in service	57
	3 The 1847 limited enlistment act	70
3	The soldiers: punishment, education and reward	79
	1 Punishment	79
	2 Godliness and good learning	85
	3 Rewards	97
4	The rising professionalism of the officers	109
	1 Appointment and promotion	109
	2 Education	121
5	The staff and training for the field	146
6	Matching manpower to commitments	180
	1 Imperial defence	180
	2 Home defence	196
	3 Regimental organisation	211
	4 The Crimea	220
7	The administration of the army	229
	1 The system	229
	2 Its reform	246
	Conclusion	267
	Bibliography	272
	Index	290

Manchester University Press would like to thank the Managers of the Political Science Fund, Faculty of History, University of Cambridge, and the Master and Fellows of Corpus Christi College, Cambridge, for generous grants towards the publication of this book.

PREFACE

This book is about the reform of the British army before the Crimean war. It concentrates on its organisation and structure rather than on its tactics and fighting methods. Although this second theme is no less important than the first, considerations of space have excluded it.

A note on sources is required. The military press and pamphlet literature have been of disproportionate value. This is not simply the result of their own intrinsic (and considerable) contribution to reform. It is also because the official papers of the Commander-in-Chief's department, the Horse Guards, are inadequate. The main collection, the Adjutant General's out-letters in the Public Record Office (W.O. 3), are terse and unenlightening. The correspondence of the two other military departments, the Military Secretary's and the Quarter Master General's, are even less illuminating. Both Hardinge, as Commander-in-Chief, and Sir George Brown, as Adjutant General, referred to a semi-official series of correspondence, of which no trace, except possibly a few fragments in W.O. 30, now survives. The submissions made to departments and the memoranda passed betwen them are not to be found in the Public Record Office, nor do they appear in the private papers of the officers concerned. Although Commander-in-Chief for fourteen years, Lord Hill's papers contain almost nothing appertaining to that period; Hardinge's only have a few stray items apart from his letters to Prince Albert, which he tells us he kept separately; Wellington's are fuller, but principally in relation to his political life, and military matters are discussed where the two intertwine. Of the subordinate Horse Guards officers, the archives of Sir Willoughby Gordon and Lord Fitzroy Somerset are thin. Sir George Brown, the Adjutant General, stands out as a beacon in all this gloom: his full private correspondence with army officers, now in the National Library of Scotland, provides the best insight into the military administration that has survived.

The Royal Archives go far to make up the deficiencies of the official papers. I must therefore acknowledge the gracious permission of Her Majesty the Queen to quote from them. Miss V. J. Langton at Windsor proved an admirable guide to their contents. Others owners of private papers to whom I am indebted, not only for allowing me to consult the documents but also in many cases for extraordinarily generous hospitality, include Major-General the Earl Cathcart, Dr A. E. Clark-Kennedy, R. E. Howard-Vyse Esq., J. E. Colborne Mackrell Esq., the Earl of Pembroke and Lord Raglan. I must thank the Earl of Clarendon and Lord Dalhousie for permission to quote from their family papers, now deposited in public collections. The Duke of Wellington allowed me to see the first Duke's papers while they were at the Royal Commission on Historical Manuscripts, and I am grateful to John Brooke and Julia Melvin for their guidance in handling them.

The staffs of the following archives and libraries all assisted in various important ways: the Bodleian Library, Oxford; the British Library; the Department of Palaeography and Diplomatic, Durham University; Hereford County Record Office; the India Office Library; McGill University Library; the Ministry of Defence Whitehall Library; the National Army Museum; the National Library of Scotland; Nottingham University Library; the Public Record Office; the Royal Engineers Museum, Chatham; the Scottish Record Office; the Scottish United Services Museum; the East Yorkshire County Record Office. In many cases I am grateful for permission to quote from papers in their care.

Professor Derek Beales, Brian Bond, Dr. Bruce Coleman, Dr. Johann de Villiers, and Professor Michael Howard all advised on specific points. Catherine Kennett and Margaret Blackburn typed many preliminary drafts. I beg forgiveness from all those others whose aid I have enlisted but failed to acknowledge (and think in particular of the prolonged but abortive search for the papers of Lord Frederick Fitzclarence).

Most of my research has been centred in Cambridge. My debt here is fourfold. The holdings of the University Library are only rivalled by its efficiency. My own college, Corpus Christi, elected me a Research Fellow, and thus granted me the leisure to continue my work. My colleagues in Dr. G. Kitson-Clark's and Dr. Henry Pelling's seminar kept the research in its wider perspective: I think especially of Dermot Gleeson on the political context and Dr. Iain Hamilton on the naval. Finally my greatest debt of all is to Clive Trebilcock: whatever rigour and objectivity this book may have is in large measure his.

H.S.

ABBREVIATIONS USED IN THE NOTES

B.M.	British Museum
C.R.O.	County Record Office
N.A.M.	National Army Museum
N. & M.G.	*Naval and Military Gazette*
N.L.S.	National Library of Scotland
P.P.	Parliamentary Papers
P.R.O.	Public Record Office
R.A.	Royal Archives
S.R.O.	Scottish Record Office
U.S.G.	*United Service Gazette*
U.S.J.	*United Service Journal*
U.S.M.	*United Service Magazine*
W.O.	War Office records in the Public Record Office

The humbug of the present day is to scout anything that contemplates a state of war — but what is the use of keeping any force at all either naval or military in time of peace if it is not in a state to be efficient when suddenly called upon to act in case of war or rebellion? — Colonel the Hon. George Cathcart (later Lieutenant-General Sir George Cathcart, successively Governor at the Cape, Adjutant General and commander of the 4th Division in the Crimea; killed at Inkerman) to his brother, Lieutenant-General the Earl Cathcart, 12 February 1851.

INTRODUCTION
VIEWS OF THE CRIMEAN ARMY

The ease with which the Crimean war can be taken as an historian's dividing line has obscured the military activities of the previous twenty years. It stood on 'a watershed between old fashioned methods ... and modern twentieth century warfare';[1] it was a campaign fought with railways and rifles, telegraphs and trenches, by generals who had been brought up to the eighteenth-century tactical precepts of Wellington and the Peninsula. Thus in the British case, developments in the art of war and in military institutions do not constitute some indeterminate evolutionary process but have a stark landmark in the harsh facts of the winter of 1854-55. The emergence of the Victorian army of Cardwell and Wolseley has therefore been viewed as a post-Crimean phenomenon rather than as a continuous process dating from the 1830s and '40s.

The image is an easy one. A long post-Waterloo sleep ends in a rough awakening in the Crimea and a round of reforms follows. Despite aspersions on her scholarship, the influence of Cecil Woodham-Smith's *The Reason Why* on modern historians has been profound. After a study centring on three characters who took part in one charge in one battle in the war, she comes to the sweeping conclusion that 'Army welfare and Army education, Army recreation, sports and physical training, the health services, all came into being as a result of the Crimea'.[2] Asa Briggs refers to Woodham-Smith and finds 'the army machine was creaking and inefficient'.[3] The latest historian of the British army writes of it in the Crimean war as 'simply the Peninsular Army brought out of its cupboard and dusted down'.[4] And the work of more recent scholars, such as Gwyn Harries-Jenkins and Edward M. Spiers, has not revised these conclusions.

The degree to which the picture of inefficiency and torpor has been accepted might have surprised two distinguished but now unfashionable military historians, Sir John Fortescue[5] and C. T. Atkinson[6], both of whom were careful not to damn the army of the 'Long Peace'. Even more would they have astonished the British public of 1854, as it exuberantly waved farewell to the expeditionary force.

However, the popular confidence in the fitness of the army on its departure for the Crimea was itself a cause of the Crimea assuming an exaggerated place in the history of army reform. For in assuaging the public's desire for news, *The Times's* correspondent, W. H. Russell, was not merely reporting facts but also creating opinion. It was he who fired the outcry on matters of transport, medicine and supply, and did so as a conscious attack on the existing state of the army. Even more do such comments apply to Delane, the editor of *The Times*. He called for the invasion of the Crimea in June 1854, vilifying the reluctant generals as grumblers. Six months later, when the soldiers' doubts were being realised, he wrote to Russell, 'I have at last opened fire on Lord Raglan and the General Staff. According to all accounts, their incapacity has been most gross ... Leave such comment as may be dangerous to us who are out of danger.'[7] As Russell's biographer has justly observed, war correspondents become war correspondents 'because they are, or are thought to be, competent journalists, not necessarily because they understand war'.[8]

It is in this context that Russell's accounts must be treated as evidence. Dr. Andrew Smith, the Director General of the Army Medical Department, referred to a press report that 1,500 wounded were put on board the ship *Kangaroo* for transport to Scutari, with no medical officers in attendance and that in consequence hundreds died. In fact, 450 were on board, accompanied by three doctors, and twenty-two died on the voyage.[9] Even Florence Nightingale complained that the reports of conditions at Scutari were exaggerated.[10] C. E. Kennaway, in a lecture delivered in 1856, cited a report on the lack of drunkenness among the troops that was published in the second edition of *The Times* of 6 December 1854, but which was withdrawn from the copy for the 7th as an article associating drunkenness and recruiting was scheduled for publication.[11] Herein is full justification for the conclusion, albeit in a different context, of the Marquess of Dalhousie, the Governor General of India, on *The Times* at this period: 'Did you ever know a clap of thunder correct itself? Did you ever know the inky thunderer unsay what it had said? Correct a calumny? Make amends for a wrong? or, in short, do anything fair, or just or manly.'[12]

The views of soldiers themselves were as forthright. The Hon. Charles Addington, of the 38th Foot, writing in February 1855, when the winter was still at its fiercest, agreed with his father 'that the "Times" paper has written most scandalous and groundless articles about Lord Raglan ... I assure you, and I speak advisedly, that everybody here is furious at seeing the infamous lies circulated by the columns of that news-paper.'[13] The complaints of Nigel Kingscote, Raglan's A.D.C., do not therefore seem as biased as might at first appear. Also writing in February 1855, he exclaimed, 'Did you ever see such villainous articles and letters as that abominable Times publishes the latter I really think are often concocted in London.'[14]

Nonetheless, almost uniquely, historians of the Crimean war have looked less to official and semi-official dispatches and correspondence than to *The Times* and to the evidence accumulated by the select committee on the army before Sebastopol. The call for an enquiry, which had brought down the Aberdeen government, was moved by the radical, J. A. Roebuck, and the committee itself therefore engineered a confrontation where all the ill-feeling between the Cobdenites and the military, generated by twenty years of governmental parsimony, could explode. The witnesses were heard from 5 March to 15 May 1855 and thus few who had actually fought in the Crimea could be interviewed. At the start of the second report we find the evidence of George Dundas, M.P., who visited the Crimea from 15 to 29 December 1854, and later there appeared John C. Macdonald, who was in the Crimea for one week (1-9 February 1855). Civilians completely uninitiated in the horrors of war descended on Scutari for a few weeks and then returned with a catalogue of woes — the Hon. and Rev. S. G. Osborne, the Hon. J. W. Percy, M.P., and A. H. Layard, M.P. The less eloquent soldiers were thrown on the defensive by Roebuck and Layard, whom Hardinge, the Commander-in-Chief, found 'very vindictive'.[15] As one M.P., Henry Drummond, at least realised, 'idle civilians, ignorant of the realities of war, which, under the most favourable circumstances are horrid to witness, painted with colours more vivid than accurate, all they saw, as if human suffering was peculiar to this campaign, or could be effectively prevented by any care or foresight whatever'.[16]

The finally accepted report did indeed preface its observations by remarking that the evidence disagreed, that many important witnesses had not been seen and that the fulness of the investigation had been checked by state policy. It is notable that the commissioners should eventually have reached such moderate and fair conclusions. Raglan himself was exonerated in the light of his own reluctance to make the attack on Sebastopol central to his strategy, and the Aberdeen administration blamed for undertaking a European war with a peacetime establishment.[17]

The evidence taken before the McNeill and Tulloch commission on supplies in the Crimea was of an equally tenuous sort. No shorthand writer accompanied the commissioners on their visit to the east, and therefore the statements made to them were much condensed, in cases what was said was apparently altered and explanations for certain lines of conduct were removed.[18] The deficiencies of the evidence thus presented to the public were pointed out both in the final reports, and also by the so-called 'White-washing' Board of General Officers in 1856, but these clarifications appeared after the heat of debate on the war had died down.

It was consequent upon this decline in popular interest in military matters that soldiers themselves began to attack the Crimean army. As Brian Bond has pointed out, even on a question canvassed as widely as the competence of staff officers, interest ebbed immediately after 1855-6.[19] If soldiers were to ensure the continuance of government and public support for army reform, that had been so hard won on the uplands before Sebastopol, then they would have to stress the low quality of the army in order to frighten the politicians into continued action. Thus Sir Evelyn Wood, who had served in the Crimea, wrote as late as 1894, 'We must not shut our eyes to the moral of such grim lessons. A great country should not tolerate the possibility of a recurrence in a campaign, of such failures as those which discredited Representative Government for some months in 1854-5. Far above all Party questions should be the efficiency of our Forces.'[20] General Sir Edward Hamley, who as a young officer, in an endeavour to offset the influence of *The Times* and to defend the army, had written articles from the Crimea for *Blackwood's Magazine*, was more gloomy: 'Upon the return of the Army [from the east], the reduction of its establishments was effected in the usual reckless fashion. We soon reverted to our customary condition of military inefficiency.'[21]

In addition to the selfless motive of keeping alive in the country a concern for defence policy, the writings of these Crimean veterans, and particularly of the Wolseley ring, were aimed to show up in higher relief their own subsequent achievements. Wolseley's *Story of a Soldier's Life*, written with the benefit of hindsight, is most scathing about the Crimean army. He used to compare the Crimean and Abyssinian campaigns with his own much smaller and simpler Red River expedition in order to increase his military influence.[22]

Thus a smokescreen was — partly deliberately — thrown across the true state of the army at the start of 1854. It makes the claim of the *United Service Magazine*, reviewing Chobham camp in 1853, appear mere bombast. 'How is it,' it had asked, 'that after forty years of peace, the organization of our troops should be so much more perfect than it was after some twenty years of constant warfare? Most soldiers degenerate — ours have improved in every way.'[23]

Yet these were the words of a journal whose *raison d'être* of the previous decade had been an assault on the existing military system with a view to army reform. At much the same time, Colonel W. G. Cochrane wrote to the Adjutant General from Dublin, 'Our Army is nearly as perfect as it need be'.[24]

This book is an attempt to explain the reasons for Colonel Cochrane's complacency.

Notes

1. R. L. V. Ffrench Blake, *The Crimean war*, London, 1971, p. 145.
2. Cecil Woodham-Smith, *The reason why*, p. 274.
3. Asa Briggs, *The age of improvement*, London, 1959, p. 382.
4. Correlli Barnett, *Britain and her army*, p. 290.
5. John Fortescue, *History of the British army*, XIII, pp. 345, 309, 525.
6. C. T. Atkinson, *Regimental History, the Royal Hampshire Regiment*, I, p. 174.
7. J. B. Atkins, *Life of Sir William Howard Russell*, I, p. 186.
8. Ibid., I, p. 89.
9. P.P. 1854-5, IX, part I, pp. 424-5.
10. P.P. 1854-5, IX, part III, *4th report*, pp. 172-80.
11. C. E. Kennaway, *The war and the newspapers*, pp. 54, 74.
12. Letter of 30 March 1854, in J. G. A. Baird (ed.), *Private letters of the Marquess of Dalhousie*, p. 293.
13. *Journal of the Society for Army Historical Research*, XLVI, 1968, p. 170.
14. Raglan private papers, box 7, no. 232, Kingscote to Lord Richard Somerset, 6 February 1855.
15. Hereford C.R.O., G/IV/A/429, Hardinge to Airey, 11 May 1855. For Layard's attitude, see especially P.P. 1854-5, IX, part III, *5th report*, pp. 54-5.
16. P.P. 1854-5, IX, part III, *5th report*, p. 88.
17. Ibid., pp. 4-6, 88.
18. P.P. 1856, XXI, pp. 101, 220, 267.
19. Brian Bond, *The Victorian Army and the Staff College 1854-1914*, p. 82.
20. Evelyn Wood, *The Crimea in 1854, and 1894*, p. viii.
21. Edward Hamley, *The war in the Crimea*, p. 303.
22. Adrian Preston (ed.), *The South African diaries of Sir Garnet Wolseley 1875*, pp. 22, 49.
23. *U.S.M.*, 1853, II, p. 500
24. N.L.S. mss 1848, f. 121, Cochrane to Brown, 8 October 1853.

CHAPTER 1
THE IDENTITY OF THE REFORMERS

The accusation particularly levelled in 1855 and subsequently was that the army had rested unchanged on its Peninsular laurels. A member of Roebuck's committee said in exasperation, 'I cannot find out that any new invention has been taken up. You always refer to the Peninsular war — we have never got nearer to the present time than that war.'[1] However, the way in which William Napier's *History of the War in the Peninsula* had caught the popular and the military imagination was — for Britain at least — quite without precedent. It was perfectly natural that the state of the army in 1814-15 should be the main point of comparison: the army's victories had represented a peak of British military efficiency and it had been engaged in no subsequent European conflict.

The jibe that the Peninsular influence was dominant from 1815 was reinforced by the succession of Commanders-in-Chief after the Duke of York's death in 1827. Wellington's tenures of command, in 1827-8 and 1842-52, were sandwiched around that of one of his most distinguished divisional commanders, Lord Hill. But Hill found it as difficult to throw off his habits of subordination as Wellington did those of command. Although the Duke's stated rule was only to give his opinion when it was asked,[2] Hill's political naivety meant that this was frequent. In the Horse Guards' clash with the War Office over army administration, Hill pathetically requested instructions as to what 'he as Comr in Chief might properly say in answer'.[3] Even in matters of discipline, Hill would request and follow Wellington's suggestions. Moreover, the fault was not all on one side: the Duke's recommendations were so specific that, although Hill was of course at liberty to ignore them, he was unlikely to do so. Therefore little sympathy can be accorded Wellington when he wrote in 1833: 'Do what I will I cannot keep clear of Lord Hill's Affairs ... Nobody will believe that I do not command.'[4]

The recipient of these words was Lord Fitzroy Somerset, whom Hill had inherited from Wellington as his Military Secretary. If the

Commander-in-Chief tried not to consult the Duke, he found himself relying instead on the great man's amanuensis. Hill had refused the post of Master General of the Ordnance in 1827 on the plea of ill health, and consequently his long periods of absence for convalesence after he took on an equally onerous appointment were not surprising. The burden fell on Somerset's shoulders, and he in many cases either took Hill's decisions for him, even composing his letters, or naturally consulted the Duke. The situation, although not commented on by outside observers, seems to have been delicate within the Horse Guards itself. In 1835 General de Lacy Evans, commanding the British troops in Spanish service, issued a general order that implied a slur on the British army. Wellington advised that the Horse Guards comment publicly in answer, and Somerset was at some pains to urge Hill himself to mention this to Sir John Macdonald, the Adjutant General, to avoid the appearance of the opinion having originated with Wellington.[5]

Hill's real troubles, however, came from a totally different quarter. The Whigs felt that the powerful patronage at the disposal of the Commander-in-Chief was being used in the Conservative interest. Therefore, in 1835, with Joseph Hume at its head, the radical wing of the government's supporters demanded that the Commander-in-Chief should be politically attached to the administration, and pointed, rather dubiously, to the example of Marlborough's removal for political reasons. Thereafter, for the remainder of his command, rumours of Hill's replacement by the Whigs abounded and were given credibility by Hill's own state of health. In 1837 Hume renewed his attack, and Roebuck, more bluntly, said, 'The army has been made a mere appanage to a family hostile to the popular cause.'[6] A peg was provided on which to hang this radical bombast by the recall of the future Lord Cardigan to full pay as commanding officer of the 11th Hussars: Hume actually called for Hill's resignation.

Much of the problem lay in the undefined nature of the Commander-in-Chief's powers, especially in the realm of military reform. He had the right of access to the King and he took the royal pleasure on matters ranging from the army's establishment to its dress and equipment. As the King's officer he was independent of the administration: instead he was seen as an intact example of the operation of the royal prerogative. This point was reinforced by the special association of the royal family with the army, particularly in the persons of the Dukes of York and Cambridge.

The history of the office, however, was a short one, and for much of the eighteenth century the army had survived without any Commander-in-Chief at all. Thus the antics of the Duke of Wellington in 1827-8 had done it much harm, and had in particular, despite the theoretical denials of the constitutionalists, politicised it. Briefly, Wellington had accepted the job in January 1827 and then resigned because he had been rebuked by Canning. He denied that this was a political move but in August reaccepted the office on the King's repeated insistence. In the New Year he again resigned, as it was clear that he would have to head the government, but he had wished to retain the command of the army at the same time as being Prime Minister.

This trend was in part checked by Hill's refusal to rise to the tauntings of the radicals. Wellington's return as Commander-in-Chief in 1842 was, however, a cruel blow to the army's supra-political pose. Peel was most anxious not only for the Duke to head the army but also to retain his services in the cabinet.[7] At first Wellington very properly refused to associate with the government, on the grounds that the Commander must be impartial, as the Duke of York and Lord Hill had been.[8] Unfortunately his objections were too easily overcome. In July 1843 it was noted in the House of Commons that, although Wellington claimed his position was apolitical, he attended cabinet meetings and spoke on government policy in the Lords. Peel, in reply, tried to claim that Wellington's status as an individual placed him above politics, but affirmed that he had 'great control over the administration of public affairs' and that he was 'a Minister of State'.[9] Certainly Peel thought Wellington might have to resign when Lord John Russell formed a Whig government in 1846.[10] However, in the event Wellington was retained and promised not to express himself on political subjects in the Lords.[11]

His equivocal conduct had done irreparable damage to the position of the serving soldier *vis-à-vis* that of the civilian politician in the administration of the army. The attempt by soldiers to control their own destinies, even on the apparently professional subjects of discipline, promotion and training, was a rearguard action throughout the nineteenth century. By involving himself in politics, Wellington brought the army more under parliamentary control. Sir John Macdonald, the Adjutant General, had expressed the soldier's fears of the consequences of such a political Commander-in-Chief. In a memorandum of 1839, in which he argued that promotion should be taken out of the latter's hands for fear of it being granted for political, not military merit, he thundered, 'The Lord defend me from a Treasury Field Marshal recommended by a servile Commander in Chief.'[12]

Macdonald failed to observe that a large part of the military forces of Great Britain already lay outside the Horse Guards' control. Quite apart from the Royal Artillery and Royal Engineers, who were answerable to the Master General of the Ordance, a vast semi-military force of yeomanry and militia was controlled by the Home Secretary, with the Commander-in-Chief merely providing inspecting officers. In addition, the entire disposition of the regular troops in Britain, their movements, and even the issue of arms to them, had to be approved by the Home Secretary.

In all other military matters, the Secretary of State for War and the Colonies was nominally supreme. It was he who approved the annual establishment of the army before the Commander-in-Chief submitted it to the monarch. Each year in the late 1840s Wellington complained of the deficiency of manpower but to no avail. Furthermore, just as the Home Secretary approved the troops' distribution in Britain, so the Colonial Secretary vetted that for the colonies. As Hill rather feebly wrote to Stanley in 1841 on the subject of colonial reliefs: 'My official position does not entitle me to be informed of, and to offer any opinion upon the reasons which may justly require this proportion of troops in our several foreign possessions.'[13]

The same powers deprived the Commander-in-Chief of everything relative to the administration and employment of colonial troops except responsibility for the details of their internal management. In 1851, when asked for his views on the strategy that should be adopted at the Cape in dealing with the Kaffirs, Wellington wrote to the Secretary of State, Lord Grey, that 'I have never had any information of the Causes of the War in the Cape Colonies, of the objects of the Government in carrying it on, or the Views of the Government in relation to a frontier at its termination'.[14]

The employment of British regiments in the colonies was a matter decided between the Secretary of State and the governor of the colony. This officer, though normally a soldier, was appointed not at the instigation of the Horse Guards, but at that of the Secretary of State. It was Grey's decision to recall Sir Harry Smith from the Cape, despite Wellington's defence of him, and it was Grey who interviewed and appointed Sir George Cathcart in Smith's stead.[15] In the event the choice was a happy one, but Grey confided to his brother, 'I know nothing of the character of our General Officers myself & unhappily I cannot rely on the advice I should get at the Horse Guards.'[16]

Grey, however, was an exceptional Secretary of State in his attempts to integrate colonial and military policy. Until the division of the two fields between separate cabinet appointments in 1854, the true extent of his ministerial powers over the appointments in the army and the dictation of strategy were not fully realised. Frequently the Secretary of State was too closely involved in purely colonial or cabinet matters to give the army more than perfunctory attention. Lord Glenelg, who held the office from 1835 to 1839, did not even bother to write to one of his colonial governors on the matter of troop movements in 1838.[17] Even the normally diffident and discreet Somerset was prompted to describe him 'as weak as water'.[18]

This ineffectiveness increased the responsibility of the Secretary at War, who during Glenelg's tenure of office was Lord Howick, the future third Earl Grey referred to above, and the son of the Whig Prime Minister. His duties were officially confined to the preparation of the army estimates, the administration of army finance, the answering of questions in Parliament on military matters, and the drawing up of the Mutiny Bill and the Articles of War. In many hands, the work was repetitive and dull, especially as it rarely carried with it cabinet responsibility. Howick's wife wrote that her husband, soon after entering the War Office, was 'a good deal disquieted with the business in his office — He says it is all details & of the most disagreeable nature — refusing pensions ... & signing ones name thousands of times.'[19]

Financial control, however, gave the Secretary at War considerable leeway in the interpretation of his duties. As it was, he had under his aegis (in part) the Army Medical Department and (after their organisation in 1843) the Enrolled Pensioners, the latter even to the extent of receiving inspection reports on their military efficiency. In 1832 Sir J. C. Hobhouse asserted his right to appoint Commissioners to the Royal Military Asylum and the Royal Military College, Sandhurst, although Hill, as he himself pointed out, must have had a better idea of the military capabilities of the appointees.[20] Although related to discipline and morale, it was the Secretary at War, as a financial minister, who controlled pensions, rewards for long service and good conduct, allowances for married soldiers, and travelling expenses for field officers to visit troops on detached duty. The fact that he framed and carried through Parliament the Mutiny Act and the Articles of War, on which not only the army's discipline but even its very existence depended, was therefore no more than the final confirmation that through the Secretary at War 'the Govt. has ... full power'.[21]

Although officially superior, the Horse Guards laboured under few illusions as to its client position. Lord Fitzroy Somerset, giving evidence to the 1833 commission on the pay and appointments of the army and navy, affirmed that the Secretary at War had the greatest real power in the military administration. That year, he said, the reduction of the Royal Waggon Train had been at the Secretary at War's instance, and no great measure submitted by the Secretary at War to the Commander-in-Chief on financial grounds was refused on military grounds.[22] The corollary, he might have noted, was not equally true.

Thus, in the hands of an ambitious politician, such as Howick, the effective control of the army passed more and more to a civilian. In the case of an interregnum, following the resignation or death of a Commander-in-Chief, as happened in 1827 and 1852, the Secretary at War assumed overall control of the Horse Guards. It was but a short step to the aspiration of permanent military control, and this Howick tried to effect in 1837-8 and 1849-50. His dissatisfaction on taking up office was compounded by, as he saw it, the obstruction of the Horse Guards in the reform of the Army. 'I know too well,' he wrote, 'how utterly powerless in the present state of things the unhappy occupant of this office is to carry anything to which the military people on the other side of the building are opposed ... I shall therefore try to preserve the status quo for the present, with the full determination if I shd stay here of by & bye insisting upon such a change in my position as wd give me some real control.'[23]

The dissatisfaction on the part of the Secretary at War with his lot and the increasing assertion of his power added to the distrust widely felt at the Horse Guards, and in the army as a whole, for politicians in general. This had its roots in Hume's continued claim that the army was too large, Bright's view that military men were the worst authorities on the question of military punishment, and Cobden's organisation of the Liverpool Reform Association for reducing defence expenditure while at the same time spouting aggression for Russia. General Sir Robert Gardiner wrote in 1848: 'The Inefficiency of the English Army and Present Defenceless State of the Country is entirely owing to the erroneous and prejudiced opinions of Members of the House of Commons, who in general view suggestions coming from Military Men as not worthy of consideration.'[24]

Soldiers felt particularly vulnerable under the Whigs, especially as the 1830s progressed and the ministry became more dependent on the radical M.P.s for support. In 1834 Sir Willoughby Gordon, the Quarter Master General, wrote to Colonel George Brown, of the Rifle Brigade, that the government has 'a rooted dislike to the Army, which is manifested upon every occasion where it can be shown without positive injustice to Institutions or individuals'.[25] In 1842 the same officer wished his Commander-in-Chief a speedy return to health, 'when', he wrote, 'we may talk over all our successful wrangles with those authorities whose views of military affairs were not always in accordance with our own'.[26]

Both parties therefore slandered each other with the freedom born of closed minds. Hill's evidence to the commission on military punishments Howick called 'most shuffling' and referred to its 'shabbiness & falsehood'.[27] Writing to Melbourne he attacked the current administration at the Horse Guards, quoting in support examples of mismanagement in the commissariat and in the erection of barracks, but failing to note that the former was under the Treasury and the latter under the Board of Ordnance.[28] The tragedy of this situation was that it obscured the relative unanimity of views between the two departments.

Howick consulted the regimental experience of his brother, then the commanding officer of the 71st, on the introduction of good conduct awards. He is also to be credited with the employment of Lieutenant A. M. Tulloch at the War Office in the amassing of medical statistics, which in turn led to improved diets, better barracks, the employment of more local colonial regiments and the rotation of battalions for tropical service. The extent of his vision can be gauged from a letter to Melbourne of December 1837: 'I have the strongest conviction from what I have observed while in this office, that during the two & twenty years of peace which we have enjoyed much might have been done to raise the character & improve the composition of the Army by taking measures to secure a higher standard of education for Officers & to encourage professional merit & knowledge both in Officers & Men, that means might have been taken to improve the system of discipline, & the modes of punishment in use so as to check the growing feeling against corporal punishment, that the extent to which desertions have prevailed from the troops in Canada might have been checked & that a very great saving of public money might have been effected by adopting a more judicious system for the defence of the colonies.'[29]

This is an impressive testament, and one to which he was to return in 1846, but it ought not be construed from Grey's writings in later life that Hill and the army opposed his measures. Sidney Herbert reminded the House of Commons in 1854 that Lord Hill had not prevented Howick from carrying through a large measure of reform,[30] and indeed the official correspondence, in so far as it has survived, does not contain any note of obstruction. Howick's only specific complaint was to be that the Horse Guards and Macaulay (his successor in office) had altered the character of the local Canadian regiment he proposed.[31] Indeed Lady Howick recorded in their combined journal how polite Hill was to her husband, and that he called to thank Howick for his attention to military business.[32] The Quarter Master General, Sir Willoughby Gordon, continued to correspond with Howick even when he was out of office: 'It is very agreeable to see you take so great an interest in our military affairs ... You are ... the only political man who in his communications with me has not shown an abhorrence of detail.'[33]

Although, therefore, the military press bestowed a due measure of praise on Howick, Hill also was credited with reforming work in the soldier's conditions of service and earned the sobriquets, 'the soldier's friend', and 'Daddy Hill'. The institution and encouragement, under his command, of regimental libraries, of regimental savings banks, of recreations such as cricket and fives, and of the good conduct warrant, were among the first attempts, beyond the regimental level, to treat the soldier as a human being.

In 1841 Peel and the Conservatives were returned to power. The army was now entitled to feel less threatened. Peel counted among his personal friends Sir George Murray, Wellington's Quarter Master General in the Peninsula and the new Master General of the Ordnance, and Sir Henry Hardinge, who as a young officer had secured the victory at Albuera. Peel was to show an early concern for national defence as well as a more emotional admiration for feats of arms: of the five peers he created between 1841 and 1846, three were soldiers (Keane, Hardinge and Gough).

Soon after Hardinge embarked on his second term as Secretary at War (his first had been 1828–30), Hill became iller and, much to Peel's relief, offered his resignation. Speculation as to his successor was confined to Sir George Murray, who had in fact been tipped for the post as early as 1841, the Marquess of Anglesey, the Duke of Cambridge (senior), Sir Edward Paget and Prince Albert. Peel actually submitted to the Queen as candidates only Murray and Paget of the above named, but added Londonderry, Combermere and Beresford. With such a solid phalanx of Peninsular heroes, it is perhaps not surprising that he should have reserved his strongest recommendation for Wellington.[34] On 10 August 1842 Peel offered the post to the Duke[35] and it was accepted.

The press greeted the idea with some reserve and explained to their readers that Wellington's appointment was temporary, pending the young Queen's decision on the talents of the other candidates. It did not require a very perspicacious correspondent to observe that 'A man who is walking by the lamp of years ... is not the fitting person to labour through the wear-and-tear duties of a chief-in-command'.[36]

Agreement is united that the Duke's subsequent decade in office, is, certainly in military terms, the least attractive phase of his career. But explanations resting on the infirmities of old age, and the caprice and conservatism traditionally inherent in it, are insufficient. His memoranda, in an admittedly increasingly illegible hand, retain their common sense and logic, but too often the logic is a self-perpetuating one that does not look to broader questions. Over one issue alone, that of Britain's home defences, did he display the energy and grasp which had distinguished the victor of Waterloo. But while he urged an increase in the regular army and the balloting of the militia, he showed little concern for the quality of the troops, for their training, armament and equipment.

An obvious reason for the Duke's lack of activity in these spheres was his involvement in cabinet affairs. The Horse Guards staff in consequence attempted to settle even exceptional matters by themselves, without recourse to the Duke. Although Wellington demanded to be kept properly informed in October 1843,[37] he and his Adjutant General, Sir John Macdonald, were not on good terms.[38] Not until the collapse of Peel's government does his attention to the army seem to have been fairly regular: in December 1851, he told Grey that he attended the Horse Guards every day[39] and this was confirmed by Colonel Richard Airey, then Deputy Quarter Master General at the Horse Guards.[40]

The Duke, however, even in the Peninsula, where he had not employed a chief of staff and rarely delegated responsibility, had shown a remarkable lack of ability to assimilate and use the ideas of others. The Horse Guards staff were too frequently rejected or too sycophantic to compensate for this defect. On one occasion, Wellington expressed a willingness to see a new system of bayonet exercise, but when he forgot his subordinates were too frightened of the great man to remind him.[41] In 1852, although far removed from the events, he poured scorn on the reports in the press and private letters that the arms, clothing, equipment and training of the troops at the Cape were inadequate. Open contradiction was impossible: 'Field Marshal the Duke of Wellington has qualified these opinions as unjust prejudices however high the official quarters in which entertained'.[42]

An additional factor checking his acceptance of the demands from within the army for reform, or even expressing them to his political masters, was his own long political experience. In the heyday of the political economists, and to a nation which he himself repeatedly called unmilitary, it was his bounden duty as Commander-in-Chief to lobby continuously for reform, improvement and expansion. This he refused to do on the grounds that making the army a centre of public debate would either withdraw from it what little public support it still had or so inflate it as to make its cost to the nation crippling. 'Depend upon it, gentlemen,' he would say, 'that the greatest enemies the army has in this country are those who add unnecessarily to its expense.'[43] As a former Prime Minister, he saw too much the force of the cries for reduction. He candidly wrote to Sir Willoughby Gordon, 'I am one of those who think that oeconomy in the administration of the Affairs of an Army is very desirable.'[44]

It was no doubt political experience that also prompted him to interpret the position of the Commander-in-Chief in so derogatory a fashion that it provided a foolproof excuse for inaction. He saw it as his duty to give advice to the Secretary at War only when it was requested.[45] He claimed that it was only in his capacity as Lord Warden of the Cinque Ports that he inspected coastal defences at all,[46] and in 1845 he professed to abdicate all responsibility to the Secretary of State.[47] Such behaviour ill accords with his view that the Commander-in-Chief 'is supposed to be and ought to be able to go upon the Parade of the Troops, mount his Horse and carry into execution with the Troops, any strategy which would have been fixed upon in council between him and the Secretary of State!'[48] By 1850, although maintaining that he only clung to office to please the Queen,[49] he had not reserved to himself sufficient power in policy-making nor had he the physical strength left to implement it.

Therefore, while conservatism does not necessarily mean atrophy, in Wellington's case the instinct gave birth to it. 'His Grace,' his last Adjutant General recalled, 'was accustomed to adhere strictly to precedent; to the decisions he may have previously come to on similar cases. This practice greatly facilitated the task of those who had to transact business with him, seeing that all we had to do in concluding our statement of any particular case, was to refer to his decision on some similar one.'[50]

The most famed example to his contemporary soldiers was the report of the 1840 commission on promotion, which was two years in preparation, and from which much was expected, but of which the *United Service Gazette* concluded: 'The mountain has brought forth at last ... not only a mouse, but a mouse of the least possible dimensions — an absolute *topolino*, hardly discernible to the naked eye.'[51] Wellington was chairman of the commission and his stamp pervaded it. His thinking is conveyed in the introduction to the report: 'Recollecting that the results of a war unexampled in its duration ... afford ample testimony in favour of the general efficiency of the existing systems in both Navy and Army, we have rather endeavoured to amend where we thought amendment was required, than ventured to propose the adoption of material changes (however plausible the arguments by which they were supported), the effects of which we were apprehensive might not realise the hopes and expectations of the projectors.'[52]

The impeccable logic to Wellington's conservatism could lead to ridiculous conclusions. The privileged pay and rank of the Foot Guards were throughout the 1830s and '40s a subject of contention, especially for the deprived Line. Wellington's reply was that 'His Majesty sometimes sees His Guards before Breakfast in the Garden of St. James's Palace and I have seen Battalions paraded there at nine in the morning brought from Brothels and Gin shops in Pimlico as sober and clean, and in as good order as if brought to the Parade at St. Petersburgh or Berlin from the Barracks in those Towns. This is the effect of a system and we must be cautious that we do not break it down.'[53]

It was understandably hard, however, for a generation brought up to see Wellington as the greatest commander not only of its own times but of its own nation's history, to contradict him, especially on military questions. His published despatches showed not merely his grasp of tactics but also of logistics. His victory in the Peninsula was as much a victory over the system and in spite of the politicians. Thus we find Ripon writing to Ellenborough about the occupation of Scinde, a land which the Duke had never seen: 'Of course upon a subject of that nature I took the opinion and advice of the Duke of Wellington.'[54] Lord Strafford, who alone of the soldiers giving evidence to the 1837 commission on War Office organisation had favoured consolidation, retracted as soon as he gathered that Wellington had opposed it.

Although these considerations inevitably blunted any opposition to his conduct as Commander-in-Chief, in 1846 Wellington ceased to deal with his political friends, first Hardinge and then Sidney Herbert, as Secretaries at War, and instead faced a combination of Fox Maule, a former army officer himself, as Secretary at War, and Grey, as Secretary of State.

Grey drew up a memorandum[55] that was printed for circulation among the cabinet in November 1846. In it he advocated the employment of pensioned soldiers in colonial forces, the introduction of limited enlistment, and promotion examinations for officers. It is a tribute to Grey's refusal to give in to the Duke and to his limited respect for the military opinions of the great general, that all these reforms were implemented before Wellington's death, despite the latter's opposition. Moreover, in January 1852, Grey even dared to tackle the subject of military training with the Horse Guards. Convinced that 'the effects of a long peace had began to make themselves felt in our whole military establishment', he told the Adjutant General — no doubt well aware that his words would be reported back to the Commander-in-Chief — that 'if we do not mend our system & alter our mode of proceeding, we shall be left behind by all the world, and become the laughing stock of Europe, & the reproach of our own country'.[56]

Grey alone brought to defence policy an inclusive approach which enabled him to deal thoroughly and imaginatively with the problems of the army and the empire. Whether his search for efficiency was motivated by the traditional Whig desire to concentrate patronage in his own hands, or whether, more altruistically, it emanated from the rationalism of the thoroughgoing free-trade principles he had espoused by 1845, it enabled him to try to weld a coherent machinery from an inchoate mass. Unfortunately, however, his certainty, in this case justified, in the correctness of his own opinions could render him cantankerous, and 'too proud & vain to like it to be supposed that he has anything to learn'.[57] When conversing with him in 1852, the Adjutant General, Sir George Brown, an officer of Wellingtonian proclivities, found that Grey listened to his arguments 'with the self complacency of a man that was fully satisfied he understood all about these matters much better than I did, & spoke with the confidence of one who, from his superior knowledge of the subject under discussion, never doubted that he had the best of the argument'.[58] In consequence, even soldiers disposed to approve his objectives could be offended.

Maule's position was more ambivalent. When himself Secretary of State as Lord Panmure in 1855, he showed he was no respecter of the office of Commander-in-Chief, simply riding roughshod over Hardinge. In the 1846-52 ministry, however, his views about reform vacillated, and he would express half formulated notions in Parliament which he seems to have had little intention of fulfilling. Although he wrote to Wellington of the 'invariable harmony' between their respective departments,[59] his efforts to implement the army reform programme drawn up by Grey in 1846 imbued him with a considerable degree of scepticism for the Duke. In January 1850, he wrote a memorandum on the Commander-in-Chief's opposition to the consolidation of military departments, having the temerity to suggest that not only had Wellington misrepresented the suggestions of the 1837 committee but that also his 'recapitulation of our various wars is amusing and in his own peculiar fashion'.[60]

For soldiers, the decision to oppose or criticise the Duke was more traumatic. The problem was aptly summarised by Lord Fitzroy Somerset: 'It would not do to say that the Duke of Wellington is wrong. We must then be silent I presume and yet there is danger in silence, for silence, it is said, gives consent.'[61] Two of Wellington's most ardent supporters, the Marquess of Anglesey and Sir George Brown, both disagreed with him on the subject of rifle bores and yet were frightened to state their objections directly.[62] For, as Sir George Napier wrote in 1847, 'The Duke is a very difficult man to deal with, in his old age, & if once made angry, there is an end to everything'.[63] Henry Havelock, briefly home from India in 1850, attended a dinner for Gough at which he 'never witnessed so affecting a spectacle of mouldering greatness. He [Wellington] is so deaf, that he seemed to me to utter prolonged inarticulate sounds without being aware of it. He begins, but rarely concludes a sentence, and where he breaks off in a period, the spectator doubts from his manner whether he will commence another, or fall down apoplectic in the next effort to begin one.'[64] Sage counsel seemed unlikely to emanate from a source such as this, and if it did it would be met by prejudiced listeners. For the Secretary at War was told by his brother, Lieutenant-Colonel Lauderdale Maule, commanding the 79th Highlanders, 'The D.[uke] of W.[ellington] has never done one simple thing to improve the condition and status of officers in the Army — He will go down to the grave with the imputation on his character, that he has been grossly ungrateful to that body which made him what he is.'[65]

In 1850 Lieutenant-Colonel Hort, veiling himself in a nom-de-plume, published a major attack on Wellington's command, entitled *The Horse Guards*. Favouritism for Peninsular and well-connected officers and lack of sympathy for the hard-working line were the main complaints. Wellington's sins were attributed to 'the defective state' of his head, itself the product of old age. Hort culminated his diatribe on the military administration with a reminder of 'the urgent necessity existing for substituting a younger and more vigorous mind in place of the waning intellect, which at present rules the destinies of the British army'.[66]

The Horse Guards received a rapturous welcome from the military press, for it supported a campaign against Wellington which the anonymity of a newspaper could protect. This had had its origins in the outraged sensibilities of the Peninsular veterans who were refused a medal, while the victors of the brief Waterloo campaign were not only granted a decoration but distinguished as such in the *Army List*. Agitation by the Peninsular officers was not encouraged by the Duke, who defended his opposition to the award of a medal by saying that he was no longer their commander. The riposte was immediate: 'The Duke, as their leader, is dead.'[67] In the subsequent lobbying, the grievances of the Peninsular officers became fused with a concern for the future of the army. A certain Captain D. O'Halloran,[68] who called himself the vice-chairman of the Veterans Association, warned Wellington: 'Your Grace ... may aid in the attempt to keep down the services a little longer, and the consequence may be the extinction of your influence with both, — the day of reckoning will come at last.'[69]

All this, while producing a demand for reform, anticipated Wellington's actual appointment as Commander-in-Chief. When this came, it led to a less direct personal attack, and instead there arose more specific discussion of the types of reform required. The *Naval and Military Gazette*, in its annual review of the past year's progress, said of 1844: 'In no year ... have we had fewer changes to remark on ... The Duke of Wellington has ever been in the Army disposed to a conservative system ... Whenever his Grace issues orders to the Army, we observe that they are generally to enforce the existing regulations or to restore a lapsed discipline; but Reform in its usual sense never comes under his consideration ... We somewhat regret that his Grace is not a Military Reformer — for there *is* much to reform.'[70] At the conclusion of 1845 it had abandoned this restrained tone for a desperate appeal: 'Oh! Wellington, in opposition, a "great war" man (in theory); in power, a "little war" man (in practice); how much have you retrograded with your assumption of office!'[71] It hoped that a change in ministry in 1846 would bring a change in the Horse Guards: Wellington's departure would be no source of regret.

Although the *Naval and Military Gazette* did not waver from this attitude, the cudgels were really taken up by the *United Service Gazette*, which launched a most vitriolic attack on the venerable Commander-in-Chief. He was accused of giving in to the government too easily, of possessing 'infirm' judgement, and of not granting interviews to officers, with the result that he was out of touch with military opinion. In February 1850 its tone became even more strident. 'It is contrary to the laws and dictates of Nature that a man, however superlatively gifted, shall reach fourscore years of age without becoming obstinate, querulous, partially incapable of active duties, given to procrastination, and prone to seek excuses for altogether putting aside matters which levy a contribution upon the thinking faculty.' The government should instal a vigorous replacement, for 'the Horse-Guards is rapidly becoming an "Hotel des Invalides"'. It had shown itself incapable of examining new inventions or of giving 'the Army the benefit of the ingenuity of philanthropic and zealous Soldiers ... Verily the hour is come for the intervention of the Army Reformers.'[72]

These attacks established for the military press a position as the leading advocates of army reform. It was an awareness born after the arrival of Wellington as Commander-in-Chief and in the wake of the disaster to Elphinstone's force at Kabul in January 1842. A writer in the *United Service Magazine*, Colonel Firebrace, claimed that 'The best friend the Army ever had has been the military press ... It is scarcely too much to say that, with very rare exceptions, all the improvements ... in the moral and physical condition of our military force have had their origin here.'[73]

The journal from which this quotation comes was launched in 1827 as the *Naval and Military Magazine*. It filled a vacuum created by the demise of periodicals such as the *Royal Military Calendar* and the *British Military Library*, and its editor, Sir John Philippart,[74] had also been editor of the first-named. Its weighty monthly format seems from the first to have commanded respect. In 1829 the publisher, Henry Colburn, bought it and it was rechristened the *United Service Journal*, undergoing a third change of title in 1842 to the *United Service Magazine*. The editor from 1829 to 1842 was Major T. H. Shadwell Clerke, K.H., F.R.S., a veteran of Rolica, Vimiero and Corunna, who had lost a leg in the Peninsula in 1811, and was a vice-president of the United Service Institution. Clerke's impeccable military credentials gave the magazine a status even in the upper echelons of the army. Colonel George Brown wrote to thank Clerke for the *United Service Journal*'s favourable notice of the discipline in his regiment, the Rifle Brigade. 'I am sure,' he added, 'it will be gratifying to the men to find that their good conduct has been observed, & is remarked upon, in a work so highly estemed & so universally good.'[75]

Although John Mitchell, the controversial writer on tactics, was introduced to the public under Clerke's aegis, and in addition added considerably to the fame of the journal, the plethora of Peninsular memoirs and reminiscences of half-pay officers began to deprive it of some of its professional attractions. But in 1842 a new editor was appointed. His identity is not positively known, although there is very strong evidence that it was again Philippart.[76] He revitalised the *United Service Magazine*, and grafted on to it a campaigning attitude for the reform of the army. In particular, Colonel Firebrace was commissioned to produce regular articles 'on the errors and faults in our military system', and from 1842 to 1844 threw out proposals on battalion organisation, the retirement of officers, the structure of cavalry squadrons, staff training, the need for a centralised ministry of war, the status and pay of noncommissioned officers, the recruiting system, the desirability of limited enlistment, promotion from the ranks, drill, the construction of barracks and the transport system. He did not quibble with details but slammed the entire military organisation — the staff, for example, was a 'product of patronage, sycophancy, nepotism, impudence, money, and chance, without either unity or consistency'.[77]

Henry Colburn, the owner of the *United Service Journal*, was also the proprietor of a newspaper, the *Naval and Military Gazette*, first published on 9 February 1833. Colburn had, he claimed, noticed the need for a military newspaper as early as 1829. However, it was not until the *United Service Gazette* threatened to attract customers because of the similarity of its title to Colburn's own monthly publication that he rushed the *Naval and Military Gazette* into print. It was to complement the monthly magazine by appearing weekly, and in addition to the body of the newspaper, formed of editorials, it carried columns of naval and military intelligence and a lively correspondence section. Politically, it described itself as unattached, but then added the proviso that, as 'liberal conservatives, we are necessarily reformers'.[78]

John Philippart was the editor continuously from its foundation until 1868.[79] Despite the profession of political detachment, William Napier, albeit in a moment of pique, called Philippart an 'old pompous Silly Tory',[80] and Philippart himself saw political bias in his removal by the Whigs from his post at the War Office. Allegedly with Sir Herbert Taylor's and Palmerston's support, he had for twenty years acted as a semi-official leak between the government and the press on military matters.[81] His dismissal in 1833, whatever the grounds, prompted him to take up military journalism properly, his previous forays having proved short-lived. Initially his writings were cautious, and, perhaps in a bid to win readers, he condemned Hume's idea of abolishing the Board of Ordnance as 'too absurd for serious argument',[82] and defended the pay and privileges of the Foot Guards. But Philippart soon realised that in his leaders he wielded a most influential stick for improvement and in 1836 pointed out 'the necessity of a salutary reform in the administration, organisation, and constitution of the Army'.[83] Thus it was that attacks on the Foot Guards and cries for the consolidation of military departments repeatedly adorned articles of the following decade.

Philippart's system was to write a leading article, propounding in full not only the problems but also his solution, and then in subsequent leaders to incorporate the views expressed by officers in their letters to him. He would take hold of the subject and terrierlike repeat the case *ad nauseam*, until eventually he felt some action was being taken. The subject of field artillery — its strength, training and armament — was accorded extended treatment on sixteen occasions in the first half of 1847, and then resumed in 1848. The fact that the latter year marks the beginnings of an increase in rearmament in the Royal Artillery cannot be entirely coincidental.

The *Naval and Military Gazette* had a constant rival in the *United Service Gazette*, whose first issue was published on the same day, 9 February 1833. Its guiding force and proprietor until 1843 was A. A. Watts, although he only described himself as editor from March 1838.[84] Watts was angered by Colburn's rivalry, and directed a storm of abuse, principally against the *Naval and Military Gazette*, but also aimed at the *United Service Journal*. One correspondent of the *Naval and Military Gazette* called Watts 'a crabbed, crankey, irritable being, whose morose disposition is always labouring under a fit of gout, so that no one can approach him, look at him, or even breathe near him, without exciting his waspish propensities'.[85] That there was some truth in this description is shown by the fact that a number of officers, including Lieutenant Hart (editor of *Hart's Army List*), as well as Colburn himself, rewarded Watts' own preference for litigation by bringing libel actions against him.

Nor was the content of Watts' paper of any real moment for the army. Claiming to be apolitical, on the grounds that in support for the throne and the institutions of the country no more need be said, the *United Service Gazette* showed itself to be an ardent defender of protection and no friend to army reform. Its negative attitude found the present management and system in the army perfect: of the move for educating the soldier and reducing corporal punishment, it said 'the moral agency of a soldier is ... an inconvenience to the great military machine'.[86] Such journalism did not appeal to soldiers. Captain Sir J. E. Alexander of the 14th Foot wrote to Hart that he hoped sincerely 'that you will make that Black-guard Editor of the U.S. Gazette lick the dust — blacken his countenance & "do the needful" to his Father's grave'.[87]

The rivalry between the two journals is reflected in the stamp duty returns, which distinguished individual newspapers (instead of listing by publishers) for the first time in 1837. In that year the *Naval and Military Gazette* had stamps issued for 63,336 copies as against 62,000 for the *United Service Gazette*, and by 1840 the lead was 94,665 to 86,500. 1842 was the all-time peak of the *Naval and Military Gazette*, when 96,920 stamps were issued to it.[88] This circulation, which represents, in round figures, about 1,300 copies a week, must be considered in the light of a much wider potential readership. Ensign C. R. Chichester read (and, incidentally, made notes from) the *United Service Journal* in the officer's mess,[89] and the United Service Club took three or four copies of the *United Service Gazette* a week. Watts claimed that half his weekly print went to such institutions, whether mess rooms or clubs, and that there each copy was seen by fifty to a hundred readers.[90]

From 1846 to 1850 the *Naval and Military Gazette*'s annual figures fell from 95,000 to 60,320 copies, and by 1852 had only recovered to 70,325. This might suggest declining support amongst soldiers for the reform movement, but in fact the total body of readers of the military press remained fairly constant (as indeed did the establishment of the army) and merely changed its allegiance. The *United Service Gazette* reached its low point in 1848 with 63,072 readers and by 1852 had increased this figure to 92,700.[91]

The rise in popularity was due to a change of editor. The issue of the *United Service Gazette* for 8 April 1843 is marked 'Published by Alaric Watts, but forcibly withdrawn from his control during the week'. A month later, on 6 May, a declaration was made that 'Personalities and vituperative phraseology are deformities which we purpose studiously to avoid'. In December 1843, the paper was sold by auction to Andrew Spottiswoode and Watts' dissociation from it (although he apparently was retained to write the occasional political article) was formally announced on 3 February 1844.

The identity of the new editor remains obscure for the next two or so years. Over this period the *Gazette* still espoused conservative principles. But at the beginning of 1846 there came a turning point. In his opening leader for the year, the editor said Britain had never done justice to her army and that Wellington was 'the greatest enemy, perhaps, to innovation'. The percussion musket should be more widely adopted, the infantry tactical manuals should be revised, the purchase of commissions abolished, and the condition of other ranks be attended to.[92] On the parallel occasion a year later the editorial declared that 'Our object is to aid in breaking down that fatal apathy to Military affairs which has so long distinguished us as a nation'.[93]

It seems very likely that the author of these remarks was J. H. Stocqueler.[94] Stocqueler had been a journalist in India, and editor of the *Calcutta Englishman*. Stocqueler's articles were less closely reasoned than Philippart's, and perhaps relied on the pitch to which the other military papers had brought the profession. As can be seen from his views on the Horse Guards, which have already been quoted, his attacks were personal and uncompromising. He did not prepare detailed schemes such as were offered in the *Naval and Military Gazette*, but instead threw off ideas in a racy, direct style. In addition he proved his good faith by concerning himself with military education, and by the compilation of such books as *A Catechism of Field Fortifications, The British Officer* and his *Military Encyclopaedia*.

On Watts' departure, the differences between the two military newspapers were forgotten. In 1845 both jointly organised a petition to the Queen on the subject of a medal for the Peninsular war, and thereafter the *United Service Gazette*'s more courteous attitude won the other's respect. Broadly the two agreed on the need for the reform of the army: 'We are always sorry,' wrote the *United Service Gazette*, 'when we cannot ... aid our contemporary in the advocacy of a certain line of Military polity ... It cannot be doubted that the joint exertions of the two journals are always powerful for good.'[95] In 1871 Stocqueler attributed the success of the military press 'unquestionably' to Philippart.[96]

In addition their ranks were closed by the appearance in July 1848 of a potential rival, the *British Army Despatch*, also a weekly newspaper, whose proud boast was that it ignored the navy to devote itself solely to the army, and that its editors and writers were ex-army officers. Its protectionism, conservatism and contentiousness, aimed mostly at its rivals in the field of military newspapers, suggest a parallel to Watts's *United Service Gazette*. It supported the Wellingtonian administration of the Horse Guards, attacked the *United Service Gazette* as 'the Wellington-street Radical print' which dared to impugn the privileges of the Foot Guards,[97] and saw the abolition of purchase and the introduction of officers' examinations as an attempt to 'plebeanize the profession, which would render the Army unfit to maintain the Throne'.[98]

The author of most of this was A. W. Sleigh, a cornet in the Middlesex Yeomanry and at one stage an ensign in the 77th Foot.[99] Like so many conservative officers, his affection for the army was real, and he compiled a most detailed survey of the yeomanry and militia in 1850. Moreover, he was not totally inimical to reform and in particular urged the formation of volunteer units and the reorganisation of the Army Medical Department. However, his finances were in a parlous state and he lost the proprietorship of the *Despatch* in 1850 and the editorship at the same time or a year later. His successor from September 1851 until 1853 was A. B. Richards, a barrister,[100] whose conduct of the paper was marked by an almost total neglect of military matters. In September 1853 Sleigh, after bankruptcy and a sojourn in Canada, but now styled lieutenant-colonel (a commission he had gained in the Prince Edward's Island Militia), was recalled as editor. A humbler man, he sided with the other military papers, and almost alone in April 1854 dared to speak of 'an imperfect Military organization — the natural results of a system which clings with tenacity to old forms and hearkens to the advice of antiquated commanders'.[101]

Other short-lived magazines helped confirm the army's self-awareness and its desire for reform. As periodicals bidding to rival the *United Service Magazine*, there were *The Military Magazine*, of which four numbers only seem to have appeared, from 1846 to 1847, *The Military Review*, edited by Captain N. S. Shrapnel, which survived from 1852 to 1853, and *The Royal Military Magazine*, which started life as the *British Soldier* and ran for six numbers in 1852. This last was edited by Lieutenant-Colonel Hort, the author of *The Horse Guards*, and definitely belongs to the reforming literature of the period. *The Military Review* was less a polemical journal than an answer to the newly awakened awareness in the British soldier of the science of his profession, and paid attention to strictly technical subjects, such as artillery, signalling, small arms and intelligence on foreign armies. Also serving this objective were two ventures established on surer foundations. The *Professional Papers of the Royal Engineers* was produced by the Corps for its own internal use and the first of its annual volumes appeared in 1837. The main concern of its papers was to circulate scientific and professional information among Engineer officers scattered all over the world, but they were also published for the general market. The Royal Artillery Institution, founded in 1839, produced the first of its similar 'Proceedings' in a volume for 1848–57.

An officer could affix his name to articles in the last two without risking official displeasure, but in the more disputatious military prints the matter was proportionately doubtful. Wellington refused to read the *United Service Journal*,[102] let alone contribute to the *Naval and Military Gazette*,[103] and he even indirectly berated the United Service Club for subscribing to the military journals at all.[104] His attitude to officers having dealings with the press was therefore categorical. King's Regulations, while not banning communications to the newspapers, did prohibit 'Deliberations or Discussions among any Class of Military Men, having the object of conveying Praise, Censure, or any Mark of Approbation, towards their Superiors'.[105] Thus Lieutenant-Colonel Senior of the 65th Foot, who in 1838 wrote to the *United Service Journal* to praise the newly introduced system of colonial reliefs but referred to the previous method as one of favouritism, was called to account by the Adjutant General and had to submit a statement in writing to justify this allegation.[106]

However, it was equally clear that certain military authorities noted what was said in the military press: Sir Hussey Vivian, when Master General of the Ordnance, replied to criticism of the Royal Military Academy, Woolwich, in a letter to the *United Service Gazette*,[107] and Lieutenant-General Sir Charles Dalbiac, the Inspector General of Cavalry, had his letter to Hardinge on the privileges of the Foot Guards published in the *Naval and Military Gazette*.[108] The most extravagant claim was 'that from the residence of the most illustrious soldier England ever knew, communications have been received containing suggestions in regard to Military measures which even that mighty Chief believed the *United Service Gazette* capable of promoting',[109] but this surely requires further corroboration, especially in view of Stocqueler's outspoken attacks on Wellington. The best proof of all lay in the remarkable correlation between the proposals carried by the military press and the changes eventually implemented. It seems likely that Hardinge did read a series of open letters addressed to him as Commander-in-Chief by the *United Service Gazette*, and of course the military press itself was not slow to trumpet its influence.

The incentive for the officer to publish was therefore strong, if the penalties were also dire, and consequently most of those on full pay submitted their writings under a nom-de-plume. However, it was the contribution of the half-pay officers that added a sting to the military press. As in France, where many reforming periodicals devoted to the army also flourished in the 1830s, unemployment in the face of peacetime reduction prompted such officers to forsake the sword for the pen. In Britain, they were not liable to military law, and thus vitriol could replace ink. The *Naval and Military Gazette* enjoyed continued correspondence on the inadequacies of infantry training annd armament from two heroes of the Light Division in the Peninsula, Major J. Bentham, 52nd Light Infantry, and Colonel Jonathan Leach, C.B., Rifle

Brigade. A more famous case was that of Colonel John Mitchell.[110] His series of controversial articles on tactics appeared in the *United Service Journal* from 1830, and were reprinted in book form as *Thoughts on Tactics* (1838). He offered to act as arbitrator in the Watts/Hart dispute,[111] and thereafter contributed fairly regularly to the *United Service Gazette*, attacking the purchase of commissions, the lack of officer education, and including a series of letters containing his prognostications on the Eastern Question and the Crimean war.

Other examples are not so well documented. The Duke of Cambridge, at this stage of his life a young general much admired by the press as a reforming officer, used to read the military papers, and the *United Service Gazette* claimed he had a close link with it.[112] Generals or future generals among the *United Service Magazine*'s contributors included Lord Munster, Sir John Burgoyne, George Brown (later the Adjutant General), Sir Charles Pasley (the organiser of the school of engineering at Chatham), Lovell Badcock Lovell, Sir Samford Whittingham (who contributed on the recommendation of Sir Edward Paget, the Governor of Sandhurst), and possibly Lord Cathcart. Writers of manuals were predictably a well represented category — Staff Surgeon Frederic Roberts, author of *Cursory Remarks on Recruiting and Recruits*, C. de Ainslie, a future general and author of *The Cavalry Manual*, and Captain T. F. Simmons, R.A., Deputy Judge Advocate and writer on military law, heavy ordnance and artillery promotion. A. M. Tulloch first came to Howick's notice through his articles in the *United Service Journal*. The *United Service Gazette*, under Watts' editorship, claimed four generals on its lists — the Earl of Strafford, Sir Charles Napier, Sir Howard Douglas and Sir Willoughby Cotton.[113]

Owing to the success of his *History of the War in the Peninsula*, William Napier was probably the most widely read military writer of the age, and he was never slow to reply to either his own critics or those of his brother in the most blistering terms. Often under the pen-name 'Elian', he bombarded *The Times* and other newspapers with his contributions, and in addition wrote frequently for the *United Service Journal*. He attacked Mitchell's thesis on the uselessness of the bayonet and, since Shadwell Clerke agreed with Napier, thus secured on *entrée* to the editorial heart.[114] Elsewhere in Sir William's papers, it is interesting to note how the journal provided a common vocabulary in correspondence with soliders such as General Shaw Kennedy, Major J. P. Hopkins (author of a manual on infantry drill), General Sir Rufane Donkin, General Sir William Gomm, and General Sir Hussey Vivian.

By 1854 Napier's ideas on military developments had stagnated. This was not surprising, since his only active employment throughout the peace was as Lieutenant Governor of Guernsey. It was more as the propagandist of his brother, Charles, the conqueror of Scinde, that he deserves our attention. To have William as scribe and defender was a mixed blessing: his fraternal passion and bias knew no legitimate bounds. 'This Napier family,' Wellington observed with his customary terseness, 'is a most inconvenient one to have any relation with. It has great pretensions: but the indiscretion of General William Napier exceeds all bounds! and is a clog upon each and all of them.'[115]

Nonetheless, for the Duke and for the country at large, Sir Charles Napier was the only general obviously fitted to command in the field. This reputation rested on one battle, that of Miani fought in Scinde in 1843. Coming in the wake of the Kabul disaster, the victory of a man with long hair, beard and spectacles commanded rapturous applause. Moreover, Napier had shown himself well aware of the broader requirements of an army. His book, *Remarks on Military Law*, published in 1837, revealed an understanding of the importance of morale, rewards and a good regimental system. As a major-general he had been in command of the Northern district and, quite apart from peacetime novelties such as brigade training and the combined use of cavalry and infantry, he proved a most able supporter of the civil power, when the army was called out against the Chartists. In Scinde two innovations were particularly noteworthy. His attention to the building of barracks had been fired by a tour to prepare a report on them in England. In addition, in 1843, he wrote to William, 'I have long since proposed to form the army baggage ... into a regular corps, able to manoeuvre as well as the army, and if necessary defend itself.'[116] This foresight, so commendable in view of the fact that the Royal Waggon Train on the British establishment had been disbanded a decade previously, received official sanction in 1845. McMurdo, Napier's son-in-law, who was his quarter master general in Scinde, was to be the first commander of the Land Transport Corps, established during Crimean war.

During the wrangles with the East India Company which marked Sir Charles' period of command in India, the two brothers secured as publicists the services of the *Naval and Military Gazette* and, to a lesser extent, the *United Service Magazine*. In 1837 Charles Napier had conducted a full correspondence on military matters with Captain Frederick Robertson, a half-pay artillery officer, who wrote for the *United Service Gazette* under the nom-de-plume 'Ubique'. In 1835 Watts attacked William as a Whig, and in 1850 Stocqueler inveighed against Charles' egoism. The Napiers therefore preferred the *Naval and Military Gazette*, and in 1842 Robertson too transferred his loyalties. He wrote a series of articles entitled 'Musings in Camp' by 'Matross'[117] and in the late 1840s was directly responsible for a series of trenchant leaders on the Royal Artillery.[118] While Charles fed Robertson with confidential or controversial information,[119] William won over the friendship of Philippart.[120] Both brothers wrote for his two journals[121] and so close did the relationship become that William claimed the *Naval and Military Gazette* as 'prompted by me'.[122] The fruits of their labours were amply borne out in that newspaper's columns. Philippart chose to exalt Charles Napier above all as a trainer of troops, seeing him as the spawner of Britain's future generals, and suggesting an obvious parallel with the Napiers' hero, Sir John Moore.[123]

After his controversial sojourn as Commander-in-Chief in India (1849-51), Charles Napier returned home to retirement. In the invasion scare of 1852, it was widely believed that Napier would receive the command of the Kent district, and his own views on the immediacy of the situation were demonstrated in his pamphlet, *A Letter on the Defence of England by Volunteer Corps and Militia*. His death in 1853 deprived the country of, in the popular estimation, Britain's ablest general and it is interesting, if idle, to speculate whether he would have received the Crimean command in preference to Raglan. His lasting contribution, however, as perhaps even the panegyrics of the *Naval and Military Gazette* suggest, depended too much on his *persona* and not enough on the actual establishment of institutions. Dalhousie observed in 1849 — when he was still on friendly terms with Napier — 'His slashing onslaught is efficient to commence the breakdown of the system; but unless followed up firmly and steadily when he goes, no good will have been effected.'[124] He exacted the highest standards from both the officers and men under him, but his bad relations with the authorities, especially the East India Company, ensured that none of the reforms he would like to have seen introduced — improved officer instruction, the abolition of corporal punishment in peacetime, proper brigade and field training — were implemented thanks to his support: even his baggage corps was broken up in 1851.

The real doyen of the military press and of the army reformers was a much more unlikely, and correspondingly neglected, candidate — Lord Frederick Fitzclarence.[125] An illegitimate son of William IV, he profited from all the aristocratic connections and purchase possibilities which critics of the army have so stigmatised. Born in 1799, he secured an ensigncy in the Coldstream Guards while still only fourteen, and as a lieutenant he rounded up the Cato Street conspirators in 1820 — the nearest he was ever to come to active service. Via a captaincy in the Cape Corps which he never took up, he entered the 11th Foot in 1820, and was promoted lieutenant-colonel in 1824, at the age of twenty-four.

For just over a year he commanded the 11th Foot, and then from 1825 to 1832 he was commanding officer of the 7th Royal Fusiliers. In this capacity he attacked the traditional vice of drinking by the introduction of an evening meal in the soldier's diet and by only gradually increasing the apprehension and punishment of drunkards. Regimental medals were given in the 7th, and Lord Frederick established at his own expense company schools and a regimental library. The result was 'a system of discipline tempered by justice and a conciliatory bearing which rendered those corps [the 11th and 7th] models of good order and harmony'.[126]

In 1832, as a colonel, he was put on half-pay, unattached, and was promoted major-general in the 1841 brevet. The lengthy period of half-pay service which all officers had to undergo till their employment in a general officer's command was a particular deficiency of the British system of promotion. Many generals, by the time they were re-employed, were out of touch even with basics such as words of command, quite apart from the general development of military thought. Fitzclarence, however, determined this would not be his lot, and set about assiduously preparing himself for higher command. He secured employment at the Horse Guards as Assistant Adjutant General, and in 1833 he was on the Board of Officers that revised the infantry drill movements, one authority implying that the evolutions as adopted were in the main of his devising. He also visited the Prussian and French armies and came back, as he testified in later years, much impressed with their potential and equally convinced that the British army had fallen behind its continental counterparts.[127]

In 1847 Fitzclarence was appointed the general officer commanding the South Western District, and the Lieutenant Governor of Portsmouth. The time had now come to implement the ideas he had formulated over a long period of time, and, to secure support in his bid to improve the condition of the army, it was desirable that he should have the coverage and attention of the military press. No papers have survived to prove that Fitzclarence definitely aimed at this result but the circumstantial evidence is strong. His relations with the *United Service Journal* were close. Shadwell Clerke wrote a biographical note on him for Lieutenant Hart in 1846, calling him one of the best officers in the service,[128] and Lord Frederick reciprocated by describing Clerke as 'one

The identity of the reformers

of my oldest friends'.[129] Colonel Elers Napier recorded that Fitzclarence urged him to submit his proposals for the improvement of the soldiers' clothing and equipment to the *United Service Magazine*.[130] There is nothing, apart from adulation, to link the *Naval and Military Gazette* directly with Lord Frederick, but J. H. Stocqueler and the *United Service Gazette* clearly enjoyed a special relationship. Almost week by week accounts of the doings at Portsmouth, and later at Bombay, were reported, and in 1853 an editorial claimed a close but unspecified link with Fitzclarence.[131] Stocqueler in addition delivered a lecture at Fitzclarence's Portsmouth District School.[132]

The full contributions made by Fitzclarence will be discussed in their relevant places, but some explanation must be given here of the totality of his views on military reform and of why, for Sir Charles Napier among others, Portsmouth was a model garrison, and why it was expected, when Fitzclarence went to India, that Poona would become 'the modern Potsdam, the great school of instruction'.[133]

Lord Frederick conceived of military education in terms of a professional rather than a moral training. Whereas the reform of the regimental schools in 1846 concentrated on reading and writing, the school Fitzclarence formed (at his own expense) for other ranks in the Portsmouth District covered field work. The aim was twofold — to fit the army for active service and to make commissioning from the ranks a real possibility and not an ideal. The extension of this was the implementation of the Horse Guards schemes for officer education and Lord Frederick used publicly to examine regimental officers in outpost work or light infantry drill, to request reports and surveys on outlying country and to test each rank in the duties of the rank above it. The chief objective he saw accruing from this preparation was the training of senior officers to handle large bodies in the field. 'If you place 4 rgts. of Infy. 1 of cavalry & 6 guns any where, you have not the people who can move them ... I know *our* erronious system so well, & the *excellent system* of the foreign armies, particularly of the French, where *all* know their duty, that I am determined to make all my *superior* officers learn their work, & give them opportunities to do so.'[134] Brigade drills were held on average every week and, to avoid exposing the men to the nuisances of their seniors' ignorance, practice in this essential art was given by a system of skeleton drill evolved by Fitzclarence while in the Royal Fusiliers.[135] The culmination was the camp of exercise organised by Fitzclarence for 10,000 men in the Bombay Presidency in December 1853.

In his work, Lord Frederick was handicapped by the absence of manuals, the official volumes being vague even on brigade formations. He urged Sir William Napier to write a 'philosophy of war', presumably on Clausewitzian lines, but Napier was reluctant to be dogmatic on the subject of strategy.[136] In the event, thanks to Napier, Fitzclarence enlisted the aid of General Shaw Kennedy (a Light Division veteran of the Peninsula) in producing his *Manual of Out-Post Duties* (1851). His purpose, Kennedy said, was 'to publish something practically useful, and so simple and plain that all ranks may understand'.[137] In it he urged the need for practical peacetime training and called the attention of officers to the best military works in print. In 1851 Lord Frederick also published *Suggestions for Brigade and Light Infantry Movements*. Of his *magnum opus*, however, we possess only a fragment, his *Memoranda ... for the use of Young Officers assembled at Poona during the Period of Exercise in December 1853, including Instructions applicable to a combination of the three Arms*. This apparently was a prelude to a major work, then in preparation, of a one volume guide to army movements.[138]

Fitzclarence's post at Portsmouth was an enormously influential one. The regiments in the district had just returned from foreign service, and were thus often deprived of their veterans, had a large influx of recruits and lacked discipline or *esprit de corps*. Here battalions were remoulded before going on to further service. At the outset Fitzclarence brought to the work a harshness and impatience which seemed to take no account of distinguished or debilitating service overseas.[139] He was inclined to assume all his officers were fools and all his regiments in need of correction. This was compounded by his assumption of royal state: he tended to pose as a beneficent despot. A. W. Sleigh, the editor of the *British Army Despatch*, had formerly been in the 77th, one of the first regiments to come under Fitzclarence's control, and the most notable feature of that newspaper's first year was its defamation of Lord Frederick. Officers of much service had 'to rise at six and improve their military knowledge' and 'not a moment is secure from a visit or inspection' by the major-general.[140]

These grumblings were gradually stilled as Lord Frederick learned to temper his approach and as his charges began to realise the benefits conferred by his training. Nonetheless official support for Fitzclarence remained never more than reluctant. Fox Maule, the Secretary at War, chose to ignore a scheme of officer education Lord Frederick submitted to him and his visit to the Portsmouth District School did not lead to the establishment of comparable institutions elsewhere in the army. The Duke of Cambridge, who referred to his relative as 'the Great

Frederick',[141] wrote only just after the latter's arrival in the South West District that the Horse Guards did not appear to like Fitzclarence much: 'He bothers them a good deal & I think myself that he has pulled them up rather too abruptly.'[142]

However, on his promotion to lieutenant-general, which automatically disqualified him from holding the Portsmouth command and after which he himself expected a long period on half pay (as he showed by declaring himself a 'reforming' parliamentary candidate for Portsmouth), he was flattered to be offered the post of Commander-in-Chief at Bombay. Soon the Adjutant General's nephew was reporting from India that Fitzclarence was 'working like a drill sergeant'[143] and 'taking a most zealous & energetic surveillance of the drill & discipline of the Army'.[144] Opinions in India were as divided as they had been in Portsmouth. However, Henry Havelock expressed himself very pleased with his new chief, likening him to the Duke of York and being favourably impressed by his knowledge of his profession.[145] He reported to the Governor General, Dalhousie, that Lord Frederick expected to be the next Commander-in-Chief in India, but Dalhousie himself, although admiring his work, found him a little 'too pipe-clay' and preferred Sir George Anson.[146] In the event Fitzclarence did not live to be disappointed, for, long troubled by gout and weakened by overwork, he suddenly succumbed on 30 October 1854.

Fitzclarence perhaps therefore never realised his full potential, and certainly this is the case if it is a soldier's ambition to captain an army in the field, for he had never even heard a shot fired in anger. But when in a public address to the people of Portsmouth a son of William IV announces that the French army is better and more scientific in its training than the British, and that the defences of Portsmouth are inadequate,[147] ripples appear on the smooth surface of British military complacency. His contribution to army reform justified one newspaper's description of him as 'the most promising general in the British Army'.[148] The eulogies of the obituaries were reflected in the writings of a private soldier, who said, 'He was a true soldier himself, and a soldier's true friend. In him the British army lost one of its best generals, and the troops in the Bombay Presidency a commander who looked after their interests, as a father would after the welfare of his children.'[149]

The press emphasis on Lord Frederick's work aroused jealousy as well as support. Colonel Armine Mountain, the Adjutant General of the Queen's troops in India, complained that at times Fitzclarence received credit for improvements 'which have been in the Queen's regulations for the past 10 years'.[150] The feeling only serves to show that many officers, operating within the regulations and extending their interpretations of them, established much of the bedrock of reform. Regiments served so much in isolation that the onus lay on individual commanding officers to establish good 'systems' of discipline and training. Mountain himself quoted with approval the opinion of Sir Edward Blakeney, 'that there was no situation so gratifying to a soldier as regimental command, — none which brings with it so much immediate authority, or in which a man has so much direct influence for good'.[151] For his own regiment, the 26th, two influences were predominant: that of Moore, received from Sir John Colborne when Mountain had been a young officer in the 52nd, and that of Oglander, his predecessor in command of the 26th. Oglander was 'a father' to his regiment,[152] and, although Mountain saw himself as a reformer where necessary, it was a paternal interest in their men and the efficiency of the service that was the driving force for him and his contemporaries. Colour-Sergeant George Calladine of the 19th Foot said of his commanding officer, Henry Hardy, that 'he was the father of the regiment, visiting the sick, clothing the children, watching over the men in their barrack rooms to see that they were comfortable, taking care that they changed their linen and clothing when wet, taking women and children when sick to his own quarters, and supplying them with everything that was requisite'.[153] Calladine was serving in the pestilential conditions of Trinidad in 1835, and the shared rigours of colonial service helped buttress this relationship. Thus Derinzy of the 86th won praise not only from Sir Charles Napier[154] but also from an n.c.o. of the 13th Light Infantry.[155] Many of these commanding officers had as young men been with the Light Brigade at Shorncliffe under Sir John Moore: the emphasis there had been on the encouragement of individual initiative. It led, on a regimental basis, to the establishment of efficient schools, libraries, savings banks and good conduct rewards. Many officers spent large sums on their regiments, as Cardigan did on mounting the 11th Hussars. Colonel W. G. Cochrane wrote in 1853 that 'now-a-days all Commanding Officers are innovators'.[156]

With the commanding officers must be coupled the majors and captains. Sir Hussey Vivian gave out in 1831 that 'The Captain or Officer in command of each Troop or Company stands to the Soldier belonging to it, in the relation of a Parent, and should consider himself called upon, as far as lies in his power, to fulfil the duties of one'.[157] This too was the product of Moore's influence. Tactically light troops were often employed in small formations, and administratively the burden of garrisoning large areas in the long peace could scatter the battalion and make the company the prime unit. The 52nd Light Infantry in particular delegated much to the captains,[158] and evidence exists of a similar bias in the other constituents of Moore's Light Brigade, the 43rd Light Infantry,[159] and the Rifle Brigade.[160]

One such young officer, George Higginson, a subaltern of the Guards, wrote of the end of 1851, 'A feeling that all was not right with our army began to find expression about this time, and the comforting assurance which invariably followed any proposal of reform in its administration — that "no man could be so foolish as to think we should ever again see active service" — was ceasing to be the conviction of thoughtful people.'[161]

While Wellington lived, this groundswell of reform, generated by the military press and certain enlightened officers, remained unrecognised and unacknowledged. But in September 1852 there occurred, in the words of one officer, 'A happy release for the Army'[162] — the Duke died. The *United Service Gazette* viewed Prince Albert, the Duke of Cambridge, the Marquess of Anglesey, Lord Hardinge and Lord Fitzroy Somerset as potential successors. Of these, only Anglesey was an unrealistic candidate, being of a similar age to the Duke and not really the reformer which it was known was needed.

The argument for a Commander-in-Chief of royal blood was based on the fact that it would best preserve the Queen's prerogative, while at the same time freeing army appointments from the imputation of political influence. Wellington saw it as the best arrangement 'to counteract the growth of Democratic Power'.[163] The candidature of the Duke of Cambridge carried this weight, but as a young major-general it was felt he lacked influence in the army and respect with the public.

That of Prince Albert was correspondingly stronger, especially as he had always displayed an interest in military matters and had indeed been the press's favourite if Wellington had resigned in 1846. In 1850, on Sir Willoughy Gordon's death, Lord John Russell had proposed that the offices of Adjutant General and Quarter Master General be merged to create a chief of staff for the Horse Guards. Wellington was opposed as he felt that the two divisions would have to continue under the chief of staff, and that consequently the new office would simply be a prelude to the redundancy and eventual abolition of the Commander-in-Chief's post. The Duke was only prepared to sanction the scheme if Prince Albert was to succeed him as Commander-in-Chief, since a chief of staff would release the Prince Consort from many of the more mundane duties. Albert rebutted this suggestion, since he felt any controversy regarding the army would cast imputations through him onto the Queen. But to this he noted a rider, that as the Queen was a woman and her relations with her army were consequently weaker than if she had been a man, 'the army might become more especially an object of my care and attention', and more military papers might be put before Prince Albert to give him a fuller idea of the army's workings. The object of this would be superfluous, he tactfully pointed out, while Wellington remained alive, but would be important when he was succeeded. To this proposal Wellington and Russell agreed.[164]

Thus, with the royal candidates discounted, the army's two main contenders, Hardinge and Somerset, alone contested the field. The latter, who had proved himself ever urbane as Military Secretary at the Horse Guards, clearly boasted great personal charm as well as the acquaintance of most of the officers of the army. In this respect he was the favourite of the military press, especially of the *Naval and Military Gazette*. The *Gazette* failed to note the contradiction therein, since Lord Fitzroy was 'Caesaris comes et alumnus',[165] and it was this very Wellingtonian influence to which the military press had been so opposed and which in the event seems to have been responsible for Somerset not becoming Commander-in-Chief. The fact that he was passed over hurt Somerset deeply, especially as Hardinge was a junior officer. But his feelings were somewhat salved by the Master Generalship of the Ordnance, and also by the army's subscription which helped give him the financial resources to accept the offer of a barony (as Lord Raglan).

The decision therefore of the Prime Minister, Derby, and of the Queen was unanimous in favour of Hardinge. Prince Albert noted that all were 'agreed that for the loss of authority which we had lost with the Duke, we could only make up by increase in efficiency in the appointments to the different offices. That Lord Hardinge was the only man fit to command the Army.'[166] Derby, when in February he had asked Hardinge to be Master General of the Ordnance, had acknowledged that politically Hardinge would exert no influence, but stressed his desire to secure 'the services of our ablest military administrator'.[167] The Queen herself wrote triumphantly to her uncle, 'We ... are highly satisfied; he is full of courage & energy, & at the same time very ready by degrees to make improvements wh. are very necessary.'[168]

Hardinge himself, although a friend of the Duke (and indeed the second in his duel with Lord Winchilsea), avoided the imputation of being too much in his thrall. Sir John Moore had in all probability been as great a military influence on him since Hardinge had served on his staff at Corunna. Ellenborough, Hardinge's predecessor as Governor General of India, acknowledged his abilities as a man of business, but doubted his powers of originality or independence of character.[169] His belief that Hardinge would bend before a press onslaught was certainly true to the extent that he respected the importance of newspapers — he was in touch with Delane on national defence in 1852.[170] Ellenborough's suspicions, although not always so explicitly expressed, were common among politicians, who had seen Hardinge's complete devotion to Peel. In that sense, he was perhaps, above all, a pragmatist, his two periods as Secretary at War showing him first as the spokesman of economy (1828-30) and then as the harbinger of crisis in imperial defence (1841-44), without any apparent contradiction. The first Sikh war had given him recent experience of a field command, and, while not revealing him as 'a great Captain of Commanding Genius', Charles Napier rated him 'far above the ordinary run of English Generals'.[171] His work for the European forces in India, praised by Mountain, the Adjutant General of the Queen's troops, demonstrated that the lessons of the War Office were well learnt.

On his return, he had at first felt his public career to be over. But by 1851 he was manifesting an ambition to command the army,[172] and accordingly, in 1852, on the second offer, he accepted Derby's request that he become Master General. Hardinge experienced deficiencies in artillery in the Punjab and, imbued with a strong sense of the vulnerability of Britain's coastline, he launched into the re-equipping of the Royal Artillery and the organisation of the home defences with vigour.

His appointment as Commander-in-Chief earned praise because he was viewed as a reformer. The *United Service Gazette* predicted that the 'Army will doubtless witness a most important amelioration in many branches of its organisation and equipment',[173] and addressed a series of open letters (which it claimed Hardinge read) on aspects requiring change. The *United Service Magazine* took a moderate and, in the event, a justified line: 'A friend to improvement, the practical knowledge he has acquired in the field, in the presence of a vigilant and indomitable enemy will guard him from adopting the delusions of a shooting-gallery, or the equipments of a masquerade. We may expect to see alterations, but they will neither be hazardous nor ill-considered.'[174]

To meet these hopes, Hardinge was fortunate to have strong support. The wranglings of Grey with Hill and Wellington, although they had reform as their object, had induced an acrimonious spirit that was harmful to Grey's original wishes. Hardinge had to deal with Sidney Herbert as Secretary at War. They had shared a close personal friendship and regard for Peel, and Herbert was also in accord with the move for well considered improvements. In March 1854, Herbert testified to this unanimity in the Commons. 'At the present day,' he said, 'there is a complete harmony between the military and civil departments, arising out of more enlightened and extended means on the part of the military authorities; the indisposition to change has entirely disappeared.'[175]

The other great prop to Hardinge's power — although he resented it initially — was the unwavering support he received from Prince Albert, as the latter had promised the Duke he would do in 1850. The Queen wrote in September 1852, 'We shall keep the whole more under our own eye now; Ld Hardinge will communicate details of importance to Albert who has taken gt. pains with all these Army affairs.'[176] The Prince Consort's role rarely seems to have been to initiate, although he did suggest the formation of Chobham camp and also secured a Belgian shell fuze for trail. His action was more discreet: Hardinge would use him as a sounding board for ideas and for confirmation of half-formed views. The Prince then gave his weight to the implementation of these plans — when Hardinge was trying to reform the artillery, he told Albert that his aid had gained four months in the casting of ten-inch guns.[177]

However, by 1854, the Prince Consort's intervention had become more direct. He gave specific advice, particularly if it related to the Guards, in which he took a personal interest. 'I must unreservedly state,' Hardinge wrote, 'that I owe much to suggestions made by Your Royal Highness, which appeared officially as acts of my own ... I could not have stood my ground 6 months if I had not been thus sustained by Your Royal Highness.'[178] Public rumours of courtly intrigue were therefore not totally misplaced. The Raglan lobby was not yet appeased and Hardinge's confidential correspondence with the Prince seemed to prove that he was no more than the tool of a foreigner. Furthermore, while the royal prerogative might justify the Prince's intervention at the Horse Guards, he was also distributing advice — that was accepted — to the Secretary at War and to the Secretary of State for War. At the beginning of 1854 Hardinge and Aberdeen were obliged to make public statements in the Lords on Prince Albert's position in the army.[179]

If Hardinge risked censure on the grounds of toadying to the court, it was an accusation that he was open to in many other directions, for he was remarkably eclectic in his sources of inspiration for ideas on improving the army. He apparently worked on the 'principle of "trying everything'".[180] He maintained the interests in home defence and arms development which had so preoccupied him as Master General. Colonel Leach found that after his years of press campaigning his views were at last forwarded to the Horse Guards.[181] The schemes of foreign governments for arming, clothing and equipping their armies were scrutinised, and the support of manufacturers and tradesmen enlisted to the same end. By reviving the practice of Commander-in-Chief's levées, which Wellington had stopped, he came into contact with officers and their opinions.

However, in so doing he upset the Wellingtonian rhythm of the Horse Guards. The headquarters staff found that, after a long period of independence, Hardinge 'disturbed existing systems of business — put an extinguisher on routine — interfered with ancient usages and privileges'.[182]

Particularly offended by this was Sir George Brown, who had been Adjutant General since Macdonald's death in 1850. As a regimental officer, Brown had shown himself conscientious and alive to the needs of his men. His appointment as Deputy Adjutant General in 1841 had been a deliberate move by Hill and Somerset to employ a regimental officer, without connections, who 'had acquired a thorough knowledge of the general concerns of the Army — its arming, training, discipline, and equipment'.[183]

In 1850 he had overcome royal opposition and a field that included Hardinge, Fitzclarence, Sir Harry Smith, Sir Joseph Thackwell and, Albert's favourite, Sir Frederick Stovin.[184] He owed his appointment largely to Somerset and Gordon, for whom the overwhelming argument in his favour was that he had 'the advantage of being acquainted with [Wellington's] mode of doing business', and who tended in consequence to play down his unpopularity and reputation for bad temper.[185] This identification with the Duke caused Brown to an increasing degree to regard himself as the custodian of the worst Wellingtonian precepts. Lord Seaton found that in their extensive dealings in 1853, Brown was 'insolent & overbearing' and was never heard to speak in favour of anything.[186] In 1837 Brown supported the *United Service Journal*, but in 1848 he denied reading or taking any notice of the press.[187] He upset the War Office staff. There existed ill-feeling between him and Fitzclarence.[188] The Duke of Cambridge, on a visit to the Horse Guards, was discussing infantry drill with the Adjutant General, when it transpired that the latter only had the edition of Dundas (1792), although there had been two subsequent editions (1824 and 1833).[189] Two weeks previously Cambridge wrote that 'Why or wherefore he [Brown] could not himself explain except that it was so 50 years ago in his younger days, which in my humble opinion is the wost arugment in the world'.[190]

It cannot have taken Brown long to realise that an Adjutant General inimical to reform and to the War Office, and reputed to lack both tact and a control of his temper, would not fit into Hardinge's scheme of things. To this suspicion he added his own doubts as to Hardinge's fitness for office, expressing his extreme annoyance at Somerset not being appointed Commander-in-Chief,[191] and concluding that a conspiracy was being organised against him by Hardinge.[192] His feelings soon became known: nor could they fail to enlist some support, for, as Colonel Orlando Felix said, 'the old lamp' that was being replaced at the Horse Guards 'shed such lustre on the British Army'.[193]

In December 1853 Brown tendered his resignation. He wrote in a private memorandum that Hardinge 'knew nothing whatever about the Army, & that he was jealous & distrustful of those who happened to be better informed!'[194] To this fatuous claim Brown added that he had been neglected and his advice not sought: probably this was valid, since, when the Adjutant General's opposition became manifest, Hardinge drafted his own orders and seems to have avoided argument by consulting other authorities — such as Prince Albert — with increasing frequency.

Although in his private letter to Hardinge, Brown claimed that he was not opposed to reform as such, merely to 'the projects of visionaries', it was indeed over army reform that he was resigning. His departure is a barometer of the extent to which things had swung against the Wellingtonian school and in favour of change. As he himself remarked in the same letter, the views which he held and over which he was resigning 'were always entertained and repeatedly expressed by the Great Duke'.[195] 'All [Hardinge] had to do,' Brown added two years' later (with his anger even more deeply embedded), 'was to leave well alone, & to carry on the Command of the Army as he found it, but it is not in his nature to remain quiet or to conduct any office or Depmt with method & regularity [but with] his inherent love of change, his restless propensity towards innovation.'[196] In Brown's mind, the words 'vision' and 'innovation' were associated with mischief and recklessness, and were the attributes of Hardinge and a number of other officers who ought to have known better. In his private memorandum on his resignation, the irate general added that without waiting, Hardinge 'seemed to have determined that every thing must be changed — talked of "progress" & "reform" & fancied that alterations must be made & innovations introduced ...

because he had been placed at the Head of the Army, & because the "Times" news paper had undertaken that he should accomplish all this ... & devise expedients by which all future apprehension in respect to the invasion of the country should vanish'. In particular Brown opposed the establishment of proper musketry training on the grounds that it was an insult to the abilities of regimental officers, he resented the fact that the Commander-in-Chief had taken over control of clothing and equipment from the Adjutant General and had sent 'such a quantity of rubbish' to Chobham for trial, he opposed the idea of the Commander-in-Chief attending meetings of the Board of General Officers in person, and he was insulted by the employment of Lord Seaton on a revision of brigade manoeuvres.[197]

In the course of his memorandum, Brown confirms that Hardinge was indeed paying heed to the reforming agencies already outlined. Hardinge's opinions on musketry training were stigmatised as 'picked up in the military newspapers & stupid pamphlets'. He took advice from War Office men or Colonel Airey, his Military Secretary. Seaton, whom Hardinge closely involved in his plans in 1853, was quoted as asking for the opinion of Colonel Eyre, who had won a tremendous reputation as a brigade commander in the Kaffir war: 'We wanted,' Seaton was said to have added, 'an infusion of young blood', and he said that '"progress" & "reform" were necessary in the Army as in any other institution in the country.'

Hardinge's belief in this view was evinced by his appointment of Lieutenant-General Sir George Cathcart, then commanding at the Cape, in succession to Brown. Cathcart was comparatively young, had made a success of subduing the Kaffirs, and had shown himself an enterprising commanding officer of the King's Dragoon Guards, Cathcart, Hardinge told Airey, 'has the bump of invention'.[198]

Indeed, the greatest indication of Hardinge's talents lies in his own conduct over Brown's resignation. He retained the loyalty both of Cathcart and of the Deputy Adjutant General who was now bypassed, G. A. Wetherall. He paid generous and magnanimous tribute to Brown's qualities in a letter to his successor. The breathless way in which he went on to tell Cathcart of the recent developments in the army betrays his own excitement: 'We have,' he wrote, 'within 18 months equipped the field arty with nearly 300 field pieces & 600 Amn. Waggons new from our Woolwich Estabt. — We have 20,000 New Rifled Muskets, now making, which carry an ounce Ball, the weapon, with 60 r. of Ball Cartridge, being as long & as strong as the heaviest Musket, but weighing

3 lb 5 oz. lighter with its Ammunition than the Minié — The School of Musketry is prospering ... We hope to purchase abt 8000 acres of very wild waste land between Farnham & Godalming, admirably situated for purpose of Strategy towards the Coast, & from the great variety of the ground, well suited for Tactical Instruction — We hope to acquire this ground for a Permanent Camp of Instruction.' He expatiated on the qualities and energy of his staff, concluding, 'You will find your very existence elevated & invigorated by all these matters which are of the highest interest.'[199]

Just, however, when it seemed that Hardinge had established a good working team at the Horse Guards, the Crimean war broke out. Cathcart was sent, almost on arrival in London, to command a division in the east and to be killed at Inkerman. Airey, the man who had forged a life in the Canadian backwoods only to give it up to be Deputy Quarter Master General and then Military Secretary at the Horse Guards, went out with the force and was to become Raglan's mentor and Quarter Master General. Meanwhile Herbert's position as Secretary at War was emasculated by the Duke of Newcastle opting to be Secretary of State for War, and not for the Colonies, when the two were divided. Furthermore when the Aberdeen administration fell Newcastle was replaced by Panmure, who simply ignored the Commander-in-Chief, leaving him to rely on the newspapers for intelligence of the Crimean army.

Thus the programme of reform changed course in mid-stride, but Hardinge achieved sufficient to give the lie to the Crimean war being the catalyst for change. 'We have done more in two years,' he wrote to Palmerston in November 1854, 'than during the last century.'[200] He above anybody else was responsible for the introduction of an efficient rifle into the entire British service, thus working the most important single change in tactics in the British army until the appearance of heavier field artillery following the Boer war. To ensure its efficient use he established the Hythe School of Musketry, so as to disseminate an approved and uniformly higher standard of shooting throughout the army. He organised the first camp of exercise since the peace, at Chobham, and as a result of its success initiated the purchase of Aldershot. Just as the war began, he had approved in outline a scheme for the proper professional education of junior officers, and for a system of staff training. Throughout 1853 both he and Herbert were expressing suficient alarm over the absence of young and efficient general officers to suggest that the 1854 commission on promotion did not spring immediately from the difficulty of officering the expeditionary army.

The identity of the reformers

These were reforms of the first magnitude — to be set above even his work as Secretary at War on the good conduct warrant, on saving banks, pensions and rewards, or as Master General of the Ordnance, when he increased the effective artillery force approximately sixfold. As the *Naval and Military Gazette* said at the start of 1853, 'A very few years, we doubt not, will remove the antiquated follies which have too long been cherished even by our greatest Generals.'[201]

In the event Hardinge's reputation was to be eclipsed by the Crimean war. When in 1856 he resigned and, shortly after, died, the *Naval and Military Gazette* recalled its original preference for Raglan (the erstwhile Lord Fitzroy Somerset), 'but', it added, 'we must be just. Lord Hardinge has been a great Military Reformer, and he has devoted his time, his talents, and his very life to effect those organic changes for which his genius long had devised the remedy.'[202] General Sir Charles Grey, who, as the Prince Consort's secretary, saw Hardinge regularly in his official capacity, told his brother in July 1856, 'There is no man in England who has such a thorough acquaintance with the wants & requirements of an Army whether at home or in the field, or who wd have been more sincerely desirous of going hand in hand with the Minister for War in effecting any improvements that might be thought desirable in our system — And had he been more consulted things would have been infinitely better done.'[203] Earl Grey, never, as we have seen, a believer in the existence of any soldier reformers, was by his own lights most complimentary in reply: 'I do entirely agree with you as to his being a great loss at this moment, & as to the injustice of imputing to *him* the enormous errors & mismanagement of the war.'[204]

Notes

1 P.P. 1854-5, IX, part III, *3rd report*, p. 104.
2 Wellington papers, Wellington to King Leopold I of the Belgians, 8 September 1837; Lord Broughton, *Recollections of a long life*, IV, p. 203, V, pp. 211-13.
3 Wellington papers, Wellington to Somerset, 30 December 1837.
4 Raglan private papers, box 4, Wellington to Somerset, 9 March 1833.
5 Raglan private papers, box 5, Somerset to Hill, 24 September 1835.
6 Hansard, 3rd series, XXXVII, cc 813-16.
7 B.M. Add. Mss 40459, f. 273, Peel to Wellington, 10 August 1842.
8 B.M. Add. Mss 40459, ff. 279-84; Wellington papers, Wellington to Peel, 10 August 1842, and reply, 11 August 1842.
9 Hansard, 3rd series, LXX, cc 611-14.

10 B.M. Add. Mss 40461, ff. 371, 477, Wellington to Peel, 15 December 1845 and 2 July 1846.
11 Grey papers, journal of Earl Grey, C3/12, entry for 1 July 1846.
12 S.R.O., GD 45/8/3.
13 W.O. 1/596, p. 209.
14 Grey papers, Wellington to Grey, 13 November 1851.
15 Ibid., 9 January 1852; Wellington papers, Somerset to Wellington, 9 and 10 January 1852; *Correspondence of Lt. Gen. the Hon. Sir George Cathcart*, p. 1; Seaton papers, Cathcart to Seaton, 15 January 1852.
16 Grey papers, Grey to Sir Charles Grey, 13 December 1851.
17 Ibid., Sir J. W. Gordon to Howick, 16 February 1838.
18 Raglan private papers, box 3, no. 142, Somerset to Egerton, 8 November 1835.
19 Grey papers, Grey's journal C3/1B, entry for 24 April 1835.
20 W.O. 43/533, ff. 59, 62.
21 Wellington papers, Hardinge to Wellington, 13 July 1836.
22 P.P. 1833, VII, evidence pp. 150-4.
23 Grey papers, Howick to Charles Grey, 16 December 1835.
24 R.A. E 42/51, pp. 5-6, Gardiner to Russell, 26 January 1848.
25 N.L.S. mss 2839, ff. 122-3, Gordon to Brown, 29 September 1834.
26 B.M. Add. Mss 35060, f. 547, Gordon to Hill, 10 August 1842.
27 Grey papers, Howick's journal, C 3/2, 8 and 19 April 1836.
28 Grey papers, Howick to Melbourne, 15 December 1837.
29 Ibid.
30 Hansard, 3rd series, CXXXI, c 234.
31 Grey papers, Charles Grey to Grey, 18 October 1840.
32 Grey papers, Grey's journal, C 3/1B, 23 May 1835.
33 Grey papers, Gordon to Grey, 22 September 1840.
34 A. C. Benson and Viscount Esher, *Letters of Queen Victoria*, I, p. 527
35 B.M. Add. Mss 40459, f. 273, Peel to Wellington, 10 August 1842.
36 'Caleb' to *N. & M.G.*, 3 September 1842, p. 570.
37 Wellington papers, Wellington to Macdonald, 24 October 1843.
38 Sir George Cathcart papers, Sir George Cathcart to Earl Cathcart, 14 October 1846.
39 Grey papers, Wellington to Grey, 15 December 1851.
40 P.R.O. 30/46, box 3, ff. 102-3, Airey to Eyre, 2 November 1851; Seaton papers, Seaton to Walpole, 1 September 1851.
41 E. A. Angelo, *Observations on the military exercises formed by Henry Angelo*, London, 1853, pp. 15-16.
42 Herbert papers, II Add., Wellington to Prince Albert, 20 February 1852.
43 M. Brialmont and G. R. Gleig, *Duke of Wellington*, IV, p. 102.
44 Gordon papers, B.M. Add. Mss 49480 (10), Wellington to Gordon, 1 February 1832.
45 Wellington papers, Wellington to Graham, 9 October 1843, and Wellington to Anglesey, 17 July 1844.
46 Ibid., Wellington to Graham, 3 November 1845.
47 Ibid., Wellington to Stanley, 1 August 1845.

48 Ibid., Wellington to Lord John Russell, 30 November 1849.
49 Ibid., Wellington to Russell, 29 July 1850.
50 M. Brialmont and G. R. Gleig, *Duke of Wellington*, IV, p. 100.
51 *U.S.G.*, 11 April 1840, p. 4.
52 P.P. 1840, XXII, report, p. iii.
53 S.R.O., GD 45/8/124, p. 1, Wellington to Ellice, 18 January 1834.
54 B.M. Add. Mss 40868, f. 12, Ripon to Ellenborough, 4 April 1844.
55 S.R.O., GD 45/8/21.
56 Wellington papers, memorandum by Brown, 28 January 1852.
57 Sir George Cathcart papers, Sir George Cathcart to Earl Cathcart, 17 July 1846.
58 Wellington papers, memorandum by Brown, 28 January 1852.
59 Wellington papers, Maule to Wellington, 25 February 1851.
60 S.R.O., GD 45/8/66/7.
61 B.M. Add. Mss 49503, Somerset to Gordon, 9 September 1834.
62 Second Earl Cathcart papers, J. 26, Brown to Cathcart, 8 January 1852, and the same, 12 June 1852; George Wrottesley. *Life of Sir John Burgoyne*, I, p. 493.
63 B.M. Add. Mss 54524, f. 124, George Napier to Charles Napier, 25 April 1847.
64 J. C. Marshman, *Memoirs of Sir Henry Havelock*, p. 195.
65 S.R.O., GD 45/8/18.
66 The Two Mounted Sentries [Lt.-Col. Hort], *The Horse Guards*, p. 81.
67 *N. & M.G.*, 21 November 1840, p. 761.
68 Identified by William Napier as 'Colonel Mackie', Napier papers, B.M. Add. Mss 54526, f. 36.
69 *N. & M.G.*, 8 February 1840, p. 92.
70 Ibid., 4 January 1845, p. 8.
71 Ibid., 6 December 1845, p. 777.
72 *U.S.G.*, 2 February 1850, p. 4.
73 *U.S.M.*, 1846, I, p. 481.
74 J. H. Stocqueler, *A familiar history of the British army*, p. 219.
75 N.L.S. mss 2840, f. 85, Brown to Clarke, 12 August 1838.
76 B.M. Add. Mss 54525, f. 72, William Napier to Charles Napier, 15 January 1844, identifies Philippart as editor but conceivably confuses the *United Service Journal* with the *Naval and Military Gazette*. However, on f. 76 William Napier again states Philippart had become editor, and this is also suggested in 54526, f. 69. The surprising absence of any papers from the editor of the *United Service Magazine* (as the *United Service Journal* became) in the collections of military correspondence heightens the suspicion that Philippart was editor of both, particularly since both were also published by Henry Colburn.
77 *U.S.M.*, 1842, III, p. 556.
78 *N. & M.G.*, 16 February 1833, p. 12.
79 J. H. Stocqueler, *A familiar history of the British Army*, p. 219.
80 B.M. Add. Mss 54525, f. 72, William to Charles Napier, 15 January 1844.
81 Wellington papers, Philippart to Wellington, 29 December 1834, and

reply, 30 December 1834; also 31 January and 13 April 1835, and reply, 13 April 1835.
82 *N. & M.G.*, 4 May 1833, p. 108.
83 Ibid., 13 February 1836, p. 105.
84 *U.S.G.*, 3 March 1838, p. 4. Watts' son, however, said his father was editor from 1833 to 1841, when financial troubles led to the loss of his share under a decree of the Court of Chancery: Alaric Alfred Watts, *Alaric Watts*, II, p. 211.
85 *N. & M.G.*, 25 February 1837, p. 120.
86 *U.S.G.*, 7 February 1835.
87 W.O. 211/7, f. 145.
88 P.P. 1851, XVII, pp. 536-7, 542-3.
89 Chichester papers, East Riding C.R.O., DDCH 95, pp. 27-36.
90 *U.S.G.*, 30 October 1841, p. 3
91 P.P. 1851, XVII, pp. 536-7, 542-3, and P.P. 1854, XXXIX, no. 479.
92 *U.S.G.*, 3 January 1846, p. 4
93 Ibid., 2 January 1847, p. 4.
94 *British Army Despatch*, 22 March 1850, p. 280, describes the editor of the *United Service Gazette* as being named in *The Times* in connection with Fitzclarence's school at Portsmouth. Of the four lecturers at the school listed in *The Times* for 4 March 1850, p. 3, only Stocqueler was not a serving officer, and the almost weekly references to Fitzclarence suggest he had a link with the *Gazette*. The supposition that Stocqueler was editor is supported by two further clues. The *British Army Despatch*, 16 November 1849, p. 1131, calls the editor of the *United Service Gazette* 'a private in a Company's Regiment of European Infantry' — a reference perhaps to Stocqueler's journalistic work in India. Furthermore his book, *A catechism of field fortifications*, was published at the *United Service Gazette* offices, and the *Gazette*'s review of another of his works, *The British officer*, identifies the author of the introduction as J. Mitchell, a frequent correspondent to the newspaper, although in the book itself the introduction is unsigned. In the *United Service Gazette*, 14 May 1853, p. 5, the writer speaks of the editorial policy of the last seven years, which supports the suggestion that Stocqueler was editor from 1846.
95 *U.S.G.*, 13 October 1849, p. 4.
96 J. H. Stocqueler, *A familiar history of the British Army*, p. 219.
97 *British Army Despatch*, 11 January 1850, p. 37.
98 Ibid., 4 January 1850, pp. 11-12.
99 *British Army Despatch*, 23 September 1853, p. 617; *U.S.G.* 2 October 1852, p. 5.
100 *Journal of the Society for Army Historical Research*, XLI, 1963, p. 94.
101 *British Army Despatch*, 28 April 1854, p. 4.
102 Wellington papers, Wellington to Sir Arthur Paget, 21 January 1837.
103 Ibid., editor of *N. & M.G.* to Wellington, 3 April 1834, and reply, 8 April 1834.
104 Ibid., memorandum by Gurwood, 3 February 1841.
105 *King's Regulations*, 1 June 1837, p. 448.
106 W.O. 3/92, p. 347

107 *U.S.G.*, 26 June 1838, p. 6.
108 *N. & M.G.*, 14 March 1840, p. 165.
109 *U.S.G.*, 14 May 1853, p. 4.
110 For a discussion of his work see Jay Luvaas, *The education of an army*, pp. 39-64.
111 W.O. 211/23, ff. 377-9.
112 *U.S.G.*, 14 May 1853, p. 4.
113 Watts, *Alaric Watts*, II, pp. 218-9.
114 Bodleian Ms Eng. Lett., c 252, ff. 45-6, Clerke to Napier, 28 December [? 1838].
115 Wellington papers, Wellington to Ellenborough, 11 May 1847.
116 William Napier, *Life of C. J. Napier*, II, p. 417.
117 B.M. Add. Mss 54536, ff. 32, 37, 43, Robertson to Napier, 29 January, 29 April and, 18 September 1842.
118 Ibid., 54536, ff. 79, 93-4, 5 March and 2 July 1847.
119 B.M. Add. Mss 49107, ff. 53, 73, Napier to Robertson, 8 February 1841, 10 August 1843. Charles 'leaked' his views on affairs both in the Northern District and in Scinde.
120 Ibid., 54525, ff. 70-1, 72, 76; 54526, ff. 14, 23, 25, 27, 34, 36, 69, 71, 74; 54536, f. 86; Bodleian Ms Eng. Lett. d. 230, ff. 85, 90, 94, 119, 160, 181-2, 195, 206; c 243, ff. 85, 90, 91, 118, 122; c 252, ff. 187, 193; H. A. Bruce, *Life of General Sir William Napier*, II, pp. 462, 476.
121 Charles in *N. & M.G.*, 16 February 1839, p. 105, and 4 May 1839, p. 286, and in *U.S.J.*, 1839, II, p. 106, see B.M. Add. Mss 49107, f. 25; William in *N. & M.G.*, 30 December 1848, p. 845; 26 August 1854, pp. 543, 548-9; for William and *U.S.M.* see also B.M. Add. Mss 54525, ff. 59, 64, 66, 72, 79.
122 B.M. Add. Mss 54526, f. 36, William Napier to Charles Napier, 20 November 1848.
123 *N. & M.G.*, 3 June 1848, p. 360.
124 J. G. A. Baird (ed.), *Private letters of the Marquess of Dalhousie*, p. 97.
125 Fitzclarence does not warrant an entry in the *Dictionary of national biography*, although there is a brief factual account in F. Boase, *Modern English biography*, I, col. 1057. Obituaries are to be found in *The Times*, 18 December 1854, *The Gentleman's Magazine*, March 1855, p. 304, *N. & M.G.*, 16 December 1854, *U.S.G.*, 16 December 1854, but, surprisingly, not in *U.S.M.* No modern work appears to have dealt with him.
126 W.O. 211/14, f. 91.
127 W.O. 211/14, f. 91; General de Ainslie, *Life as I have found it*, p. 79.
128 W.O. 211/14, ff. 86-91.
129 *U.S.G.*, 13 July 1850, p. 4.
130 *N. & M.G.*, 7 May 1853, p. 295.
131 *U.S.G.* 14 May 1853, p. 4.
132 *U.S.M.*, 1850, II, p. 53.
133 *N. & M.G.*, 8 May 1852, p. 296.
134 Bodleian Ms Clarendon Deposit, c 103, ff. 61-5, Fitzclarence to Clarendon, April 1853.
135 *U.S.G.* 4 September 1847, p. 3.

136 H. A. Bruce, *Life of General Sir William Napier*, II, pp. 277-8.
137 Bodleian Ms Eng. Lett. c 247, ff. 183, 188, 195-6, Kennedy to William Napier, 28 October 1850, 30 December 1850, 11 August 1851.
138 See *N. & M.G.*, 30 April 1853, p. 284; *Military Review*, II, 1853, p. 228.
139 R. P. Dunn-Pattison, *History of the 91st Argyllshire Highlanders*, pp. 170-2.
140 *British Army Despatch*, 15 September 1848, p. 152.
141 R.A. Add. E/1 no. 124, Cambridge to Forster, 26 August 1851.
142 Ibid., no. 42, 19 May 1847.
143 N.L.S. mss 1857, ff. 101-2, F. Brown to father, 18 May 1853.
144 Ibid., 2852, f. 175, Helen Brown to Brown, 3 June 1853.
145 J. C. Marshman, *Memoirs of Sir Henry Havelock*, pp. 215-6.
146 J. G. A. Baird (ed.), *Private letters of the Marquess of Dalhousie*, pp. 294, 306, 320, 354.
147 *U.S.G.*, 22 May 1852, p. 6; 5 June 1852, p. 4.
148 *U.S.G.*, 16 December 1854. p. 4.
149 William Douglas, *Soldiering in sunshine and storm*, p. 15.
150 N.L.S mss 1855, f. 89, Mountain to Brown, 3 January 1854.
151 Mrs A. S. H. Mountain (ed.), *Memoirs of A. S. H. Mountain*, p. 227.
152 Ibid., p. 222; Seaton papers, Mountain to Seaton, 27 March 1841.
153 M. L. Ferrar (ed.), *Diary of Colour-Sergeant George Calladine*, p. 188.
154 B.M. Add. Mss 40474, f. 240, Charles Napier to Hardinge, 9 January 1845.
155 [J. McMullen], *Camp and barrack-room*, p. 272
156 N.L.S. mss 1848, f. 154, Cochrane to Brown, 29 October 1853.
157 N.A.M. 7709-6-10, at end, p. 6, C.-in-C.'s confidential circular, Dublin, 21 July 1831.
158 W. S. Moorsom, *Historical record of the 52nd Regiment*, pp. 306, 311, 315.
159 W.O. 3/307, p. 63.
160 J. B. Atkins, *Life of Sir W. H. Russell*, I, p. 129.
161 George Higginson, *Seventy-one years of a Guardsman's life*, pp. 55-6.
162 B.M. Add. Mss 49117, f. 65, Maugham to Charles Napier, 30 October 1852.
163 Grey papers, D 5/2, journal of Gen. Charles Grey, 7 April 1850, p. 90, noting conversation between Prince Albert and Wellington.
164 R.A. E 1/43-46, quoted in part in Theodore Martin, *Life of the Prince Consort*, II, pp. 253-62.
165 *N.& M.G.*, 2 October 1852, p. 632.
166 A. C. Benson and Viscount Esher, *Letters of Queen Victoria*, II, p. 476.
167 Hardinge papers, Derby to Hardinge, 23 February 1852.
168 R.A. Y 97/37, Victoria to King Leopold, 30 September 1852.
169 B.M. Add. Mss 49105, ff. 141-2, Ellenborough to C. Napier, 8 February 1850.
170 A. I. Dasent, *John Thadeus Delane*, I, pp. 130-1.
171 B.M. Add. Mss 49140, f. 154, Napier's journal, 14 March 1846.
172 J. G. A. Baird (ed.), *Private letters of the Marquess of Dalhousie*, p. 158.
173 *U.S.G.*, 25 September 1852, p. 4.

174 *U.S.M.*, 1852, III, p. 305.
175 Hansard, 3rd series, CXXXI, c 235. See also P.P. 1860, VII, pp. 444-57.
176 R.A. Y 97/37, Victoria to King Leopold, 30 September 1852.
177 R.A. E 44/59, Hardinge to Albert, 29 November 1852.
178 Hardinge papers, Hardinge to Albert, 25 September 1855.
179 *U.S.G.*, 4 February 1854, p. 7. There is no reference to this in Hansard.
180 Hardinge papers, Torrens to Hardinge, 30 July 1853.
181 Seaton papers, Seaton to Leach, 2 November 1853(?), and Seaton to Hardinge, 4 November 1853.
182 *U.S.G.*, 7 January 1854, p. 4.
183 N.L.S. mss 2841, ff. 304-5, Macdonald to Brown, 25 November 1841.
184 R.A. C17/53, Albert to Russell, 31 March 1850.
185 Wellington papers, Somerset to Wellington, 3 April 1850.
186 Seaton papers, Seaton to Hardinge, 23 June [? 1856].
187 Bodleian Ms Eng. Lett. d 240, f. 203, Brown to William Napier, 27 December 1848.
188 N.L.S. mss 2851, f. 128, Cochrane to Brown, 8 November 1852.
189 R.A. Add. E/1 no. 113, Cambridge to Forster, 11 January 1851, quoted in Willoughby Verner, *Military life of Duke of Cambridge*, I, pp. 29-30.
190 R.A. Add. E/1 no. 106, Cambridge to Forster, 26 December 1850.
191 W.O. 37/13-101, f. 28, Brown to Scovell, 23 September 1852.
192 N.L.S. mss 1848, f. 79, Somerset to Brown, 25 September 1852.
193 Ibid., 2853, ff. 38-9, Felix to Brown, 7 November 1853.
194 Ibid., 1849, f. 11, memo by Brown, 15 February 1854.
195 Ibid., 1848, f. 177, Brown to Hardinge, 6 December 1853.
196 N.A.M. 6210/94/4, Brown to Wetherall, 9 February 1856.
197 N.L.S. mss 1849, ff. 9-27, memo by Brown, 15 February 1854.
198 Hereford Record Office, G/IV/A/382, Hardinge to Airey, 22 July 1854, and 436, 18 July [1854].
199 Sir George Cathcart papers, Hardinge to Cathcart, 14 December 1853.
200 Hardinge papers, Hardinge to Palmerston, 5 November 1854.
201 *N. & M.G.*, 1 January 1853, p. 9.
202 Ibid., 12 July 1856.
203 Grey papers, Charles Grey to Grey, 12 July 1856.
204 Ibid., Grey to Charles Grey, 15 July 1856.

CHAPTER 2
THE SOLDIER'S LIFE

Throughout the nineteenth century there existed a fundamental division of approach as to where the emphasis in reforming other ranks' conditions of service should lie. On the one hand there were those who argued that the army could attract better recruits in the first place. What was needed was an improvement in the soldier's terms and conditions of service, so that they conformed to (or even exceeded) the expectations of the better paid operatives in the civilian sector. As far as possible diet and accommodation, pay and pensions, should rival standards outside the army.

On the other hand were those who shared Wellington's notorious views on the lowly origins and doubtful motives of his men. They accepted that the likelihood of any improvement in the quality of those who enlisted was remote. Therefore the army's job was to try to forge from this unpromising material the type of soldier it required; it could do this by a mixture of punishment and reward, and also through the army's own system of education. Circumstances in the 1830s and '40s, favoured this approach. The duties imposed by imperial responsibilities put the emphasis on the regiment, which by its corporate sense of identity conveyed to the recruit a sense of moral worth and higher purpose. In addition the size of the army was relatively constant, and thus the alternative thesis, that greater inducements should be offered to attract not only better but also more recruits, carried relatively less weight.

Nonetheless the dialectic between the two was continuous. It is not a clear-cut distinction: corporal punishment was a feature of military discipline that could be seen as a discouragement to recruits. It is, however, a division around which the principal improvements in the soldier's welfare can be grouped. The present chapter will consider the first approach — the quality of recruits, their terms of service, and their standard of living. The unspectacular gains here confirm the argument that greater advances are to be found in the succeeding chapter, devoted to the improvement and education of the soldier while in service.

1. *Recruits and recruiting*

Each commanding officer would send out parties to beat up for recruits, and, since regiments were in most cases not tied to a locality and changed their stations regularly, a heterogeneous collection resulted. Generally, however, the stated preference was for Scotsmen. They were found to be more literate and, in Highland units, to be better behaved owing to the ties of kinship and the likelihood of misconduct being reported home. A higher proportion of them became n.c.o.s: in 1840, in the Royal Artillery 16 per cent of the Scots were n.c.o.s, but only 11·8 per cent of the English and 9·75 per cent of the Irish.[1]

Unfortunately, however, the supply of Scottish recruits began to dry up. As early as 1835 the 71st (or Highland Light Infantry) had found recruiting very sticky in locations as far apart as Aberdeen and Lanark.[2] By 1845 two nominally Scottish regiments, the 26th and 78th, had opened their recruiting to all parts of Britain, and in June 1845 three more, the 72nd, 79th and 93rd, although each regiment had six parties out, had not enlisted one man. The 74th alone of the Highland regiments was up to its establishment but only a third of its men were now Scots.[3] The 78th Highlanders, who had numbered 1,041 Scots out of 1,086 other ranks on their raising in 1793, fell from 810 Scots out of 840 in 1840 to 448 of 1,059 in 1850: it never recovered its true nationality following malaria and disease in 1844-5.[4]

Scots were proving progressively more reluctant to join the army. In 1830 13·5 per cent of the army were Scots, when Scots formed 10 per cent of the United Kingdom population: in 1870 the figures were 8 per cent and 10·5 per cent.[5] This trend can in part be explained by the employment possibilities offered by major railway construction in Scotland. But some other related phenomena need to be noted. The first is the falling away of specifically Highland recruits. The kilted regiments were in origin clan levies: thanks to the clearances that obligation of military service no longer existed and the families that had met it had deserted their glens. Those that remained were said to be reluctant to wear the kilt: the military form of Highland dress was impractical and excessively fussy, with the result that the maintenance of their uniform imposed a greater financial burden on the members of kilted regiments than on their trousered colleagues. Therefore the Highland regiments that did retain their national character increasingly relied on recruits from south of the Highland line. In 1830-4 the 42nd (Black Watch) took 26 per cent of its recruits from the Highlands, but 56 per cent from the rest of Scotland.[6] Even this solution presented problems. The relatively higher standard of national education meant promotion prospects were better for Scotsmen in units that were not native to Scotland. Those that remained could of course be Highlanders disappointed in their search for employment in the metropolis, but they could equally be Glaswegians, whom one commanding officer described as 'the greatest blackguards in the army'.[7]

For other units, however, the virtues of the Lowlander were extolled; he was said to be harder working, more intelligent and more adaptable to foreign lands than the Highlander. In 1836, Major du Bourdieu, who as commandant of the Provisional Battalion saw recruits for twenty-four different regiments, thought the Northern Irish as good as any Scots, and Yorkshiremen and Northumbrians were said to possess similar characteristics.[8] London produced the most recruits — twice as many as any other district — but these were often men from elsewhere in the country, who had failed to find all they had hoped for in the city. Although separate figures were not kept for Welshmen, such evidence as there is suggests they were reluctant to don the red coat — in 1843-4 of 17,450 recruits only 167 were Welsh[9] — although this may have been due to the lack of recruiting stations in Wales.

To an increasing degree, full employment in Britain, especially during the railway boom, forced the army to look across the water to Ireland for its men. The growing numbers of Irish caused alarm. Two-thirds of all courts-martial concerned them and, if of dominant proportions in a regiment, they rendered it unsafe to post that unit to Ireland.[10] Nonetheless the army's debt to them was great — of 677 men in the 1st Battalion of the Royal Scots in 1836, 289 were Irish,[11] and in 1854 the 23rd, nominally a Welsh regiment, had 331 Irish of a total strength of 809.[12]

But the Irish too were a wasting asset. Famine and emigration meant that, although the number of Irish recruits remained in proportion to their share of the United Kingdom population, their dominant position in the army was eclipsed. In 1830 42·2 per cent of the infantry were Irish, in 1840 37·2 per cent, in 1868 30·8 per cent and in 1896 12·2 per cent.[13] The biggest fall in population occurred in the 1840s, and in February 1854 Hardinge noted with some alarm the startling decline in Irish recruiting since 1852.[14] The Irish had in fact helped to obscure the difficulty of procuring soldiers from elsewhere in the country. In eighteenth-century Europe military service was the preserve of landed society. In nineteenth-century Britain the centres of social activity were the towns, and even the large estates had to conform to some of the rules of political economy. Ireland before the famine allowed the army to ignore this shift.

The army's ideal recruit therefore bore increasingly little resemblance to logical expectations. For, when officers expressed a desire for a better class of recruit, they seem not to have meant men of a different background or of a higher social class, but better types from the trades who already fed the army. It was reasoned that a gentleman's son or a clerk would only enlist if he were in some sort of trouble. Much to be preferred were agricultural labourers, and, especially since they were the victims of seasonal unemployment or of disappointed expectations in towns, they did constitute the majority of army recruits. The occupational origins of 113 recruits enlisted into the 80th Foot in 1839 were reasonably typical: sixty-four were labourers, nine servants, six tailors, six potters, four colliers and twenty-four from unspecified trades.[15] The usual orthodoxy was that recruits from 'the manufacturing districts and large towns are frequently idle and dissolute'.[16] But Dr Robert Jackson argued that artisans made good recruits, since mechanical work set them up better for the handling of arms and made them quicker to learn.[17] An interesting example of a battalion following this advice was the 42nd, which between 1830 and 1854 only took 38 per cent of its recruits from the labourer or servant class, as opposed to 11 per cent weavers, 7 per cent from shops or offices, 15 per cent craftsmen, 10 per cent cobblers or tailors, 5 per cent cloth-workers, 4 per cent from industry, 4 per cent miners, and 6 per cent from unknown trades. This regiment at least seems to have drawn skilled artisans from the depressed crafts, although it made little headway among the more successful industries.[18] Furthermore, if this pattern was repeated among the other Highland regiments, it would have buttressed the reputation of Scots recruits, since literacy (never below 50 per cent in all Scotland) was almost universal among artisans, mechanics and skilled labourers in Scotland.[19]

Urban recruits were physically less fit than those from the country. In the London District in 1838-9, 85 per cent of country recruits were approved, but only 62·5 per cent from the town.[20] Therefore, after the mid-century and as the centres of population swung to the English towns, officers came to recall the soldiers of the pre-Crimean army as physical paragons. General Sir William Butler mourned, 'Prior to the Crimean War ... strong men were easily obtained and no soldiers equalled ours in strength, courage and endurance. That day is gone ... men are now taken who would have been rejected with scorn a few years ago; we get recruits no longer from the rural districts, but from the slums of the big cities ... The old soldiers were men of splendid physique and well-chiselled feature. I often look now as soldiers pass and marvel what has become of those old Greek gods, for not only are the figures gone, but the faces have also vanished — those straight, clean-cut foreheads, the straight or aquiline noses, the keen, steady eyes, the resolute lower jaws and shapely turned chins. What subtle change has come upon the race? ... All I know is that they are gone as the buffalo are gone from the prairies.'[21] Behind Butler's romanticism lies a hard kernel of truth. The soldier must be inured to physical fatigue, be accustomed to the vagaries of the weather and must see the open country as a friendly, not an alien, place. Whatever his virtues in the handling of equipment, the urban recruit needs to develop these powers, both physical and psychological, during his service, and is in this respect inferior to him who has been brought up to them from his earliest days.

The recruit was inspected at the district headquarters by a staff surgeon. The rejection rate on health grounds could run as high as forty per cent,[22] but few were failed for moral or intellectual reasons. Of 6,026 rejections in 1843-4, only twelve were because of 'weak intellect'.[23] However, in general terms, the educational and social backgrounds of cavalry recruits were superior to those of the infantry. Moreover, some regiments — including the Grenadier Guards and the Royal Artillery — checked the previous characters of their soldiers, and the Royal Sappers and Miners, many of whose men were employed independently on surveys and in similar work, expected their recruits to be of good character, to be able to read and write, to have some knowledge of a mechanical trade, and to be aged eighteen to twenty-five (as against the unspecified age for the Line).[24]

It may seem a fruitless quest to ask why men enlisted, when the remainder of the recruits were 'thoughtless youths, petty delinquents, men of indolent habits, persons who are unable to procure work, or who are in very indigent circumstances'.[25] There was every ground for this being the case when debts of under £30 were remitted on joining up. Although extreme cases of desperation were the popularly accepted reasons for a man's enlisting, in such accounts as we have they were rarely the true cause: a lawyer enlisted in the 13th Light Dragoons owing to a 'difference' with friends,[26] and Sergeant David Reid, who was in any case something of a prig, wished to achieve more in life than manual labour, to see foreign lands and to gain promotion.[27] John Ryder, whose father had been in the army and tried to persuade him against it, said he was drawn into the 32nd Foot by its uniform.[28] Security of lodging and sustenance, and the promise of a pension at the end of the day, were advanced as causes by philanthropists but seem rarely to have crossed the recruit's mind.

The immediate — and deceptive — attraction for the recruit was the offer of bounty money. This was, however, earmarked to cover the cost of his 'necessaries' (the equipment not provided by the colonel of the regiment). In the cavalry the bounty fell approximately £1 6s. short of the sum required, and in the infantry it was about 12s. too little.[29] The soldier not unnaturally felt that he had been cheated, and in addition to the toughness and shock of adjusting to a new way of life found himself with a debt that with care would take six months to liquidate. In 1843-4 Hardinge attempted to remove this abuse, but he was only partially successful, as no more than minor increases in bounty were forthcoming.

The feeling therefore continued to predominate that the recruiting system was one of 'so much deception & trickery'.[30] This view, although common enough in military circles, was widespread among a civil population fed on the image of Sergeant Kite. Drink was an important element in the recruiting sergeant's repertoire. Although no recruit could be attested within twenty-four hours of being enlisted, so as to give him a chance to regain sobriety, this provision could be overcome by keeping the man in a constant state of intoxication.[31] In any case the recruit was often trapped by the requirement to produce £1 'smart' money and to repay the money he had received on enlistment before his discharge.

Common sense, however, told commanding officers that recruits brought in by trickery would make reluctant soldiers. Often n.c.o.s were chosen for the duty and carried with them instructions from their commanding officer on the type of men required. William Lucas, who, despite the customary family opposition, was very much a willing entrant to the 6th Dragoons, found that the recruiting sergeant gave 'a very good description of a soldier's life' before enlisting him.[32]

Apart from direct recruiting, regiments also raised men by 'volunteering', or the transfer of men from one regiment to another on payment of a bounty. The purpose of this was to augment the strength of the regiment more rapidly for service in India (where battalions were maintained on a stronger establishment than at home). It gave a regiment men seasoned to the climate, experienced veterans who would help the newly arrived unit adjust quickly. Those homeward bound would form a nucleus round which fresh recruits could be gathered and trained. In a sense, rather than have local colonial regiments, the Horse Guards instead condoned permanent postings for individuals. In 1837 Howick and

Hill agreed to extend the system to Canada,[33] and, when recruiting became difficult for Highland regiments, Scottish volunteers were called for to meet an augmentation in the 42nd Highlanders.[34]

However, the arrangement undermined the whole emphasis on regimental *esprit de corps* which commanding officers were trying to inculcate. The regiment returning to Britain to re-form would often lose as many as half its men, and in 1836 the 38th took back only 300, leaving 509 in the sub-continent.[35] Thus there was precious little on which to graft a recruit. In a very real sense, battalions in Britain were often little more than training units. Once abroad again, this carefully nurtured flower was brought up to strength by incomers, some of whom were married to local women and others of whom had enjoyed bad reputations in their previous regiment, the bounty attracting them to a new home and their former commanding officer only too pleased to be rid of them. Veterans proved more resistant to the absorption of regimental values than young recruits. Of twenty-seven volunteers received by one regiment in 1836, eight had been invalided within three years, eleven were dead and two transported: of the seven still with the regiment, six had been before a court-martial.[36] Although the Deputy Adjutant General announced in 1842 that he was going 'to knock on the head the volunteering system',[37] it still persisted. This was one nettle which was not firmly grasped.

With the army averaging only 100,000 men in total strength, the normal number of casualties per year, including discharges, was only 13,140, and the *ad hoc* system of recruiting produced an average of 12,885 recruits.[38] No cause for immediate alarm existed here but it was evident a rapid expansion of the army would find the machinery wanting. Although a total revision was at times suggested — the one attracting most support being a replacement of regimental recruiting parties by district recruiting staffs and employing pensioners to 'bring' men — when the Crimean War came, the customary peacetime shortfall in recruits of 2 per cent widened to 25 per cent. In March 1855 90,000 men were required but only 4,514 were procured. Apart from surrogate soldiers — foreign corps in Britain pay, the formation of non-combatant corps for labouring and other duties, and the embodiment of the militia — the only sanctions in the government's immediate power were temporary expedients, such as short service (February 1855), additional pay on active service (June 1855), or, in particular, the increased bounty that had been refused Hardinge a decade previously. The cavalryman's bounty rose from £5 15s. 6d. to £10 by January 1855 and the infantryman's doubled to £8. From March 1854 to March 1855 43,735 recruits were procured.[39] But this figure obscures the continued crisis since the bulk of these were drawn from the embodied militia, and had therefore already undergone the most painful aspects of adaptation to military life. Although the press's exposé of sufferings in the Crimea influenced an increasingly literate population, the fundamental problems were more deeply etched. Irish depopulation was now following in the steps of the Scots; high farming meant full employment for those still on the land; the recruit of the future lay in an as yet barely exploited area — the English towns. In the boom years of the 1850s and '60s even he would be hard to catch. However, of those serving in Scotland in 1851, 56·1 per cent of the English and Welsh were from cities, the cavalry were predominantly from the cities (74·1 per cent of the English) and, whatever their nationality, more n.c.o.s had an urban background. By 1891, this trend would be even clearer: 83·3 per cent of English infantry serving in Scotland were city-born. But in 1854 the assumptions behind army recruiting had not yet followed the shifts in population.[40]

2. *Life in service*

Recruits, thrown into a new life among strangers, probably away from home for the first time, began their military careers in low spirits. Marshall reckoned that nine-tenths now regretted the step they had taken.[41] Certainly desertion among them was far higher than for any other class of soldier — of 1,757 deserters in 1846–7, 1,177 were recruits and only 212 men of five years' service or over.[42]

Probably the least of their worries was their diet. The ration was regular and sufficient, comprising a pound of meat and a pound of bread (or three-quarters of a pound in Britain) per man per day. By modern standards it was low in vegetables and dairy produce, and it provided insufficient calories for daily hard work. But its main drawback was its monotony, totally unrelieved by any culinary competence in its preparation.

What rendered it irksome to the soldier, as his service progressed, was the system of supply. At home in 1848 the stoppage for rations was 6d. from a daily payment of 1s. 1d. (the additional 1d. being granted in 1800 in lieu of beer). Beyond this price, however high the cost of food, the soldier could not be charged, but should prices fall, then the difference was reimbursed, and in fact in 1849 he was only paying about $4\frac{1}{2}$d. Abroad, however, and in Ireland during the famine, the stoppage was fixed at 5d. (it was reduced from 6d. rather than add the 1d. beer money to the pay), but this did not respond to local market prices, thus leaving the soldier serving in foreign climes relatively poorer.[43]

The reason for the fixed stoppage abroad was that the Commissariat provided food by contract, and thus established a uniform standard, whereby the troops were guarded against fluctuations in price or availability. Consequently, however, the soldier's diet abroad assumed a stereotyped nature unjustified in the face of local fruits, fish and vegetables. The meat issued in the West Indies was salted for all but two days of the week, and therefore encouraged scurvy and stimulated the soldier's thirst. In 1836, Sir Andrew Halliday, Deputy Inspector General of Hospitals in Demerara, issued fresh meat to the troops on his own initiative and was charged with needlessly incurring heavy public expense.[44] He was acquitted, but the case gave additional momentum to an improvement in the soldier's diet. In 1837, Howick secured fresh meat every day for the troops in Jamaica, where mortality was highest, and in the Windward and Leeward Islands the ration was to be fresh meat five days a week, and salt pork for the other two.[45]

During the 1830s many regiments began to provide a third meal in the day, to supplement the main ones of breakfast and lunch. Since it provided an alternative occupation in the evening and stilled the pangs of the stomach, it acted as a means to reduce drunkenness. In 1844, as a result of memoranda by Tulloch, which showed just how many medical officers supported the introduction of a third meal and how far it had already progressed,[46] the Queen's Regulations stated that 'an evening meal of tea or coffee, with a portion of Bread, should be furnished ... when the price of Provisions and other circumstances admit',[47] that is to say without exceeding the regulated stoppage from the man's pay. On this basis a third meal was available in all the tropical stations, and in most of Great Britain and Ireland. But in stations such as Gibraltar and North America the price was too high to permit its provision, and the Treasury refused to heed the pleadings of regimental medical officers for an extra allowance.

The contract system itself was yet another source of discontent. In the competition to win a contract, purveyors often tendered such low prices that they could not meet the terms. Bread of the specified quality had its weight made up with cigar ends, candle wicks and stale crusts.[48] The result was that in the United Kingdom regiments and even companies preferred to make their own contracts rather than use the Board of Ordnance — especially in the late 1840s when cheaper food made the security of an Ordnance contract undesirable. The Ordnance undertook the distribution of perishable stores because the Commissariat did not have depots at home. Thus not only did the stoppage and consequently the quantity of the rations vary, but also so did the supply system. An expeditionary army for the field would be fed by the Commissariat, but it would be formed from regiments used to being supplied by the Ordnance or to fending for themselves. What had been a system had become, through Treasury penny-pinching, an anarchic free-for-all, only operable in optimum peacetime conditions. Furthermore, even within Britain, ridiculous anomalies appeared in the variety of costs between corps.[49]

The restoration of regimental contracts to regiments in Ireland that had adopted the Commissariat system during the famine was the subject of a committee formed of Sir Willoughby Gordon, Hardinge, and two Commissaries — Sir Randolph Routh and Mr. William Booth. Their report, dated 12 January 1849, favoured the establishment of a uniform and consistent practice throughout the empire, and suggested that the whole question of provisioning be entrusted to the Commissariat, who would thus be better prepared for their duties in the field and would at the same time ensure a regular supply during any emergency at home. Three meals per day should be provided in all stations, and the type of bread should be improved to white, not brown, of the quality known as 'seconds'. The stoppage for rations should be fixed at $4\frac{1}{2}$d. at home and $3\frac{1}{2}$d. abroad, so low that the soldier would cease to have any interest in market forces and would also (allowing for the 1d. difference in beer money) be no worse off if stationed overseas.[50]

Eminently sensible though the report's suggestions were, it would have been naive to imagine that political economists could underwrite the principle of true utility. The Select Committee on Army and Ordnance expediture opposed the provisions of the report that related to the Commissariat,[51] although a royal warrant of December 1850 did accept that $3\frac{1}{2}$d. be the stoppage abroad.

Some order was restored by Hardinge. Although he was disgusted at the government's miserliness and felt that regimental contracts would serve the men better, he was convinced of the military virtues of a uniform system and, as Master General of the Ordnance, fought in 1852 for the restoration to the Ordnance of the control of food contracts in Great Britain.[52] As a result, during 1853, the Ordnance contracted for 'seconds' bread, thus enhancing the attraction of its supplies for the regiments. In 1854 Hardinge completed the work of putting the soldier's ration on a uniform and equitable basis by finally prevailing upon the Treasury to sanction a stoppage of $4\frac{1}{2}$d. at home.[53]

The complexities of the rationing system no doubt worried the soldier only on a change of station. Much more forbidding to the new recruit was the initial appearance of his barracks. 'The usual construction of a soldier's barrack-room is an oblong apartment, having a door at one end and the fire-place at the other, with rows of iron bedsteads on either side, which are folded up with the beds in the day-time; there are also tables and benches. This oblong chamber serves as a dormitory, a dining-room, and washing-place for the women.'[54] The *United Service Journal* concluded that 'At present the jails and bridewells are far beyond them; and they rank only with asylums for the insane or some of the new poor-houses'.[55]

In 1822 the barracks had passed over to the control of the Board of Ordnance, and the result was that, when any complaints arose, a regiment's Quartermaster blamed the Barrack Master. He in turn blamed the Royal Engineers, who were nominally in charge of construction work but who usually found they lacked the means or the artificers to effect any improvement.[56] The Barrack Master was responsible for assessing the damages when a regiment quitted the area, and tended to charge it for fair wear and tear as well as for restoring the buildings to their 'original' condition. Consequently even new paintwork put on by the regiment had theoretically to be stripped and the commanding officer was thus discouraged from improving his regiment's accommodation.[57]

In fact, however, although the regulations were pettifogging, the true author of the discomfort was again a miserly government. Overcrowding was chronic: in 1847 five hundred men were crammed into barracks in Jersey built for 386, and ophthalmia was the consequence.[58] The regulation one-foot gap between beds was thus rarely observed. The bad air was compounded by the small fuel allowance and the difficulties of heating the large room, with the result that it was never properly ventilated. An Ordnance circular laid down that each man should be allowed four to five hundred cubic feet of space, but this bare minimum was only to apply to barracks under construction. Washing facilities were often confined to a pump in the barrack yard and, it was averred, 'The Ordnance Department do not recognise such a thing as a water-closet.'[59]

To prove the moral consequences of bad buildings was difficult. One commanding officer cited a barrack room thirty feet by twenty feet, to hold sixteen men; the fire was sufficient to heat five of them, and one halfpenny candle was meant to illuminate the room. It being impossible even to read there in any comfort, the soldier resorted to the canteen.[60] The immediate and more demonstrable consequence of this niggardliness in barrack construction was bad health. The London barracks were particularly associated with sickness. In a tropical climate, any deficiencies in construction were multiplied by overcrowding and in India (where the East India Company was responsible) Sir Charles Napier found that this caused more fatalities than did the 'climate, battle, drunkenness, or any other cause of death'.[61]

It was therefore in the colonies that improvements were first made in barrack construction. Wellington, when Master General of the Ordnance, appointed a committee to prepare plans of accommodation for troops in the West Indies,[62] but little was done until the pioneering work of Dr. Henry Marshall and his pupil, A. M. Tulloch. They showed by the tabulation of statistics not only that mortality was higher in tropical climates but also which localities had proved healthier and pointed out some conclusions on the site and style of barracks both at home and abroad.[63] Captain Smyth, R.E., reduced mortality in Demerara from approximately twenty per cent to 5·25 per cent, by constructing buildings that were well insulated against extremes of climate, cut off from marshes, and had high ceilings and wire gauze over the windows to exclude insects.[64] In 1841 Sir George Murray, Master General of the Ordnance, took the evidence of Marshall's report in hand and it became Board of Ordnance policy that barracks should not necessarily any longer be placed in the most strategic positions but in the more elevated and healthy spots.[65]

At home, the arguments for reconstruction could not rely on the same volume of statistical evidence. Sir Hussey Vivian, Murray's predecessor as Master General of the Ordnance, had been so shocked following a personal tour of the temporary barracks in the north of England that in 1840 he asked Sir Charles Napier to prepare a report. In the wake of Chartism, Napier condemned the existing small barracks scattered among the new towns as divided and weak against a potentially rebellious population, and equally useless for efficient military training if the people were quiet. Fresh sites should be chosen near railways and on the edge of towns, so as to render the troops rapidly disposable but safe from sudden attack. Large garrisons could be established and thus discipline and training would prosper.[66]

With Vivian's support, Napier justified his plan to the Home Secretary, Lord Normanby, and between 1841 and 1845 £212,000 was allocated for barracks in the disturbed areas of England.[67] By 1845 the new barracks at Bury and Ashton were ready, and those at Preston progressing. Good schools and reading rooms were included in their plans, and they became the first of a gradual improvement. A grant of £5,000 was taken in the 1847 Ordnance estimates for wash-houses.[68] Horfield barracks boasted such luxuries as a chapel, baths, and a horse infirmary.[69] The barracks of the new construction were reckoned to accommodate twenty per cent less men in the same area than those of the Napoleonic wars: the estimated cost of lodging each man was £100 and sergeants were allowed separate rooms.[70]

However, alongside the new buildings, the old barracks continued in use. In 1847 the Army Members launched a fresh attack in the Commons,[71] and in 1848, Burgoyne, the Inspector General of Fortifications, revealed that only £1,606,983 had been spent on barracks in the previous two decades.[72] Napier's prognosis was repeated, with particular reference to the Northern District, by Sir Harry Smith, Lord Cathcart, Sir George Brown and Sir Howard Douglas in 1853.[73] It is therefore no surprise that Raglan, in virtually his last act as Master General before departing for the Crimea, proposed a committee to increase the comfort of the barracks.[74] The report of the committee, submitted to Panmure in June 1855, while noticing the improvement in the newly constructed buildings, confirmed that 'the accommodation hitherto provided in barracks ... has been generally inadequate both for the comfort and convenience of the soldiers, and for the creation of a higher tone of social habits amongst them, and while [the committee is] aware that it is their duty to endeavour to reconcile the claims of the soldiers' comfort with the economical expenditure of the public money, they feel certain that considerations of economy should not be allowed to overbear the demands of a sanitary and moral character.'[75] The evidence presented a picture which the soldier of the 1820s would not have found unfamiliar. The committee's recommendations confirmed that, whatever the accusations levelled against the Board of Ordnance by angry soldiers, the real fault had been that no ministry was prepared to implement a major building programme.

In particular a question much debated in the army but almost totally ignored in the plans for barracks was the provision of married accommodation. Women were obliged to live with their husbands and children in the same crowded barrack room as the unmarried soldiers. At the best, they might have awnings for privacy. In 1847 a report for the Inspector General of Fortifications proposed the alternatives of lodging money for married soldiers or, preferably, the establishment of cottages within the barracks.[76] The former promised to be cheaper and in the estimates for 1849 Maule provided £4,000 as lodging money. However, this only allowed 4d. per week per family.[77] Although the sum was raised to 2d.

per day in the 1851 estimates, Colonel Chatterton observed that few took up the grant on sound financial grounds: by living out of barracks a soldier forfeited any claim to fuel and candle allowances and to the use of barrack bedding and furniture, benefits whose total value he thought exceeded 1s. 2d. per week.[78]

Moreover, on disciplinary grounds, it was highly desirable that all the men should live within the barrack compound. The preference of most officers — including Fitzclarence, who was one of those who had already tried to force the official hand[79] — was therefore for the provision of houses. In 1851 Maule approved suggestions in the service papers that trial model barracks for married soldiers be constructed by officers acting in conjunction with public companies.[80] One proposal in the following year — to form a society to provide married lodging houses by subscriptions within regiments — fell foul of the Articles of War.[81] However, another, sponsored by the officers of the Guards, raised £4,000 immediately (including money from Fitzclarence). With the £9,000 eventually collected, tenements of two rooms with a kitchen were leased at 2s. 6d. per week. However, difficulties were raised on military grounds because officers were acting as landlords to their subordinates, and on financial grounds, over the difference which existed between the low rentals and the value of the debentures in which the money was invested. Thus the War Office was eventually forced to buy out the officers of the Foot Guards and take over the first approved married quarters for the army.[82]

Part of the official reluctance to sanction married accommodation was due to the feeling that 'the more comfortable [the women] are made the greater is the inducement to marry'. This attitude was born not merely from a desire to reduce the number of regimental hangers-on, but from the philanthropic feeling that a soldier who was paid only a shilling a day could ill afford to keep a wife and two or three children. Hardinge felt that a necessary preliminary to the provision of married accommodation was a ration allowance for the soldier's family.[83] As Sir Charles Chichester of the 81st wrote in 1845, 'There seems reason to fear that Raikes is going to commit matrimony: it would be better for himself & the Regt it was murder.'[84]

Queen's Regulations, while charging commanding officers to discountenance marriage among their men, encouraged soldiers to apply for their commanding officer's approval. Permission was usually contingent on a number of years' good service. If the soldier married without approval, the indulgences normally granted to married men were withheld and consequently his wife would have to live out of barracks and he, most probably, in. When the regiment was ordered overseas, the wife's position became even tougher. Only six women could go with each company, although the proportion was increased to twelve if the regiment was posted to New South Wales or India. The general practice was to draw six names by lot from those 'legally' married. Women not chosen were returned to their parishes. When foreign service was at least a ten, and perhaps a twenty, year span, it was unlikely that husband and wife would meet again. So regimental officers tended to help their men by taking wives as servants for their families or by turning a blind eye to women smuggled aboard the transport vessel. Sir Charles Napier thought that in peacetime all women should accompany the regiment[85] and this seems to have been sanctioned by 1849 on the condition that the husbands of those not chosen paid the cost of their wives' rations.[86] Although regulations stated no women should follow the regiment on active service, four per company were allowed to sail with the army in 1854.[87]

To compensate for the vagaries of the life of a soldier's wife, a number of regiments established funds for them. These were made redundant in 1842 with the universal establishment of savings banks.[88] Ten years later the fears of military wives were further allayed by the formation of the Royal Cambridge Asylum for Soldiers' Widows (so named after its instigator, the Duke of Cambridge) and of the Wellington and United Services Benevolent Institution, pledged to the same cause.

The gradually improving position of the soldier's wife, even if her lot still remained a comparatively hard one, was due to the growing awareness of the correlation between marriage and good conduct. The Royal Sappers and Miners had the highest of marriage rates (about twenty per cent), although in this case good conduct could be attributed to their highly selective recruiting.[89] Officers nonetheless reported that married men proved to be steadier in the ranks and the moralists added that marriage would discourage prostitution, make the soldier save his pay, prevent him from deserting by giving him an additional tie, and also provide an alternative to drink. Statistics, based on one regiment over a three-year period, showed that 19 per cent of the single men had been court-martialled, but only 3·5 per cent of the married men. Over five years 35,501 hospital diets had had to be prescribed for 512 single men but only 1,044 for the 204 married men. Finally of 356 n.c.o.s, 200 were married, including all the staff sergeants and eight out of the ten colour-sergeants.[90] These figures themselves show how far some commanding officers found it advantageous to exceed the ideal of six women per company. In a long-service army, marriage to some extent was unavoidable, but, probably more than any other of the devices tried, it was the best method of sustaining good conduct.

Short of marriage, the soldier's most popular alternative means of coping with the bleakness of his lodging, the boredom of his existence and, in particular, the midday heat of the tropics, was drink. By the nineteenth century, excessive consumption was a habit so engrained in British military life that its antecedents no doubt lay as far back as Hogarth's gin shops and society's expectations of a soldier. Contemporaries in the 1830s were nonetheless drawn to the explanation and eradication of a phenomenon that bedevilled the army at every turn. For while many commanding officers felt that the soldier's demand for drink was such that to attempt to curb it was merely to encourage illicit consumption, they still heartily longed for a cure, since, in Wellington's words, drunkenness was 'the parent of every other military offence'.[91] The Rifle Brigade, although enjoying an excellent reputation for good conduct and high morale, had 121 cases of drunkenness in its 2nd Battalion and 124 in its Reserve Battalion in December 1842 alone — that is to say, about one in eight men was arrested on this charge in one month.[92] With such a large proportion of a regiment either incapable or under guard at any one moment, drink was a severe drain on a unit's effectiveness.

Much of the concern about the soldier's drinking habits was engendered by the medical officers, especially Fergusson and Marshall, who saw the consumption of alcohol, particularly in tropical climates, as the main cause of disease. Sir James McGrigor awoke Hill and Howick to this situation in 1835, but it was of course hard to quantify to what extent intemperance was responsible for illness.[93] However Captain Henry Havelock, of the 13th Light Infantry, admittedly himself an abstaining Baptist, unequivocally claimed that the absence of a spirit ration had allowed the beleaguered Jellalabad garrison to gain 'full one-third in manual exertion'.[94] It seemed too that resistance to disease was weakened by drink, for in Scinde forty-two teetotal women of the 86th, a regiment where half a bottle of arrack a day was deemed temperance, suffered only one slight attack of cholera between them while their menfolk were ravaged by the disease.[95]

Explanations for the soldier's addiction varied, but many felt the root cause of the habit to be the rum ration. Hardinge, when Secretary at War in 1829, had endeavoured to persuade the Horse Guards to allow a soldier to draw a money allowance in place of his ration, but the recruiting warrant of 1830 only granted such powers to commanding officers whose units were in the field or in cases where a medical board approved it.[96] Fergusson noted that the grog was officially taken with three parts water but that thirst encouraged the consumption of more and habit increased the proportion of alcohol. Nominally to render the water safer, a half pint of rum was the daily issue to soldiers on board ship, and even their children received an eighth of a pint. Fergusson concluded by likening the ration to the inoculation of the entire army with an incurable disease.[97]

Further official encouragement to drink was given in the barrack canteens. Since the entire regiment tended to drink in the canteen, a man's absence was commented on and he was pressurised into going. As a part of the barracks, it was administered not by the Horse Guards but by the Board of Ordnance, who sold the lease to the highest bidder. In addition, 'privilege' or 'head' money was levied in accordance with the number of men in the barracks, and this could rise to as much as £1 1s. per ten men per month.[98] To recoup, the lessee would charge high prices (although in 1847 it was ordered that prices should accord with those in neighbouring shops),[99] or go to a brewer to raise the rent and, as a tied house, purvey the brewer's worst beer. He had no interest in the comfort, health or discipline of the troops. However, it was felt infinitely preferable to have the men drink in approved establishments under the eye of their n.c.o.s, than to abolish the canteens and force them into the town. Therefore, since the canteen was a necessary evil, attention shifted to the improvement of its administration. It was often suggested that an n.c.o. should run it, with the profits being devoted to a regimental fund for the purchase of library books or the reward of good conduct. A wider range of commodities might be stocked so that it acted as the regimental shop for food, coffee, tea and soap.

The chief problem was the high consumption of spirits in preference to malt liquors or beer. In particular West Indian rum and East Indian arrack provided temptations in stations where illness, heat and monotony all combind as inducements to drink. In India, in 1845, over three pints of arrack cost about two shillings, only slightly more than the cost of one bottle of beer,[100] and this was in spite of the East India Company's suggestion that the canteen fund be used to subsidise the price of beer.

Pressure on the Horse Guards to take action came from two sources, on the one hand the Army Medical Department and on the other the flourishing regimental temperance societies. Hill's decision to ban these societies,[101] on the grounds that he could not condone regimental clubs with their own codes of behaviour, increased the onus on the central authorities. Howick favoured the abolition of the sale of spirits in canteens, and he had the support of twenty-six commanding officers, who had given evidence to the 1836 commission on military punishments.[102] However, his departure from the War Office forestalled any action. In 1845 the new principal Chaplain, the Rev. G. R. Gleig, quoted the success of a ban at Nottingham in order to call for the abolition of the sale of spirits and to summon up cosy images of the canteen's replacement by a general shop and coffee room.[103] The following year, albeit anonymously, Gleig published his views in the *Quarterly Review*, and gained the parliamentary support of Colonel Lindsay. In 1848 Gleig carried the day and the sale of spirits in barrack canteens was banned.[104]

A single solution to these twin problems, the welfare of the soldier's family and his own propensity to drink, seemed to lie in the institution of savings banks. If the soldier could be persuaded to invest the residue of his daily pay (about five pence after stoppages had been made for his rations and his laundry), he would not dissipate it in the canteen. He would also either provide himself with a lump sum on discharge or make provision for his widow and orphans. Regimental funds devoted to these ends proliferated, and they were particularly popular in Canada where the additional tie checked the investor from deserting to the United States.

In 1838, after a number of false starts, Hill proposed the establishment of a uniform scheme. He felt it undesirable to have an authority independent of the commanding officer (in those cases where separate committees administered the funds) or alternatively a system subject to the caprice of successive commandants. The Treasury favoured a central savings bank, with the regiments as branches. On this basis, with an interest rate of £3 15s. per year, allowable on as small a deposit as 6s. 8d. per quarter, a savings bank act was passed in 1842 and a warrant published in 1843.[105] However the slowness of the Horse Guards to act meant that by now large sums were involved, as well as a great many units.[106] Once again the regiments had anticipated the Horse Guards, and, although most of the funds were dissolved by instruction, it required an act of Parliament to effect the final merger with the approved savings banks in 1849.

These divided interests only in part explain the sluggish start made by the banks. By 1845 there were no more than 2,000 depositors in the whole army.[107] The men themselves feared that a good rate of deposits would suggest that their pay was too high and that it could consequently be reduced; their officers dreaded funds being accumulated for a massive debauch. Regimental influences were predominant, a low rate perhaps reflecting the existence of some alternative fund as much as a high rate did the encouragement of a paternal commanding officer. Neither Life Guards regiment had a single depositor in 1846, while the Blues were good subscribers.[108] By 1849, however, no doubt largely owing to the suspension of regimental funds, there were 5,756 depositors, with a total £75,128, and by 1853 this had grown to 10,728 and £124,249.[109]

Perhaps an element in the reluctance to save was attributable to the fact that at least the soldier was in pensionable employment. For many, it was this alone that explained why men enlisted. Whether this was true or not — the evidence that the soldier was careless of the future is strong — it provided a useful argument in the hands of the military reformers. On the one hand, in the aftermath of Waterloo, demobilisation and the cries for retrenchment had in effect produced a constantly growing bill for pensions, that in turn became the focus for radical attacks. In 1829, the 'non-effective' estimates for the army were paying 85,756 men — almost as many as there were effective.[110] The recruiting argument served to deflect some of these barbs. On the other hand, the reformers could suggest that much might be done to prevent an increase in the list, if Parliament would care to take note of the medical officers' arguments. They held that the debilitating effect of imbibing in a tropical climate or the disease fostered in ovecrowded barracks might not necessarily impair a man's effectiveness in the field but would certainly wear him out in the long run. Thus the pension bill was swollen by men incapacitated not through enemy action but through largely preventable circumstances.

Therefore the attack on pensions was two-pronged. One prong was the improvement of barrack construction and the ban on the sale of spirits in canteens. The other approach was a revision of the pension warrant itself. In 1829 Hardinge, as Secretary at War, established a board to define closely the nature of disabilities qualifying for a pension, retaining as its object the need to have the regiment effective for the field, and to make, in Wellington's words, 'service & not *disability* ... the criterion'.[111] The result was a military not a financial warrant, that established long and good service as the basis of reward. After twenty-one years' service (twenty-four in the cavalry), the pensioner received 1s. a day, or 10d. a day if discharged at his own request. Additions were made for wounds and rank. Partially disabled men of less service were no longer allowed to be parasites on the state: in the past 'men who had been discharged as blind were restored to sight, the deaf heard, and the lame ceased to halt'. In future their pensions were to last for a period of up to three years to enable them to secure a civilian job.[112]

In 1833, however, Sir John Hobhouse to some extent reverted to the principle that disability be the standard. The private discharged after twenty-one years now received 6d. per day, although this could rise to a shilling after additional service, or be added to for disability. The 1833 warrant appalled all shades of army opinion. In military terms a soldier was worn out after twenty-one years. Only about a dozen men per regiment had served that long at any one time, and in 1845 only two of 27,000 soldiers in the United Kingdom had served the twenty-seven years required for a shilling pension.[113] Consequently either the soldier dragged himself painfully through a few years' extra service, or he was encouraged to drink or in some other way induce disability. In both cases, the effectiveness of the regiment was impaired, and the good recruits needed to compensate were unlikely to be forthcoming. If the veteran of twenty-one years' service left on the minimum pension, pauperdom was his likely lot. Sixpence a day was totally insufficient for him to maintain himself. The only job open to the discharged soldier without a trade would be on the land, but a farmer was always more anxious to take on local labour than employ the pensioner so as to save on poor rates.[114]

The restoration of adequate pensions had to wait until 1847. This warrant, drawn up by Maule, virtually reverted to the 1829 scale, establishing 1s. as the basic pension (or 10d. if the soldier was discharged at his own request), with reductions for those of less than twenty-one years' service. It was less of a sop to the ire of the army than a manifestation of Grey's wish to introduce limited enlistment. Although men of over ten years' service were reluctant to take their discharge, the Horse Guards wanted a guarantee that this leavening of experience would be preserved for the army and the attraction of an increased pension after twenty-one years was the simplest method.

The combination of pension rights and savings banks could make the soldier the possessor of capital and thus in theory elevate him into the higher echelons of working-class employment. In addition the army offered him job security and guaranteed food and lodging. But none of these attractions seems to have been sufficient to attract the elusive 'better class' of recruit on a regular basis. The press and popular opinion played on the accompaniments of military service — disease, death in foreign climes, the lash. By the 1850s the standard of living in towns had probably improved little on that a century before, and the worst features of barrack life would not have been too shocking. But his pay was closer to that of soldiers in Europe than to prevailing levels in working-class employment. The 1832 poor law commission calculated the weekly wage of an agricultural labourer at 12s. and that of the artisan as 33s. In Leeds in 1838 the weekly wage of a skilled labourer was often over £1.[115] That of the soldier remained a shilling a day. Even if the massive capital investment in barracks and living conditions that the reformers wanted had been made, the easing of cyclical unemployment after the mid-1840s put the 'better class' even further beyond the recruiting sergeant's wiles.

3. *The 1847 limited enlistment act*

The introduction of limited enlistment in 1847 was not — as it was to be later — a response to a shortfall in recruiting. The only way in which it resembled the logic of the 1870 short service act was in the hope that it would create a reserve. In the event this aspect was not fully developed. Its principal motive was to equate military service with other working-class occupations, to remove the implications of loss of liberty implicit in an indefinite period of service, and it was thus a manifestation of the desire to attract a better class of recruit. It was an acknowledgement of the failure to draw in a higher standard of soldier by other means.

The military doctors, Fergusson and Marshall, were the principal advocates of limited enlistment. They mingled the cause of justice and humanity with the pressures of a market economy. Marshall claimed that a soldier's average service before he was invalided out was only ten years.[116] Therefore manpower would not be affected by a reduction in the period of service. Charles Grey thought that about half the strength of every regiment had served under seven years,[117] and in any case the Rifle Brigade at the Cape found their more experienced but middle-aged soldiers faring badly under fatiguing duties.[118] The reluctance of those of over ten years' service to take their discharge supported the theory that there would be no sudden exodus from the army. From 1809 to 1828, a period when limited enlistment was permitted, Marshall found that only 2·4 per 1,000 at Dublin opted for it in preference to unlimited enlistment, although this figure rose to eighteen in London and 145 in Glasgow.[119]

The anticipated effect on the army would be a purely moral one. It would restore hope to the men and consequently reduce desertion. It would make parents less reluctant to part with their sons, and the sons more willing to join the colours; as well as a better class of recruit, if the soldier did take his discharge after the expiry of his initial commitment, the govenment would have the benefit of a reduced bill for pensions. The length of service advocated ranged from seven to fourteen years, with the option to re-enlist for a further term.

Although canvassed in the 1820s and early 1830s, it was neglected by the 1836 commission on military punishments and not until 1837 did the *Naval and Military Gazette* take up the cudgels and then cling to the cause with its customary pertinacity. The *United Service Magazine* followed suit, and could count among its sympathisers such famous Peninsular warriors as Sir John Colborne[120] and Sir Hussey Vivian.

'If you desire to effect such a great moral change in the Army,' Vivian felt, 'if you hope to preserve discipline & to get rid of a mode of punishment by the power of which it has in a great degree been hitherto maintained — you must take means to better the condition of the soliders so that a class of men of a superior description in point of character may be induced to enter your ranks you must limit the period of his service — & secure to him an adequate maintenance in his old age.' What Vivian had in mind was no more than an absolute limit of twenty years' service, to be reduced by three months for every year spent in a tropical climate. On his discharge the soldier would be sufficiently young and fit to learn a new trade, and he could thus be given a progressive rate of pension, which would increase in accordance with his age and incapacity for work. Apart from the benefits to the individual, Vivian envisaged his scheme removing the large number of ineffective, old soldiers cluttering the army in the 1830s, and instead creating a reserve force of pensioners in counties and enhancing the attractions of a military life for recruits.[121] Significantly, among the Secretaries at War he wrote to on the subject was Howick. Unlimited service, he told him, was one of the greatest obstacles to improvement: limit the period of service and all else would follow.[122]

However, the chief advocate of limited enlistment in the Commons was Captain Layard, and in 1845 he called for an enquiry into the value of a set period of ten years' service. Citing Marshall, Jackson and the military press, he believed a better class of recruit would enlist, and desertion and crime would fall. Sir Howard Douglas reminded Layard that the current rules for discharge 'amounted, virtually, to an optional system of limited service' and the motion was defeated.[123] However, the following year, when Layard returned to the attack, he found himself pre-empted by the government's own actions.

Grey, perhaps remembering Vivian's views of seven years earlier, told

Maule in September 1846, that 'I have always been for limited enlistment; and what is more for practically short service from our soldiers. Limited inlistment wd make the service most popular, & if the men served but a short time, say 10 years, you wd have these gt. advantages — 1st. An army always young & vigorous — 2d. great relief from the heavy burthen of the out pension list — 3d. the maintenance of a reserve force both at home & in the colonies of a very cheap & most effectual kind.'[124]

In looking for the creation of a reserve as well as an incentive to enlistment, Grey was aiming for much more than his contemporaries. He embodied the proposal in his memorandum on the army circulated to the cabinet, and, on 14 December 1846, he wrote officially to Maule and Wellington filling in the details. The ten-year period would be expandable for two years if the troops were on active service and for one year if abroad. On discharge, the soldier would serve in a reserve until aged fifty-five and qualified for a pension. Those now serving were to have the benefit of limited service, provided that no regiment lost more than twenty-five men in the case of the infantry or ten for the cavalry.[125] To the Master General of the Ordnance, he proposed terms of twelve years for the Royal Artillery and fourteen for the Royal Sappers and Miners, in view of their more extended training.[126]

Predictably, Wellington opposed. At the moment, the Duke argued, those of over ten years' service amounted to 12,000 cavalry and infantry at home alone. The settled rhythm of military life would be upset, 'the most intelligent, the most efficient' men would be lost, and those elegible but debarred by the limitation of numbers from taking their discharge immediately would become discontent. He suggested, by way of compromise, that the experiment be limited to recruits only.[127]

Grey relented sufficiently to suspend the part relating to serving soldiers,[128] and thus in effect met the Duke's objections. With his customary lack of tact, however, he tried to suggest that the Duke's prognosis was wrong. After fourteen years' service a man was already entitled to apply for a free discharge, and therefore the futures of only 6,798 soldiers were being discussed — that is, those of more than ten but less than fourteen years' service. Even after fourteen years, only $2\frac{1}{2}$ per cent of the infantry at home took their discharge, while, apart from the Cape (9 per cent) and North America ($7\frac{1}{2}$ per cent) where men settled, less than one per cent took it in the colonies.[129]

Wellington was not to be pushed. He reminded Grey that the army was already overstretched owing to its small size and insufficient battalions, without in addition losing its most experienced and valuable men. He

The soldier's life

wrote to Russell, refusing to 'destroy the efficiency of the small Army which Her Majesty's Govt has at its disposition', and threatened to tender his resignation to the Queen.[130] Both Russell and Grey hastened to assure the Duke that they would not adopt the plan of discharging soldiers then in the army without consulting him, and that they would only progress with a bill for prospective ten-year enlistment.

On this basis, Maule introduced the bill in the Commons, proposing ten years for the infantry and twelve for the other arms, with provision to re-enlist for a further eleven or twelve years. A number of soldiers supported the first reading, but Sir Howard Douglas rushed to the defence of the *status quo*. If the measure were genuinely good, why was Wellington's approval not trumpeted forth and why were the bill's provisions not extended immediately to all ranks? It was unfair to enlist men for a period, at the end of which no pension was available, but which might nonetheless leave them broken in constitution. Sidney Herbert, while not supporting Douglas in all his arguments, did agree that 'it was not a superior class of men, but superior men of the same class, that they wanted', and thought a limit of fourteen years would meet the requirements of the bill and at the same time not upset the existing balance. Douglas proposed this as an amendment to the bill, but it was defeated.[131]

In his winding-up speech on the third reading, the Prime Minister, Lord John Russell, reflected a wider spirit of reform: 'It is not an answer to us to say that there was a good Army thirty or forty years ago, in the Peninsula or at Waterloo, for we must make all the different institutions of the country conform to the general spirit of the times and the advancement of the day.'[132] In the Lords, Grey, facing the phalanx of now ennobled Peninsular heroes, explored the same vein. The bill, he urged, must be seen as 'part of a course of policy and of a series of measures which for the last twenty-five years had been passed with the object of raising the character of the Army, and improving the condition of the soldier'.[133] The Peninsular peers, especially Combermere and Londonderry, looked to Wellington to smash the Secretary of State's case. But Wellington, who had only assured Grey of his support four days before,[134] tersely shattered their expectations; old soldiers would not be lost to the service as the incentives to re-enlist existed, and consequently the measure had his backing.

Stanley and Brougham tried to gather the pieces by publicising the Duke's private opinions. Of the military peers, Wellington carried with him only Seaton and the Master General of the Ordnance, Anglesey, leaving in opposition Cardigan, Lucan, Beresford, de Ros, and, of course, Londonderry and Combermere. But in such a narrow majority as 108 to 94 his views must have been the crucial factor for the civilians.

Of course, Wellington, as Commander-in-Chief, had no constitutional right to do anything other than support the government or resign. The debate is important, however, because it shows his relationship with the older generation of soldiers, while a younger group — such as Layard — supported by the more far-sighted middle-ranking Peninsular officers (Hardinge and Seaton) felt able to follow their own consciences, the military press and Grey. Equally the measure, the last really important one in the whole welter of reforms to improve the lot of the soldier in the pre-Crimean period, was carried while the Duke lived, and not in the liberated years after 1852.

In the event the efficacy of the reform was marginal. In the choice between short service and a large reserve or long service and no reserve, a compromise had been reached which ensured neither. The time devoted to training, despatching troops to the colonies and acclimatisation meant that a two or three-year term on the continental model was impossible for an army with colonial duties. A large reserve for European war was therefore incompatible with continuing obligations abroad. But the alternative, a long-term commitment, seemed to deter recruits, particularly the elusive 'better class'. The provisions of 1847 did not appear to improve the quality of the intake, and one argument said that the prudent recruit feared discharge after ten years when he might be of an unemployable age. The actual terms of the act were not effective until ten years after its first enlistment — 1857 — and thus the failure of 1847 took time to manifest itself. In the event, recruiting became so difficult, that the 1867 army enlistment act sanctioned the only practicable solution, a twenty-one-year commitment. But before this had time to operate, despite the experience of 1847, Cardwell's 1870 short-service act stipulated a seven-year period, and subsequent service in the reserve. It confirmed all the doubts expressed in 1847: re-engagements were few, the better class of recruit was not forthcoming and the tough professional was harder to forge.

The relative failure of the act perhaps proved that the army's attention should be focused on improving the men who did join and not on attracting a better class of recruit: by making a good soldier from a profligate the army justified its place in society.[135] It was logical that this argument should be refined by the most successful of 'small war' generals, Garnet Wolseley.[136] Not only did it provide a variant on the

The soldier's life

army's educative role in society which so preoccupied his continental brethren, but it also constituted a doctrine which was compatible with long-service professionalism, with the peculiar strategic role of the British army.

Notes

1. Papers of Cornet Drummond, S.R.O. GD 24/1/936, return for House of Commons, 9 March 1841.
2. Grey papers, Charles Grey to Howick, 10 December 1835.
3. W.O. 1/1138. L. B. Oatts, *Proud heritage*, 2, p. 271, claims all 74th in 1851 were Highlanders, except for eighty Irishmen.
4. H. Davidson, *History and services of the 78th Highlanders*, II, pp. 167-8.
5. H. J. Hanham, 'Religion and nationality in the mid-Victorian army', p. 163.
6. Eric and Andro Linklater, *The Black Watch*, p. 227.
7. N.L.S. mss 2841, f. 271, R. Wynyard to Brown, 23 October 1841.
8. P.P. 1836, XXII, pp. 149, 164.
9. *U.S.M.*, 1845, III, pp. 107, 284; 1846, I, p. 117.
10. *N. & M. G.*, 24 June 1848, p. 411; N.A.M. 7709-6-12, p. 249, Vivian to Macdonald, 19 October 1834.
11. J. C. Leask and H. M. McCance, *Regimental records of the Royal Scots*, p. 417.
12. A. D. L. Cary and S. McCance, *Regimental records of the Royal Welsh Fusiliers*, II, p. 69.
13. H. J. Hanham, 'Religion and nationality in the mid-Victorian army', pp. 161-2.
14. Newcastle papers, NeC 10595a, memorandum by Hardinge, 6 February 1854.
15. *Journal of the Society for Army Historical Research*, XLIX, 1971, p. 186.
16. Henry Marshall, *On the enlisting, discharging and pensioning of soldiers*, p. 8.
17. Robert Jackson, *A view of the formation, discipline and economy of armies*, p. 188.
18. Eric and Andro Linklater, *The Black Watch*, p. 228.
19. R. K. Webb, 'Literacy among the working class in nineteenth century Scotland', *Scottish Historical Review*, XXXIII, 1954, pp. 100-14.
20. Marshall, *On enlisting*, p. 6.
21. William Butler, *An autobiography*, London, 1911, pp. 41-2.
22. P.P. 1850, X, p. 244.
23. *U.S.M.*, 1846, II, p. 271.
24. P.P. 1849, IX, evidence p. 416.
25. Marshall, *On enlisting*, p. 10.
26. *U.S.M.*, 1844, I, p. 523.
27. [David Reid], *Memories of the life of a soldier*, pp. 2-3.
28. [John Ryder], *Four years' service in India*, p. 1.

29 Hansard, 3rd series, LXVI, c 1370.
30 N.L.S. mss. 2842, f. 273, A. Lawrence to Brown, 29 September 1842.
31 P.P. 1836, XXII, p. 208.
32 Lucas's ms autobiography, quoted by Marquess of Anglesey, *A history of the British cavalry*, I, p. 123;
33 W.O. 43/745, f. 150; W.O. 3/96, p. 396.
34 W.O. 3/98. p. 118.
35 W.L. Vale, *History of the South Staffordshire Regiment*, p. 105.
36 *U.S.M.*, 1842, III, p. 257.
37 N.L.S. mss 2842, f. 274, A. Lawrence to Brown, 29 September 1842.
38 N.L.S. mss 2849, f. 213, 'Distribution of Army', 27 November 1851.
39 P.P. 1854-5, IX, part III, *4th report*, pp. 351-2.
40 Olive Anderson, 'Early experience of manpower problems in an industrial society at war', *Political Science Quarterly*, LXXXII, 1967, pp. 526-45; Alan Ramsay Skelley, *The Victorian army at home*, pp. 289-94.
41 Henry Marshall, *Hints to young Medical Officers of the army on the examination of recruits*, pp. 89-90.
42 Hansard, 3rd series, XCI, c 1353.
43 P.P. 1850, X, pp. 1024-8.
44 *N. & M.G.*, 26 March 1836, p. 194; *U.S.G.*, 12 March 1836; *U.S.J.*, 1837, II, p. 507.
45 *U.S.J.*, 1837, II, p. 379; Grey papers, Howick to Hill, 1 February 1837; W.O. 43/656, f. 213.
46 W.O. 43/777, ff. 1-68.
47 *Queen's Regulations*, 1844, p. 138.
48 *British Army Despatch*, 23 May 1851, p. 330
49 W.O. 44/539.
50 P.P. 1850, X, pp. 1022-8.
51 P.P. 1851, VII, p. 51.
52 W.O. 43/829, ff. 260-338; Herbert papers, Hardinge to Trevelyan, 20 January 1854.
53 Herbert papers, III B (54), Treasury minute, 10 February 1854; Hansard, 3rd series, CXXX, c 489.
54 *U.S.M.*, 1846, III, p. 122.
55 *U.S.J.*, 1837, III, p. 324.
56 *N. & M.G.*, 3 June 1837, pp. 341-2.
57 Horse Guards circular, 10 December 1838.
58 W.O. 3/106, p. 45.
59 *U.S.M.*, 1846, III, p. 114. In fairness, it seems that attempts to replace privies with water-closets were confounded by the soldiers' own ill-treatment of them, P.P. 1854-5, XXXII, 37, pp. 19, 55, 76, 90, 150.
60 *N. & M.G.*, 31 January 1852, p. 75.
61 S.R.O., GD 45/8/78, Napier to Wellington, 15 June 1850.
62 *Wellington despatches*, II, pp. 126-8.
63 Marshall's earliest statistical work appeared in 1821, but the *Edinburgh Medical and Surgical Journal*, XXXIX, XL, XLII, XLIV, carried the surveys on the health of troops that led to the official reports done in conjunction with Tulloch.

64 *Royal Engineers Professional Papers*, II, 1838, pp. 232-7, also pp. 238-44.
65 N.L.S. Adv. mss 46.9.10, p. 32, Murray to Goulburn, 1 October 1841; P.P. 1849, IX, p. 427.
66 B.M. Add. Mss 54515, Napier's 'Report on barracks in the Northern District' 1840.
67 F. C. Mather, *Public order in the age of the Chartists*, p. 171.
68 Hansard, 3rd series, XC, c 653.
69 *U.S.G.*, 24 April 1847, p. 2.
70 P.P. 1849, IX, pp. 244-5.
71 Hansard, 3rd series, XCI, cc 711-2, 721, 725, 727.
72 W.O. 44/565.
73 Second Earl Cathcart papers, J. 43, Trevelyan to Cathcart, 16 February 1853.
74 W.O. 46/92, p. 15.
75 P.P. 1854-5, XXXII, 37, p. iii.
76 *Aide-mémoire to the military sciences*, III, p. 175.
77 Hansard, 3rd series, CXIII, c 363.
78 Hansard, 3rd series, CXVI, c 203.
79 W.O. 3/107, p. 314.
80 *U.S.G.*, 21 December 1850, p. 4; *U.S.M.*, 1850, III, pp. 568-71; *N. & M.G.*, 5 April 1851, p. 216; Hansard, 3rd series, CXV, cc 750-1.
81 *N. & M.G.*, 29 May 1852, pp. 348-9, and 2 July 1853, p. 426; *British Army Despatch*, 28 May 1852, pp. 341, 438.
82 George Higginson, *Seventy-one years of a Guardsman's life*, pp. 67-9; *U.S.G.*, 31 December 1853, p. 8.
83 W.O. 46/89, pp. 259-60, Hardinge to Gleig.
84 East Riding C.R.O., DDCH 82, p. 91, diary entry of Sir Charles Chichester for 26 February 1845.
85 C. J. Napier, *Remarks on military law*, pp. 187, 257.
86 W.O. 4/269, p. 306.
87 P.P. 1854-5, IX, part I, *2nd report*, p. 243.
88 W.O. 3/101, pp. 298, 457. On savings banks, see below, pp. 67-8.
89 *N. & M.G.*, 23 September 1843, p. 597.
90 *U.S.M.*, 1849, III, pp. 349-54.
91 *Wellington despatches*, V, p. 343.
92 N.L.S. mss 2843, f. 9, R. Irton to Brown, 1 February 1843.
93 W.O. 43/475.
94 J. C. Marshman, *Memoirs of Major-General Sir Henry Havelock*, pp. 107-8.
95 *British Army Despatch*, 15 September 1848, pp. 155-6.
96 B.M. Add. Mss 54517, f. 151, Hardinge to C. Napier, 21 July 1845.
97 William Fergusson, *Notes and recollections*, p.72.
98 P.P. 1854-5, XXXII, 37, p. v.
99 W.O. 3/305, p. 292.
100 Marquess of Anglesey, *Sergeant Pearman's memoirs*, pp. 27, 61.
101 W.O. 3/98, pp. 183, 277.
102 W.O. 43/592.
103 Herbert papers, I M (32), memo by Gleig, 8 November 1845.

104 W.O. 4/269, p. 399; Horse Guards circular, 27 September 1848.
105 W.O. 43/704, ff. 1-85.
106 W.O. 43/859.
107 Hansard, 3rd series, LXXIX, c 222.
108 W.O. 3/104, p. 352.
109 Herbert papers, III A (46).
110 *U.S.J.*, 1829, II, p. 317.
111 Wellington papers, Hardinge to Wellington, 15 February 1836, quoting Wellington.
112 Marshall, *On enlisting*, pp. 190-9.
113 Hansard, 3rd series, LXXIII, c 568.
114 S.R.O., GD 45/8/21, p. 18, memorandum by A. M. Tulloch, attached to Grey's memorandum of 17 October 1846.
115 E. J. Hobsbawm, *Labouring men*, p. 81.
116 Marshall, *Military miscellany*, p. 103.
117 Grey papers, Charles Grey to Howick, 6 November 1836.
118 N.L.S. mss 2846, f. 19, Lt.-Col. Michel to Brown, 24 January 1847.
119 Henry Marshall, *Military miscellany*, p. 75.
120 Seaton papers, memorandum presumed to be that written by Seaton on 12 January 1841.
121 N.A.M. 7709-11, pp. 6-7, Vivian to Hobhouse, 4 August 1832; 12, p. 247, Vivian to Macdonald, 19 October 1834; 13, p. 127, Vivian to Macdonald, 8 April 1835; 13, notes on paper by Sir John Wilson, 27 January 1836; 14, pp. 70-2, Vivian to Melbourne, 18 April 1838; 14, p. 121, Vivian to Howick, 11 April 1839; 14, pp. 194-9, Vivian to Macaulay, 25 March 1840.
122 Grey papers, Vivian to Howick, 11 April 1839.
123 Hansard, 3rd series, LXXXI, cc 1398-412;
124 S.R.O., GD 45/8/21, Grey to Maule, 13 September 1846.
125 W.O. 43/827, ff. 185-8; W.O. 30/112, Grey to Wellington, 14 December 1846.
126 W.O. 6/127, p. 297.
127 W.O. 30/112, memorandum by Wellington, 15 December 1846.
128 W.O. 30/112, Grey to Somerset, 22 December 1846.
129 Grey papers, Grey to Wellington, 20 January 1847.
130 Wellington papers, Wellington to Russell, 23 January 1847; Wellington to Queen, n.d.
131 Hansard, 3rd series, XCI, cc 281-7, 489, 646-55, 661-2, 689-96.
132 Ibid., XCI, cc 864-5.
133 Ibid., XCI, cc 1316-33.
134 Grey papers, Wellington to Grey, 22 April 1847.
135 [J. McMullen], *Camp and barrack-room*, pp. 269-70.
136 Alan Ramsay Skelley, *The Victorian army at home*, pp. 241-2.

CHAPTER 3
THE SOLDIERS: PUNISHMENT, EDUCATION AND REWARD

1. *Punishment*

In most of Europe it was the example of the French revolutionary conscripts which associated military success with more flexible battlefield formations, with an opening of the officer corps, and ultimately with an incipient sense of nationalism. However, in the case of Britain the social fabric of the state and of the army did not need to be transformed in order to assimilate some of the benefits of revolution.

Even before 1789, the Enlightenment's emphasis on the worth of the individual had made itself felt in the disciplinary systems of armies. For the British army, the shared dangers of colonial service had inculcated a comradeship between officers and men, that depended in the one case on a sense of obligation towards those less fortunate and in the other on the deference due to an increasingly professional body.[1] The outward manifestation was regimental *esprit de corps*. The application of the principles of encouragement rather than repression in British military service in the eighteenth century therefore originated paradoxically in the long-service, professional nature of the army, and its colonial duties. It was institutionalised by the reforms in the treatment of other ranks carried through by the Duke of York and Sir John Moore.

The disciplinary system thus forged was a mixture of carrot and stick, of prevention and punishment. The influences of the officers and of the regiment corporately could be long in gestation and assimilation, and were sufficiently finely balanced as to be easily upset. The process of 'improving' the soldier was therefore a gradual one. If finally successful, it might perhaps so alter the public image of the army as to attract a better class of recruit. But in the interim the army needed to justify its own position in society. The growth in the popularity of the soldier throughout the nineteenth century, which is particularly apparent from about the mid-point, may not only be a reflection of the fact that the odium of aiding the civil power was now largely shouldered by the police, or of the fact that the licentious soldiery grew in attractiveness the further it was from its native isle. It may also in reciprocal fashion suggest that colonial service was making the army more genuinely deserving of popular sympathy. The process noted in the eighteenth century was now a constant one, the interchange between officers and men fruitful in terms of the former's professional pride and the latter's sense of dignity. Quite simply the soldier was learning how to behave.

In 1851 Colonel A. W. Torrens, who commanded the 23rd or Royal Welch Fusiliers, believed that 'the attainment of moral influence ... is the great object to which officers must aspire'.[2] In consequence, as Colonel John Rolt wrote in 1842, the soldier's conduct should be influenced by 'the fear of offending their commanding officers, not the dread of punishment'.[3] These lofty ideals were not simply platitudes: in 1840, in his half-yearly inspection report, Sir George Arthur declared that 'There exists a most praise worthy desire, by kind admonition, and a careful knowledge and distinction of the men to raise the moral character of the soldiers'.[4]

However, in 1800 the lines of this development were no more than sketched in. Much in the soldier's own expectations of himself and of society's expectations of the soldier had first to be changed. In the interim the soldier might interpret benevolence as softness. Therefore the lash, an immediate and drastic threat, was in the eyes of many the sheet anchor without which discipline could not be maintained nor reform achieved.

Radical attacks on corporal punishment, often themselves a cloak for a more general assault on the military, consequently seemed a profound danger to the army's internal order. The cries of the abolitionists were such that the criminal more often than not emerged as the martyred hero, and a spate of pamphlets in the late 1820s and early 1830s reflected many a young subaltern's shock at the infliction of up to 1,000 lashes in the Peninsula. In the House of Commons motions to abolish or limit the punishment were brought forward in 1824, 1827, 1828, 1829 and 1830. The pressure had some effect. The 1829 Mutiny Act limited the maximum number of lashes awardable by a district or garrison court-martial to 300 and in 1832 regimental courts-martial were restricted to 200. In 1830 Sir John Byng could say 'the punishment is not now inflicted to one-fiftieth part of the extent it used to be'.[5]

The opposition to any further reduction centred on Wellington. He ruled comparisons with France inadmissible since there conscription had brought in a better class of recruit, and, in the absence of any more drastic sanctions, the incidence of capital punishment and long prison sentences had increased. The bedrock of the British army's discipline was centred on the regimental commanding officer: if he did not have an ultimate threat to support his use of minor punishments, 'We might as well pretend to extinguish the lights in our houses or theatres by extinguishers made of paper as to maintain the discipline of the army'.[6]

Statistics supported Wellington's claims for the efficacy of corporal punishment. In 1826, in 2,242 instances, flogging was inflicted following only 5,524 courts-martial: in 1834 (despite the establishment of the army having been reduced by approximately 8,000 men) a uniform process of decline showed 963 corporal punishments for 10,212 courts-martial.[7] Sir Hussey Vivian, who as commander-in-chief in Ireland presided over a forty per cent reduction in flogging between 1831 and 1834, found that the incidence of crime doubled. More importantly the army's efficiency was eroded. Desertion rose, and, owing to the increased use of imprisonment, the burden of duty fell on the better conducted men. Vivian concluded that, since the army's main priority had to be the maintenance of discipline for the benefit of the good (rather than for the reform of the bad), the effectiveness of flogging as a deterrent made it a more lenient punishment.[8]

However, the popular feeling against corporal punishment was itself undermining discipline. Fresh parliamentary agitation in 1833 produced a quick response. To save the principle that regimental courts-martial should have the right to award corporal punishment,[9] the Horse Guards agreed to restrict flogging to the punishment of mutiny, insubordination or violence, drunkenness on duty, the sale of equipment, stealing or disgraceful conduct. At the same time, in a bid by Wellington to still the debate once and for all,[10] a royal commission was set up. All commanding officers were asked for their views, the most distinguished of them gave evidence, other ranks appeared before the commission, and the resulting document was one that more than any other single development put the soldier on the path to improved treatment and better standards of living.

The report was published in 1836. It endorsed the views of the vast majority of commanding officers, who agreed that corporal punishment should be inflicted as rarely as possible and anticipated its eventual abolition, but who were extremely reluctant to answer for their regiments without the lash. Several argued that corporal punishment was only required for the field, since it was then essential to have as many men effective in the ranks as possible and the lash removed offenders for a briefer period than did a prison sentence. However, as Hardinge pointed out, it was inequitable, particularly in an army scattered over so many duties as the British one was, to have corporal punishment reserved only for those undergoing the deprivations and sufferings of active service. Therefore the result of the report was to limit general courts-martial to the award of 200 lashes, district courts-martial to 150 and regimental courts-martial to 100. In 1837 five out of eight regiments showed in their half-yearly returns that they had had no recourse to the lash.[11]

These conclusions received ample reinforcement from experience in the field. Colonel de Lacy Evans, who significantly had never commanded a regiment, had given evidence to the commission calling for the total abolition of flogging in the army. When, in 1835, he was dispatched to Spain to command the British Legion in the Carlist wars, he issued an order saying that such punishments would not be used in his force. But within a year drink and the rigours of service had wrought their toll, and Evans was compelled to resort to the lash.[12] Similarly, after Lord William Bentinck's abolition of corporal punishment in the East India Company's native army in 1835, discipline declined, mutinies broke out, and in 1845 Hardinge, then Governor General, was compelled to restore it.[13]

However, Wellington had not buried public agitation as satisfactorily as he had hoped. In July 1846 a private of the 7th Hussars died at Hounslow almost a month after being flogged for striking an officer with a poker. By past standards his sentence had been paltry — a mere 150 lashes — and he had been healing well. Nonetheless the coroner for Middlesex, who was an anti-flogging M.P., had the body exhumed and examined by a medical friend. The latter disagreed with the military doctors and concluded that the flogging had caused the death.[14] On 7 August the coroner led the way in a fresh Commons motion for abolition. Although the motion was defeated, it was not without its effect. Two days previously, Wellington had tried to pre-empt the attack by reducing the maximum punishment to fifty lashes and ordering it to be awarded only by general or district courts-martial.[15]

Thus the threat of flogging remained, but as a punishment it almost ceased to operate. As recently as 1825 a man had received 1,200 of a 1,900 stroke sentence,[16] but in 1850 twenty-five was the general number of lashes awarded, and that only 'in aggravated cases and at rare intervals'.[17] In 1851 and 1852, over 100 regiments of the total 132 in the army had no floggings whatsoever.[18] The figures presented to Parliament confirmed the pattern: 879 sentences of corporal punishment in 1838 had been reduced to 461 in 1846, and 206 in 1851.[19]

The reduction in flogging, of course, put a greater onus on other forms of punishment. Discounting the branding of deserters (which although barbaric was eminently practical since it prevented a man deserting and re-enlisting again to claim more bounty), these divided into minor punishments, awarded within the regiment, and major sentences given out by a district or general court-martial.

In the former category, almost every regiment was slightly different in its practice, although the Horse Guards tried to establish uniformity through the inspection of returns. To avoid breach of contract, a stoppage of pay could only be imposed to make up losses incurred by damage or for habitual drunkenness. Drill in heavy marching order or extra guards were frowned on as making a military duty more degrading than honourable. Commanding officers as frequently relied on their powers of 'billing up' men in the 'black hole' for up to two days, and of confining to barracks for up to two months. But the offences which warranted such treatment varied, especially since their entry in the defaulters' book was seen by the inspecting officer and thus reflected on the credit and conduct of the regiment and its officers. In the cavalry, it was considered a punishment to be deprived of a favourite horse, but equally a cavalry regiment would be more averse to confinement since the prisoner's horse had to be cared for in his master's absence.

Major punishments were more easily regulated. At first transportation seemed a satisfactory substitute for the lash. It had the great virtue of discharging the bad soldier without making him feel he had gained his liberty. In fact, however, especially in the days of unlimited service, it did promise eventual freedom, while the prisoner enjoyed a more relaxing life and a better diet in a more congenial climate. The idea of convict battalions, which was occasionally suggested as a military form of transportation, would leave certain areas with unreliable garrisons and was deemed inapplicable for an army which spent many years in tropical and unhealthy climates in the normal course of service. Therefore, although undesirable in that it reduced the number of men available to do duty and threw an unfair onus on the innocent, it was a main recommendation of the 1836 commission that a proper system of military prisons be established.

Imprisonment had been permitted as a court-martial sentence since the Mutiny Act of 1825, but the lack of anything beyond the barrack-cell, which was designed for forty-eight-hour sentences only, restricted its use. In the already overcrowded county gaols, soldiers, innocent of any civil crime, associated with 'the pickpockets and thieves of the suburbs of the

City of London';[20] they were consequently as often confirmed in bad habits as reformed. Therefore, in 1834 Hill suggested that a network of military prisons should be established — 400 solitary confinement cells in barracks in the United Kingdom, eight district military prisons in Great Britain, and three (excluding the existing provost prison at Dublin) in Ireland.[21] Howick was worried by the cost,[22] but in 1836 Lord John Russell took up the suggestion of Colonel Daniel Mackinnon that a wing of the Millbank Penitentiary be appropriated for military prisoners.[23] Despite initial difficulties at Millbank, spare buildings were also converted into prisons at Portsmouth, Chatham and Devonport.[24]

In 1836 Horse Guards pressure compelled Howick to accept Hill's demand for 400 solitary cells in barracks, and eventually the estimates of 1839 took a vote of £10,000 for improving barrack prisons. The new cells, which came into service in 1844–5, were to take prisoners for up to twenty-eight days and the old converted 'black holes' for seven.[25] The detailed regulations secured some degree of uniformity in punishment, and in 1851 their practice was assimilated as closely as possible to that of the by-then-established district military prisons.

In February 1844, after prompting by Hardinge, Lord Cathcart was appointed president of a committee that included Dr. Nihill from Millbank and Major Jebb, R.E., the surveyor-general of civil prisons and a commissioner of Pentonville.[26] Its immediate priority was to relieve the pressure on county gaols in the south of England by proposing a system of military prisons.[27] The committee[28] confirmed its support for the existing barrack cells, but proposed district military prisons to enforce sentences in excess of twenty-eight days. Since it would be impossible to construct sufficient single cells, it suggested that men should be classified, but according to character rather than crime. The governor was to be 'the friend and reformer of the culprit'.[29] Provision was made for the prisons in the 1844 Mutiny Act but, although £60,000 was the cost estimated for fully implementing the report, only £4,408 was included in the 1845 estimates. However, largely by the conversion of existing buildings, nine prisons had been set up within fourteen months, each providing for troops in the adjacent counties, and 4,276 prisoners had passed through.[30] By 1853, the system had been extended to ten colonial stations.[31]

Jebb calculated that over 5 per cent of the army were confined in the district prisons each year, and taken in conjunction with barrack cells it was thought 3,000 men a day were thus rendered ineffective.[32] Therefore, in order to return the men to the ranks as soon as possible, the prison regime aimed at a short, sharp shock. The inmate underwent hard labour for a maximum of ten hours a day, and was in solitary confinement for the rest. It was really the latter that impinged on the minds of men accustomed to crowded barrack rooms.

As reformatories, the prisons were relative failures. The normal sentence was 100 days, but this meant that the prison staff had little opportunity to improve their charges. On average, a third of the prisoners were men recommitted for a second sentence or more.[33] However, as a deterrent they were successful. Their presence was more immediate than the uncertainties of transportation, and they thus provided the essential corollary to the reduction of corporal punishment.

2. *Godliness and good learning*

The decline in corporal punishment and its substitution by imprisonment was only the most negative aspect of the 1836 punishment commission's work. If crime originated in drink, then the long-term solution was a more gainful occupation of the soldier's time and even mind. Originating with Sir John Moore at Shorncliffe, and embodied throughout the evidence and report of the punishment commission, was the belief in prevention rather than punishment. To avoid flogging, self-respect must be instilled in the soldier — this was the underlying theme of the report, and its circulation to every district commander in the army insured that this became the military orthodoxy of the day. 'Prevention,' the standing orders of the 2nd Dragoons said in 1839, 'is the spirit of discipline'.[34]

If prevention was to be the keynote for discipline, then clearly the onus was on commanding officers to provide alternative amusements to drink and the consequent crimes. The 1836 commissioners suggested games such as fives, rackets, cricket and football. Hill pressed their recommendation on the Secretary at War,[35] and in 1841 cricket pitches were established in the United Kingdom. However, more expensive projects met with less success. Schemes to build army gymnasia failed to win Wellington's support. The Board of Ordnance approved a plea to erect 146 fives courts, but the Treasury reduced the number to twenty-nine.[36]

In any case, mere occupation of the hands in activities other than drinking would not alone work the change in character required. What was needed was a higher moral tone in the army. The punishment commission acknowledged that the care taken of the soldier's spiritual welfare was lamentable.

Following the failure of regimental chaplains to execute their duties adequately in the Peninsula — indeed, in some cases to go out to Spain at all — only chaplains to the forces were appointed. As Secretary at War, Hardinge, although himself the son of a clergyman, reduced the chaplains' department still further. He brought chaplains from half-pay back into the service regardless of their efficiency, and he increasingly resorted to local parish clergy to conduct services at home. From 1830 no further commissions to chaplains were granted and the principle of employing civilian priests was extended to the colonies. By 1844 only five chaplains appeared in the Army List.[37]

Scotland alone was well provided for, since the Act of Union expressly stipulated that each fortress should have a commissioned chaplain on the establishment. For the rest of the army, the local parish clergy received allowances for ministering to the troops and visiting their sick. This, although cheap, was totally ineffective: the clergy were often negligent and had virtually no personal contact with the men, especially since their sojourn in each parish was likely to be short; often the civilian congregation would be so large that a special service had to be conducted in the barracks or in the church, but in either case cut off from the local population and with the minimum of ceremony. Communion, the heart of spiritual preparation, such as it was, was rarely, if ever, celebrated.[38]

Although freedom of worship was guaranteed to all ranks, allowances were only payable to the clergy of the established church of the country in which the regiment served, or, failing that, to the denomination to which the majority of the regiment belonged. Thus the 91st in Ireland had a Presbyterian minister paid for, but over four hundred Presbyterians in a regiment in the south of England were neglected.[39] Catholic priests could pose different problems: occasionally they emerged as the mouthpieces of treason.[40] Therefore advocates for the restoration of regimental chaplains argued that they would fill an interdenominational role which would overcome these difficulties and also reunite the regiment in a spiritual fellowship.

Although niggardliness was again the main reason for the lack of attention to spiritual welfare, a subsidiary cause was the absence of an effective head to the chaplains' department. At the end of 1829 Hardinge reduced the status of the office of Chaplain General to that of Principal Chaplain at Headquarters, and bestowed its ill-defined responsibilities on Dr. Dakins.[41] In 1841 the Rev. G. R. Gleig, who had served under Wellington in the Peninsula and was best known as the author of *The Subaltern*, submitted a plan for improving the religious condition of the army.

When Dakins retired in 1844, Gleig — on Hardinge's suggestion — was appointed his successor. His duties were to direct the work of the military chaplains and to supply Bibles and other books for the propagation of the Gospel.[42] This, however, was not the limit of Gleig's ambitions: 'I am quite ready to undertake the moral improvement of the army, if you gentlemen of the sword will act wisely and allow it.'[43]

Ensconced in the War Office and answerable to the Secretary at War, Gleig was well placed to win over first Hardinge and then Herbert. He memorialised Peel in February 1845, asking for promotion in the army and the church, and suggesting his pay was too low.[44] He antagonised the Commander-in-Chief, not unnaturally, when he thought that 'Every question affecting the moral conduct of the soldier seems to me to belong legitimately to my province'.[45] Notwithstanding this, his pressure was effective, and in July 1846 the office of Chaplain General to the Forces was revived: the army had effectively got the 'military bishop' for which its press had lobbied.

Gleig was energetic, bullying, and heedless of War Office procedures. Although Maule reminded him that his expressions of opinion should be left to the cabinet,[46] he was alleged to be 'Emeritus', the author of papers on army reform in *The Times*. In a series of articles in the *Quarterly Review*, written under an only thinly disguised anonymity, Gleig covered not merely religious and moral improvement in the army but also canvassed an increase in manpower, the ballotting of the militia, the establishment of camps of instruction, the increase and training of the artillery, the abolition of the Board of Ordnance, and even the demerits of the Minié rifle. His emphasis on military qualities was not perhaps surprising when, he reminded his readers, victory on the continent would be a blow to Popery and in the empire the Christian soldier was a missionary among the heathen.[47]

He was thus a curious amalgam of evangelism, without in any true sense being an evangelist, and of conservatism, having marked himself as a Tory by his anti-Reform Bill views and his association with Wellington in the early 1830s. Some indications as to his approach are perhaps to be found in that titan of ecclesiastical reform, C. J. Blomfield, who as Bishop of London had played a vital role in Gleig's advancement. Blomfield saw the spiritual duties of the priest as best performed by a full interest and concern in the education and material welfare of his parish. Gleig's parish was the army, and, while his vocation remained central, from this trunk sprouted a legitimate concern for all manner of military questions.

In fact success was to be more attendant in temporal than in spiritual matters. Gleig was no advocate of the restoration of regimental chaplains, but instead preferred each parish that contained a barrack to have the service of an additional curate whose sole responsibility would be to the army. This would make the church, not the regiment, his prime calling, but at the same time would give him a chance to exercise his pastoral duties.[48] To support the priest, Gleig wanted every barrack to have its own chapel. But the Treasury would only approve each case on its merits,[49] although it did establish as a general principle that every new barrack should have one.[50]

However, the Chaplain General's scheme of employing local curates was totally incompatible with the duties of an army on service. And so in 1846 Gleig secured four more appointments as chaplains to the forces and in 1853 the Rev. G. W. Langmeade was commissioned on the understanding 'that on all future ... occasions, he be expected to take the field'.[51] Four Anglican chaplains, two Catholic and one Presbyterian accompanied the original four divisions sent to the east in February 1854. Gleig used to maintain that he had been a chaplain once while on service in the Peninsula, and thus the reports from the Crimea of the chaplains' zeal and effectiveness must have brought him considerable satisfaction.

However, the Bible was of little value to an illiterate, and Gleig's greatest 'moral' reform for the soldier was his endeavour to secure for him a sound education, as the bedrock to all further self-betterment. It was here that the secular role of the priest was given its most immediate application, and by his intervention in this field Gleig not only benefited the army but also set a crucial example in the most controversial and most truly political area of the relationship between church and state.

In some quarters in the 1830s, such as Watts' *United Service Gazette*, the education of the soldier was still regarded as reprehensible. Many commanding officers saw educated men as 'lawyers', who could express their grievances more eloquently than the other soldiers. Indeed, as late as 1846 a survey[52] of an infantry regiment showed that of 324 just-literate men, forty-three were sergeants, but that of 123 of good education only three were, and that all seven men 'intended for learned professions' were still privates. The latter were of course believed to be less amenable to discipline, although in this instance the failure to promote was attributed to the colour sergeant's refusal to recommend those of abilities greater than his own.

On the whole, however, discrimination against learning was on the retreat. Henry Marshall argued that education should be the open path to promotion.⁵³ His contention that it would lessen crime and drinking was supported by Staff Surgeon Frederic Roberts, who quoted as evidence the higher crime rate in the infantry than in the cavalry and artillery, due to the latters' 'better education, ... the more intellectual nature of [their] duty, and the greater sphere there is for the exercise of mental qualities'. The artillery lost 0.9 per cent of its home strength each year through desertion, the cavalry 1.2 per cent, the Foot Guards 1.45 per cent, and infantry of the line 11.1 per cent.⁵⁴ Both the *Naval and Military Gazette*, and the *United Service Journal* concluded that there should be compulsory education for other ranks.

Equally, however — and this was especially true the more their demands were fulfilled — most men agreed with Sir George Arthur that, while 'the religious and moral cultivation of his mind affords the best prospect of elevating his character', it should not go 'beyond what is required for the Soldier's *station in life*'.⁵⁵ Too good an education would make all soldiers potential officers and they would therefore be discontented with their lot as privates. A grounding in reading, writing and arithmetic was all that was required. 'In making the scholar, we must not unmake the soldier.'⁵⁶

The degree of a recruit's education varied considerably according to the area in which he was enlisted. In 1843, in the Rifle Brigade, a regiment that took slightly more care about its choice of men, 27.3 per cent of its recruits were illiterate on joining — a very low proportion partly explained by the fact that only $5\frac{1}{2}$ per cent of the Scotsmen were in this class. The figures for the other nationalities were 28 per cent of Irishmen, 33 per cent of Welshmen, and 23 per cent of Englishmen. The southern counties of England showed up badly, with Sussex 'the most boorish', and half the recruits from Buckinghamshire and Hertfordshire were illiterate.⁵⁷

Such diversity makes it hard to quantify the individual regiment's contribution in educating its men. In 1838 Sir Thomas Bradford spoke of the vast improvement in other ranks' education in the previous forty years.⁵⁸ Recent research has supported his conclusions: findings for certain areas show that illiteracy in the armed forces declined from 51 per cent in 1785–1814 to 32 per cent in 1815–44, while the national average remained fairly constant, going from 39 per cent to 35 per cent.⁵⁹ The 1841 census report showed that in the army 66 per cent of those aged sixteen to twenty-five were literate (or 60 per cent excluding officers) and 78 per cent of those aged twenty-six to thirty-five (including a higher proportion of officers).⁶⁰ This was roughly equivalent to the overall national average of 33 per cent illiteracy,⁶¹ but, if allowance is made for the 66 per cent illiteracy of labourers and servants, the class which provided most recruits for the army, the result is very flattering to the service. By 1846 the picture was even better, with a survey of eleven regiments showing only 27 per cent of the 10,000 men unable to write.[62]

The credit for this situation rested with the regimental schools, established by the Duke of York in 1812 for the children of the army. Their purpose was to instil 'early habits of Morality, Obedience, and Industry', in the hope that their pupils would see fit to follow their fathers' careers. In case they did not, a trade was to be taught them, and the girls were to learn 'plain work and knitting' in so far as provision could be made for them.[63] In 1840 the request that the Cape Mounted Rifles might have a schoolmistress resulted in their appointment to every regiment, and thus the 9,371 girls in the army's care were also to learn to read and write, as well as to acquire domestic skills.[64]

The regulations for the schools made no mention of the education of adults, although a return of the number attending the school was required, and Hill was certainly anxious that those other ranks who wished to attend should. The fact that n.c.o.s were required to be literate and numerate was a spur to the ambitious. In 1827 Fitzclarence had attracted thirty men per company to the school of the 7th Fusiliers,[65] but the fifty-four of the whole regiment attending that of the 4th Foot was probably nearer the norm.[66] By the 1840s adult attendance at the regimental school was widespread — 200 from the 93rd,[67] 160 from the 67th,[68] and in the 2nd Foot all other ranks had to attend two hours a day.[69]

These attendance figures can be considered high, because for many — those both literate and numerate — attendance at the regimental school was of little use. The recommended system of education was that of the Rev. Dr. Andrew Bell — in Gleig's words, 'a solemn bore'.[70] Designed for children rather than adults and with its emphasis on learning by rote rather than by understanding, it could only appeal to those anxious to grasp the rudiments. Chichester found in the 81st that, although the pupils appeared to read fluently, 'give them a book they have not seen before, and words of three letters puzzle them'.[71] Moreover, although there were honourable exceptions, there was little chance that the schoolmaster would enliven this staple, since the job tended to cut him off from further promotion and therefore attracted only worn-out n.c.o.s.

Even if he overcame these hurdles, the keen commanding officer was bedevilled by the bad rooms furnished for the school, and, especially if his school was successful, by the high pupil-to-master ratio. Gleig wrote, admittedly grinding an axe as he did so, after his tour of five regimental schools: 'I did not find anywhere a room fit for the purpose of a school; a decent supply of books — or other implements of teaching, or of a master so trained as to be capable of communicating useful information to others. The attendance of adults is both small, and uncertain.'[72] Good individual regimental schools could not constitute a system of army education.

Some of the beleaguered Line looked wistfully across to the Royal Sappers and Miners. Grey, when Secretary of State, took them as his model for training the infantry, but as recruits for the Sappers and Miners had to be literate on enlistment, a direct comparison was not strictly valid. Attendance at the Sappers' school was compulsory for two hours a day. After a course of geometry, arithmetic and elementary fortification, the recruit progressed to the theory of sieges, while in the field he was given a practical training in its operations and in the skills required for field works, bridging, sapping and mining.[73] The Chatham system of instruction showed the rest of the army not only the value of compulsory standards of education but also that of giving the course a specifically military bias.

Certainly its influence was noticeable in Fitzclarence's great venture, the Portsmouth Garrison School, established at his own expense in January 1848. In addition to mathematics, arithmetic, algebra, geometry, plane trigonometry, English grammar, English history, mechanics and dynamics, the course reflected the military bias of the Sappers and Miners' instruction and covered field fortification, the attack and defence of outposts and positions, reconnaissance and field sketching.[74] Thirty to forty n.c.o.s. and privates from the Portsmouth district attended at a time, facing six hours' instruction a day.[75]

To the Garrison School, Lord Frederick next grafted on his Superior District School. This was established late in 1850 as a school for n.c.o.s and potential n.c.o.s, with an officers' class added on. The numbers attending and the range of subjects were similar to those of the Garrison School. The pupils were divided into two classes, according to their relative abilities. Sir Frederic Smith, the commandant of the Royal Engineer Establishment at Chatham, conducted an examination in August 1851. In addition to their extensive theoretical syllabus, the men were asked to discuss Marlborough's wars, to explain Vauban's first system of fortification, and to produce for inspection their reconnaissance reports and plans of the adjacent countryside.[76]

Cynics attributed Fitzclarence's success to his drawing off the cream from every regiment, and to the abilities of his 'Head District School — master', Scrivener.[77] In June 1852 Gleig appointed Scrivener Head Garrison Schoolmaster in Dublin, with the job of organising all the regimental and depot schools in Ireland,[78] and barely a year later, Scrivener followed Fitzclarence to Bombay, where, as Superintendent of Regimental Schools, he was given the rank of lieutenant. Fitzclarence had established at Poona a two-tier structure similar to that at Portsmouth. Three hundred pupils attended the so-called 'Central Normal School', with sixty-two n.c.o.s at the Superior School. The n.c.o.s studied a similar syllabus to that followed at Portsmouth, but with Indian history added in.[79]

Fitzclarence had proposed to Fox Maule that every district should have a school on this basis, so that regiments changing quarters could painlessly change schools.[80] But, although the press raved, the authorities were all but mute. Certainly Maule and Herbert had visited the Portsmouth School, and the former had supported the Superior School. Gleig too had praised the Garrison School and taken the best of Fitzclarence's n.c.o.s to be regimental schoolmasters, thus spreading his influence throughout the army. There, however, official support ended. The scheme was not applied to every district, largely, one suspects, thanks to Gleig. The Chaplain General's ideas on education saw moral, not military, improvement as the basis. By the time the value of Fitzclarence's system was proved, the army was already committed to a more theoretical and bookish mode of learning.

The intervention of the central authorities in the field of regimental education followed a rather perverse order, its first concern being with libraries rather than with enabling the men to use the books therein. This was because reading was regarded as a constructive recreation which kept men away from the canteen and therefore reduced crime. It was only in the later stages of their development that the corollary to libraries appeared: in order to be drawn thither in the first place, the soldier needed to be literate.

Again the idea had sprung up in regiments with good systems of discipline, but the bulk of books acquired added considerably to the regiment's baggage and transport costs. The solution lay, as the punishment commission realised, in a system of barrack libraries. Thus Howick's proposal to encourage regimental libraries, sent to Hill in November 1837, was countered by the Commander-in-Chief's suggestion that garrison libraries be established at the principal stations. Initially, in February 1840, thirty-one libraries at home and abroad were catered for, and all soldiers were to have a right of entry on payment of 1d. a month.[81]

Typically, however, the Treasury almost wrecked its own beneficence by niggardliness over the details. It was planned that the librarians would be discharged n.c.o.s, but no barrack accomodation or allowances for fuel and candles were permitted them, and few therefore undertook the job. By late 1841 some libraries were therefore still inoperative.[82] Equally no provision was made for rooms in which to house or read the books. By October 1842 Chatham had 1,000 books but no library opened, and seven other libraries were complaining about their accommodation. However, in 1844 the War Office divested itself of the issue by transferring the administration of the libraries to the Board of Ordnance: the Ordnance provided librarians and rooms, and put the whole under the charge of the Barrack Master.[83] All new barracks had a library included in the design.

The volumes selected for the barrack libraries were designed to teach the soldiery the value of 'sober, regular and moral habits'.[84] The danger was that the books would be boring. Gleig's own works were ranged alongside 'the dry, hard, mechanical rubbish of the "Useful Knowledge" people'[85] and 'a great number of books treating of abstruse, ethical, and doctrinal topics'.[86] Military works, as well as anything smacking of political or religious controversy, were eschewed. However, gradually novelists and poets, such as Defoe, Fielding, Scott, Marryat, Milton, Burns and Byron,[87] were incorporated. Under Hardinge, military books were placed on the shelves, including the abridged edition of *Wellington's Despatches*.[88] Furthermore by 1844, there were thirty-eight libraries at home and forty abroad, so that no foreign station was without one. In 1853 117,000 volumes were thought to be stored in 150 libraries, and 16,000 subscribers were said to read them.[89]

The ultimate success of the barrack libraries was in part due to the reform of the regimental schools, and the consequently growing role that the library played in an integrated system of military education.

The national debate on education in the 1830s and '40s was rooted in the position of the Church of England as the established church. The arguments between some of its members and Catholics or dissenters, over the granting of state support to schools whose religious instruction was denominational, was a crucial factor in the slow development of compulsory education in Britain. Increasingly, however, Nonconformists and latitudinarian Anglicans argued for undenominational education. The Church of England clearly did not control the spiritual lives of the entire British people, and the repeal of the Test and Corporation Acts in 1828 had definitively split Protestantism from the state. As a result, by the mid-nineteenth century a concept of generalised Christianity was widely accepted as the basis for educational reform.[90]

In 1842 a committee of officers, formed at Hill's behest and under the presidency of the Deputy Adjutant General (Brown), unanimously found the allowances for the army's regimental schools inadequate. A training school for masters should be established in the half-empty Royal Military Asylum in Chelsea. It would be modelled on the nondenominational Normal School, established at Battersea in 1840 by the secretary of the Committee of the Privy Council on Education, James Kay-Shuttleworth. At the regimental level, the schools should be geared towards the education more of adults than of children, and every barrack should have a properly fitted schoolroom. A uniform and high standard would be assured not only by the training of the masters but also by more thorough supervision on the part of the chaplains than had been customary theretofore.[91] Thus, although Kay-Shuttleworth had failed to persuade the Committee of the Privy Council to grasp the nettle of a comprehensive system of popular education, the army's own committee had launched it firmly into the current of the debate. It was motivated not least by a fear that denominational education would have a divisive and destructive effect on the army.

Hardinge put the committee's proposals to the Board of the Royal Military Asylum in March 1842.[92] There they rested until 1844 and Gleig's appointment as Principal Chaplain. It is possible that Gleig had something to do with the 1842 proposals, but, even if not their progenitor, he was destined to be their midwife. Bemoaning the lack of a uniform system in the schools, he revived the 1842 report. In almost every respect he agreed with it: with good teachers, the regimental schools could be taken in hand, Bell's system abolished and education made compulsory for all recruits.[93]

As Principal Chaplain, however, Gleig's powers were relatively limited. He tried to enforce more thorough inspections of the schools, and, so as to reward the successful masters in proportion to their efforts, and to encourage pupils to place a value on education, he made payment for adult instruction obligatory.[94] His efforts were aided by a report on the Royal Military Asylum by the Rev. Henry Moseley, which supported the conclusions of the 1842 committee. A further committee formed of Herbert, the Pay Master General and the Quarter Master General therefore proposed that the Asylum consist of a training school for thirty masters (the Normal School), with four companies of boys forming the so-called Model School.

In June 1846 Herbert suggested to Wellington that these proposals be implemented. Chelsea-trained schoolmasters should be paid 2s. 6d. a day, rising to 3s., and should rank second only to the sergeant-major in the regiment. Wellington approved. At the same time the Treasury agreed to Herbert's proposal that Gleig hold the new appointment of Inspector of Military Schools concurrently with that of Chaplain General. He was to be answerable to the Secretary at War, and his duties included administering the barrack libraries, establishing a uniform system of education, and the selection and appointment of masters.[95]

In 1847, twenty-seven civilians were accepted into the Normal School after a competitive examination among 115 candidates. The requirement of a £50 bond ensured a high social standing among the applicants, and they included the sons of clergymen, surgeons and officers, one of the first intake even leaving in the middle of the course to take up a commission.[96] Soldiers who went to Chelsea had to re-enlist and thus forfeited all the previous service they had accumulated towards their pension. The first eight were not admitted until 1849 and two years later Gleig reported that to maintain the standard fewer soldiers should be taken.[97] In due course, however, the main source proved to be neither civil nor military life, but the Model School itself: of the 178 teachers trained by 1858, ninety-three were former monitors of the Asylum, as opposed to thirty-seven civilians and forty-eight soldiers.[98]

Two years were spent at Chelsea, including six months' practical training in the Model School. The first five to complete the course went out in April 1849 as garrison rather than regimental schoolmasters — a temporary expedient so that their influence could be as widely diffused as possible. The star of the batch was Scrivener himself, who reported that within a month 130 were attending his school, including six sergeants; he was teaching the sergeant major of the 52nd two evenings a week, and working constantly from 9 a.m. to 10 p.m.[99]

These hours demonstrate the conscientiousness of the soldiers as much as of the master. For the only stipulation concerning attendance was that all recruits were to go to school for two hours a day until dismissed drill, and were to pay 4d. per month for the privilege. Therefore the remainder of the pupils were volunteers.

During the course of 1849 nineteen trained schoolmasters were sent out, and in 1850 the first eight assistants appointed. In 1853 sixty-three schoolmasters were active, and of these four were at garrisons, the remainder being with regiments. In February 1854 the average attendance for a regiment was 166, of whom only thirty-nine were recruits, and six regiments had over 300 at school, and three of these over 400. For all ranks enabled to attend the lessons of a trained schoolmaster, 24·33 per cent, or over 10,000, were doing so.[100] By 1857, when Gleig resigned as Inspector General, 20·5 per cent of other ranks were totally illiterate (the majority in the infantry), 18·8 per cent were able to read but not write, 56·0 per cent could do both and 4·7 per cent were defined as having a superior education.[101]

Furthermore, this was one reform whose impact was not lessened by financial stringency. Gleig insisted that every military station have a properly equipped schoolroom. Unlike their predecessors, which depended on their commanding officer's generosity or a regimental fund, the new schools were liberally stocked with pens, ink, slates, blackboards, paper, maps and over thirty different textbooks, their subjects themselves reflecting the new order — poetry, history, Euclid, algebra, etymology, geography and natural history.[102]

Nonetheless, there were difficulties. In some regiments, a conflict developed between the sergeant-major and the new arrival, based in the former's case on the threat to his primacy and in the latter's on his resentment at being treated as a sergeant by a less educated sergeant-major. Herbert struck a compromise whereby the schoolmaster ranked between the sergeant-major and the quartermaster and was classed as a warrant officer.[103] The attitude of the Horse Guards was obstructive. The Duke feared that as schools were administered by the War Office they would further broach the Commander-in-Chief's powers, and Gleig maintained that after 1846 he lost Wellington's favour for ever.[104] Some of the more reactionary commanding officers reflected similar views. What they resented was the schoolmaster's independence of the regiment: he had rarely been brought up in it, he was not responsible to its commanding officer, and he was introducing a system that derived from a central army authority: theirs was a cry for the regiment and its declining individuality.

However, opposition was not long sustained. At the beginning of 1850, after less than a year of operation, Lieutenant-Colonel Browne of the 21st said, 'The new system has already had a visible effect on the regiment in many ways. Men have been able to fit themselves for promotion who were previously unable to do so. Others have learned to read and write, and have found occupation for time that was formerly spent in public houses. It is very popular, and next to the good conduct warrant, is, I think, the greatest boon the Army has received since I entered it.' The commanding officers of the 12th, 13th, 14th, 27th, 40th and 93rd Regiments all agreed.[105]

The press, still holding out the hope that a better class of recruit could be obtained, crowed that army education was now better than anything the lower classes could obtain as civilians. The soldier would be more self-reliant in the field, and more employable on his discharge. Certainly Gleig demonstrated to the would-be reformers of civilian schools that a nondenominational system could be formulated, a system which communicated the scriptures but left to the clergy in their respective churches 'such crumbs of polemical doctrine as appear to be necessary'.[106] In an indirect fashion, the state had thus supported Kay-Shuttleworth's Normal School, and, *pace* Blomfield, had integrated it with a revivified priesthood. Although the argument does not appear to have been cited at the time, the army was serving as a microcosm of society in the great arguments on church and state.

3. Rewards

Immediately, however, it was education for its own sake. Within the army itself, it certainly improved the soldier's prospects, but it hardly opened up a whole new field of advancement. Clearly an n.c.o. required to be literate and numerate in order to fulfil his duties, but Wellington refused to make an educational qualification a precondition of noncommissioned rank, since it would interfere with the discrimination of the commanding officer.

Even less likely was it that education would enhance the soldier's prospect of becoming an officer. Fitzclarence reminded the n.c.o.s in the Portsmouth District School of the possibility of being commissioned from the ranks,[107] and the commanding officer of the 92nd is said to have threatened to resign if he could not reward deserving n.c.o.s with commissions.[108] But these were exceptions. Wellington, the military press and the punishment commission were all reluctant to encourage promotion from the ranks. Even Colonel Mountain, the archetypal soldier — philanthropist, who had eight ex-rankers among his officers, found that the harmony of his regiment was disturbed and reluctantly concluded that 'in nine cases out of ten a bad officer is made out of a good serjeant'.[109] Chichester of the 81st expressed himself in a similar vein: 'To my great sorrow the Sergeant Major was promoted to an ensigncy in the Regt ... Promotion from the ranks is bad in every way; bad for the officers who get a vulgar set amongst them . . . It is bad for the men who love little indulgences which other officers give & those cannot afford. But of all I think it worst for the individual promoted: it moves them out of a sphere from which they were calculated, into one for which they are not.'[110] The soldier's education might rival that of an officer, but it did not make him a gentleman.

At least until 1845, these feelings found rationalisation in a situation which made it undesirable to promote. First, the army was so contracted by the 1830s, that promotion among officers was slow and vacancies consequently few. Secondly, if an n.c.o. did qualify himself for a commission, he would be of such an age as to make it undesirable to start again with young and bumptious ensigns. Financially, as a sergeant-major, he would have 3s. per day pay, a room, fuel allowances, the use of a soldier servant and free education for his children. Although an ensign earned 5s. 3d. per day, this was more than taken up by mess and band subscriptions, the cost of his equipment, and the loss of allowances. He would start with a debt of £50 that he had little hope of ever liquidating.[111]

This is not to say, however, that promotion from the ranks ceased to operate. Certainly the main successes were those elevated young in the Peninsula, where promotion was faster. In the mid-1830s, just under twenty n.c.o.s were commissioned a year, most of them to be regimental staff officers — adjutants, quartermasters or riding-masters. Such a modest intake could be easily absorbed and served as a good example to other n.c.o.s. In 1837, thirty-five n.c.o.s were commissioned,[112] an increase perhaps reflecting the spirit of the 1836 commission. By 1839 there was difficulty in securing good n.c.o.s for the 3rd West India Regiment because nearly two-thirds of the commissions vacant without purchase were given to other ranks.[113] Between 1840 and 1847, 264 n.c.o.s were promoted from the ranks, as against 182 in the period 1830 to 1839.[114]

However, this growth did not embrace the most educated and best conducted arms, the artillery and the sappers and miners. The scientific education and slow peacetime promotion of both erected the major barrier. In the artillery the position of quartermaster was open to the gunners, and in 1853 two quartermasters were added to the establishment of the Royal Engineers so that the chances of a commission were equalised with the artillery — one in 700. Theoretically members of both regiments could be commissioned into the line, but regiments were loath to bring in outsiders and only one instance is cited for the sappers and that in 1828.[115]

The nominal blocks to promotion from the ranks were knocked down in the late 1840s. The *United Service Magazine* had campaigned for a grant to be made to the newly-elevated n.c.o. for the purchase of equipment, and in December 1845 Herbert secured grants of £150 for those entering the cavalry and £100 for the infantry.[116] At the same time the mood of the military press swung in favour of promotion from the ranks, and Captain Robertson acknowledged that this must come as soon as the Normal schoolmasters were operative.[117] In 1849 the introduction of examinations for first commissions gave a standard by which to peg the n.c.o.s' capabilities, and it was suggested that places be kept for them at Sandhurst.

But Sandhurst was too reduced in staff and the examination thought too theoretical for men of middle age already wise in professional matters. Although the new education was undoubtedly of value, it did not provide the hinge on which a commission depended. The shortage of officers for the Crimea, felt as early as March 1854, meant that ninety-four other ranks were commissioned during the year,[118] and at its close, in spite of Raglan's opposition for the traditional reasons, the Queen proposed to promote one n.c.o. per regiment.[119] The experiences of the Scots Fusilier Guards, however, suggested that, notwithstanding education and allowances, the requirements of a gentleman were not met: of twelve commissioned in the Crimea, only one 'gave great satisfaction', although only three could be described as positively bad.[120] Large-scale promotion from the ranks lay far in the future.

The need to reward good conduct therefore remained. Almost all the pamphleteers of the 1830s called for a system of increased pay and the right to wear a badge or mark of distinction. 'If rewards and badges of distinction,' the argument ran, 'were more frequently resorted to in the British army, it would tend to the abolition of flogging more effectually than all the philanthropic, though ill-judged speeches of the best intended members of Parliament.'[121] Charles Napier cited with approval the example of Sir Neil Douglas, who established a regimental order of merit in the 79th in 1815,[122] and at least twenty-two other regiments had similar systems. All these had their influence, not only in encouraging the 1836 commission to recommend a system of good conduct awards, but also in urging rapid action, since it was felt that all professional rewards should emanate from the Queen and not the commanding officer.

It was the 71st which had the greatest effect on the framing of the eventual order. The 1829 pensioning warrant had made provision for a good conduct gratuity, and the award of a long service and good conduct medal. But this had been very limited both in its effects and precepts, since only two were awarded per year per regiment, and those only on discharge. Howick therefore sounded out a proposed system on his brother, Charles, the commanding officer of the 71st. Charles consulted his sergeant major and both agreed that 'it would work *most* beneficially'.[123] The actual provisions of Howick's 1836 pensioning warrant and the additional 1839 good conduct warrant were that, after every seven years' good service, the soldier was to receive an extra 1d. a day and a ring of lace round the right arm, and that for every five years that a certain level of good conduct pay had been claimed proportionate increases would be made in the pension.[124] A warrant promulgated by Sidney Herbert in December 1845 granted the benefits of the 1836 warrant after five, not seven, year periods, and thus enabled the keen recruit to qualify sooner.[125] Consequently by 1846 9,253 men were in receipt of good conduct pay, rising to 22,642 in 1850-1.[126] Moreover the 1829 long service and good conduct medals were given as far as possible at a regimental parade, and, after April 1854, could be bestowed before discharge, so that the force of example was not lost.

Howick's warrants were really the first government attempt to assume responsibility for the soldier's improvement, and in a sense from them grew all the subsequent provisions of the 1840s. They were too the most important positive power bestowed on commanding officers. Even so, commanding officers felt constrained by a War Office system that lacked adaptability to regimental circumstances, obliging them to withdraw a privilege when perhaps they did not regard the crime as so drastic, and making it difficult to reward outwith the seven or five year interval. Several regiments therefore adopted the Prussian system of 'classification', by which each divided their privates into three classes according to conduct, those in the higher classes receiving less punishment and more indulgences. However, this system was prohibited for the same reasons as the regimental good conduct awards of the 1830s — all professional rewards must proceed from the Crown.

A much more serious defect of the good conduct warrant was its neglect of sergeants. This was noted with regret at the time of the 1836 warrant. It was however compounded by the 1845 amendment, which gave corporals and privates progressive rates of pay and pension, which at their topmost were more lucrative than a sergeant's pay. Yet the 1829 awards were limited to one n.c.o. and one private per regiment, regardless of whether two good sergeants were due to be discharged in one year. Furthermore, if the sergeant was arrested, he was likely to revert to private with all his previous good service forfeit, whereas his juniors could suffer an intermediate punishment. To offset this, Herbert's 1845 warrant had made £2,000 available for the granting of £20 annual gratuities, together with a medal 'for meritorious service', but by August 1847 117 were already in receipt of this, and the sum was so taken up that by 1851 only one more sergeant had been added to the list, and he under special dispensation.[127]

The sergeants secured an advocate in the House of Commons in Colonel Chatterton of the 4th Dragoon Guards, and in 1849 and 1851 they themselves presented petitions to the Adjutant General outlining their case. Maule brought some relief in 1851 by securing the pension element of good conduct pay for sergeants reduced to the ranks, but the Treasury adamantly refused to pay an additional £12,000 *per annum* in good conduct pay for all sergeants. It did, however, agree in 1853 to a further £2,000 for sergeants' gratuities, but to be given in staggered lots of £250 a year, so as to secure more even distribution.[128]

Overall, however, the good conduct pay and its associated medals were an equitable system, well designed for a long-service colonial army. What they did not do was make provision for service in the field. Outstanding gallantry tended to be met by promotion despite the fact that a brave man was not necessarily well adapted to lead. De Lacy Evans, Hardinge and Grey all suggested a military decoration for which all ranks would be eligible. Sir Charles Napier claimed to be the first to mention other ranks in despatches, after Miani, but, except for an isolated case in 1846, nobody was to follow his example until Raglan did so in 1855.[129] The *United Service Magazine* was a keen advocate of medals, and in 1845 presciently suggested an order named after Queen Victoria.[130] However, the Victoria Cross was not instituted until 1856.

If distinguished gallantry went unrecognised, at least some token was forthcoming for active service. All ranks present at Waterloo had been awarded a medal and a year's additional service towards a pension. While for some — particularly the jealous Peninsular veterans — this was a precedent, for Wellington it most decidedly was not. But in 1842 the East India Company forced his hand. The Queen's troops could not reasonably be excluded from the grant by Shah Shujah of a medal for Ghuznee and by the Company for Jellalabad. Having begun with a campaign as unsuccessful as that in Afghanistan, the Queen was free to extend the principle to the wars in Scinde and China in 1843, Gwalior in 1844 and the Punjab in 1846. The Peninsular heroes could now no longer be checked and, through the intervention of the Queen herself, secured approval for the so-called 'General Service Medal'.

Many senior officers felt that the indiscriminate issue of campaign medals had brought them into disrepute. 'To distribute [medals] to every officer and private of a regiment,' Colonel Luard wrote, 'defeats the object by destroying the distinction.'[131] But the force of example was not lost. In a long-service army, particularly one divided over so many theatres, the sight of a bemedalled veteran regiment met in some distant cantonment still stimulated endeavour. Long periods of dull colonial policing punctuated by a 'little war' deserved their reward.

For many soldiers, however, the best reward for good conduct was to be released from the army. As late as 1847 Wellington still felt that, apart possibly from the Life Guards, 'there is not a soldier serving in the Army, who does not desire or will not accept his discharge if offered him'.[132] When the soldier enlisted, the monarch had a claim to his service for life, and, since the soldier had no right to his discharge, it was considered reasonable that he should pay for it. Preference was therefore given 'to men according to the goodness of their character; a course, which if steadily pursued, cannot fail to operate as a strong inducement to good conduct'.[133]

With the standards of behaviour constantly rising, such an arrangement became counterproductive. The good so rewarded included promising n.c.o.s who were thus lost to the service, while the dissolute were retained. However, it was difficult to discharge bad men when good men had to pay for the privilege and when it was feared that such a system would be a direct stimulus to crime. The establishment of military prisons meant that discharge could be associated with a gaol sentence, and in 1849 for the first time the Horse Guards felt able, when ordering the reduction of regiments, to give commanding officers the power to remove undesirable and inefficient soldiers first.[134]

A further indication of the rising quality of the soldier's life was the reluctance of well-conducted men to take the release to which they were entitled. Discharge became gradually cheaper after seven years' service and after fifteen (or sixteen in the cavalry) it was granted free. No upper limit existed to the numbers buying themselves out, and some officers believed in giving their support as often as asked rather than retain reluctant soldiers. It was, however, noticed that soldiers of about ten years' service or more rarely applied, preferring to continue with a familiar way of life and to qualify for their pensions. In 1846, of 10,540 infantry eligible for a free discharge, only 264 took it, and 39 of 1,006 cavalry.[135] Even when in the same year the cost of purchasing a discharge for those of less than seven years' service was reduced, only seventy-four men took advantage of it in the next five years.[136]

However, it is not incompatible to contend that the low rate of discharge suggests some improvement in the soldier's prospects and in his quality of life. To the outsider, a military career might appear no more beguiling in 1854 than it had in 1830, and thus the better class of recruit be no nearer enlistment. But, within the army, as Stocqueler himself was prepared to admit, 'The position of the soldier is now much improved ... With the improvement of his condition, a corresponding improvement in the character of the soldier has taken place.'[137] Another reformer, the Duke of Cambridge, confirmed to the Roebuck commission, that 'the change in the men, even in my short experience [he entered the army in 1837] is very striking'.[138] In 1838 one in slightly over eleven men was tried by court-martial: in 1853, despite the declining severity of punishments, one in sixteen.[139] A much more revealing barometer of the soldier's morale is the impressive decline in desertions, from 3,527 in 1841 to 1,500 in 1850.[140]

A dramatic alteration in the tone of the soldier's life had been effected, and its authors were undeniably individual regimental commanding officers, fired perhaps by memories of Moore, but more significantly evolving systems of discipline and recreation to cope with the boredom of colonial and peacetime garrisoning. But the necessity for all favours to proceed from the Crown, and for conditions of service to be uniform, forced the government to assume responsibility for the soldier's welfare in spite of itself. Concern for the soldier and the reform of his working conditions dovetails neatly into the pattern of Victorian factory and social reform. But the prime concern of the free-trading radical was to reduce the cost of government rather than find fresh areas of responsibility. In this case, however, the government was the employer and legislation had to be supported by finance to implement the good intentions. Thus radicals were often lukewarm about change, while military M.P.s of all political persuasions urged the government's responsibilities on it.

Therefore, the assumption by the War Office, and by extension the Commons, of some degree of answerability for military welfare accords with the arguments of those who see nineteenth-century administrative reform as a succession of organically generated, pragmatic responses, rather than as a product of doctrinaire Utilitarianism.[141] The role of 'inspection' was in this case carried out by officers, men unlikely to be familiar with Utilitarian or Benthamite doctrine, who either acted on their own initiative within the regiment or exposed their grievances in the professional press. To extend the analogy, the consequent regulations were improved and adapted not by the further investigations of an inspectorate but by the more searching tests of war or colonial service.

'A measure,' the Adjutant General had told commanding officers in 1833, 'that shall commit to Parliament, or to a Committee of Parliament or to a Royal Commission (if not composed exclusively, of Military Men), the difficult, delicate and vitally important task of modelling anew the means of governing the British army, instead of leaving its Discipline, and all matters connected therewith, in Military hands, to be upheld by Military Authority and Military Discretion under the guidance of the Sovereign, must be fraught with, I would say, awful considerations.'[142] The occasion was the limitation of corporal punishment, but MacDonald — and indeed Wellington — clearly felt that here was a general principle. However, by leaving the initiation of reform to regimental officers and to the military press, the Horse Guards ensured that it was not as much the sheet-anchor of the country's military institutions as it would have liked. The officers not only awoke some degree of response in Parliament but also themselves became more dependent on Westminster than on the Horse Guards, since thence originated the money for the improvements required. By forcing legislation, they were imposing a uniform system on the varying practices of individual regiments and thus swinging the initiative for reform away from the military periphery to the legislative centre.

Notes

1 J. A. Houlding, *Fit for service*, pp. 105-15.
2 [A. W. Torrens], *Six familiar lectures for the use of young military officers*, p. 2.
3 John Rolt, *Moral command*, p. 4.
4 Charles R. Sanderson (ed.), *The Arthur papers*, letter no. 1453.
5 Quoted in Marshall, *Military miscellany*, p. 208.
6 Wellington papers, Wellington to Macdonald, 7 April 1833.
7 P.P. 1836, XXII, appendix p. 197.
8 N.A.M. 7709-6-10, pp. 56-66, Vivian to Somerset, 1 October 1831; 10, at end, pp. 3-7, C.-in-C's confidential circular, Dublin 21 July 1831; 12, pp. 3-5, Vivian to Hardinge, 11 February 1834; 12, pp. 244-5, Vivian to Macdonald, 19 October 1834; 13, pp. 125-7, Vivian to Macdonald, 8 April 1835; 13, at end, notes on paper by Sir John Wilson, 27 January 1836.
9 Wellington papers, Macdonald to Wellington, 5 and 6 April 1833.
10 Wellington papers, Wellington to Macdonald, 7 and 9 April 1833.
11 W.O. 3/91, p. 215.
12 *U.S.J.*, 1836, II, p. 462; B.M. Add. Mss 40314, f. 105, Hardinge to Peel, 9 October 1835.
13 B.M. Add. Mss 40475, ff. 45, 48, Hardinge to Queen, 23 October 1845;

The soldiers

    B.M. Add. Mss 54517, ff. 56-7, 101, Hardinge to C. Napier, 7 June 1844, and 31 October 1844.
14 S.M. Mitra, *The life and letters of Sir John Hall*, pp. 77-87.
15 S.R.O., GD 45/8/12, Macdonald to Maule, 5 August 1846; Wellington papers, Wellington to Macdonald, 3 August 1846.
16 Hansard, 3rd series, XCI, c 1319.
17 P.P. 1850, X, p. 33.
18 *N. & M.G.*, 10 September 1853, p. 580.
19 Hansard, 3rd series, CXXIV, c 676.
20 Wellington papers, Wellington to William IV, 25 March 1833.
21 Wellington papers, Hill to Secretary at War, 26 July 1834; also quoted in P.P. 1836, XXII, pp. 314-6.
22 W.O. 43/591, ff. 2-5.
23 W.O. 4/264, pp. 257-9.
24 W.O. 3/286, p. 322; W.O. 3/287, p. 441; W.O. 3/94, p. 458; W.O. 3/95, pp. 194, 310.
25 W.O. 3/103, p. 113; Second Earl Cathcart papers, H.1.
26 W.O. 43/591, ff. 76-136.
27 W.O. 4/267, pp. 35, 74.
28 Copies of the report are in the Wellington papers, Wellington to Graham, 6 April 1844, and Second Earl Cathcart papers, G. 129. See also Jebb's article on military prisons, *Aide-mémoire to the military sciences*, III, pp. 130-9.
29 S.R.O., GD 45/8/112, 'Brief sketch of what has been done for the soldier', n.d.
30 Wellington papers, Sir Thomas Fremantle to Wellington, 2 August 1844.
31 Herbert papers, III A (69), Jebb to Herbert, 18 February 1853.
32 Frederic Roberts, *Cursory remarks on recruiting and recruits*, p. 7.
33 *U.S.M.*, 1851, III, p. 294.
34 *Standing Orders of the 2nd Dragoons*, 1839, p. v.
35 W.O. 43/591, ff. 2, 20.
36 W.O. 43/595, ff. 301-33.
37 A. C. E. Jarvis, 'My predecessors in office', *Journal of the Royal Army Chaplains' Department*, III, 1931, pp. 444-80, 481-520.
38 *Quarterly Review*, 76, 1845, p. 416; *U.S.M.*, 1843, 1, p. 109.
39 *N. & M.G.*, 20 January 1844, p. 39.
40 W.O. 3/101, p. 94; 3/108, p. 165; 3/111, p. 395.
41 W.O. 43/535, ff. 80-109.
42 W.O. 43/740, ff. 220-30.
43 N.L.S. mss 2844, f. 219, Gleig to Brown, 30 October 1845.
44 N.L.S. mss 3870, ff. 159-62, Gleig to Peel, 3 February 1845.
45 Herbert papers, I M (33), Gleig to Herbert, 10 November 1845.
46 S.R.O., GD. 45/8/16, Maule, 7 December 1846, to unnamed, but from Hansard, 3rd series, XC, c 307, it must be Gleig.
47 *Quarterly Review*, 76, 1845, pp. 405-6.
48 Ibid., 76, pp. 419-21.
49 W.O. 43/819, ff. 311-21.

50 Hansard, 3rd series, LXXXI, c 1334.
51 W.O. 43/287, f 349.
52 *U.S.G.*, 31 January 1846, p. 3.
53 Henry Marshall, *Military miscellany*, p. 320.
54 Frederic Roberts, *Cursory remarks on recruiting and recruits*, pp. 7, 14.
55 Charles R. Sanderson (ed.), *The Arthur papers*, letter no. 1453.
56 *N. & M.G.*, 2 September 1843, p. 552.
57 N.L.S. mss 2843, ff. 39-40, Irton to Brown, 24 April 1843.
58 *N. & M.G.*, 23 June 1838, p. 399.
59 R. S. Schofield, 'Dimensions of illiteracy, 1750-1850', *Explorations in Economic History*, summer 1973, p. 437.
60 *N. & M.G.*, 21 October 1843, p. 661; *Military Annual for 1844*, p. 385.
61 Carlo M. Cipolla, *Literacy and development in the West*, London, 1969, p. 121.
62 Herbert papers, I Add., Herbert to Cardwell, 27 June 1846.
63 *King's Regulations*, 1837, pp. 232-4.
64 W.O. 43/752, ff. 165-81; Hansard, 3rd series, LII, c 1091.
65 *British Army Despatch*, 28 May 1852, p. 349.
66 L. I. Cowper, *The King's Own*, II, p. 50.
67 Charles R. Sanderson (ed.), *The Arthur papers*, letter no. 1234.
68 C. T. Atkinson, *Regimental History, Royal Hampshire Regiment*, I, p. 304.
69 Colonel Baumgardt, *Standing Orders for 2nd or Queen's Royals*, 1846, p. 37.
70 *Quarterly Review*, 77, 1846, p. 542.
71 East Riding C.R.O., DDCH 80 p. 264, Sir Charles Chichester's diary, 28 November 1843.
72 W.O. 43/807, f. 46.
73 W.O. 55/1931, pp. 14-16; Wellington papers, statement on Royal Sappers and Miners schools, 15 November 1846.
74 *U.S.M.*, 1848, II, p. 465; *N. & M.G.*, 17 June 1848, p. 387.
75 S.R.O., GD 45/8/42, Fitzclarence to Maule, 10 March 1848. The terms of the letter are closely reflected in *U.S.G.*, 5 February 1848, p. 4, which supports the notion of Fitzclarence's close links with the paper.
76 *U.S.G.*, 23 August 1851, p. 6; *N. & M.G.*, 23 August 1851, p. 534.
77 Herbert papers, III A (73), Gleig to Herbert, 16 September 1853.
78 *U.S.G.*, 5 June 1852, p. 5.
79 India Office Library, L/MIL/3/1907, no. 59.
80 S.R.O., GD 45/8/42, Fitzclarence to Maule, 10 March 1848.
81 W.O. 43/590, ff. 270-7, 290.
82 W.O. 3/294, p. 3; W.O. 3/195, pp. 158-363.
83 W.O. 3/300, pp. 4, 105; W.O. 43/590, ff. 304-5, 314, 327; *Queen's Regulations*, 1844, pp. 253-5.
84 General Order no. 544, 5 February 1840.
85 *N. & M.G.*, 8 June 1839, p. 361.
86 [J. McMullen], *Camp and barrack-room*, pp. 154-5.
87 *Journal of the Society for Army Historical Research*, II, 1922, pp. 37-8.
88 Hardinge papers, memo of 11 April 1853.

The soldiers

89 Hansard, 3rd series, LXXIII, c 554; CXXIV, c 675.
90 G. F. A. Best, 'National education in England 1800-70', *Cambridge Historical Journal*, XII, 1956, pp. 155-73;
91 W.O. 43/796, ff. 150-61.
92 Herbert papers, III Add., undated memorandum on the Royal Military Asylum. The proposal was leaked to *N. & M.G.*, 5 February 1842, p. 89.
93 *Quarterly Review*, 77, 1846, pp. 540-53.
94 Horse Guards circular, 16 September 1845.
95 W.O. 43/796, ff. 1-77; there are also copies of this whole correspondence in the Herbert papers, I Add.
96 N. T. St. John Williams, *Tommy Atkins' children*, p. 43.
97 W.O. 43/807, ff. 153, 223-4.
98 Alan Ramsay Skelley, *The Victorian army at home*, p. 112.
99 W.O. 43/807, ff. 120-33.
100 Herbert papers, III B (5).
101 Alan Ramsay Skelley, *The Victorian army at home*, p. 87.
102 P.P. 1850, X, p. 892.
103 W.O. 43/513, ff. 257-94.
104 G. R. Gleig, *Personal reminiscences of the 1st Duke of Wellington*, pp. 304-5.
105 P.P. 1850, X, p. 53.
106 [G. R. Gleig] in *Edinburgh Review*, 95, April 1852, p. 332.
107 *N. & M.G.*, 23 August 1851, p. 534.
108 C. Greenhill Gardyne, *The life a regiment*, II, p. 40.
109 Seaton papers, Mountain to Seaton, 27 March 1841.
110 East Riding C.R.O., DDCH 84, p. 120, Chichester's diary, 26 February 1847.
111 *U.S.M.*, 1842, III, pp. 233-4; see also *N. & M.G.*, 29 August 1838, p. 620; 9 February 1839, p. 89; 30 July 1842, p. 489.
112 *U.S.J.*, 1838, I, p. 1.
113 *N.& M.G.*, 5 January 1839, p. 9.
114 Edward M. Spiers, *The army and society, 1815-1914*, pp. 3-4. Spiers points out that this numerical increase actually constituted a smaller percentage of the total commissioned without purchase.
115 T. W. J. Connolly, *History of the Royal Sappers and Miners*, I, p. 275; II, p. 121.
116 W.O. 43/787, ff. 294-337.
117 B.M. Add. Mss 54536, f. 91, Robertson to C. Napier, 2 July 1847.
118 Herbert papers, III B (76).
119 N.A.M. 6807/289, Raglan to Hardinge, 28 December 1854.
120 N.L.S. mss 9319, f. 133, Scots Fusilier Guards, 'Crimean campaign 1854 to 1856'.
121 [T. F. Simmons], *Remarks on the promotion of officers of Artillery*, p. 31.
122 C. J. Napier, *Remarks on military law*, pp. 220-7; B.M. Add. Mss 54544, 27-31, Douglas to C. Napier, 15 June 1836.
123 Grey papers, Charles Grey to Howick, 24 April 1836.
124 Marshall, *On enlisting*, pp. 212-3, 236-42.

125 W.O. 43/787, ff. 279-337.
126 P.P. 1850, X, p. 848.
127 W.O. 43/834, ff. 19, 34-5; Hansard, 3rd series, CXIII, c 364, gives 123 n.c.o.s. in receipt of the annuity.
128 W.O. 43/787, ff. 349-404.
129 S. G. P. Ward, *Journal of the Society for Army Historical Research*, XXV, 1947, pp. 44, observes that Napier mentions them in an annexe, whereas Raglan did so in the body of the dispatch.
130 *U.S.M.*, 1845, III, pp. 80, 339.
131 John Luard, *A history of the dress of the British soldier*, p. 151.
132 W.O. 30/112, memo by Wellington for Grey, 22 January 1847.
133 General Order, 1 January 1830, quoted in Marshall, *On enlisting*, p. 77.
134 *N. & M.G.*, 17 February 1849, p. 107.
135 W.O. 43/947, p. 69.
136 W.O. 43/771, ff. 246-90; 4/270, p. 439.
137 J. H. Stocqueler, *The military encyclopaedia*, p. 262.
138 P.P. 1854-5, IX, part I, *2nd report*, p. 20.
139 Hansard, 3rd series, CXXIV, c 676.
140 N.L.S. mss 2849, f. 213, 'Distribution of army', 27 November 1851.
141 Oliver MacDonagh, 'The nineteenth-century revolution in government: a reappraisal', *Historical Journal*, I, 1958, pp. 52-67.
142 N.A.M. 6210/73/19, memo by Adjutant General on corporal punishment, 29 April 1833.

CHAPTER 4
THE RISING PROFESSIONALISM OF THE OFFICERS

1. *Appointment and promotion*

Enough has already been said of the reforming role of the regimental officer to suggest an alternative picture to the ignorant, hunting, dandified rake portrayed by Dickens and Thackeray. Of course idle fops served in the army, and the popular press and the correspondence of the Adjutant General abound with their exploits. But to imagine that the influence wrought by these reckless subalterns did much more than affront the sensibilities of Victorian worthies would be misplaced. Many were simply youthful — 'precious young ninocompoops' displaying 'the sort of faults boys coming straight from school to a messroom would normally have'.[1]

Many, moreover, were merely serving a few years, and soon sold out. In the 3rd Light Dragoons, only three officers present with the regiment in 1835 were still in it in 1840.[2] Those that lingered were forced to review their prospects when the regiment sailed on foreign service. This came round so regularly in the infantry — after a maximum of five years — that dilettantes were rarely to be found in its messes.

It was particularly abroad, and therefore out of the eye of the newspapers, that officers, removed from the social blandishments of home pleasures, were turned in upon their regiments, and became concerned for their betterment.

Many soldiers' memoirs mention a favourite officer, from whom little acts of kindness were received. Amidst all the criticism they handed out, McNeill and Tulloch still wrote in June 1855 that 'the conduct of the men is ... the highest encomium that can be passed upon their officers. They have not only shared all the danger and exposure and most of the privations which the men had to undergo, but the evidence is full of incidental indications of their solicitude for the welfare of those who were under their command ... It was always gratifying to observe the community of feelings and of interests that appeared everywhere to subsist between the officers and their men.'³

Victorian paternalism and deference formed much of the basis of this good feeling. But it would be wrong to let a class distinction lead to the conclusion then current among the radicals. It was not birth that dictated the grant of commissions, so much as the wealth to purchase and to provide a private income. In 1830 21 per cent of British officers were aristocrats, 32 per cent landed gentry and an overwhelming 47 per cent middle-class.⁴ A check of the *Army List* in 1847 revealed that of 5,000 infantry officers, only seventy-three were titled (including younger sons of peers), and even the allegedly exclusive cavalry and Foot Guards could muster only a further 103 aristocrats between them.⁵ In 1854 13 per cent of colonels came from aristocratic backgrounds, and a further 25 per cent from the gentry; but the bulk of the remainder had fathers in the professions, including 22 per cent in the armed services and 10 per cent in the clergy.⁶ Bernal Osborne, a self-avowed liberal, pointed out in 1850 that the vast majority of the officers in the heavy dragoons were 'sons of capitalists and gentlemen who had made their money fairly and honestly in their different occupations. He found, also, that the great proportion of infantry were the sons of very poor men, who entered the army as a profession; and it was only in two exceptional regiments, which were not the working branch of the service, that it was otherwise.' Richard Cobden was not disposed to disagree.⁷

The regimental system, with its ancient lineage, its landed and royal connections, and its social and sporting life, bestowed status. And it could be bought. There is no need necessarily to see the attractions of military service for the rising middle class as lying only in the aftermath of the abolition of purchase. For the successful merchant, the acquisition of a commission for his son could confer the *imprimatur* of arrival. He might, it is true, construe the army as a poor investment in terms of cash and prefer to establish continuity in his own business, with his progeny as partners. But for some at any rate the first argument held good. Sergeant J. McMullen, who did not present a very favourable picture of the army, reflected the desire for gentlemen as officers. He took as typical the man, 'who very probably, is your superior only because his father was fortunate in trade and therefore able to pay £450 for a commission for his son'.⁸

Resentment at the incursion of new wealth into the officer corps was not grounded simply on the means by which it had been accumulated: after all, the sons of professional men, officers, clergymen and lawyers had long provided a large part of the intake. The root was often jealousy, because increasingly the latter group could not afford the cost of commissions for their offspring, but the successful businessman, anxious to confer status on his family, could. Over and above this simple hostility was the feeling, reflected by McMullen, that the harmony of a regiment would be disturbed by officers who did not understand the nature of landed society. The preferred recruit was an agricultural labourer, and therefore the regiment was a sort of rural community, where deference was rewarded by solicitude for the men's welfare. Sir Charles Napier, who, although a firm commander in northern England in 1839-42, often expressed sympathy with the Chartists' case and whose brother, William, was friendly with Roebuck and advised the paramilitary formations of the Reform Bill riots, expressed this view. For him, 'a man of high breeding is hand in glove with his men, while the son of a millionaire hardly speaks to a soldier'.[9] His knowledge of radical feeling showed him the impersonal relationship between owner and employee: the commissioning of the owner's son might bring this insensitivity into the army and so undermine the mutual respect on which it rested its discipline. Therefore, despite his political proclivities, Napier preferred a 'man of ancient lineage with an empty purse'.[10]

Consequently, apart from the formal requirement that an applicant for a commission be over sixteen and not much over nineteen, and that he produce certificates as to his education, character, connections and health, the only unwritten rule was that he be a gentleman, a man of 'education, manners, Honor, and other qualities acquired by the Education which English Gentlemen receive'. 'This is *the Man*,' Wellington reminded Fitzroy Somerset, 'to whom all look in moments of difficulty and danger ... There is no greater mistake than to suppose that the Service performed by the British Army could be carried on by any other description of Man excepting one educated as is an English Gentleman!'[11]

The Duke's view bit deep. Sir John Macdonald, the Adjutant General, declared in 1840: 'It is the proud characteristic of the British Army that its officers are gentlemen by education, manners and habits.'[12] The 71st's standing orders gave the beau ideal of an officer 'as a combination of the highest military qualifications with the tastes and habits of an educated gentleman'.[13]

All these quotations stress that the characteristics of a gentleman were bestowed by education rather than birth. They made for a social equality among officers which was the admiration of foreigners. The cordiality and good feeling of mess life generated an *esprit de corps* and a sense of honour, which percolated throughout the regiment.

However, mess life presented a serious drain on the subaltern's slender resources. The efforts of the Horse Guards to control extravagance meant that in 1853 the average cost of a mess dinner was only 2s. 6d.,[14] and in 1812 the Prince Regent had established an allowance to enable officers to have wine. But the incentive to spend in the company of like-minded young men was strong. Moreover, on appointment to a regiment, an officer had to put thirty days' pay into the mess fund, and thereafter an annual subscription of up to eight days' pay was levied, and a further sum demanded on each promotion. Twenty days' pay on joining or promotion and twelve days' pay per year were also allocated to a fund for the regimental band, and 1s. 6d. per week (or 2s. 6d. in the cavalry) payable to his servant. These were the only compulsory charges on an officer, but one writer computed that annually they accounted for £99 6s. 5d. as against an ensign's pay of £95 16s. 3d.[15]

Therefore, a private income, variously pitched at £50 to £100 minimum, was essential for any rank under that of major, and 'even a lieutenant-colonel [is] paid less by the country ... than many commoners give to their servants out of livery'.[16] If the interest on the purchase value of his commission was added to the officer's losses, it reduced the pay of a lieutenant-colonel to a mere £107, as against the £73 of an ensign.[17] On top of this, there was the constant depreciation of his uniform and equipment: in 1829 the officer's uniform of the 10th Hussars cost almost £400.[18]

Foreign service produced certain allowances and reduced outgoings sufficiently to make it possible for a subaltern in India to live on his pay. In addition, war would mean a share of prize money, and penurious officers endeavoured to serve abroad. Even here, however, there were complications — an officer travelling without troops had to pay for his own passage, and in the field the comforts issued automatically to the ranks were not available to the officers, who were supposed to provide their own by virtue of their better means and their field allowances, regardless of their availability.

Nor was this financial deprivation compensated for when the benighted officer finally became a general. Up to the rank of lieutenant-colonel, his pay (and that of the other ranks) was higher than in any other European country, although the gap narrowed with seniority and was also offset by the higher cost of living in Britain. As a general he received less than his equals in every other European army except Russia.[19] Apart from those on staff employment, 120 generals were eligible to receive unattached pay of £1 5s. per day: any generals supernumerary to this establishment received the pay of their last regimental rank. In addition generals could earn pay from titular garrison appointments and as colonels of regiments, where the profits on clothing the corps, called off-reckonings, were reserved for the colonel. Both sources were under attack, particularly the latter as they created a conflict between the colonel's self-interest and the good equipment of the troops, worn-out items having to last longer than efficiency perhaps countenanced. Those in the first class that were sinecures were recommended to be abolished in 1833, and those in the second were reduced to a flat rate outwith the clothing system in 1854. At the same time salaries of employed officers had been cut, so that the Commander-in-Chief in Canada had seen his daily pay shrink from £9 9s. to £3 15s.[20]

However, as a result of an 1833 select committee, it was established in 1835 that a minimum of £400 per annum should be given to generals of distinguished service.[21] Therefore by unattached or distinguished service pay a minimum salary was established for all generals willing to be employed. However, no distinction of pay existed for rank from major-general to field-marshal, their relative incomes depending on the profitability of their individual colonelcies or on the prize money won in the waging of a successful war.

To support these poor financial returns was a system of retirement as confused and miserly. Before 1830[22] an officer could without limitation opt to transfer to the half-pay list, and only three years' service was required after 1830. No distinction was made as to his motives, whether his health had been broken by long service or his regiment reduced, or whether he had simply become bored by a couple of years' garrison duty. In the post-1815 reductions, in particular, many conscientious soldiers suffered — Wellington claimed that he knew of officers who had three times bought themselves back on to full pay, only to be reduced again.[23] On the other hand, in 1835, there were still 193 officers drawing pay for an average of forty-five months' service, and a further eighty-eight ensigns and cornets on half pay who had never served at all.[24]

In practice, the half-pay list fell into two divisions. An officer could use it as a means to retire, by receiving the difference in the value of his half and full-pay commissions, but in so doing he cut himself off from all further claim to promotion. In response to a demand for a proper system of retirement, permission to do this was, after 1840, restricted to those of at least eighteen years' service,[25] and this was increased to twenty-one in 1852, in order to align it with the other ranks' pension scheme.[26]

The true purpose of half pay, however, was not to reward past services but to retain the duties of the officer in case of emergency or the expansion of the army. This it singularly failed to accomplish. In their poverty-stricken state, many officers withdrew to the cheaper life of the continent and thus ceased to be immediately available. Although half-pay officers were used to staff the Canadian Militia in 1837, a survey in 1847, to establish their eligibility for the Enrolled Pensioners and Militia in Britain, showed that most were unfit or had by then been promoted to ranks far senior to those in which they had been actively employed.[27]

Those half-pay officers who expressed their willingness to serve again were retained on the list for promotion. Thus more than half the generals employed in the twenty years up to 1854 had been on half pay for over ten years.[28] However zealous, they were at the least out of touch with current developments, and at the worst useless and decayed — as General Elphinstone showed at Kabul after twenty-five years on half pay.

The size of the non-effective list was massive: in 1831 there were 9,404 officers drawing various forms of half and retired pay, as against 6,768 on full pay.[29] Therefore, even if the system was militarily useless (as was finally admitted in 1849 when officers of reduced regiments were retained 'en second' on full pay rather than put on half pay),[30] financially it remained desirable to bring back these nominally retired officers to full pay. Although this arrangement at least meant some return on the half-pay bill in terms of work, it too had undesirable professional consequences. The incursion from the half pay checked the already slow current of full-pay promotion and pushed up the average age of each rank. In consequence recourse was had to the commutation of half pay by buying out junior officers and by offering land in the colonies (although few accepted the latter). From 1834, in an endeavour to help promotion and reduce the half pay, for every three vacancies by death in each rank on the retired or half-pay list, one full-pay officer from the rank below was promoted to a half-pay unattached commission, while his place was in turn filled from the half pay.[31] It is doubtful whether this produced any younger officers or helped the flow of promotion in a regiment, but it did at least clear the half-pay list of those except the more genuinely deserving.

The tendency, therefore, was for the half-pay list to be less a reserve of officers and more a means to retirement. The *United Service Journal* was a keen advocate of abolishing the half-pay list altogether, and proposed instead a retiring allowance for officers of over twenty-five years' service. Sir Willoughby Gordon's evidence given to the 1840 promotion commission was eloquent in its support, but the commission compromised.

There already existed provision for retired full pay, although it was so limited as to be totally ineffective. The commission therefore proposed that retired full pay be allowed to twenty lieutenant-colonels, twenty majors and 115 captains. Although greeted as the only glimmer in the whole report, by 1844 only half the places had been taken up[32] — not because the numbers were still too low, but because in retirement all promotion ended, whereas on half pay it did not, and because by selling out altogether an officer would procure a higher rate of income from investing the capital thus realised.

These expedients were part of a much more central issue, crucial to the army's efficiency as well as to individual pride — that of promotion. An inflated half-pay list and a reduced army after a long war had left comparatively young senior officers, probably fit for a long span of service ahead, and consequently an almost imperceptible trickle of promotion. There existed no means to compel an old soldier to retire, nor little attraction for him to do so. The pages of the *United Service Journal* in the 1830s were crammed with complaints of the static roster and published ingenious expedients to solve the problem. The report of the 1840 promotion commission was so eagerly awaited that the *Naval and Military Gazette* devoted an entire special issue to it, although from the first the commission had been conceived as a means to confirm the existing system and still the debate.[33]

Without a retirement scheme, the only logical alternative to maintain the current of promotion was natural wastage through death. A death vacancy was normally, although not always, filled without purchase by seniority within the regiment. Such opportunities, however, were scarce. The annual mortality of officers at home was less than one per cent, and even for all the infantry of the line less than two per cent.[34] Moreover, its effect was indiscriminate: in five regiments over a nine-year period there were no death vacancies.[35] On this average, advancement by seniority and natural wastage would allow one major from every two corps to be promoted every twenty years. Therefore, except for the West India Regiments and units on active service, death vacancies played a negligible role.

A frequent accusation against the Horse Guards was that parliamentary and landed interest were more important factors in deciding promotion than seniority. In fact only one written hint of political interest dictating preferment has been found, and that at Grey's, not Wellington's, instance.[36] Moreover it concerns the grant of a first commission — the only point where the Commander-in-Chief could and did exercise a right of selection, since the number of candidates far exceeded the vacancies. The individual cases of fast promotion cited by the military press often involved influential personages, but, as in the example of Cardigan, it was purchase not favouritism that secured the promotion, and, whatever the social qualifications, all officers had to have served two years as an effective subaltern before becoming a captain and six until eligible for a majority.

The only case where personal whim could further an officer's career was in the award of brevet rank for distinguished service. This conferred a senior rank in the army (and thus hastened promotion to general) but left the rank and pay in the regiment unchanged. Normally granted for conduct in the field, it could also be used to place a junior but more meritorious officer over a senior. Brevet promotion does not seem to have been abused, although Mountain complained that there was a tendency in India to grant it to men for holding certain positions in an army on service rather than to those who had executed their duties well.[37]

But of course the principal vehicle of promotion was the purchase of commissions. As an inequitable and outdated phenomenon it has been cast at the nineteenth-century army by every commentator in a way that belies its comparative irrelevance.

There were admittedly abuses. All ranks up to those of lieutenant-colonel could be purchased, more often than not for prices in excess of the regulation amount, depending on the type of regiment and where it was stationed. Very often a field officer in a regiment would be bought out by the senior of each rank below him, who would thus profit from the vacancy. The losers in this system were the poor subalterns who could not afford the sum required, and for some no doubt the indignity of serving under a less experienced officer was profound. Even for those who did manage to purchase, the capital sum languished without return (estimated at an annual loss of £247 in interest for a cavalry lieutenant-colonel), and would be absolutely forfeit if the officer died or was promoted general.

With peacetime contraction and when the half-pay list had been brought under control, the proportion of bought rank was higher than that achieved by other means, and this was reflected in the 1840s by the diminishing ages in the ranks of all regimental officers.[38] It did, however, raise a spectre of an army officered on wealth alone. Foremost in the attack was the redoubtable Colonel Mitchell, who throughout the 1830s expressed his desire for the total abolition of purchase in a series of trenchant articles. Purchase was a system 'which crushes all honest emulation by showing that merit, valour, and acquirements count for nothing in its estimation, — which, forgetful that the lives and happiness of men depend upon the result, ... promotes the wealthy dunces of the honourable profession ... over the heads of all the bravest and the best who cannot purchase'. By the 1840s the *United Service Magazine* and the *United Service Gazette* were, in the name of education, repeating Mitchell's call for abolition.

In 1840 the military hierarchy, although anxious to confine the prices of commissions to their regulated limits, gave overwhelming support to the principles of purchase.[40] Purchase had stood the test of service. Moreover there was little likelihood of the government producing the four million pounds estimated as required to buy out officers' existing interests. Nor would it undertake the additional burden of a regular pension scheme to replace the security of raising money for retirement by the sale of commissions. The requirement to purchase ensured some degree of dedication on the part of the officer, and a property qualification was thought a constitutional safeguard.

It is hard to believe that, if purchase had been abolished, the army would have become radical, plebeian and 'no longer to be trusted with the maintenance of our Throne'.[41] However, the contemporary tendency to exaggerate the democratic effects of abolition has been counterbalanced by a modern image of purchase as the only method of promotion. In fact, of 5,120 officers on full pay in January 1848, only 2,411 had purchased all their commissions, although a further 1,555 had bought one or more.[42] Of these, few first commissions were granted without purchase (108 in 1844 but only 36 in 1852),[43] and most of these to Sandhurst cadets. In 1850 sixty-seven of 141 lieutenant-colonels in the infantry had not purchased that rank, and five had never bought a single step. Of 204 majors, only eighty-two had bought all their commissions.[44] For those unable to buy, there was the compensation of arriving at the top of their rank sooner by others' purchase and thus being first on the list for a death vacancy.

An additional fillip to the pro-purchase lobby was the simple fact that, given the existing circumstances, promotion by seniority alone would have wrecked the army's efficiency. Practical evidence of this was provided by the Royal Artillery and Royal Engineers, all of whose promotion rested on seniority. Consequently, in 1833, the ten senior artillery colonels had served just over forty years each; the problem was aggravated among the subalterns, the ten senior lieutenants showing over twenty years' service apiece.[45] By 1840 all the artillery lieutenant-colonels were over fifty years old, and not one of the captains had served less than thirty years.[46]

Successive Masters General of the Ordnance tried to improve the situation. In 1823 Wellington allowed artillery officers to sell their commission on the unattached half-pay list, Anglesey in 1827 abolished the rank of major to speed promotion, and Vivian extended the provision for retirement and reopened the door to permanent half pay.[47] The 1840 promotion commission conceded that none of these had produced any permanent improvement, but its own recommendations, for four lieutenant-colonels and four captains to retire each year on full pay, and for two more lieutenant-colonels to retire without further promotion, also proved insufficient. From 1828 to 1848, 478 first commissions were given in the Royal Artillery but only 191 officers retired: in the Engineers 223 officers joined but only 65 left.[48]

Colonel F. R. Chesney lobbied for a reduction in subalterns and an increase in field officers,[49] and his scheme was implemented, at least to a limited extent, when in 1848 two new battalions were added to the Royal Artillery and one to the Royal Engineers, so that further vacancies occurred in the upper echelons of the two regiments.[50] These augmentations provided temporary relief, most captains got their companies within fifteen years, and by 1854 there were no lieutenants over thirty (forty-one had been in 1838), and eighty-five captains were aged twenty-five to thirty (none had been under thirty-five in 1838). But among the field officers, the situation had worsened: although by 1854 there were seven gunner lieutenant-colonels under fifty, twenty-four of the total of fifty-two were over sixty (none had been in 1838), and in the Engineers twenty of the thirty (one in 1838).[51]

By the outbreak of the Crimean war, therefore, the junior ranks of both parts of the army were relatively healthy and young. In the field ranks and above, there were grounds for grave disquiet, for, after lieutenant-colonel, promotion went entirely by seniority. According to the date of their last commission, officers became generals by periodical brevets, often given on occasions such as coronations and sometimes postponed on political grounds owing to the sudden added cost of such large-scale promotion.

The brevets embraced all classes of commission, including those on the half-pay list. So dominant was half pay that it precluded the individual brevet affecting promotion in many regiments — it was reckoned that, of 160 to 170 lieutenant-colonels eligible in 1837, only thirteen were on the infantry full pay.[52] Nominally, an officer needed to declare his willingness to serve in order to qualify for the brevet, but it is clear that, while many in principle were ready to do so, few actually found themselves fit enough to go to India or the West Indies if the occasion arose.

Therefore in an officer's upward climb there came a long-drawn-out pause when he reached lieutenant-colonel. During the 1830s the number of general officers was reduced from 450 to 304,[53] and in this time in particular many commanding officers remained at the head of regiments they had ceased to adorn. In 1834, after twenty years as lieutenant-colonel and colonel in the Rifle Brigade, Brown was considering retirement, little aware that after the 1841 brevet over a decade of service at the Horse Guards and a divisional command in the Crimea would be extracted from him. More than half the full colonels in the *Army List* in 1846 had entered the army in the eighteenth century, and thirteen of the eighty-seven senior lieutenant-colonels.[54]

In this context, an outstanding abuse, the promotion privileges of the Guards, in fact became the boon that gave any youth at all to the list of generals. In the Foot Guards, the regimental rank of lieutenant carried with it the army rank of captain, while the Guards captain was a lieutenant-colonel in the army. This, taken in conjunction with their higher pay and almost unbroken home service, provided fuel for attacks that could only lamely be answered by referring to the more expensive commissions, the greater extent of purchase and the slower current of promotion within the regiments. 'The Guards' system of rank over the Line,' Hardinge noted, 'give to 7 Battns. of Foot Gds 70 Lt. Colonels — reared in London, trimming up to the rank of Major General. In the Line of 120 Battalions $\frac{1}{3}$ dispersed in our Colonies, we have 140 Lt. Cols. toiling upwards for the same reward!'[55] It brought a Guards officer ten to fifteen years[56] nearer general officer rank than his counterpart in the Line. Although a Guards general had rarely commanded a battalion or had field experience, the abuse provided a loophole to bring on outstanding Line officers, by transferring them to the Guards; 450 officers were alleged to have been brought forward in this way in half a century.[57] Wellington thus elevated Hardinge in 1815, and Hardinge himself countenanced it in 1854. In 1855 it enabled him to appoint one such officer, Codrington, to the supreme command in the Crimea at the tender age of only fifty-one.

This anomaly, however, provided no more than a glimmer in an otherwise gloomy picture. In 1837 the army had four generals for every 1,000 men,[58] so that fortunately only one in ten was employed.[59] Nonetheless

Charles Napier, purportedly the most distinguished of them, was already regretting his age before Miani and confessed himself too old for work in 1845, when he was still to serve as Commander-in-Chief in India.[60] At the height of the invasion scare in 1850, there was no general in Britain under sixty-one.[61]

The 1840 promotion commission had at least acknowledged the waning bodily energies of the generals, but a decade later the Secretary at War still spoke of brevet promotion as a means to reward past services rather than to create an élite for the future.[62] Fortunately his apathy was ceasing to be common. The military press called for the ending of brevets and the promotion of generals as vacancies occurred. In 1852 Prince Albert advocated the abolition of brevets, a fixed establishment for each general officer rank, a third of which were to be appointed by selection, and upper age limits for every rank above field officer.[63] Charles Grey, his private secretary, wanted all lieutenant-colonels to be promoted after six years on full pay.[64] Through Charles' mediation, the Prince Consort found an ally in Lord Grey. The latter proposed that every commanding officer should be eligible for temporary appointment as a major-general and then confirmed in this rank after three years.[65] The Duke of Cambridge wanted to stop half-pay promotion, and to retire all officers over fifty.[66] The *United Service Gazette*, perhaps on the Duke's prompting, took up the proposal of separate retired and active lists,[67] while de Lacy Evans urged the adoption of promotion by selection.[68]

All these ideas had their merits, and were no doubt considered during 1853 by a very worried Hardinge. The Burma campaign was in the hands of a septuagenarian and ill health threatened the incumbents of several other commands. In December that year he found difficulty in even appointing to the Horse Guards staff: 'In the present state of our decrepitude caused by the slow promotion of Peace, I would prefer to waive Rank in all Staff appointments, for the sake of ensuring more Youth and Energy.'[69] Two months later, in February 1854, he had to officer an expeditionary force: although brigades in the Peninsula and normally been commanded by major-generals, none of those available was sufficiently young and instead Hardinge had to appoint brigadiers, that is to say colonels with brevet rank.[70]

The problem of finding adequate officers for the eastern expedition was thus the final blow rather than the initial reason for Herbert's summoning a commission on promotion in February 1854. He and Hardinge had already agreed that its purpose was to accelerate promotion, in particular to bring up younger generals, and to introduce the principle of selection into the system.⁷¹ To save time, the 1840 commission's evidence was adopted and the proceedings conducted by a series of printed memoranda circulated among the members. The latter included Grey, who manifested his customary lack of courtesy to the military. This apart, the workings of the commission were remarkably harmonious, and, except for one minor point, all the resolutions of the committee were — at first at any rate — unanimously adopted.⁷²

Published in June, the report⁷³ recommended that three years as an active lieutenant-colonel should be rewarded by promotion to colonel, and thence by seniority to major-general. Brevets should be abandoned, the provision for retirement increased and an establishment of 234 general officers fixed. Beyond this, however, there was allowance for the maximum flexibility: brevet rank should be continued for distinguished service and should be converted to regimental rank at the first opportunity; if an officer had held temporary rank for five years in peace and less in war, it should become permanent; above all else, the committee recommended that when a general was to be appointed, 'the fittest officer that can be found for the particular duty should be selected, without reference to seniority'. For the Royal Artillery and Royal Engineers, an increased establishment of generals was proposed, and selection on a much wider scale than in the line urged, including for all ranks abroad. This last provision was the subject of a dissenting report by two members, Lord Cathcart and Sir Hew Ross (himself a gunner), who feared that it was an arbitrary system and would encourage jealousy. A third member, Sir John Burgoyne, curiously supported them in the case of the artillery but not of his own corps, the engineers.

The provisions of the report were emplemented in a warrant of 6 October 1854. A final large brevet was held in June with the immediate purpose of satisfying all existing claims but with the additional bonus of improving the pool of officers for the Crimea. For Hardinge, the report bestowed the sanction he desired, and in his appointments in 1855 early promotion and the selection of ability were the keynotes.⁷⁴

2. Education

Promotion by merit seems such an obvious solution that it is pertinent to inquire why it had not been adopted earlier. Wellington acknowledged that 'If the question was merely military, ... [a man] should then be selected for promotion only on account of his abilities'.⁷⁵ However, his great fear was that of political considerations playing any part in the distribution of army patronage. Promotion by seniority, although the best safeguard, was impracticable as a universal system. Therefore, he concluded that the exercise of his own prerogative as Commander-in-Chief was the surest guarantee that professional considerations would dominate the current of promotion.

However, some officers, particularly those toiling in the colonies, reckoned that Wellington did not neglect his own personal preferences in bestowing appointments. Selection for rank therefore threatened to widen the Commander-in-Chief's scope to abuse his patronage. From Wellington's own point of view, he would have to rely far more on the advice of others, since the army was so widely diffused and engaged in such a variety of duties that it would have been impossible for him or Somerset to maintain constant oversight of each officer's capabilities and achievements. Consequently promotion by merit promised to be the direct route to jealousy and competition for favour.

What was needed was a criterion that was constant and independent of individual whim. Despite its inapplicability to specific military requirements, education seemed the soundest alternative. It was, after all, even in Wellington's view, the principal means to the acquisition of gentlemanly qualities.

In the 1830s the existing provision for the instruction of officers had but the slightest impact on their ascent in the service. All officers of the Royal Artillery and Royal Engineers were educated at the Royal Military Academy, Woolwich, but these, the only arms with a compulsory educational qualification, were the seniority corps. Performance at Woolwich did no more than dictate an individual's initial position in each batch of new commissions. Nonetheless, the estimation in which this institution stood as a seat of military science can be gauged from the fact that the fathers of candidates in 1835 included five existing or future generals as well as Gleig himself.[76] On one level the list confirms that the predominance of purchase in a peacetime army was driving the traditional officer-producing classes into support for an educational qualification.

During the 1820s, however, the standards of the Academy had slipped. The blockage in promotion had meant the deliberate slowing down of the cadets' education, and at the same time as many as a third of them, despite having passed the entrance examination in English, arithmetic, French and Latin, failed to last the course. The education was free, the government's money had thus been wasted, and the conclusion was that 'Gratuitous education necessarily produces a majority of officers of minimum attainments'.[77] Therefore, in 1831, a scale of payments was required from the parents or guardians of cadets, ranging from £80 a year for civilians to £20 for the orphan sons of officers.[78] This had little effect on the competition for places, and in 1835, Sir Hussey Vivian, the Master General, felt sufficiently confident to undertake a programme of reform.

He set up a committee,[79] whose main brief was to ensure that the entrance examination was tougher and also that it was conducted in open competition and not simply among those nominated by the Master General to sit it. He reckoned that, 'by having a larger Field & higher Fences',[80] 'we shall obtain for the service men of talents generally superior to those obtained under the present system'. As a result cadets were to enter aged between fifteen and seventeen (not fourteen to sixteen), four candidates were examined for every three places, and they had to prove themselves in a wider ranger of subjects. A second probationary examination was held twelve months after entrance.[81]

These regulations could have been the basis for a sound system. However, often they were 'frittered down to meet the views of influential complainants',[82] and the higher standards of the examination meant that candidates were crammed, with the result that 'A reaction takes place when they find themselves admitted'.[83] Moreover, the organisation itself still contained a major defect. Bullying and a particularly disreputable form of fagging had led to an overall decline in disciplinary and even moral standards. The *Naval and Military Gazette*, in a series of extremely persistent leaders written by Roberston,[84] undertook a virulent campaign for moral and Christian training in a den of drinking and gambling.

In a clear case of the effectiveness of the military press, a committee appointed by the Master General[85] in 1846 adopted one of the *Gazette*'s own suggestions, that the age on entry be reduced again to fourteen and that the Ordnance establish its own preparatory school. This was opened at Carshalton in 1848, but, in the event, the moral faults of the senior establishment were carried over, and magnified by academic failure as well. Only thirty of the original entry passed into Woolwich, and in 1851 eleven of the fourteen candidates who failed were from Carshalton. In consequence a gunner officer was appointed headmaster and the establishment remodelled on military lines.[86]

Carshalton had been threatened with extinction and was only saved because paradoxically to it was in part attributed the dramatic improvement at Woolwich itself.[87] The true author of this, however, was Captain F. M. Eardley-Wilmot, who, following the 1846 committee's report, was appointed to command the Cadet Company. Taking Arnold for his model, his aim was a curious identification of Christianity and zeal for the service. The first objective was to give the cadets a confidence in themselves, to let them feel that they were trusted and treated as gentlemen. He prefaced a volume of moral advice, entitled *Soldierly Discipline*, with the revealing words 'Remember that the Army is truly a profession'. Within three years, crime had fallen by over three-quarters,[88] and 110 cadets held good conduct badges, as against the old average of fifteen. By 1854 bullying had virtually gone.[89]

The actual syllabus of instruction given at Woolwich charted a similar graph of gradual improvement. The cadet spent two to (at a maximum) four years in the theoretical class, before passing on to a final practical course. Until 1840 the theoretical class was divided into academies, up which the cadet advanced according to his overall knowledge. However, owing to the dominant position of mathematics in the syllabus, progress in other subjects could suffer in proportion, and therefore in 1840 separate classes were established for mathematics, for fortification, and for history, geography and modern languages. The final examinations were held when the cadet had reached the first of each of the three classes. Following the 1846 committee this structure was abolished and replaced in 1848 by four theoretical classes each studying every subject, although split into sections according to individual talent. In the final assessment mathematics still held the dominant position, carrying a possible 5,000 marks; fortification was worth 4,500, and each of the other subjects 1,300, except chemistry, mechanics and geology which rated 400 each.[90]

In view of the relatively rigorous entrance examination, standards were demanding. Seven hours a day were devoted to study,[91] and, of an annual establishment of over a hundred cadets, ninety-eight were removed between 1841 and 1854 on academic grounds.[92] The staff, which in 1827 numbered twenty-four (of whom six were teachers) for about a hundred cadets, had expanded by 1848 to forty-five, including twenty-eight teachers, for only double the number of pupils.[93]

However, none of this refuted the principal attack on the Woolwich education — that it was too narrowly theoretical. Indeed it was apparently only the need to slow up the supply of officers in the post-war years that led Wellington to introduce a practical course in 1820, and from 1836 to 1847, with the adjustment to contraction over, the course was reduced in length from one year to six months.[94] It was the 1846 committee which gave the practical course any real bearing. The year was devoted to the exercise of heavy artillery, the firing of guns, the throwing up of field works, equitation, surveying, making gabions and fascines, and the manufacture of guns and gunpowder.[95] From 1848 the marks gained on the course influenced the cadet's placing for a commission. Captain Dixon was appointed Professor of Artillery and in 1853 Captain Boxer produced his *Treatise on Artillery* for the cadets' use.

However, the bias of even this improved practical course was heavily towards the gunners. Practical engineering and fortification were neglected. Consequently, although those who passed out top almost invariably opted to join the Royal Engineers, future sappers were told that Woolwich was 'grievously defective' as a place of scientific instruction.[96]

Such strictures must severely qualify any estimate of Woolwich before the Crimean war. Its monopoly of commissions in the Royal Artillery and Royal Engineers meant that, owing to the Academy's inbuilt slowness to adjust to the demands of war, those two regiments were short of seventy second lieutenants in December 1854.[97] It also meant that, since in effect their intake was trained to a certain pattern of thought from their early 'teens, there was a danger of sterility. On an absolute level it is hard to judge its products, when so few had the longevity to reach the army's higher ranks, let alone overcome the reluctance to bestow staff appointments on gunners or sappers. But, Lord Seaton, while admitting that individuals such as Pasley, Jones, Burgoyne and Dixon were 'stars', said he found 'very few of them ... brilliant ... fine fellows [but] thick headed, without military capacity'; then he added the proviso, 'although they had had the advantage of Woolwich'.[98]

Herein lies the problem. Criticism and comparison of Woolwich on any objective level are hard when it was in a sense the only truly thoroughgoing military education in the land, and was undeniably efficient as a theoretical training for regimental officers. Sandhurst was most certainly none of these things, and, unlike Woolwich, virtually no effort was made to render it effective.

For many, the Royal Military College, Sandhurst, was little more than a wartime expedient. This was especially true of its Junior Department, which had been approved in 1802: in 1815, its estimate was £34,000 but by 1832 the whole college was self-financing.[99] In 1829, Hardinge knocked thirteen men off the staff, including five professors,[100] with the result that the staff were too few for the number of pupils. To reduce costs further, contributions were levied from parents according to their income and background, in a fashion similar to that adopted at Woolwich.

It was only the charging of fees that enabled Sandhurst to continue at all. A board of general officers,[101] established in 1832 to consider the Secretary at War's demands for more reductions, felt that Sandhurst could only be preserved by an increase in the higher-paying class, the sons of civilians. With a limitation on the overall establishment, this implied a proportionate decrease in the other classes. Undermined by the theories that those who paid for their education worked harder, and that it was wrong to train destitute boys for a profession that demanded a private income, the gratuitous education of orphaned sons was ended in 1838. A subaltern, let alone his widow or a half-pay officer, could not afford the lowest scale of fees (£40 per annum), and it was found that general officers' sons were normally too old to take up the places available to them. Despite the cries of the military press for government expenditure on Sandhurst, the Secretary at War refused to restore the free orphan class and as late as 1851 a committee suggested further reductions.[102]

Few officers therefore were able to consider educating their sons at the Junior Department, and this in itself pointed to an emasculated role for the college in the army. Between 1834 and 1838, of 397 commissions given in the line, only eighty-six were to Sandhurst cadets.[103] The college boasted few distinguished names between 1832 and 1854, and by 1851, of the 420 cadets that passed through between 1813 and 1837, only three had become lieutenant-colonels and they were all Foot Guards officers.[104]

Although budgetary requirements were perhaps the principal reason for Sandhurst's decline, blame also rests with the Board of Commissioners, which, ridiculously, was responsible to the Secretary at War and not to the Commander-in-Chief. The extent of the Board's subordination can be the only further excuse for the neglect of Sandhurst by the army itself.

The entrance examination in arithmetic and English, with Latin as an optional extra, was regarded even by Sir George Scovell, the Governor, as ridiculously simple. Although geography and algebra were added in 1851, and in 1853 French and German became optional,[105] the Professor of Military Science said in 1855 'any boy from a British School in any country village' would pass.[106]

To obtain a free commission, the cadet had to undergo a *viva voce* examination in six 'steps'. Three of these were compulsory — Euclid, fortification and surveying — and he could choose his other three from history, Latin, French, German, the attack and defence of fortresses, analytical geometry, calculus and mechanics.[107] However, the structure of the course contained a number of major faults. The cadet would take each step as soon as he felt able to do so, and therefore he was continually dropping subjects and not taking them up to the final examination. The only counterweight to this was no more beneficial, since in promotion from class to class mathematics and arithmetic tended to be the regulators of progress. Furthermore, much of the cadets' early time was wasted owing to the slack entrance examination and the low age at which pupils were admitted. A strong lobby existed for raising the starting age from thirteen to fifteen or sixteen, and J. M. Spearman suggested a junior school be established on the lines of Carshalton.[108]

Quite apart from controlling bullying and fagging, a preparatory school would also have encouraged the Junior Department proper to concentrate on the more military parts of the education. The department was divided into two companies with their own military staff: they learnt infantry drill and a cavalry detachment was attached to the college to teach equitation. From 1829 men of the Royal Sappers and Miners assisted in instructing the cadets in the construction of field works, in bridging and pontooning, and in the use of voltaic batteries for explosives. They also learnt to work and manoeuvre guns. But all this practical activity was little use when not allied to theory. The compulsory step in fortification was old-fashioned and concentrated on permanent systems such as Vauban, which were of little use to an infantry subaltern in the field; the methods of attack, although integral to an understanding of the defence, formed a separate and optional step. The cadets learned drill as private soldiers, not as field manoeuvres applicable to tactical problems. Apart from the occasional reference, military history formed no part of the course, and it seems that, despite the Governor's request, the cadets did not even attend the adjacent camp at Chobham in 1853.[109]

The *United Service Magazine* advocated that, in spite of these deficiencies, all officers should pass through Sandhurst. A course with a military bias, emphasising the sciences rather than classics, seemed likely to produce better officers than the public schools. But few agreed. Sir Edward Paget, the Governor,[110] and Colonel Prosser,[111] for many years the Lieutenant Governor, acknowledged the merits of a public school education. Hardinge, when Secretary at War in 1830, doubted 'the expediency and justice ... of granting a monopoly of Commissions to

Boys educated on a particular system, over the Sons of the Gentry, and Clergy, who may prefer a Classical Education'.[112] He counselled his friend, Sir Robert Peel, not to remove his son from Eton since 'the Education of an English Gentleman is the best ground work for an English officer. The professional knowledge is better acquired at a later period ... The Commanding officers of Regts. generally find boys from a public school better officers than the cadets from Sandhurst.'[113]

With Sandhurst itself in many respects an adapted public school, and with the emphasis on gentlemanly as much as on professional virtues, an opening existed for private establishments to teach boys for the army, especially if they could do so at a price adapted to the pocket of the regimental officer. Although Wellington opposed such schools, on the grounds that they would make officers a caste separate from the rest of society,[114] from about 1832 there appeared various projects for a school for officers' sons. Ironically the fruit of these ideas was a college, initially for the orphaned sons of officers, launched as a memorial to the Duke in 1852, and which has continued to bear his name since opening in 1856.

The schemes were stimulated by the slowness of the public schools to capitalise on the expense to parents of an education at the Junior Department. Only Cheltenham made a concerted effort to train its pupils destined for the army in subjects other than classics, and from its foundation in 1840 had a thriving military department.[115] The days of the army class in public school education lay further in the future, but in 1851 Harrow and Westminster both ran a course of military instruction.[116] King's College, London, began its continuing interest in military studies in 1848. Although its syllabus had a strong professional orientation, the department struggled from the outset and in 1864 was abolished.[117]

These and many lesser establishments received a powerful impetus in 1849, when, after much lobbying in the press, examinations for first commissions were introduced. The plan was simply to ascertain that a candidate has 'the elementary principles of a liberal education',[118] as a security, in the words of the *Naval and Military Gazette*, 'against the introduction of gross irremediable weakness of intellect'.[119] Although it was hoped that such an examination would make officers view the army as a profession for life, it was felt that a candidate for a commission should only be required to prove a general education; military knowledge would come later.

Official interest had been roused in October 1846, when Grey proposed an examination for potential officers to ascertain that they had 'the education of a gentleman', including one European language and the elements of military drawing.[120] Wellington's reaction was not unfavourable. In 1836 he had advised Queen Adelaide that in preparing her son, Prince George of Cambridge, for the army, her main attention be on 'a gentleman's education', for 'such studies must facilitate and promote the acquirement & knowledge [?] of the scientific branches of the Military Art.'[121] He therefore vowed to consider Grey's suggestion.[122]

The following month Gleig rendered Grey most powerful and opportune support. In his report on the military educational establishments of the continent, he stated: 'Not in any one of [Holland, Prussia, Belgium or France], nor I believe in any other nation of Continental Europe are young gentlemen permitted to hold commissions . . . till they shall have satisfied competent judges appointed by the government for the purpose, that they possess a sufficient extent of information to qualify them for the right discharge of their duties, and intelligence enough to give them a proper moral influence in their corps.' It was a matter of indifference, Gleig continued, whether Britain endeavoured to catch up with the continent's advance in military education by reorganising the military academies or by introducing commissioning examinations. In either case, the result would be that 'Young gentlemen will be brought to regard the Army as a great profession, for which it is becoming that they should prepare themselves by a previous course of study'.[123]

However, it was not until the beginning of 1849 that the commissioning examination was introduced, and even then, according to Stocqueler, only thanks to a single orthographical error which converted Wellington to support the proposal.[124] The candidate had to know the first four rules of arithmetic, proportion, fractions and the use of logarithms; algebra, Latin or French or German translation and, in the modern languages only, prose; the histories of England and the Ancient World; geography, particularly of Europe, Britain and the Empire; and fortification but only to the standard of sketching Vauban's first system. He had also to produce a certificate of religious instruction, and to pass a superficial medical examination.[125]

The proceedings were held at Sandhurst before a board of examiners drawn from the college staff. Except in arithmetic, algebra and fortification, the questions were put *viva voce*. The standard was meant to be easier in the first than in subsequent years, but only in some subjects was the progressive standard imposed. If the candidate failed, but in less than three subjects, or it was felt that he had had 'the education of a gentleman', his case was forwarded to the Commander-in-Chief, who could allow a second chance. The failures were said to be 'very bad indeed'. However, generally speaking, commissions were never given to those who failed in languages, and a pass mark of twelve out of eighteen in geography and history (the subject in which most failures occurred) set a reasonable level of competence. Certainly the failure rate suggests not only that some very doubtful intellects had been commissioned before 1849, but also that the examination was not a mere formality: between May 1852 and April 1855 there were 456 failures to 1,444 passes. Until May 1854, when pressure on the reduced numbers of officers lowered standards, the failure rate averaged about half the candidates, and on occasion rose to two-thirds.[126]

Criticism nonetheless abounded: one newspaper said there was too much emphasis on fortification, while another felt there was too little. It was anomalous that cadets from Sandhurst were commissioned on the basis of a tougher examination. The real fault lay in the publication by the Horse Guards of a recommended book list, and, although later proscribed, it still provided a reasonable basis for cramming since some of its titles were the works of Sandhurst examiners. Gleig wanted the whole conduct of the examination put in the hands of a board totally unconnected with the Royal Military College.[127] He reiterated the original purpose of the exercise, that candidates should show judgement and willingness to learn, rather than specific knowledge.[128] In January 1854 Sidney Herbert embodied Gleig's views in a letter to Hardinge. The machinery encouraged cramming rather than general education, and Herbert concluded, 'My own belief is that the examination is too technical, too limited, within its limits too severe.' He secured Hardinge's approval in principle to Gleig's plan for a board of military education.[129]

There, however, the matter rested, a victim of the need for rapid commissioning in the Crimean war, that made even the existing examination virtually a dead letter. It could not be denied, however, and Herbert's proposals of 1854 confirm, that a means of continuous improvement among the officers had been introduced. Whatever its defects, the commissioning examination ensured that all new officers for the army had at least some education. But what they did not have, particularly given the problems with Woolwich and Sandhurst, was the opportunity to acquire professional expertise. This was the outstanding desideratum in an officer's education.

The nascent feeling of the army as a profession meant that an officer should study his calling, just as did a lawyer, physician or divine. Weight was added to this vague impulse by the rising levels of other ranks' education and by 'the shame attending the possible superiority of the servant

The rising professionalism of the officers 131

over his master'.[130] In 1838 a lieutenant of the 9th Foot noted in his diary, 'Like all other professions, men only of superior intelligence and talents gain a station for themselves,' and he therefore resolved to 'show and ... feel ... an honest zeal in *professional* pursuits'.[131] In 1835 Lord Seaton's son was cautioned, 'Remember that as you have chosen your profession, you must endeavour to acquire perfect knowledge of every part of it,'[132] and in 1844 Charles Napier advised Ensign Campbell that 'A man may talk and write, but he cannot learn his profession without constant study'.[133]

Admittedly it could be hard for the dedicated officer: his fellows saw him as 'a perfect nuisance at mess ... [without] a particle of information or amusement in his composition, save in eternally drilling into your ears his confounded stories of campaigns and sieges'.[134] His study would often be solitary and unsupported, relying for its success on his self-discipline. Ensign Chichester confessed in 1841, 'I am & ought to be anxious to learn my profession. But what have I done very little.' Commencing with Caesar, his military reading was catholic in the extreme — Napier's *War in the Peninsula*, J. Jebb on outposts, and a series of French manuals acquired on a visit to Paris.[135] Harry Smith's idea of a military education was to read Caesar's Commentaries, Condé, Turenne, Wellesley's and Wellington's correspondence,[136] and he took in hand the education of the young Henry Havelock, who in consequence devoured Vauban, Lloyd, Tempelhoff and Jomini.[137]

Those so motivated could look to the military press for inspiration, as did Chichester, or to one of the growing band of military clubs, themselves symptomatic of a new-found professional identity. One of their finest offshoots was the United Service Institution. Born in 1829 of an idea in the *United Service Journal*, the Institution's membership grew continuously until 1840, when it stabilised at about 4,000. But during the 1830s only the library served to foster professional ends: the rest was swamped with the stuffed animals and geological specimens collected by officers when overseas. The Institution was concerned with 'things which have no more to do with the art of war and either public or professional benefit, than we have to do with Hecate or Hecuba'.[138]

It was only in about 1845, with the opening of new premises and the chairmanship of Major T. Shadwell Clerke, that the swing in favour of military science became pronounced. A new lecture room was opened in 1850, and at the same time the bias of the talks — often up to sixteen a year were delivered[139] — moved from natural history to military matters. N.c.o.s were encouraged to attend, Major Adams gave a course on tactics, and Wilkinson, the gunsmith and sword-maker, lectured on firearms. In 1853, at the first of a series of evening meetings, a forum was provided for James Fergusson to outline his controversial ideas on fortification: present on that occasion were many of the most distinguished officers of the day. Only the addition of its journal (first published in 1857) was required for the Institution truly to be fulfilling its objects.

Without the journal, the importance and active membership of the United Service Institution was confined to London. Powerful agent though it potentially was for the discussion and fertilisation of military ideas, it was no more than an optional aid in the professional education of the regimental officer. Furthermore study prompted by it or the individual conscience could not ensure any uniformity of standard or guaranteed body of knowledge. As in the case of the other ranks, the protagonists of officer education looked wistfully across to the Ordnance.

The instruction of Royal Engineer officers had been comparatively complete and uniform since 1812. The Corps' feelings on the inadequacy of Woolwich, coupled with the early failings of the Engineers in the Peninsula, had encouraged a group of young officers to lobby successfully for the formation of the Royal Engineer Establishment at Chatham. One of these reformers, C. W. Pasley, was responsible for formulating a syllabus and producing manuals of instruction that remained relatively unchanged under his successors, Sir Frederic Smith (1842-51) and Colonel H. D. Jones (1851-5). Newly commissioned from Woolwich, the Engineer officer underwent a complete course of surveying and reconnaissance; as a member of the corps responsible for the maintenance of the army's buildings, he was required to study practical architecture; he translated French accounts of famous sieges, drew plans of them, and prepared projects for the attack and defence of fortresses; with the aid of the Sappers and Miners also instructed at Chatham, he was trained in siege operations, mining, bridging, pontooning, and in the infantry battalion movements. He was likely to spend about 500 days at Chatham, devoting the mornings to indoor work, the afternoons to practice and the evenings to reading.[140] Once on service, qualified officers could refer back to their 'Aides Memoires', which each prepared while at Chatham, and could expand their wisdom by studying the *Royal Engineers Professional Papers*.

The fact that in 1847 the Royal Artillery boasted forty-eight subscribers to the *Royal Engineers Professional Papers* underlines the suggestion that, while a similar desire for education existed among the gunners, it was only in part met. As in the Engineers, it was tacitly acknowledged that the Woolwich course, although better orientated towards the Artillery, was not in itself sufficient. Second lieutenants were instructed 'to attend sedulously to their professional studies, and to report weekly to their Commanding Officer the nature of each day's study and occupation'.[141] But the only provision for ensuring this was done was a half-yearly return on the young officer's progress, and that might be hampered by the remoteness and limited equipment of the garrison or station to which he belonged. In 1848 Eardley-Wilmot wrote to J. H. Lefroy, 'How many officers are there who know what guns are in the service? or who could tell you anything about ordnance? and have they any chance of learning?'[142]

For the consideration of higher artillery questions and indeed, before 1852, for all commissioned instuction, the gunners had to look to their own creation, the Royal Artillery Institution. In 1838 Eardley-Wilmot and Lefroy, inspired by the Royal Engineer Establishment at Chatham, proposed a scientific institution for the study of artillery matters and for the further education of the Royal Artillery. The Master General approved the idea but only contributed a building site towards its expense. Therefore, although the Institution should have been a properly constituted part of the regiment, membership was by subscription and voluntary. The Institution was formally founded in 1840,[143] and its immediate role was to continue the professional and practical education of second lieutenants newly commissioned from Woolwich. Eardley-Wilmot objected to the description 'a Scientific Institution', as it 'frightened men away from the real objective of an *Artillery* Institution for professional purposes'.

By the late 1840s, however, even Eardley-Wilmot had to admit that the Institution was not fulfilling its potential. A better building was needed, but the estimated cost in 1850 was in excess of £5,000. The members rapidly collected £1,050, a testimony to the gunners' commitment to their profession, and the Master General, Lord Anglesey, was persuaded that the Treasury should bear the remaining cost.[145] The inclusion of a printing press in the plans bears testimony to Eardley-Wilmot's ambition to spread the Institution's influence beyond the immediate environs of Woolwich. In 1854 it published Lefroy's *Handbook for Field Service* and from 1847 the minutes were printed, and included papers read at the Institution's meetings.

The Institution has thus received an acknowledged role in the formation and future of the regiment. Eardley-Wilmot and Lefroy had attracted 600 members, and they finally consolidated its position with yet another contribution to professional education. In 1849 Eardley-Wilmot asked the commission on Ordnance expenditure for a course in artillery similar to that at Chatham.[146] In a frank conversation two months later with the Deputy Adjutant General of the regiment, Sir Hew Ross, he recommended taking Dixon's practical class as its starting point, and that it then proceed to cover strategy, military history, and visits to the Ordnance workshops and factories. His scheme was adopted, and in 1852 it was constituted as the Department of Artillery Studies.[147]

In the cavalry and infantry, the only compulsory professional training was a requirement to pass in drill within two years of being commissioned. Reasonable diligence and competence ensured that the new subaltern was proficient in this respect within two or three months. Guidelines certainly existed for further professional instruction. The 1833 *Field Exercise* urged officers to study topography and map-reading, to post picquets, to reconnitre, to patrol and report on their findings, and to defend and fortify field posts. Queen's Regulations suggested that junior officers should practise the duties of ranks senior to their own, for example captains should command battalions, and said that it was beholden on every officer to know the *Field Exercise* and the interior economy of a regiment: commanding officers were to ensure that their officers were trained in light infantry drill, out-post duty, patrolling and taking up ground.

However, no means were provided for acquiring this knowledge, since 'It is impossible to lay down any rule for the mode of conveying Instruction, with respect to which some Commanding Officers may possess greater facilities than others'. The onus lay once again on the initiative of a good commanding officer. Generals, especially on their half-yearly inspections, were encouraged to be conscientious in ascertaining the true state of the education of a regiment's officers. However, again means were not specified, and sadly few availed themselves of the infinite powers thus available to them.[148]

To leave the vital question of professional instruction so much to individual zeal, not only meant that officers of similar rank and service had no common body of military knowledge but also that there was no yardstick by which professional competence could qualify for promotion. From 1838 the *United Service Journal* in particular called for promotion examinations, citing the Prussians as an example, and adding the rider that such a system would give security against the threat of incompetent officers inherent in purchase.[149]

Promotion examinations were of course the logical corollary to examining candidates for commissions. In addition they provided a reasonable basis for assessing merit that would cut the ground from under the feet of the seniority and purchase protagonists. Consequently, in 1846, Grey lobbied for examinations for the rank of captain, to be a test of 'at least a moderate knowledge of the theory and science of his profession, as well as of its practical duties'. A certain proportion of each promotion should be reserved to those distinguished in the examinations, thus supplying 'that motive for endeavouring to improve themselves, which with officers of our army is now altogether wanting'.[150] Wellington was bound, albeit reluctantly, to acknowledge the potential advantages.[151]

Meanwhile, at the War Office, Gleig thought that languages, tactics, military drawing, surveying and fortification should form the subaltern's syllabus, with an increase in standard according to rank. A committee of general officers should draw up a reading list, and the second major of every regiment should be trained at the Senior Department of Sandhurst before becoming the regimental superintendent of military instruction.[152] Gleig probably influenced Herbert, who raised the subject in the Commons in March 1847, but the latter's successor, Fox Maule, proved remarkably ineffectual in prosecuting the topic. Possibly he was swayed by his brother, the commanding officer of the 79th, who rightly observed that the Horse Guards already had 'checks quite sufficient in their hands, if they would use them', without 'fresh trammels to hamper the service': the potential officers from the ranks would 'be disgusted and put to the blush by an examination in grammar, syntax, or prosody', and the standards of such an examination would be variable owing to foreign service rendering it hard for one board to administer.[153] Nonetheless, the initial story of Gleig having fathered the scheme was subsequently denied, but at the same time nobody at the Horse Guards seemed willing to be answerable for it.[154] The *United Service Gazette* claimed that the War Office pushed the plan on the Horse Guards, who in reply pitched the requirements so high as to make the examinations inoperable.[155]

Whoever was the author, it was the Horse Guards that on 14 May 1850 issued a confidential memorandum laying down the syllabus for promotion up to the rank of captain. Candidates for lieutenancies were to be examined by a board of officers formed of the commanding officer, the senior captain and another field officer or the next senior captain. They were to know the regimental standing orders, the duties of regimental orderly officers, the manual and platoon exercise, company drill, the Queen's Regulations, the Mutiny Act and the Articles of War, and the warrants concerning, and the weights of, the soldier's equipment and necessaries. In the cavalry, the would-be lieutenant had also to have completed a course of instruction in the riding school and to know the stable duties.

In all probability, most subalterns already acquired this modicum of knowledge in the course of their regimental duties. However, a captain who had entered the army after July 1849 had to show an advance on the theoretical knowledge required for his first commission. His examination covered geography, history, the first six books of Euclid, the properties of the circle, algebra (to quadratic equations), logarithms, plane trigonometry, mensuration, fortification (but only to the first system of Vauban), the form and proceedings of courts-martial, regimental and light infantry drill, the interior economy of a company, the regulations governing transports and convict ships, and the warrants concerning the pay, provisions, pensions, rewards, periods of service, clothing and equipment of the soldier. He had in addition to be fit to take charge of a company in any situation. Those who joined before July 1849 or had been less than a year in the United Kingdom were required, if to be promoted captain after July 1852, to pass the full requirement of practical knowledge but were only to be tested in a modified version of the theoretical part. They still, however, had to pass the full theoretical examination before being eligible for their majority.

To say that the demands of the examination were not great may be true, but it also obscures the enormous stride forward that the examination represented. The general tone, particularly of the captain's requirements, was of cautious welcome, even if it was felt that greater stress could have been put on modern languages and on the more technical subjects such as ballistics and the construction of firearms. There was regret that field officers were not included, as an opportunity had thus been lost to drive incompetence from the army at a stroke. There were, too, doubts about the advisability of regimental boards conducting the examinations.

However, it was the negative criticism to which the Horse Guards proved susceptible, resisting it so weakly that the impact of the reform was considerably lessened. It was argued on many fronts that senior subalterns — eighty had more than twelve years' service — were too old to start learning Euclid, algebra and mathematics. Despite the strenuous opposition of the *Naval and Military Gazette*, a number of officers, including Lieutenant-Colonel F. Markham, a commanding officer of distinguished field service,[156] Colonel Reid, who was voluble in the

Commons,[157] and Lieutenant-General R. Ellice,[158] managed, perhaps by playing on the Horse Guards' original doubts, to procure two concessions, first that the entire theoretical part be suspended for two years, and second, in 1851, that no officer commissioned before 1849 be examined at all in the theory.

Although the Horse Guards gave way more than they needed to — waiving the requirements on mathematics for senior subalterns would have been ample concession to hostile opinion — they had not yet wrecked the long-term prospects for the order. The responsibility for this must be shared with the War Office, which, in conceiving the syllabus, had paid no attention to the means to enable officers to be instructed, let alone subsequently examined. This omission, blighting any prospects for the scheme's immediate full-scale implementation, is especially curious, since Grey, its progenitor, was still Secretary of State and still expatiating 'at some length on the ignorance and want of insturction of our officers ... the least instructed body of officers in Europe'.[159]

The *Naval and Military Gazette* was in favour of a system of garrison instructors, the grant of study leave, and a central London board of examiners established to secure uniformity. It advocated a structure that made the maximum use of existing facilities and was therefore relatively cheap. Its rival newspaper was in broad agreement. But the government seems barely to have considered the matter. Rumours existed that central or garrison boards had been approved to replace the regimental ones, but Fox Maule simply threw out a vague proposal for regimental 'captains of instruction', only to withdraw it a month later.[160] A few regiments held examinations, and a subaltern of the 43rd was actually tested by a regimental committee in the field in 1852.[161] But the Adjutant General's claim that the system was operational, and that officers who had failed had been passed over for promotion, presents a less than truthful picture.[162] Sir John Burgoyne and the editor of the *Naval and Military Gazette* were under the impression that no promotion examinations of any sort were conducted.

Maule's equivocation is even less excusable in the context of a letter to him from Lord Frederick Fitzclarence in March 1848, outlining a system of district instruction that Lord Frederick himself was to prove perfectly practicable. Assuming the existence of a commissioning examination, Fitzclarence proposed that young officers should spend one winter and one summer under a captain instructor, who would be a Royal Engineer officer appointed to the district. He would teach permanent and field fortification; the attack and defence of houses, villages, bridges and forts;

pontooning and military drawing. In addition all regimental officers would be required to attend lectures on strategy and tactics.[163]

It is possible that Maule was offended by the fact that these proposals had already been published in the *United Service Gazette*.[164] Certainly Fitzclarence was left to plough his own furrow. The provisions for officer instruction in the 1833 *Field Exercise* were apparently of his devising.[165] It was therefore natural that he should implement them, and he examined officers in the duties of the rank above and requested reports on reconnaissance and outpost work. The type of lectures Fitzclarence suggested to Maule were given at Portsmouth in 1850, and in December that year his District School opened its doors to fifteen officers (including seven captains). They were taught arithmetic, algebra, geometry and fortification for the first two weeks, before progressing on to field works, military sketching and other practical training. Although the Adjutant General was said to be opposed to other ranks teaching officers, their mentor in these labours was the indefatigable Scrivener.[166] When transferred to Bombay, Lord Frederick could progress even closer to the ideal he had sketched for Maule in 1848. Up to six months' study leave was permitted to two officers per regiment, who were attached to a unit at Poona for the duration of the course. On 1 June 1853 a general order to the Bombay Army stipulated regimental examinations and instruction for officers in the practical topics covered in the Horse Guards captaincy examination,[167] and by the end of the year Fitzclarence felt sufficiently far progressed to be able to make such knowledge a precondition of promotion.[168]

In the context of the controversy at home on the mechanics of promotion examinations, Fitzclarence's timing made his scheme a model to would-be reformers in Britain. In particular, Gleig's thinking, as already suggested by his views in 1846, followed similar lines to those of Fitzclarence on the education of officers, if not of other ranks. In May 1851 the Chaplain General urged Maule to set about training 'officers of instruction', whether they were to be appointed to a regiment or to a garrison. They should study a full range of academic and military subjects and then devote six months to a practical course at Chatham. Gleig suggested that each district have a school (including a lecture room and library) staffed by two such officers of instruction, and a third to a quarter of the subalterns in the area could attend at a time. The syllabus in the schools would be identical, and half-yearly promotion examinations could be held in them, with the papers being sent, under cypher, to a central board of examiners. Marks would be allocated in proportion to the importance of the subject, military subjects bearing the greatest weight and Latin the least. Officers would be placed in three classes and the results would guide the Commander-in-Chief in their subsequent employment.[169]

Although neglected by Maule, in 1853 Gleig reiterated his proposal to Herbert, being even more specific on the nature of the resulting promotion examinations,[170] and introduced the public to them in an article in the *Edinburgh Review*.[171] In his proposed scheme for officer education of January 1854, Herbert adopted Gleig's plan almost intact, although he added military history and strategy to the syllabus in the captain's course. Beyond the opening of the barrack libraries to officers in 1852, Herbert was right to stress that no means of study or examination yet existed 'to carry out the second portion and the most important portion of the Duke's plan' of officer education. Hardinge approved the Gleig/Herbert proposals on promotion, just as he had done those on first commissions. Herbert planned to send out potential officers of instruction to spend the winter of 1854–5 on the staff in the Crimea to learn 'the art of war', informing them that they would return as majors to take charge of all the military education, including regimental schools, in a district.[172] Not surprisingly the first two so chosen were both Ordnance officers.[173]

The reform in the appointment and promotion of officers therefore came too late to have bitten deep into the bulk of the army by 1854. This is not to say, however, that its origins lie in the Crimea. In as far as it was an internally generated change, it was due to the fast improving conditions of the other ranks, which gave rise to a genuine fear that their capabilities might outstrip those of their officers and lead to ill-feeling and contempt for their decrepit generals. The movement won support because the long peace and colonial garrisoning had stressed that the army was, for some at any rate, a lifetime's profession, which should consequently have a career structure of its own.

As regards promotion, the arguments in favour of an educational criterion were purely pragmatic and professional. For the grant of first commissions, however, motivations were more complex. The chief reformer of the army in this respect was Grey, who shared with Sir Charles Trevelyan, its advocate for the civil service, a commitment to Whiggism. Neither therefore can be seen as the most likely advocates of middle-class entry to a bastion of the aristocracy. In the army's case, owing to purchase, the son of a wealthy businessman could, under prevailing circumstances, already procure a commission more easily than could the impoverished younger son of a nobleman. That this was so is perhaps reflected in the higher proportion of aristocrats in the artillery — whose commissions were free — in 1830 and 1852 than in 1780 or 1810.[174]

Nonetheless the popular image, propagated by many radicals, was that the army served to prop up aristocratic power. The adoption of an education qualification for entry could therefore silence this argument, while perhaps even having a contrary tendency. Trevelyan was no advocate for professional training as a means of entry to a particular job — disliking Woolwich's monopoly of artillery and engineer officers for this very reason.[175] Both he and Sir James Graham thought that tests of professional merit should come later[176], after the selection of the officer had taken place. The basis for the first step should be that the candidate had the education of a gentleman. Both Trevelyan and Grey wished to apply this standard to the army, and it was a yardstick also set by Wellington and Hardinge. Furthermore, being derived from existing academic curricula, it had the twin virtues of pleasing the schools and discouraging cramming. Thus the aristocratic element could be retained with popular consent. The adoption of an educational qualification for officers was a means not only to stop the *nouveau riche* from buying up the army, but also to restore the sons of the professional middle class — the clerics, lawyers or soldiers, who had provided so many officers in the past — to a position of equality once again. Maule might argue that commissioning examinations had been adopted in deference to public opinion,[177] but the motivation was anything other than populist. Trevelyan expected competitive entry to bring in men of ability but he saw the effect of this as increasing the numbers of gentlemen, not reducing them.[178] His evidence to the 1857 purchase commission, so often taken as naked advocacy of middle-class interests, confirms this analysis. Those with a liberal education, the sons of farmers, clerics and doctors, found a spokesman in Sir Charles. But 'the great industrial class' were consigned to being promoted from the ranks into the Military Train and other auxiliary corps. The same classes therefore would officer the army, but would do so as a professional body, rid of incompetence.[179]

Thus, although not related by contemporaries, the parallel reforms in the administration of the civil service point more clearly to the grounds for selection and promotion examinations than do any accusations of professional incompetence on the uplands of Sebastopol. Furthermore in this context the ease with which Grey carried the defences of the Horse Guards is more readily explicable. The standard which he was seeking was that which Wellington said he had always demanded of officers in the British army. It was one moreover which allowed a neutral expansion of the officer corps and certainly precluded it becoming the preserve of the landed gentry. Nonetheless, it remains true that the 'education of a gentleman' carried connotations as to behaviour and deportment which prevented it becoming the other ranks' passport to a commission.

Notes

1 'Of cornets in the 17th Lancers depot mess', 1854, *Journal of the Society for Army Historical Research*, XXXVII, 1959, p. 186.
2 *N. & M.G.*, 29 September 1840, p. 136.
3 W.O. 33/1, p. 484.
4 P. E. Razzell, 'Social origins of officers in the Indian and British Home Army, 1758-1962', *British Journal of Sociology*, XIV, 1963, p. 253.
5 *N. & M.G.*, 16 October 1847, p. 665; 13 November 1847, p. 728.
6 Spiers, *Army and society*, p. 8.
7 Hansard, 3rd series, CIX, c 683.
8 [J. McMullen], *Camp and barrack-room*, p. 309.
9 W. Napier, *General Sir C. J. Napier*, IV, p. 325.
10 C. J. Napier, *Remarks on military law*, p. 237.
11 Herbert papers, Wellington to Fitzroy Somerset (copy), 8 December 1845.
12 *The Times*, 24 October 1840, quoted in Gwyn Harries-Jenkins, *The army in Victorian society*, p. 16.
13 Quoted in L. B. Oatts, *I serve*, p. 131.
14 W.O. 3/321, p. 331.
15 A Regimental Officer, *A few remarks about the British army*, p. 40.
16 *N. & M.G.*, 14 October 1837, p. 648.
17 Hansard, 3rd series, CIX, c 650.
18 *U.S.J.*, 1829, II, p. 242.
19 Archives Historiques de Guerre, MR 1947/31, memorandum of 1843.
20 P.P. 1833, VII, pp. iv, 143, 163-5, 273-5.
21 Warrant of 28 May 1835, quoted in *U.S.J.*, 1835, II, p. 563.
22 P.P. 1833, VII, p. 147.
23 *Wellington despatches*, IV, p. 118.
24 *U.S.J.*, 1836, I, p. 145.
25 P.P. 1850, X, p. 141.
26 P.P. 1851, VII, pp. 37-9; General Order of January 1852, quoted in *Royal Military Magazine*, 1852, p. 393.
27 Grey papers, Tulloch to Grey, 15 July 1847, 8 December 1847.
28 P.P. 1854, XIX, 833, p. 10.
29 P.P. 1840, XXII, pp. 110-11.
30 W.O. 6/128, p. 67.
31 Warrant of 27 October 1834, quoted in *U.S.J.*, 1834, III, p. 563.
32 *U.S.M.*, 1844, II, pp. 356-8.
33 Wellington papers, Melbourne to Wellington, 5 May and, 14 March 1838, and Wellington to Melbourne, 5 and 23 March 1838.

34 *U.S.J.*, 1835, II, p. 145.
35 Ibid., 1835, III, p. 145.
36 Wellington papers, Grey to Wellington, 11 September 1849.
37 N.L.S. mss 2846, f. 319, Mountain to Brown, 28 July 1849.
38 P.P. 1854, XIX, 833, p. 7.
39 *U.S.J.*, 1838, I, p. 168.
40 P.P. 1840, XXII, pp. xxvii-xxviii.
41 *British Army Despatch*, 4 January 1850, pp. 11-12.
42 *U.S.G.*, 26 August 1848, p. 4.
43 Herbert papers, III B (135).
44 P.P. 1850, X, p. 313.
45 P.P. 1833, VII, p. 251.
46 P.P. 1840, XXII, pp. xi-xiv.
47 P.P. 1840, XXII, p. 37; *Naval and Military Magazine*, III, p. lxviii.
48 P.P. 1849, IX, pp. 47, 646, 700-1.
49 P.P. 1849, IX, pp. 369-73, 385, 397; F. R. Chesney, *Observations on the reconstruction of the Royal Regiment of Artillery.*
50 P.P. 1849, IX, pp. x, 27-8, 65-6.
51 P.P. 1854, XIX, 833, pp. 20-1.
52 *U.S.J.*, 1837, I, p. 1.
53 B.M. Add. Mss 40474, f. 15, Hardinge to Peel, 12 November 1841.
54 *U.S.M.*, 1846, III, p. 161.
55 B.M. Add. Mss 40474, f 262, Hardinge to Peel, 7 April 1845.
56 Grey papers, Gordon to Howick, [? 1836]; P.P. 1850, X, p. 290.
57 P.P. 1850, X, p. 236.
58 *N. & M.G.*, 11 February 1837, p. 88.
59 Hansard, 3rd series, XXXIII, c 1220.
60 B.M. Add. Mss 49140, f. 19, C. Napier's journal, 28 March 1845.
61 F. B. Head, *The defenceless state of Great Britain*, p. 84.
62 P.P. 1850, X, p. 138
63 Grey papers, Charles Grey to Grey, 14 November 1852.
64 Herbert papers, III Add., Charles Grey to Herbert, 13 October 1853.
65 Grey papers, Grey to Charles Grey. 16 November 1852; R.A. E 44/24, the same, 14 November 1852.
66 W. Verner, *The military life of H.R.H. George, Duke of Cambridge*, I, p. 56; R.A. Add. E/1 no. 156, memo by Cambridge, December 1853.
67 *U.S.G.*, 5 November 1853, p. 4.
68 Hansard, 3rd series, XCI, c 714.
69 R.A. E 3/17, Hardinge to C. Grey, 13 December 1853.
70 Newcastle papers, NeC 10060, Hardinge to Newcastle, [10 February 1854].
71 Hardinge papers, Hardinge to Prince Albert, 4 February 1854; Earl Cathcart papers, J.54, Herbert to Cathcart, 11 February 1854.
72 The proceedings are best followed through the Herbert papers, III B (92), (93), (94), (99), (101), (112).
73 P.P. 1854, XIX, 833.
74 Hardinge papers, Hardinge to Prince Albert, 26 and 29 June 1855; 1 November 1855.

75 *Wellington despatches*, VIII, p. 404.
76 N.L.S. Adv. Mss 46.8.17, ff. 112-14.
77 *U.S.J.*, 1831, III, p. 233.
78 N.L.S. Adv. Mss 46.8.17, f. 172.
79 W.O. 44/541, for the committee's proceedings.
80 N.A.M. 7709-6-13, p. 177, Vivian to Palmerston, 7 September 1835.
81 N.L.S. Adv. Mss 46.8.23, f. 97, G. Whitmore to Murray, 12 January 1842.
82 Colonel Portlock, quoted in F. G. Guggisberg, *The Shop*, p. 47.
83 N.L.S. Adv. Mss 46.8.23, f. 61, Whitmore to Murray, 7 January 1842.
84 B.M. Add. Mss 54536, f. 79, Roberston to Napier, 5 March 1847.
85 P.P. 1849, IX, p. 444.
86 Guggisberg, *The Shop*, p. 69.
87 W.O. 46/86, pp. 234-5; 46/90, pp. 290-1.
88 *N. & M.G.*, 12 October 1850, p. 647.
89 *Memorials of Fredk. M. Eardley-Wilmot*, pp. 65-74, 82-3, 86-7, 91-4, 101-10, 115-20.
90 Guggisberg, *The Shop*, pp. 69, 269.
91 W.O. 44/541.
92 Guggisberg, *The Shop*, p. 72.
93 P.P. 1849, IX, pp. 1061-2.
94 Guggisberg, *The Shop*, pp. 48, 78-80.
95 W.O. 55/1931, pp. 23-4.
96 *Royal Engineers Professional Papers*, I, 1837, p. xii; Sir Frederic Smith, in P.P. 1849, IX, p. 434.
97 Newcastle papers, NeC 10340, Monsell to Newcastle, 16 December 1854.
98 Seaton papers, Seaton to Hardinge, 23 June [1856 ?].
99 P.P. 1854-5, XII, 311, p. iv.
100 *U.S.J.*, 1829, I, p. 374.
101 W.O. 7/58, pp. 1-15; copy also in Murray papers, N.L.S. Adv. Mss 46.8.16, f. 25.
102 P.P. 1851, VII, 735, p. 30.
103 *N. & M.G.*, 9 June 1838, p. 355.
104 *U.S.M.*, 1851, II, pp. 380-90.
105 W.O. 99/9, nos. 79, 92.
106 P.P. 1854-5, XII, 311, p. 76.
107 [Lt.-Col. Prosser], *A letter, by authority, on the Royal Military College at Sandhurst*, p. 11; P.P. 1854-5, XII, 311, pp. v-vi, gives history, geography, Latin, French and German as the optional subjects.
108 J. M. Spearman, *Notes on military education*, pp. 11-12, 32, 37.
109 Seaton papers, Scovell to Seaton, 8 July 1853.
110 W.O. 99/22, Paget to Sir H. Taylor, 6 February 1829.
111 P.P. 1854-5, XII, 311, p. 14.
112 W.O. 43/514, f. 316.
113 B.M. Add. Mss 40474, ff. 76-7, Hardinge to Peel, 7 January 1843.
114 N.L.S. mss 1848, f. 99, Wellington to Lachlan, 3 December 1833.
115 M. C. Morgan, *Cheltenham College*, pp. 3-4, 11, 21, 70, 221-2.
116 *N. & M.G.*, 9 August 1851, p. 501.

117 *N. & M.G.*, 24 February 1849, p. 122; F. J. C. Hearnshaw, *The centenary history of King's College, London, 1828-1928*, pp. 176-7, 260.
118 *U.S.M.*, 1842, I, p. 394.
119 *N. & M.G.*, 14 October 1848, p. 664.
120 S.R.O., GD 45/8/21, memo by Grey, 17 October 1846, p. 14.
121 Wellington papers, Wellington to Queen Adelaide, April 1836
122 Grey papers, Wellington to Lord John Russell, 11 November 1846.
123 S.R.O., GD 45/8/16, 'Report on military education on the continent', 7 December 1846:
124 J. H. Stocqueler, *A familiar history of the British army*, p. 243.
125 J. H. Stocqueler, *The British officer*, pp. 185-6.
126 P.P. 1854-5, XII, 311, pp. x, 27, 107-15, 172.
127 Herbert papers, III A (44), 'Education and examination of officers' headed in Gleig's writing, and referred to in III A (73), Gleig to Herbert, 3 October 1853.
128 [Gleig] in *Edinburgh Review*, C, 1854, pp. 554-5.
129 W.O. 43/865, ff. 296-311; see also Hansard, 3rd series, CXXX, c 1286.
130 *U.S.M.*, 1847, II, p. 323.
131 J. S. Cumming, *A six years' diary*, pp. 34, 91.
132 G. C. Moore Smith, *Life of Lord Seaton*, pp. 268-9.
133 W. Napier, *Life of Sir C. J. Napier*, III, p. 39.
134 Phelim O'Doodle, *The subaltern's check-book*, p. 50
135 East Riding C.R.O., DDCH 95, C. R. Chichester's diary, 1847, pp. 1, 2, 14, 20-1; DDCH 96, 1847, p. 30, and 1848, pp. 30-8.
136 W.O. 135/3, Smith to D'Urban, 8 August 1844 (copy).
137 J. C. Marshman, *Memoirs of Major-General Sir Henry Havelock*, p. 9.
138 *N. & M.G.*, 28 March 1835, p. 201.
139 W.O. 43/833.
140 W.O. 55/1931; P.P. 1849, IX, pp. 433-6.
141 *Standing Orders for the Royal Artillery*, 1847, p. 7.
142 *Memorials of Fredk. M. Eardley-Wilmot*, pp. 64, 81.
143 *Minutes of Proceedings of the Royal Artillery Institution*, I, 1857, pp. i-xvi, 5, 150.
144 *Memorials of Eardley-Wilmot*, pp. 76-7, 90, 113.
145 W.O. 44/542.
146 P.P. 1849, IX, p. 451.
147 *Memorials of Eardley-Wilmot*, pp. 120-1, 127; Hansard, 3rd series, CXV, c 832.
148 *Queen's Regulations*, 1844, pp. 124-7.
149 *U.S.J.*, 1838, III, p. 111; 1840, I, p. 1; *U.S.M.*, 1842, I, p. 395, II, pp. 37, 113, III, pp. 20, 115, 520; 1843, I, p. 372.
150 S.R.O., GD 45/8/21, Grey's memorandum of 17 October 1846, pp. 14-15; see also Grey papers, Grey to Tulloch, 22 September 1847.
151 Grey papers, Wellington to Russell, 11 November 1846.
152 *Quarterly Review*, 77, 1846, pp. 560-1.
153 S.R.O., GD 45/8/18, L. Maule to F. Maule, c 1849.
154 Bodleian Ms. Eng. Lett. c 247, ff. 173-4, Shaw Kennedy to W. Napier, 4 July 1850.

155 *U.S.G.*, 12 April 1851, p. 4.
156 N.L.S. mss 2847, f. 334, Markham to Brown, 13 August 1850.
157 Hansard, 3rd series, CIX, cc 689-690; CXV, c 820.
158 N.L.S. mss 2848, f. 200, Ellice to Brown, 9 May 1851.
159 Wellington papers, memorandum by Brown, 28 January 1852.
160 Hansard, 3rd series, CXV, c 751.
161 P.P. 1854-5, XII, 311, pp. 103, 131, 134.
163 S.R.O., G.D. 45/8/42, Fitzclarence to Maule, 10 March 1848.
164 *U.S.G.*, 5 February 1848, p. 4; also 21 July 1849, p. 4. This is further corroboration of Firzclarence's links with that journal.
165 *N. & M.G.*, 6 April 1850, p. 216.
166 Ibid., 7 December 1850, p. 776, and 12 April 1851, p. 235; *U.S.G.*, 14 December 1850, p. 7, and 1 March 1851, p. 5.
167 *U.S.M.*, 1853, III, p. 139.
168 *U.S.G.*, 14 January 1854, p. 6, quoting Bombay Army General Order of 12 November 1853; India Office Library, L/MIL/3/1753, p. 269, 1754, pp. 448-9, 1907, no. 50.
169 S.R.O., GD 45/8/95, pp. 9-12.
170 Herbert papers, III A (44) and (73), Gleig to Herbert, 3 October 1853.
171 *Edinburgh Review*, 100, 1853, pp. 556-60.
172 W.O. 43/865, ff. 296-324.
173 N.A.M. 6807/289, George Ramsay to Sir Hew Ross, 17 November 1854 (enclosed by Ross to Raglan).
174 Razzell, 'Social origins of officers', p. 235.
175 Edward Hughes, 'Sir Charles Trevelyan and civil service reform, 1853-5', *English Historical Review*, LXIV, 1949, pp. 225-6.
176 G. Kitson Clark, 'Statesmen in disguise', *Historical Journal*, II, 1959, p. 21.
177 Hansard, 3rd series, CIII, c 963.
178 Hughes, 'Sir Charles Trevelyan', pp. 71-3.
179 P.P. 1857, sess. 2, XVIII, pp. 290-1, 293, 294, 296, 298.

CHAPTER 5
THE STAFF AND TRAINING FOR THE FIELD

For the modern reader, the role of a general staff in the correct application of each component of the army has become self-evident. In the eighteenth century, however, one general could observe and orchestrate his forces in a way that the larger bodies of men and more disparate formations of the Napoleonic wars began to render not only undesirable but also unnecessary. Napoleon himself seems never to have realised the full implications of his own corps system, so tight and indefatigable was his own personal control. Wellington too was slow to delegate, although his army was of course smaller and his style of command more suited to the eighteenth century. Thus the genesis of a capital staff, in the Moltkean sense of a supreme co-ordinating body, was slow. In none of the major European powers was it slower than Britain.

Britain after 1815 did possess a headquarters staff (the Horse Guards) and a body of general officers. It also possessed officers whose duty was to advise and help the commanders of combined forces. But it would be mistaken to describe these officers as forming a cohesive group. An officer with a staff appointment retained his regimental rank and seniority. He thereby roused ill-feeling amongst his brother officers, who felt that he was foregoing the rigours of normal duty, loading its burden on to them, and yet still retaining his pecking order in the regiment. The only educational requirement made of him was that he be thoroughly acquainted with his regimental duties. Even if this standard was applied, the lack of any other test of scientific attainment meant regimental particularisms, rather than a common staff doctrine, predominated.

The types of appointment he might hold fell into three categories. First, each general officer in employment was entitled to aides-de-camp, the number being in proportion to his rank. These formed a part of the general's household and in the field delivered their commander's orders: they were, in a sense, apprentices. Sir George Cathcart admirably summarised the caricature of the a.d.c., 'amiable & gentlemanlike but is *very idle* & not by any means bright — he will I fear only do for domestic purposes & possibly as a galloper in the field'.[1] Secondly brigade, divisional or district staffs aped the organisation at the Horse Guards, the officers either belonging to the Adjutant General's department and therefore responsible for military returns and the enforcement of discipline, or to that of the Quarter Master General, concerned with quartering, encamping and moving troops. The third category was that of major of brigade, the only staff appointment with individual responsibilities, since 'he is considered as an Officer attached to the Brigade, not personally to the Officer Commanding it'.[2] However, outside India, brigades were too rarely formed for this to have practical effect. No officer existed to co-ordinate the efforts of these three groups, except the general himself, nor was their remit sufficiently wide to encourage original thought.

Since those with the best military education — the Engineers and Artillery — were effectively precluded from staff appointments, ignorance and inexperience made the staff much more dependent on its commander's skills than vice versa. However, the general himself was perhaps old, recently brought from the half pay, and probably little better informed than his subordinates. In practice high-sounding ideals stood or fell on the strength of one man's initiative. Even should the general have been competent, the qualities of good field command and of administrative ability were rarely combined. 'Gough,' Hardinge wrote, 'has no capacity for administration. He is at the outpost wonderfully active, but the more important points, which he dislikes, of framing proper orders and looking to their execution are much [neglected].'[3] On innumerable occasions in the Sikh wars, a Gneisenau to match his Blücher would have saved Gough from planning mistakes which had to be recovered by hard fighting. At Mudki, Bunbury, the commanding officer of the 80th Foot, was warned by Hardinge's a.d.c. that no reserve or second line had been formed. As the 80th was posted on the extreme left flank, it seemed sensible for it to move to the right and rear so as to be able to support the rest of the line. However, the a.d.c. could give no specific orders, Bunbury did not wish his regiment to be accused of shirking the fight, and he could find no general officer to give him the order. So he stayed where he was. Planning therefore was at a premium. 'It is the duty of general officers,' Bunbury angrily concluded, 'to make these necessary dispositions, but if they do not, and they prefer the system, shove on, keep moving, no matter where, and so break up a well drawn out order of battle, their officers can have no alternative but to follow the leader's example.'[4]

More seriously, the lack of a trained staff meant the absence of a foil for individual incompetence. At the outset of the Cape war in 1847 'There was no military man to conduct operations,' since the commander, Sir Peregrine Maitland, was 'A simple clog upon every operation ... In the Army at this moment, there is nothing there should be & everything there ought not to be. Sir P.M. let nobody have a proper staff: consequently all work is improperly done.'[5] The larger the army, the more did the absence of a general staff compound the sins of omission. The Kabul disaster is a clear example, although responsibility must also lie with the division between civilian and military control. In the Crimea, the quality of staff work was probably greater than anything hitherto achieved by Britain at the outset of a war, but the scale of the problems outdistanced the improvement. Responsibility was simply divided over too many heads — the Adjutant General, the Quarter Master General, the Commissary General and the Admiralty. Not all focused on Raglan, in any case already burdened with questions of strategy and too sensitive of department protocol.

Nonetheless, the idea of a more corporate staff was struggling to find expression. The French *état major* was occasionally suggested as a model for the British. 'The staff of our army,' Colonel Campbell wrote in 1840, 'ought to be a distinct and permanent branch of the service, and no officers should be employed upon it but those who had received such an education, as is usually given to our Engineers.'[6] Newcastle apparently wished to establish such a body in 1854, but in peacetime, as Fitzroy Somerset pointed out in 1833, this scheme would have proved expensive and would perhaps even have left officers underemployed.[7] Furthermore there were good reasons to doubt the value of the French system. Sir Samford Whittingham, writing in 1831, observed that by taking staff officers from the line the widest possible choice remained available and the staff had a good grounding in regimental duties.[8] The reform required was less an élite divorced from the rest of the army, and perhaps therefore planning in ignorance of its true worth, than a regular rotation of officers between staff and regimental employment. Admittedly any desire to integrate the two duties had its origins less in doubts about the French system than in indignation at the nepotism and refuge from foreign or regimental duty that the staff offered. The 1833 appointments commission called for a rotation of duties but, although reaffirmed by the 1850 commission on army expenditure,[9] it was still not mandatory by 1854.[10] Periods of three to seven years on the staff were mooted, and the expectation was that such a cross-fertilisation would not only produce a healthy staff — as Prussia was to prove was the case — but would also provide a good stock of staff officers in case a punitive expedition had to be mounted in a colony at short notice and with limited resources.

That some idea of a homogeneous staff — whether on the French or Prussian model — was beginning to emerge in 1854, is witnessed by two developments. At the Cape in December 1853, Sir George Cathcart had preferred to employ two deputy assistant quartermasters-general to one assistant adjutant-general, as he was thus able to get not only two young officers instead of one older one but also two whose duties could be interpreted as ranging over the whole orbit of staff work rather than the more restricted functions of the Adjutant General's department.[11] The next stage, which followed in April 1854, was that in the lower grades the two departments — the Adjutant General's and the Quarter Master General's — were instructed to regard their duties as interchangeable.[12]

The second improvement was more dramatic: the appointment of a chief of staff, so long in germination, finally blossomed in 1855. Wellington had of course gone through the Peninsular and Waterloo campaigns without one, and there was a consequent tendency to misunderstand the nature of his functions. When Murray was proposed by Taylor as chief of staff at the Horse Guards in 1827 it was as a caretaker Commander-in-Chief in the interregnum. Similarly, when, in 1850, Lord John Russell suggested that the vacant Adjutant Generalship provided an opportunity to combine the post with that of Quarter Master General to create a chief of staff, Wellington opposed on the grounds that it 'would be to appoint two different persons to do the same duty', and would only be the prelude to the abolition of the Commander-in-Chief's office.[13] However, in a field command the need for a chief of staff was more overt. In 1840 Colonel Campbell thought it essential that a chief of staff marshal the work of the Adjutant General's and Quarter Master General's departments, and so act as a filter for the detailed reports that would otherwise monopolise the attention of the army commander.[14] In the Crimea, Britain's French allies served to underwrite the pre-war rumblings of the military press. On 6 December 1854 Claremont, a liaison officer with the French, wrote to the Horse Guards that the fundamental fault in the British army lay not in its parts but in its organisation and administration. 'The whole,' he wrote, 'should be at the beck and call not of the Quarter Master General but of the *Chief [of] the Staff* who should be the only mouth piece of the Commander in Chief and main spring of the whole army.'[15] Claremont's was not an isolated voice. De Lacy Evans came out in favour of a chief of staff.[16] More significantly, Estcourt, the

Adjutant General, saw clearly the danger of Raglan being his own chief of staff. He wrote to Wetherall, 'I wish he would let me act without him, and let Airey do the same: But he is determined to know everything: and he has wonderful powers of deciding cases and disposing of business. Still the General in Command has other things to think of, the object of the campaign. I think therefore the French system far better than our's.'[17]

Raglan had been too long another man's aide to be anything other than his own worst enemy. His accessibility meant that commanding officers went to him rather than to his departmental heads. In February 1855 Panmure appointed a chief of staff to Raglan, to 'superintend the whole routine of staff duties',[18] but it was not so much an imitation of the French model as a bid to have a spy at the Crimean headquarters, especially to look over the suspect qualities of Airey and Estcourt. Airey himself fulminated: 'A mere Chief of the Staff suddenly adopted without the whole of the rest of the machinery is pure nonsense — the 5th wheel to a Coach, without power of working.'[19] Thus Raglan was afforded little relief, and it was left to Codrington, his successor, to make this sop to the press the co-ordinator of the different departments, and the only channel between himself and the army.

The dominant cause of this limited progress was the nature of the British army's service. In the case of both France and Prussia, a large army was concentrated in the homeland, the frontiers readily definable and the potential enemies marked out. But, for the British, colonial garrisoning meant that each field army was small, and each force's potential requirements, especially in terms of maps, intelligence and transport, very different. Only in India was the likely application of a general staff really apparent, and yet here most appointments (except, paradoxically, actual commands) went to East India Company officers. On other stations, the variation in arrangements was enormous. In Canada, a large staff was kept in being to serve as a nucleus for the sudden accretion in strength should a threat materialise from the United States. The result was that in 1832 three regular battalions were commanded by twelve staff officers.[20] But when an emergency arose elsewhere, as in South Africa in 1852, the local establishment could prove woefully inadequate and senior officers were drawn off from their regiments at a time when they were most needed. In Britain itself a small staff sufficed, both on financial grounds and because troops were so rarely exercised together. The regiment or battalion being the core of the army, staff officers seemed superfluous. In 1839 in Scotland one officer fulfilled the duties of assistant adjutant-general, assistant quartermaster-general, major of brigade and inspecting field officer of the Edinburgh recruiting district.[21] The consequently denuded state of the staff in Britain was well illustrated in 1854, when Newcastle complained that of the senior officers at the Horse Guards and the Board of Ordnance only Hardinge was left behind to proffer advice. Despite the small size of the expeditionary force, the Adjutant General, the Quarter Master General, the Master General of the Ordnance and the Inspector General of Fortifications were all despatched to the east.

This represented a considerable decline on the Horse Guards' position at the start of the century. Then the threat of invasion had made its strategic advice most important. By 1803 the Quarter Master General's department was developing as a fully fledged central staff. It had a school of its own, a permanent nucleus of officers and a formal body of engineers to assist in the field (the Royal Staff Corps). In the Peninsula the department had boasted the cream of the army's intellect, and its chief, Sir George Murray, has been described 'as the principal staff officer of the Army'.[22]

Nonetheless Wellington's staff depended on him alone for its spark and its officers were in fact subordinate to the divisional generals. After 1815, as a creation nurtured by wartime practice rather than one grounded on an established system, the Quarter Master General's department withered. Gordon, the Quarter Master General at the Horse Guards, was intelligent enough, but unpopular and sycophantic. In addition to the department's more mundane duties of arranging quarters and troop movements, it continued to collect books and topographical information. But little evidence appears of information on the new colonies being fed back to it, and the efforts made in out-stations themselves were very variable. In 1853 Hardinge had to ask the Adjutant General's department to sift through *Le Moniteur Militaire*, as the Quarter Master General's staff was predominantly civilian.[23]

The department's tasks in the Crimea showed that at best it had marked time since 1815. Murray's Peninsular instructions were rapidly reprinted as an official manual. Airey's definition of the role of his department reflected only a part of a general staff's responsibilities.[24] The functions were advisory rather than executive, with little guarantee of conformity to the department's suggestions. In July 1854 Brown saw fit to complain to de Ros, Airey's predecessor as Quarter Master General, that his officers had been giving orders in their own names to divisional staff.[25] Raglan, admittedly when under the peculiar strain of explaining why the Light Brigade had charged the wrong guns, seemed to condone Brown's view: the written order sent by Airey 'did not exact that Lord Lucan should attack at all hazards', and, rather than interpret it as such, Lucan should have reprimanded Airey's a.d.c., Nolan, for assuming an authority he did not have.[26] Poor Airey felt increasingly frustrated by his powerlessness. At Inkerman, Cathcart was killed and his division badly mauled, having acted in direct contradiction to the orders the Quarter Master General had given him five minutes before.[27] Thus not even central direction was guaranteed.

The notion that the Quarter Master General's department constituted a general staff rested in part on its close links with the Senior Department of the Royal Military College, Sandhurst. In the Peninsula, the latter had fed the former with a number of distinguished officers. But the close correlation declined during the peace, and in 1852 only seven graduates of the Senior Department were employed on the staff.[28] However, the spurt towards officers' education in the late 1840s demanded a connection between specific qualifications and staff employment, and it was logical to look once again to the Senior Department for such a training. In 1853 Sir George Scovell, the Governor of Sandhurst, requested Hardinge that Senior Department officers be granted staff appointments.[29] The Commander-in-Chief, who was himself one of its products and who entertained a high view of the establishment, duly obliged in his recommendations for staff employment in 1854. De Lacy Evans, on the prompting of the Horse Guards, selected as a.d.c.s two Sandhurst graduates and a Russian linguist.[30] In appointments to the expeditionary army as a whole Raglan was urged to choose from Senior Department men and he tried to seek out any other officers so trained lurking in regimental appointments. No effort therefore was spared to appoint the best qualified officers to the staff in the Crimea.[31]

However, the opprobrium heaped on the staff suggests that, since apparently the choice was made from the best available, there existed a fault in the professional training as much as a limited view of the staff's duties — in short, that the Senior Department did not constitute a staff college.

In 1820 the department had been moved from High Wycombe, in order to share premises with the Junior Department at Sandhurst — a move which in itself was said to have detracted from its growth as a staff school. At the same time the entrance examination was made harder so that a reduction in the length of the course from two years to one (or one and a half if not previously at the Junior Department) would be compatible with a constant output of qualified officers, the total strength being reduced from thirty to fifteen. In fact the places were so hard to fill and extensions had to be granted so regularly that in 1833 the one and a half or two year course was restored. The standard of the entrance examination was low and its range limited to arithmetic and geometry. In 1849 Scovell suggested that it be equivalent to the proposed captaincy examination,[32] and in consequence history, geography, fortification and languages were added as entrance requirements.[33]

In the main, however, a tolerably experienced and willing set of officers found their way to Sandhurst. Furthermore there is no doubt that once there their knowledge in certain branches of science was considerably enhanced; unfortunately these subjects did not include tactics or strategy. At the time of the 1820 reorganisation, the professors were reduced from seven to two. No replacement was procured for General Jarry, not only the institution's first commander and joint founder but also its principal instructor in higher military matters. The bulk of the teaching was borne by the astronomer and mathematician, John Narrien, F. R. S. Narrien was on the staff at Sandhurst for over forty years, and undoubtedly won the affection of his pupils and the respect of his superiors, but so pervasive was his influence that even Jarry's lectures were neglected as mathematics began progressively to grow in dominance.

Before 1820 the syllabus was summarised as covering mathematics, fortification, castramentation, military topography, the reconnaissance of ground, the estimation of the military resources of a country, the disposition and movements of troops in attack and defence, French, German and military drawing.[34] By 1844 the subjects were Euclid, the drawing of plans, trigonometry, permanent and field fortification, algebra, surveying, practical geometry, conic sections, practical astronomy, and the attack and defence of fortresses. The standard attained was high, tough examinations were held at the end of each period, and after 1834 the final results were graded into three classes — by 1852 only nineteen officers (including Patrick MacDougall, the first commandant of the Staff College) had been placed in the top class. However, the texts for the achievement of this accolade were not Jomini or Lloyd, but Poisson's *Traité de mécanique*, Airey's *Mathematic tracts* and La Place's *Mécanique céleste*. The mapping duties of the Quarter Master General's department in the Peninsula had been allowed to surpass all others in subsequent importance. The problem was that a staff officer in the saddle had little time for detailed surveying: an ability to make rapid sketches without instruments was the prerequisite.

Some awareness of this criticism was manifested by the early 1850s. In 1848 the Governor ordered that in future plans must be accompanied by a report on the military capabilities of the roads, the defensive potential of the villages, and the availability of billets. In short, details were required 'which could be relied upon by a general officer about to conduct operations in the country surveyed'. In addition field fortifications were thrown up, gabions and fascines made, and sapping and pontooning practised. Nonetheless there remained little in the course that specifically qualified an officer for a staff appointment, and, to justify the hard work involved, there had to be a closer correlation with professional advancement. This could only be achieved by creating a proper staff college.

The mainspring, as in so many other facets of military education, was Gleig. After his tour of the continental schools in 1846, he reported to Fox Maule that 'In the armies of Continental Europe employment on the Staff is the recognised reward of superior talent, and of a successful endeavour to improve it. In Berlin and Paris, especially, Officers go through a laborious course of study in order to qualify themselves for such employment, and the staff is in consequence supplied exclusively by men who have more or less distinguished themselves at the higher military academies — this also is a wise regulation for it not only awakens a spirit of honourable emulation among all the Members of the Profession, but it secures for the service of the staff the elite of that body.'[35] However, it was some years before Gleig formulated his application of this idea to Britain. In a paper for Herbert, probably written in October 1853, Gleig saw the Senior Department as the finishing school for those who passed into the first class in promotion examinations. Only officers educated there, in a syllabus orientated more towards languages and staff duties, should be eligible for staff employment — although the interchange between regimental and staff appointments should continue.[36] Opportune support for Gleig came from Captain J. H. Spearman's book, calling for a separate staff school, located in London and basing its syllabus on a purely military education.[37]

As a result, Herbert, in his memorandum on officer education of January 1854, noted that a change might be made at the Senior Department, whither those who passed well in the captaincy examination would go for further study with a view to staff employment.[38] The Senior Department would thus become the brightest star in the military educational firmament. In the ensuing two years, the scheme that initially came to the fore was a long-standing demand for the intakes of Woolwich and Sandhurst to be amalgamated, so that the Junior Department of the latter could give primary and theoretical education to cadets of all arms and the Royal Military Academy could complete a subaltern's practical training. To this a staff college would provide the logical third tier, and introduce the more outstanding young officers — after some regimental experience — to higher questions. In the event the amalgamation of the two cadet colleges was defeated in 1858, but in the interim J. H. Lefroy had stepped forward with his recommendation that the Senior Department should be the obligatory path to staff employment.[39] Largely through Lefroy's efforts, the Staff College was eventually established in 1857.

Part of the pre-Crimean lack of interest in staff education sprang from the deep-rooted conviction that — in the words of Sandhurst's leading apologist, Colonel Prosser, — 'nothing but actual experience would bring out the real staff officer'.[40] However, doses of staff experience in combat were too few to remain the only path to training.

As the Peninsular generation grew older, the stock of learning gleaned in European war became less, and for a fresh generation anxious to learn their profession a substitute needed to be found. The benefits of the Senior Department were confined to a few and of limited value even for them. The United Service Institution was the prerogative of those fortunate enough to be at home. A manual could provide a common base for officers, whatever their service, but the profusion of unofficial publications could not make for a uniform system, and the official regulations were inadequate. Only the interior economy of a regiment and the movements of the infantry and cavalry were covered. Brigade and light infantry evolutions were but sketched in and divisional matters totally neglected. No approved manuals on higher tactics, administration or transport existed.

A reasonable corollary of the dominance of 'the school of experience' might have been an emphasis on practical training for the field. Extended field manoeuvres would at least have provided some substitute for a diminishing stock of combat experience. But whether judged as individual training in the skills of cooking or encampment or as the collective responsibilities of outposts and field manoeuvres, little was done.

As so often it was less a question of the inadequacy of the regulations as of the failure to apply them. In a section credited to Fitzclarence himself, the 1833 *Field Exercise* had given 'a general outline of field training', that embraced patrols, reconnaissance, foraging parties, field fortification, picquets and the use of ground. Some commanding officers were said to oppose hard work in the field as it made the men less well set up in the ranks and wore out the clothing more rapidly (thus displeasing the colonels who paid for it). On a false application of the division of labour theory, Hill would not approve the employment of soldiers as their own bakers, carters or labourers — although all were tasks which field service might impose.[41] Similarly entrenchments and field fortifications were viewed as the Engineers' responsibility. These nostrums could often be buoyed up by the difficulty of procuring an adequate exercise area. Public antipathy to the soldiery and fears of damage to crops were sufficient block to the loan of land, and parliamentary parsimony precluded the purchase of training areas for an army so scattered. Therefore, however much military reformers bemoaned the excessive drill and called for instruction in field duties, the barrack yard imposed an automatic limit to their ambitions.

In 1845 the *Naval and Military Gazette* advocated the creation of a school of infantry. Every regiment should pass through it before proceeding on foreign service, and its syllabus should embrace ball-firing, escalading, field fortification, entrenching, siege work, and the attack and defence of positions. An inspector of infantry should be appointed, similar to the existing inspector general of cavalry, so that he could make 'the Army at home ... a school of instruction for service abroad'.[42] The central school would be accompanied by local 'schools of practice'. The *Gazette*'s inspiration for these was Fitzclarence's Portsmouth garrison. Portsmouth was a major training centre because it was there that battalions recently returned from foreign service began to rebuild. In addition, Fitzclarence had strong views on the importance of tough and extensive field training.[43] The two commands which were possible candidates for the central school were Dublin and Chatham.

Ireland was normally the last home station before foreign service. The battalions there had completed the process begun four or so years before at Portsmouth. In 1847 the Duke of Cambridge, one of the *Naval and Military Gazette*'s candidates for the inspectorship of infantry, was given the command of the Dublin garrison. The barracks were large, Phoenix park provided an extensive exercise area, and Cambridge saw Dublin as 'the school for the whole of the British Army'.[44] However, high expectations proved ill-founded. Occasional divisional exercises were held, but even Dublin was too remote to make a considerable impact on the military press or the Horse Guards. Furthermore, Sir Edward Blakeney, Ireland's commander-in-chief, had been born in 1778 and held the appointment from 1836 to 1855, with the result that by the late 1840s youthful enthusiasm was unlikely to be his *forte*.

The staff and training for the field

The other great entrepôt for troops training for foreign service, Chatham, was the locale of the provisional battalion, which fed the Queen's regiments in India. It was also the home of the 'engineer school of field instruction': somewhat stylised siege operations were held there at least annually from 1830, and the school boasted facilities for escalading, pontooning, field fortification, mining and manoeuvres. The practice of infantry attending the Engineers' school was officially approved in 1821,[45] but until 1852 instances were few. In 1846 Grey urged that 'every soldier in the army should receive precisely the same instruction which is now given to the Sappers and Miners'.[46] Wellington approved the idea and did nothing. In January 1852 Grey returned to the charge, and in the following month Prince Albert added his support.[47] In March the Adjutant General's defences crumbled. At his instigation the Master General agreed that detachments of up to 300 men with their officers could be relieved of all garrison duties at Chatham in order to be instructed in throwing up field works and in the operations of a siege. Men from infantry battalions were then sent in rotation.

The progress at Chatham was accompanied by an enormously important development at Hythe. In the days of the Brown Bess musketry instruction was poor, the victim of inadequate ammunition allowances and insufficient ranges. In 1846 the Royal Engineers conducted the first full experiments on the smooth-bore musket,[48] and one conclusion from their report was that some of the musket's defects could be overcome if the men had a better understanding of the capabilities of their arms. Therefore, Burgoyne, the Inspector General of Fortifications, called for proper training with the Brown Bess.[49] Shortly afterwards, British observers conceived an exaggerated respect for the regimental musketry instruction of France's *chasseurs à pied*, and for the central *école du tir* at Vincennes. The spur to action came in May 1851, when Wellington accepted Lord Anglesey's recommendation that all the infantry should be armed with a muzzle-loading rifle, the ·702 inch Minié. The Minié transformed the firepower of the infantry. The maximum effective range of the soldier's firearm moved from 150 yards to 800, and its accuracy quadrupled. In 1853 Hardinge secured the adoption of an even better weapon, the three-grooved ·577 Enfield rifle.[50] But there was little point in possessing a reliable and accurate arm if its owner was not trained to use it effectively. In February 1852 all regiments due to receive the Minié sent an officer and two n.c.o.s to Woolwich in order to be instructed in its use. When Hardinge arrived at the Horse Guards, he determined to put the Woolwich course on a permanent footing, and to establish a uniform system of musketry in the army.[51] To this end, in February 1853 a range of 1,400 yards was secured at Hythe and in May it was opened as the school of musketry.[52] In the first year of its existence the school produced a revised *Platoon exercise* (published in June 1854) and, more important, the first official manual on regimental musketry training (February 1854). Each battalion had to have two Hythe graduates, an officer and an n.c.o., as its instructors of musketry. With the adoption of the Minié, the annual ammunition allowance per man was increased from thirty to ninety rounds, and in 1853-54 Hardinge set about procuring safe ranges close to all the main military stations.[53] Although effective musketry training had only just begun to be adopted, its impact in the Crimea was immediate. At the battle of Vittoria in 1813, one bullet in — at the best — 459 took effect; at the Alma and Inkerman one in sixteen.[54]

A parallel development occurred in the artillery. Gunners above all needed training. Field instruction was conducted in four field batteries stationed at Woolwich. Between 1846 and 1848 the strength of the Royal Artillery was increased from 6,709 to 11,347; the number of companies to be rotated through these four batteries (of which — thanks to the demands of the Woolwich garrison — only two were efficient) rose from seventy-two to ninety-six.[55] The annual ammunition allowance was thirty rounds per gun and there was little opportunity to expend even that. The range at Woolwich, on Plumstead marshes, had a line of fire that crossed the river Thames: maritime traffic prevented firing on about three out of every five visits.[56] In 1845, twenty-eight consecutive days' shooting was lost.[57] Furthermore the maximum range at Plumstead was 1,500 yards. This was sufficient for smooth-bore field guns but for the trial of the heavier ordnance adopted in the 1840s it was totally inadequate. Attempts in 1838, 1842 and 1843 to realign the Woolwich range failed,[58] and from 1844 the artillery began to search for a new site. In 1845 two officers recommended the sands of Shoeburyness.[59] Shoeburyness was first used as an experimental range in 1847, but it was Hardinge, when Master General, who planned the sands as a great instructional and scientific centre for Britain's gunners.[60] Furthermore it was also Hardinge who, in response to the threat of invasion, established field batteries elsewhere in the United Kingdom, and so decentralised and augmented the field instruction of the regiment. His work was completed by his successor at the Ordnance: in 1848 the ammunition allowance had been increased to eighty rounds per gun, and in 1853 Raglan raised it to 140.[61]

But both Hythe and Shoeburyness were concerned with the parts, not the whole. Neither they — nor Portsmouth, Dublin and Chatham —

were concerned, in the words of Charles Napier, 'to show the application of *tactics* to *strategy*: that all manoeuvres have an object ... the one teaching what the moves are; and the other how to apply them'.[62] Field training had not only to accustom the battalion to applying its manoeuvres and to fending for itself, but also to train leaders and staff officers. The staff was the hinge and yet movements by individual battalions along pre-ordained grooves — as was the custom at the Chatham siege operations — provided little test of its abilities. Sir Charles Chichester put it thus: 'Commanding a brigade is easy but commanding a battalion in a brigade makes you sharp.'[63]

However, as he acknowledged when he wrote it, almost fifteen years had elapsed since Chichester had last done drill in brigade, and his experience was not exceptional. In 1850 the 95th Foot had not been brigaded with any other battalions for thirteen years.[64] The single battalion was both organisationally and tactically the core of the British system, so much so that a reading of the *Field exercise* seemed to suggest that each regiment was to operate in isolation. Colonial service and garrison duties made the principal higher formation, the brigade or perhaps even the division, forfeit pride of place to a declining tactical unit.

The brigade was therefore an *ad hoc* organisation, depending for its existence on the coincidence of regiments — in a fashion that could almost be described as random, unless the meeting presaged an emergency or the outbreak of war. J. H. Stocqueler in his *Military encyclopaedia* defined 'brigadier' as a 'title, in England ... suppressed in time of peace, but revived in actual service in the field'.[65] It existed as an appointment not a rank. Nor could the prudent officer prepare himself for the honour since, although the 1824 and 1833 *Field exercise* disarmingly confined themselves to general principles, the latter edition stated that 'all subjects connected with the manner of applying specific formations, embrace points of consideration much beyond the detail of tactical arrangement'.[66]

The cavalier attitude to the brigading of troops in peacetime was bound to have untoward consequences in war. Hardinge told Ripon that at the start of the first Sikh war, 'The troops ... had only been brigaded on paper. [They] therefore were not in that state of organization and formation so essential to discipline and field movements. The brigadiers and their staff were unknown to the men, and the men to their brigadiers.'[67] And yet Harry Smith's experience at Ferozeshah demonstrates how important and self-sufficient the command of a brigade might be. His two brigades were a mile apart, with the result that he could not control both effectively. As he did not have a clear idea of the overall plan himself, Smith could not delegate very much authority to the brigadier who would perforce have to operate independently. In consequence, Smith concluded, 'The army was one unwieldy battalion under one Commanding Officer who had not been granted the power of ubiquity.'[68]

Such brigade field days as were conducted came only a very short way towards meeting these deficiencies. Brigades were normally formed of one arm only — three battalions of infantry or ten to twelve squadrons of cavalry. Their movements were an attempt to assimilate those of the greater body to the lesser, a logical step that rendered the principles easy to grasp but communication difficult indeed. To make himself heard, the brigadier had to stand upwind, and it is hard to see how the power of his lungs, or indeed of drums or bugles, could in action have overcome the noise of firearms. He and his staff rarely had to deploy arms of a nature different from their own, since artillery was only occasionally attached to cavalry or infantry brigades for training. There were of course exceptions — principally in Dublin — but manuals, both official and unofficial, offered guidance for the movements or brigades of one arm only, and therefore the field days put little pressure on the brigadier's tactical sense, let alone his organisational ability.

Furthermore the field days did not provide opportunities to assemble divisions, formations which the larger armies of the Napoleonic wars had rendered desirable for purely administrative reasons. With its own transport and supply, not to mention light troops and artillery, the division could pursue an independent role and the army's staff could delegate many of its more tedious responsibilities. In British practice, the Peninsular war was the first major campaign in which a divisional system was evolved. However, as in the case of brigades, their composition and the duties of their staffs were not formulated except in war. Only the unofficial publications — those of Inigo Jones, J. H. Lefroy and Lord Frederick Fitzclarence — spoke of them, and so rooted were those in continental practice that they assumed cavalry would form part of a British division, although neither in the Peninsula nor in the Crimea was this the case. The maintenance of an independent cavalry division before Sebastopol can be construed as a sign of immaturity in the development of higher military formations, particularly since the roles of reconnaissance and patroling for which British cavalry were particularly destined implied a subordination to other arms. Nonetheless, in the Crimea the division was the principal administrative unit. It was on this level that the Commissariat and the Army Medical Department operated. Therefore the limited scope of brigade field days was not such an egregious fault as the lack of even a temporary divisional organisation or some such administrative equivalent. The problems of communication imposed a tactical limit on both higher formations, but the growing size of armies and their maintenance requirements put a premium on their potential organisational simplifications. The need for brigade and divisional manoeuvres was not simply, in the pregnant words of Charles Napier, so that 'Men and officers, more especially commanders, thus acquire the habit of acting in great bodies' but so that they also acquire that 'of drawing their supplies'.[69]

In such a large unit, complications would be magnified, and therefore peace afforded the opportunity for a harmonious system to be evolved. Whittingham in 1831[70] and Smith in 1844[71] both urged that in India divisions should be kept continuously in being, so that the army would always be ready for the field. Russia and Prussia had permanent divisional systems, with the result that confidence and familiarity were encouraged. France, however, provided the most forceful example. 'Since I have seen the French army move their masses with such ease,' Lieutenant-Colonel Torrens wrote in 1852 to the Adjutant General, 'I would venture to say that it appears to me that what is wanted in our military system ... is an organisation of our Troops at home in Brigades & Divisions, & such a disposition of our Regiments as shall bring them frequently together under their Generals.'[72]

In the same year the Duke of Cambridge submitted a memorandum to Hardinge, which took as its premise, 'that no army can be considered as in a proper state to take the field ... unless a Brigade and Division system be introduced, which is to be found in every Continental army'. As Torrens had also seen, the police rendered local garrisons at home less necessary and the railway provided a means of rapid movement and concentration. Therefore, with minimal disruption to the existing distribution of troops, and with no addition required in manpower or in barrack accommodation, three divisions could be formed in London, south and south-west England, each formed of one brigade of cavalry and two brigades of infantry. Both Torrens and Cambridge advocated the annual concentration of a large proportion of these men so that they 'may have an opportunity of really learning their duties in combined bodies'.[73]

What really gave force to these proposals was the fear of French invasion. Plans for entrenched camps and rings of fortresses made little sense without the means to assemble the men they would require. Railways meant this concentration could be rapid, but their very speed added to the complexities of the staff problem. Regiments not previously arranged into higher formations 'will be beaten in detail, and the whole country thrown into confusion and dismay'.[74] Consequently a number of schemes similar to that of the Duke of Cambridge were mooted. In 1848 Sir George Cathcart insisted on a prior brigade organisation to counter the French threat.[75] In 1853 Major Bedford spoke of the army of the United Kingdom being divided into four corps, based on Portsmouth, Manchester, Edinburgh and Dublin. Each should be complete with artillery, commissariat and pontoon train, and have sea and rail transport available. That for Ireland would be an expeditionary force.[76]

Therefore, to meet the twin strategic responsibilities of imperial defence and countering French invasion, Britain was to become an armed camp. Clearly it rang too much of Cromwell's major-generals to please the constitutionalists. But the strategic argument coincided with three major and interrelated training requirements. First, and most basically, came the failure to prepare the individual soldier in the field, whether it was on the level of self-sufficiency under canvas or the correct use of cover in action. Secondly extended movements by combined bodies of men were rarely experienced — 'We seldom fight regimentally, and we seldom drill except regimentally.'[77] The third defect was a direct consequence of the second. Large bodies of troops were not assembled, and so 'it would indeed be surprising to find our General Officers otherwise than ignorant of the practical portion of their duties in the field'.[78]

The panacea put forward to cure all these ills was the same as that adopted on the continent. 'Camps,' the *United Service Journal* pontificated in 1832, 'are the order of the day.'[79] The Prussians had one at Berlin, the Austrians one at Milan, the Dutch one on the Belgian border, and the British should follow suit at Portsmouth, Blackheath or some other site where at least a division might be assembled for a month in the summer and put through a continuous course of instruction. Different regiments could pass through each year, and thus the benefits of the camp be disseminated.

The late eighteenth-century camps of instruction at Warley and elsewhere had come to a fitting climax in 1803 at Shorncliffe. But, from then until the 1850s, such camps as were held consisted of little more than pitching and striking tents. At Dublin, where the troops were regularly encamped, the purpose was confined to the assembly of troops in case of famine-based insurrection. In 1848, the Chartists spread the fear of rebellion to England. Camps were held at Kersal Moor and Everton but, although apparently Ordnance and Commissariat supply problems were beginning to emerge, the full benefit of the lesson was lost by the premature dissolution of the lines as the troops were suffering owing to bad weather.

There was of course an outstanding exception to this catalogue of missed opportunities in the person of Lord Frederick Fitzclarence. His attention to brigade exercises led logically to a desire to draw all the elements of his training schemes together. As he told Lord Clarendon in 1853, it was useless to blame British generals for being 'incapable of moving, handling, or placing, a few regiments when *assembled together*, and for combining the three arms together ... unless G1. officers have *opportunities given them* to learn their duty by having troops brought together, and staff officers *equally instructed*'.[80] In January the same year he had implored the governor of Bombay for more barrack accommodation at Poona. This would allow him to bring together larger bodies of men for training. He concluded his letter with an impassioned and prolix plea; 'I know the wants and I might even say errors in the system of the British army and I can affirm with confidence that the greatest want is that of giving Corps and Regiments an opportunity of acting together particularly with reference to the manoeuvring of the Three arms in concert each knowing its part so as to mutually assist and support one another, the highest and most essential attainment of thoroughly instructed officers without a knowledge of combination in these component parts even the most highest drilled Regiments and most perfect artillery and Cavalry become useless as compared with what they might, and ought to be impeding each others movements and paralysing attacks from want of system and ignorance on the part of those who I humbly conceive are unfairly treated by never having an opportunity afforded them of learning the art of manoeuvring Troops.'[81]

Therefore, in November and December 1853, a camp of exercise was held at Poona for a force of almost 10,000 men.[82] The programme of operations was said to have considered 'every branch of professional science'. Progress was deliberately gradual so that confidence could be established. The first week was devoted to manoeuvres based on part IV of the *Field exercise* and was held on the divisional parade ground. In the second week, the cavalry and horse artillery in brigade proceeded at an accelerated pace, and the combined force manoeuvred on extended lines on the bank of the river Moola-Moota, practising changes of front, position and direction, covered by artillery, cavalry and light infantry. In the third week the division went up to the hills to attack, defend and assume positions against a token 'enemy' force. Escalading, night operations, the combined movements of columns, their assembly and the maintenance of contact in rough ground were all tested in the hills. In the fourth and final week the work of light troops, outposts and picquets predominated. For the benefit of officers reared in the duties of one arm alone, Fitzclarence drew up a memorandum, subsequently published, for the use of the three arms in combination, establishing an order of priorities in movements and suggesting the correct use of each. Predictably the brigadiers were found old and sleepy, but this was reported as the only blemish. The cavalry and horse artillery worked well together, the principles of support were grasped, and in all 'The Force here at present can be handled and manoeuvred like a Regiment'.[83] Perhaps some credit is due to Lord Frederick for the loyalty and effectiveness of the Bombay army in the Mutiny. Certainly he set an example for India, that was followed in 1854 at Ambala and again at Poona.

At home the impact of Fitzclarence's work was muted but not totally lost. The basic professional requirements had not *per se* elicited financial support from Parliament or moral support from the public. Nor were they likely to, when 'No sooner does his Majesty assemble his guards for a few days' exercise at Windsor, than the event is hailed by the radical press as the harbinger of military despotism'.[84] However, the opprobrium thus incurred by troops when they moved round their native land was diminished as the country's need for them became clearer. When soldiers were finally concentrated in numbers near the capital — at Wellington's funeral in 1852 and at Chobham in 1853 — far from being vilified, they were the object of zealous attention on the part of a fascinated populace. Foreign threats were a more idealistic rallying cry than a ritual suspicion derived from historical and literary allusion.

The defenceless state of Britain therefore formed the justification for a memorandum by Prince Albert in 1847. He posed Wellington the simple question: 'Would not a concentration of a part of our Land forces in England for a short time be a very useful & admissible measure?' In particular an invasion would have to be countered by troops assembled by railway, 'an operation, which is comparatively new and will want some practice and experience before it can be satisfactorily performed'. A camp, for two weeks or so, at Winchester, Salisbury plain or Bagshot could draw together 10,000 men from garrisons south of Weedon, and would provide a good test of 'Our Commissariat arrangements ... & ... what may be wanting in that respect'.[85]

Wellington's response characteristically reminded Albert that 'Such measures may cost the public some money'. In any case, he felt, 'The mere exercise and mechanical discipline of the Troops themselves might be as well carried on possibly in their Garrisons and Stations as at present in their existing numbers; as these objects could be attained in a camp.'[86] Wellington was not in principle opposed to camps of exercise. In 1843 he had advised Lord Ripon on the expediency of holding one to cover Gwalior. However the cost of the camp could not be justified as an exercise in itself but only as an answer to the specific problem of Gwalior. For, the Duke believed, 'It will be found that a Regt. taken from the immediate performance of the duty of guarding in small bodies Convicts in transports on their Voyage to Penal Colonies, or others taken from the Occupation of half Billet stations in the Mountains and Cross Roads in S. Wales, or from their cantonments [?] in Publick Houses & Brothels in the Suburbs of London, Westmr. & Southwark would be equally trained and prepared to perform any duty manoeuvre or Operation in Line with others, as were the British Troops when under my Command in the Army of Occupation in France'.[87]

The Duke was hardly likely to progress the idea of camps of exercise. It does not seem unfair to associate with him Sir George Brown's dictum of as late as February 1853: Sir Harry Smith, Sir Charles Napier and Lord Cathcart all favoured the concentration of troops in large barracks for the purposes of training, but Brown feared that 'if your troops are concentrated in masses, they will more readily attract the notice of the economists, who would assuredly soon get up a further cry for reduction! In fact, it is only by keeping the troops scattered and out of sight, that we are enabled to keep up any army at all in this country.'[88] Furthermore the Duke had the support of Lord John Russell, who, although in sympathy with Prince Albert's idea, was not prepared to support it in the winter of 1847, since he felt that in conjunction with the invasion scare it might have caused panic among the public.[89]

However, the memoranda of men such as the Duke of Cambridge and Colonel Torrens were not lost on Hardinge. In December 1852 he proposed that in order to repel an invasion, the army in the south of England should be concentrated on Reigate, with its flanks stretching through Tonbridge and Ashford to Dover in one direction and to Guildford, Farnborough and Basingstoke in the other. In the summer these troops should be brigaded and encamped.[90]

It is hard to trace quite how the idea developed from there. Hardinge subsequently and repeatedly passed credit for the origins of the camp of exercise to the Prince Consort, but he may of course have had in mind the Prince's 1847 memorandum as much as anything that followed in

December 1852. In January 1853 Sidney Herbert, as Secretary at War, agreed to take a vote in the army estimates to cover the expenses of a camp for 7,000 men that summer.[91]

The approximate location for the camp was clear. It needed to be in the south of England, accessible by rail and suitable for troops concentrating to repel a landing on any point of the south-east coast. In March, Torrens prepared a report on the Bagshot area,[92] while Captain Higginson of the Grenadier Guards covered the ground from Sunningdale to Woking, including Ascot Heath.[93] Although Higginson reported the land as boggy and short of drinking water, Hardinge discounted his own original preference for Bagshot and opted for a site on Higginson's beat, called Chobham. On 15 April he inspected it personally, and reported favourably to the Prince Consort.[94] Albert chivvied the Commander-in-Chief constantly on progress, even hoping to command the Guards in the camp, and it is interesting to note that the selection of Lord Seaton as commander at Chobham seems to have been decided between these two, on Hardinge's instigation, and without any reference to Herbert or Newcastle.

It was nonetheless a happy choice. Of the generals who combined sufficient field experience with relative fitness, he was probably the only feasible possibility, Sir Charles Napier — a likely contender — being at death's door, and others, such as Sir Harry Smith and Raglan, already holding active and strenuous appointments. Hardinge, distressed by his difficulty in finding incumbents for the brigade commands, took solace in his relationship with Seaton. The feelings of regard and community of thought, fostered by their shared education in the school of Sir John Moore, were well expressed in memoranda that each of them appears to have written separately but which were close not only in spirit but often in words. On 4 June 1853, Hardinge told Seaton that 'The object to be attained is to accustom the Officers, and Troops to move over rough and undulating ground, with that freedom, and ease, which should be practised before an enemy in the field — to take up ground in reference to its shape for defensive purposes — or to attack a position by such a combination of the three arms, as may best be adapted to bring each into action in its proper place, and at the most appropriate moment'.[95]

More detailed objectives were also in view. The camp was to be the practical test for proposed improvements. Hardinge sent to Chobham for trial new ammunition waggons, that were designed to cope with the expected increase in ammunition expenditure consequent on the adoption of the Minié, oblong wooden boxes to store the rounds, so that unlike the barrels then in use they could be conveniently carried on pack saddles, items of clothing that were looser in cut and designed to afford better protection against the varied elements to which the British soldier was exposed, and finally a selection of knapsacks and equipment that might not only be more comfortable to bear but also reduce the total weight carried by an infantryman from sixty pounds to forty. Seaton also encouraged officers to look at the construction and transport of the camp equipage, and in particular the field cooking kettle. They should give thought to the likely impact of the new rifled musket on tactics and whether it should be issued to all infantry.[96]

Finally Hardinge's other great object was to capitalise on the support for the army already awakened in the nation by Wellington's funeral and the fears of French invasion. 'The Camp is keeping alive a martial spirit,' he told Seaton, '& the good effect will not be limited to the training of the Troops — it is pervading the whole population.'[97] Despite the interference with training, the public should be allowed 'the most liberal freedom of the Camp, to make it as popular as the [Great] Exhibition'. If the main events could be conducted on Saturdays, M.P.s would be free from parliamentary duties and therefore able fully to appreciate the need to unlock their coffers for further improvements.

In April Colonel Torrens was put in charge of preparations for the camp. With a party of Sappers and Miners he mapped the general area, then marked out the camp, channelled springs into reservoirs and sunk wells. The Sappers built camp kitchens and, with the aid of fatigue parties sent in advance of their regiments, erected stables and put up huts and marquees.[98] These preparations certainly facilitated Seaton's wish to have the whole force on the ground and encamped in one day. Unfortunately, they also deprived many men of practice in the arts of encampment. However, without them the army might have found itself very embarrassed in the full glare of publicity on the first day. The 95th, for example, came to the ground ignorant of how to establish a camp kitchen.[99] The emphasis should be on the degree of improvement gradually imparted while the camp was in progress. In retrospect Stocqueler, not necessarily a favourable critic, concluded that 'The men showed considerable skill and alacrity in hutting themselves ... out of the brushwood and earth available, and on the whole imparted a confidence to the country that they would not be found wanting when their services might be needed in the field'.[100] Despite the heavy rain, only 1·7 per cent of the force were sick over the two months. Discipline was equally impressive: of the total 17,658 men who were at Chobham from

June to August only four underwent corporal punishment and there were no cases of disgraceful conduct or robbery.[101]

Hardinge chose a division as the unit for encampment. Not only was it a self-sufficient formation with its own reserves, transport and supply, but it also enabled successive divisions to be trained individually, so that as many troops would be ready to act in line as if a larger body had been assembled in the first place. From 14 June to 14 July Seaton had under his command a cavalry brigade, a brigade of Guards, two infantry brigades (each of three battalions), one troop of horse artillery, three field batteries, a company of Sappers and Miners and a pontoon train. Sir Randolph Routh, a deputy commissary-general in the Peninsular war, administered the provisions to universal satisfaction. On 14 July all the troops were replaced by fresh regiments, new staff officers were brought in (with the exception of Seaton, the Duke of Cambridge, Routh and the sapper, Jones) and thus almost as many men at home as could be brought to Chobham received the benefit of its instruction. The operations were concluded a month later.

The heath and wastelands round Chobham in 1853 formed very rough and broken ground, and, although without trees, varied from bog in the low-lying areas to scrubby, dry turf. The demands made by the terrain were seen in themselves to justify the choice of site. However, while the infantry benefited from the variety of manoeuvres the broken ground imposed, the cavalry were reduced to meekly following them. They could only move in threes, and not in troops, and not one charge was executed during the entire two months. This subordination only conformed to what in any case amounted to national practice but it was unfortunate that mistakes in the application of the arm had to be reserved for the war itself. The criticism that the light infantry was badly employed — on one occasion they were only thirty to forty paces in front of the main body, and on another a brigade advanced without any skirmishing screen to cover it — can probably be explained in Seaton's wish to try all infantry as riflemen. This, however, was no excuse for the lack of out-post work (perhaps conceived as something that could as well be practised by regiments individually), nor for the failure to fire live ammunition, whether at a target or not, since as much ball as could possibly be obtained was taken to camp. Only the second contingent had the opportunity to throw up field works and even these were not as extensive as planned for fear of 'doing any mishap to the Land'.[102]

The instructional value of the camp was therefore less for the soldiers and junior officers than for the generals, brigadiers and field officers.

The principal aim was to manoeuvre a division and its brigades. Hardinge observed that 'The attempts to move three Brigades of three Battalions each, by the voice of their respective Brigadiers giving the words of command from the rear, would in action when firing had commenced lead to great confusion'.[103] Instead the troops learnt the system used in the Peninsula, whereby staff officers passed messages along the rear. Although Hardinge instructed Brown to incorporate it into a revised brigade exercise,[104] this procedure was not yet enforced in regulations by 1854. Its impact was twofold: first it was of course quieter and more certain, and secondly it put greater emphasis on the duties and qualities of the divisional and brigade staff, while removing the initiative from the regimental commanding officer. The consequence, of what was perhaps an over-rigid ruling, or an over-rapid switch of system, was that at least one regimental officer complained that he had little idea of the overall purpose of the manoeuvres he was meant to be putting into operation. This in turn resulted in confusion in manoeuvring, with, on one occasion, cavalry exposing their flank, artillery getting embroiled in the ranks of the 79th and troops firing on each other.[105] Seaton also seems to have observed too readily the Adjutant General's advice that sham fights led to bad blood between the regiments concerned,[106] and, although not conforming to the very limited field days Brown therefore saw as practicable, the 'enemy' forces in manoeuvres tended to be so restricted as 'only to indicate in the vaguest manner how battles are lost', and certainly to give little idea of attack and defence.[107] Therefore, although the schemes for operations were varied, the implementation rested so much on the divisional staff as to give little practice to other rising officers. The Duke of Cambridge, already marked for higher things and one of the few senior officers sufficiently young to seem likely ever to go on active service, was the only man apart from Seaton who wielded the division itself. Hardinge's system of giving orders was the best adapted for war and it was right to test it at Chobham, but it was a pity that the man who in consequence learned most was never again to command in the field.

Mistakes abounded. The *Naval and Military Gazette* concluded that Chobham 'has told us a tale not the most agreeable to hear, but which ought to be instructive. We have treated, tried and found defective, much that we fancied perfect in the organisation, training, clothing, equipping, and arming of all branches of the Service ... We have seen, too, how easily mistakes can be made through ignorance of first principles of manoeuvre, and through inexperience in those officers who are the best instructed in the theory of strategy and tactics.'[108] This, after all, was the purpose of Chobham. Errors once revealed could be put in order. New equipment was introduced, although in most cases not until 1855. The artillery had shown that it was still unfit for war, but this could be rectified. It was only a pity that the Commissariat had been in such capable hands and been so little taxed in the transport and procurement of supplies.

The problems Chobham raised served to confirm the necessity for continuing the practice. Little doubt existed but that an even better camp would be held in 1854. Hardinge, however, was more ambitious. A permanent camp of instruction was required that could function all the year round and would be relatively independent of annual parliamentary grants. His initial plan, in June 1853, was to purchase three or four localities similar to Chobham in the maritime counties.[109] One site in particular had taken his fancy. The land at Aldershot was surveyed at the beginning of 1853 and by July the Commander-in-Chief had secured the support of the Prince Consort for its acquisition.[110] On 26 September Hardinge wrote a memorandum on the advantages of Aldershot. Chobham justified the recommendation that the government acquire eight to ten thousand acres in which brigades, divisions and even militia battalions could be encamped or hutted for five months of the year. Hiring such a large tract of land was clearly an unreliable system, and Hardinge therefore favoured the purchase of the Aldershot site. It was adjacent to railway lines for London, Portsmouth, Chatham and Dover, and surveys in March, April and August had convinced the Commander-in-Chief that 'This tract of land is therefore suited for a permanent camp of instruction in peace, and of concentration in war'.[111]

Time was of the essence. By late August Hardinge was aware that the parishes around Aldershot were discussing the enclosure of the land,[112] but not until the beginning of September did he find out that twenty-seven enclosure acts, passed less than two weeks previously, had included Chobham.[113] He feared Aldershot too would be lost. At this juncture Prince Albert stepped in and persuaded Palmerston, the Home Secretary, to take the matter up.[114] By the end of November Hardinge was more confident of success and on 11 December Gladstone, the Chancellor of the Exchequer, committed the government to the purchase of 3,000 acres as a start.[115] Acquisition could only be gradual. By May 1854 3,933 acres had been bought, with a further 2,519 to be agreed on.[116] £100,000 was voted in 1854-5 for these purchases, but land continued to be added until 1861.[117]

Hardinge was anxious to make Aldershot operational as soon as possible. It was already realised that the most important objective was an extended period of instruction, and to this end huts were decreed more appropriate than tents. Furthermore, as Prince Albert pointed out, 'Put permanent buildings on the land, and the country will never be allowed to sell it. The state of popular feeling engendered by the war is such, that you can now ask Parliament for anything you want. Strike while the iron is hot.'[118] The Belgian camp at Beverloo was the only hutted camp in Europe, and in 1852 and 1853 the Commander-in-Chief received two reports on it.[119] In addition he sent his son and Colonels Wood and Torrens (both of whom had been on the staff at Chobham) to the French, Austrian, Prussian and Russian camps of 1853, presumably with a view to gaining information for his own creation,[120] and Raglan dispatched Engineer and Artillery officers to those of Austria and Prussia.[121]

By 1854 therefore British opinion was reasonably well grounded in the principal desiderata. These were embodied in a memorandum by Hardinge in May. Adequate barracks were needed for the troops to defend the south coast, and he therefore dismissed huts as being only available in summer and requiring frequent repairs. An intermediate construction, to last thirty or forty years, should be decided on by a committee. The barrack would be occupied throughout the year, but in the warmer weather an equivalent force could be under canvas and so two or three divisions of 10,000 men each could be exercised in the four or five months of summer.[122]

The committee sat in July 1854; it considered a smaller barrack built at Portland by Jebb and it interviewed Cubitt and other distinguished civil engineers.[123] Construction started in September and in January 1855 the Board of Ordnance authorised £250,000 to be spent on the barracks.[124] The immediate wartime requirement of housing the militia and despatching troops to the east meant that huts — admittedly of a substantial construction — were also put up. Thus Britain's 'improved Potsdam'[125] entered service. The appointment of its first general officer commanding, Sir William Knollys, who, as commanding officer of the Scots Fusilier Guards, had initiated the Prince Consort in the mysteries of the British military system, confirmed the Albertian influence that had been so strong throughout. It is hard to judge from the correspondence whether Hardinge was too deferential to the Prince, but an attempt to apportion relative degrees of credit would in any case be superfluous, when both had a common identity of motive.

However, Chobham and Aldershot were too little and too late. Taken in conjunction with the Staff College almost as much was done or planned for the higher education of the army in 1853 and 1854 as was to be carried through for the next half-century. Nonetheless, as the impact of Hardinge's brigade exercise at Chobham showed, the habits of parade manoeuvres or the ignorance of communicating orders in the field were too ingrained for a brief flurry of reform to have a noticeable impact in the Crimea.

Broadly speaking, the senior officers appointed to the expeditionary army were the best available. Hardinge had settled on Raglan for the command early in February 1854, largely because the latter's urbanity would stand him in good stead in joint councils of war with Britain's French allies. The attributes that Raglan lacked would, at this early stage of the expedition's planning, have been provided by Hardinge's other two recommendations: Burgoyne would contribute strategic wisdom and the Duke of Cambridge youthful dash.[126] Raglan should clearly have remained at the Ordnance but his nearest rivals were either too old (Hardinge, Seaton, Combermere and Anglesey) or were the legitimate cause for some suspicion. Hardinge's doubts about Gough as a field commander had been reinforced by Chillianwallah;[127] the excitable Sir Harry Smith had the shadow of Buddiwal over his subsequent victory at Aliwal and had recently been recalled from the Cape.

The growth of the expedition from a force of 10,000 men, destined perhaps to go no further than Malta, to an army of 25,000 men for the invasion of mainland Russia, meant that the difficulties of making satisfactory appointments were compounded. Assuming the threat of mutiny in India, and given that the most important of the wars of the 1840s had been in that theatre, it would have been foolhardy on Hardinge's part to denude the subcontinent of its best commanders. As it was he had to pillage Woolwich and the Horse Guards to find satisfactory appointees. The only officer who had successfully and recently held an independent field command — Sir George Cathcart — was not merely torn from his new post as Adjutant General to take the 4th Division but also was given a dormant commission to command the army should some accident have befallen Raglan. Torrens had one of the 4th Division's brigades, and Goldie, whose service had been strictly regimental, the other. The remaining infantry appointments were equally logical — the Duke of Cambridge, as the rising star of the army, had the 1st Division, which included the Highland Brigade under the old campaigner, Colin Campbell, and the Guards were under Bentinck, who had held a similar appointment at Chobham. Experience at the camp of instruction presumably weighed in the choice of de Lacy Evans to command the 2nd Division, and his service in Spain with the British Auxiliary Legion gave him more recent knowledge of European war than any general of comparable rank. His brigades were in the hands of H. W. Adams, who had commanded the 18th Foot in China, and Pennefather, a scion of the Napier school in Scinde. Another Chobham product was the veteran of the Cape and Afghanistan, Sir Richard England, who took the 3rd Division. Macdonald, when Adjutant General, thought him 'one of the most zealous, ardent, intelligent men I ever saw at the head of a Regt.',[128] although this was not always the prevailing view. His brigadiers were Sir John Campbell, who had fought in Burma and was a competent regimental officer, and William Eyre, who as the commander of an independent column had emerged very much the hero of the latest Kaffir war. The Light Division was entrusted to the former Adjutant General, Sir George Brown, its brigades going to Buller (a Rifle Brigade officer who had fought the Kaffirs) and — albeit only briefly — Airey. Airey was appointed Quarter Master General on de Ros' withdrawal, and Codrington, the future Commander-in-Chief but at this stage 'a dark horse', took Airey's brigade. The Napier school was further represented by Simpson, *'a real good sound head'* as the conqueror of Scinde had called him,[129] who was sent out as chief of staff and succeeded Raglan. Less method can be found in the choices for the Cavalry Division, although Lucan had served with the Russian army in the Balkans in 1828. The cavalry's lack of foreign service left only Sir Joseph Thackwell as an experienced officer: he was fully employed as Inspector General of Cavalry, and had in any case failed to exploit the opportunities which had come his way in the second Sikh war. At the time, therefore, the selection for the cavalry was perhaps more credible than the choice of Adjutant General, Estcourt. His recent career had been predominantly parliamentary, which perhaps explains his full correspondence with Herbert, but he never wrote to Hardinge, who not unnaturally concluded that he must have had 'his fingers shot off'.[130] The appointment was due to Raglan, who thought Estcourt 'the best of men and a very nice fellow'.[131] The junior staff appointments were, as we have already seen, given as far as possible to the graduates of Sandhurst.

In the circumstances, then, the best men were chosen. However, the difference between commanding a brigade in a colonial war and a division in a European one was more than some allegedly competent officers were capable of. Sir Colin Campbell, whose reputation had not emerged unscathed from the second Sikh war,[132] was not a commander of large formations. 'An excellent Brigadier' told Panmure that Campbell was 'unfit for individual responsibility', and this opinion was supported by Raglan and Simpson.[133] The decision later in the war to bypass him for the supreme command in favour of Codrington, a Guards officer of little previous foreign service, did not therefore rest on a prejudice against officers of Indian experience, Campbell's cause in fact being espoused by the Queen. Moreover, the decision of Panmure and his advisers was subsequently justified by Campbell's questionable strategy in the Indian Mutiny. The same applied to Simpson. His elevation to the command in this case did rest on the fighting reputation he had forged in the subcontinent and, on his own admission, he was totally inadequate to the task.[134] It is hard therefore to substantiate the accusations of bias against 'Indian' officers. But equally Dublin and Chobham were shown to have provided insufficient training. At the Alma the Duke of Cambridge first so lengthened his line as to cramp the neighbouring divisions and contribute to the faulty alignment of the whole British army, and then proved slow to fulfil Raglan's instructions to support the Light Division. Nor did he retrieve his reputation at Inkerman.

These criticisms of leadership and command are, however, secondary to the greatest staff failing in the Crimea. In any war communications between the various units of a force are perhaps the most crucial area of staff work, and they were accordingly the field in which the British officers most showed their inexperience. At Chobham, Hardinge had endeavoured to overcome the tradition of brigade or divisional independence of the Commander-in-Chief's staff, but Cathcart's unhurried approach to the battle of Balaclava and Sir George Brown's refusal to be dictated to by staff officers suggest that his success was limited. In any case the a.d.c.s proved themselves inexplicit in conveying their orders: Cathcart should have been left in no doubt as to the urgency of the situation and Nolan must surely bear the blame for the vagueness of the instructions he conveyed to Lucan and Cardigan. The failure, therefore, of the Quarter Master General's department to develop into a proper staff had its inevitable consequence in the transmission and implementation of even simple executive commands. The cavalry at Balaclava of course provided some of the best examples of the failure to communicate. In instructing Paget to give him his best support, Cardigan forgot to repeat himself to the other regiment in the second line, the 8th Hussars, with the result that it conducted virtually a separate charge. Scarlett was twice the victim of his Heavy Brigade being given orders which were not also communicated to him.[135]

Even given the relatively unsophisticated interpretation of a staff's

The staff and training for the field 175

composition and duties, the failings here instanced are ones which the Crimean army would have acknowledged as its province. Transport and supply were less thought of as a staff officer's currency, but every British officer knew that the manoeuvring of troops in the field with success was the summit of his profession. This, beyond the level of a regiment or battalion, the economies of the 'long peace' had left him unfit to do.

Notes

1 Of Captain Curzon, Sir George Cathcart papers, Cathcart to his wife, 1 March 1852.
2 *Queen's Regulations*, 1844, p. 59; see also pp. 53-62 on staff generally.
3 Quoted in J. W. Fortescue, *The last post*, p. 167. Fortescue gives 'reflected for 'neglected', but to make sense the latter must be meant.
4 Thomas Bunbury, *Reminiscences of a veteran*, III, pp. 272-3.
5 N.L.S. mss. 2846, f. 15, Michel to Brown, 24 January 1847.
6 James Campbell, *A British army, as it was, —is, —and ought to be*, p. 131.
7 P.P. 1833, VII, pp. 168, 188.
8 Portland papers, Pw Jf 2196, Whittingham to Bentinck, 13 March 1831.
9 P.P. 1850, X, pp. 76-7, 988; P.P. 1851, VII, p. 27.
10 P.P. 1854-5, XIX, p. 16.
11 Sir George Cathcart papers, Cathcart to the Military Secretary, 30 December 1853.
12 W.O. 3/322, p. 309.
13 See above, pp. 35-6.
14 James Campbell, *The British army*, p. 145.
15 N.A.M. 6210/94/5, Claremont to Wetherall, 6 December 1854.
16 Newcastle papers, NeC 10487, Evans to Newcastle, 4 February 1855.
17 N.A.M. 6210/95, Estcourt to Wetherall, 3 March 1855.
18 W.O. 33/1, p. 55.
19 N.A.M. 6210/94/1, Airey to Wetherall, 6 June [? July] 1855.
20 Sir George Cathcart papers, I 33, Cathcart to his father, 7 September 1832.
21 W.O. 3/94, p. 258.
22 S. G. P. Ward, *Wellington's headquarters*, p. 131, also pp. 17-18, 24-31, 110.
23 N.L.S. mss 1848, f. 171, Hardinge to Brown, 30 November [? 1853]. Hardinge perhaps meant *Le moniteur de l' armée*.
24 W.O. 33/1, p. 173.
25 N.L.S. mss 1849, f. 182, Brown to de Ros, 14 July 1854.
26 Newcastle papers, NeC 9893, Raglan to Newcastle, 28 October 1854.
27 N.A.M. 6210/94/1, Airey to Wetherall, 22 July 1855.
28 P.P. 1854-5, XII, 311, p. 158.
29 Hardinge papers, Scovell to Hardinge, 7 February 1853.
30 P.P. 1854-5, IX, part I, *2nd report*, p. 42.
31 P.P. 1854-5, XII, 311, pp. 25, 61, 94, 97, 127; Hereford C. R. O., G/IV/A/408, Hardinge to Airey, 5 January 1855; Hardinge papers,

Hardinge to Prince Albert, 27 November 1854 and 18 June 1856; J. A. Ewart, *The story of a soldier's life*, I, p. 247.
32 W.O. 99/19.
33 P.P. 1854-5, XII, 311, p. 21. For much of what follows see also pp. 20, 22, 58, 61, 125-6, 145, 157-8.
34 Charles Dupin, *Military force of Great Britain*, II, pp. 84-9.
35 S. R. O. GD 45/8/16, [Gleig] to Maule, 7 December 1846.
36 Herbert papers, III, A (44); see III A (73), Gleig to Herbert, 3 October 1853.
37 J. M. Spearman, *Notes on military education*, pp. 34-5, 38-9, 56.
38 W.O. 43/865, ff. 300, 302, 303.
39 Newcastle papers, NeC 10728, Lefroy to H. Roberts, 23 December 1854.
40 P.P. 1854-5, XII, 311, p. 22.
41 Burgoyne papers, EC 73, Trevelyan to Burgoyne, 8 September 1854, quoting Hill, January 1842.
42 *N. & M. G.*, 6 December 1845, p. 777; 14 February 1846, pp. 104-5; 18 April 1846, p. 250; 20 October 1849, p. 664; 20 July 1850, p. 456; 7 June 1851, pp. 361-2; 22 November 1851, p. 745.
43 Lord Frederick Fitzclarence, *A manual of outpost duties*, p. vi.
44 Willoughby Verner, *Military life of Duke of Cambridge*, I, pp. 31-2.
45 W.O. 55/970, Adjutant General to Secretary to Master General of Ordnance, 18 March 1852; see also *Royal Engineers Professional Papers*, II, pp. 8-9.
46 S. R. O. GD 45/8/21, memo by Grey, October 1846, pp. 9-11.
47 Wellington papers, memo by Brown of conversation with Grey, 28 January 1852; memo apparently by Prince Albert, with comments by Brown, 17 February 1852.
48 Copies in P.R.O. 30/46/2/4 and W.O. 1/477, p. 451.
49 George Wrottesley, *Life of Sir John Burgoyne*, I, pp. 429-31.
50 C. H. Roads, *The British soldier's firearm 1850-1864*, ch. I-III.
51 R.A. E 2/51, Hardinge to Prince Albert, 20 January 1853.
52 R.A. E 44/89, Hardinge to Prince Albert, 31 January 1853; R.A. E 2/61, same, 11 February 1853; Hansard, 3rd series, CXXIV, cc 679-80.
53 W.O. 3/116, pp. 128, 279, 284, 305, 343, 444, 458, 478, 482; W.O. 3/320, pp. 181, 208.
54 *Journal of the Society for Army Historical Research*, XVI, 1937, p. 120.
55 P.P. 1849, IX, pp. ix, x, 20, 24-5; W.O. 44/522; R.A. B 10/219.
56 P.P. 1849, IX, pp. 456, 608.
57 *N. & M. G.*, 2 January 1847, p. 2.
58 W.O. 44/298.
59 W.O.44/644.
60 W.O. 46/89, pp. 118-9, 192-3.
61 P.P. 1849, IX, 264; W.O. 46/90, p. 389.
62 B.M. Add. Mss 54561, f. 45, memo by C. Napier on review at Kersal Moor, 30 October 1840.
63 East Riding C.R.O., DDCH 80, diary of Sir Charles Chichester, 14 July 1843, p. 177.

The staff and training for the field

64 U.S.G., 26 October 1850, p. 6.
65 J. H. Stocqueler, *The military encyclopaedia*, p. 43.
66 *Field exercise and evolutions of the army*, 1833, p. 223; *Queen's Regulations*, 1844, p. 54, is just as unhelpful.
67 R. S. Rait, *Life of Gough*, II, p. 7.
68 Joseph Lehmann, *Remember you are an Englishman*, pp. 234-7.
69 C. J. Napier, *Defects, civil and military, of the Indian government*, p. 392.
70 Portland papers, Pw Jf 2197, Whittingham to Bentinck, 18 March 1831.
71 W.O. 135/3, memo by Smith, 24 February 1844 (copy).
72 N.L.S. mss 2850, f. 188, Torrens to Brown, 13 May 1852; see also A. W. Torrens, *Notes on the French infantry*, p. 60.
73 R.A. E 44/85, quoted in Willoughby Verner, *Life of Duke of Cambridge*, I, pp. 39-44.
74 Colonel Lewis, in *Royal Engineers Professional Papers*, X, 1849.
75 Sir George Cathcart papers, Cathcart to Somerset, 3 February 1848.
76 W. D. Bedford, *Some suggestions for the cheap defence of the kingdom*, pp. 5-7.
77 *N. & M. G.*, 31 July 1847, p. 494.
78 Ibid., 29 September 1849, p. 621.
79 *U.S.J.*, 1832, III, p. 1.
80 Bodleian Ms. Clarendon Deposit c 103, f. 62, Fitzclarence to Clarendon, April 1853.
81 India Office Library, L/MIL/3/1910, no. 2.
82 Ibid., L/MIL/3/1753, p. 550, and L/MIL/3/1909, no. 109; *N. & M. G.*, 5 November 1853, p. 716; R. S. Liddell, *Memoirs of the Tenth Royal Hussars*, p. 255; H. Davidson, *History and services of the 78th Highlanders*, p. 148; *U.S.G.*, 8 October 1853, p. 5, 7 January 1854, p. 4.
83 *U.S.G.*, 21 January 1854, p. 6.
84 *N. & M. G.*, 12 October 1833, p. 291.
85 Wellington papers, 5 November 1847; copy also in R.A. E 42/7.
86 Wellington papers, Wellington to Prince Albert, 8 November 1847; copy also in R.A. E 43/6.
87 Wellington papers, Wellington to Ripon, 3 November 1843.
88 Second Earl Cathcart papers, J. 43, Trevelyan to Cathcart, 16 February 1853.
89 R.A. E 42/4.
90 R.A. E 42/72, Hardinge to Albert, 11 December 1852.
91 R.A. E 44/89, Hardinge to Albert, 31 January 1853; Hansard, 3rd series, CXXIV, cc 679-80.
92 R.A. E 45/13, Hardinge to Albert, 22 March 1853.
93 *Military Review*, II, p. 176; *N. & M.G.*, 5 March 1853, p. 148; George Higginson, *Seventy-one years of a Guardsman's life*, pp. 71-2.
94 R.A. E 45/25, Hardinge to Albert, 16 April 1853.
95 Seaton papers, Hardinge to Seaton, 4 June 1853; copy also in R.A. E 2/87.
96 W.O. 3/320, p. 253; W.O. 3/321, p. 9; R.A. Add. E/1 no. 152a, memo by Seaton, 3 June 1853; Seaton papers, Seaton to Hardinge, 8 June 1853 (copy in R.A. E 2/88) and 10 June [1853].

97 Seaton papers, Hardinge to Seaton, 16 June 1853; he expressed himself in similar terms to Prince Albert, R.A. E 2/97.
98 T. W. J. Connolly, *History of the Royal Sappers and Miners*, II, pp. 130-5; Charles Macfarlane, *The camp of 1853*, pp. 23, 29-30.
99 *U.S.G.*, 4 June 1853, p. 6.
100 J. H. Stocqueler, *A personal history of the Horse Guards*, p. 211.
101 N.L.S mss 2852, ff. 221-2, memo by R. B. Wood, 25 August 1853; see also Seaton papers, divisional after-order, 18 August 1853.
102 Seaton papers, Jones to Seaton, 19 July 1853; see also *U.S.G.*, 13 August 1853, p. 4; A Regimental Officer, *A few remarks about the British army*, pp. 45-6.
103 R.A. E 2/87, Hardinge to Seaton, 4 June 1853.
104 R.A. E 2/87; N.L.S. mss 1849, f. 24, memo by Brown, 15 February 1854.
105 *British Army Despatch*, 29 July 1853, pp. 486-7.
106 Seaton papers, Brown to Seaton, 22 May 1853.
107 Charles Macfarlane, *The camp of 1853*, pp. 48, 51.
108 *N. & M.G.*, 20 August 1853, p. 536.
109 Seaton papers, Hardinge to Seaton, 18 June 1853.
110 Hardinge papers, Prince Albert to Hardinge, 21 July 1853.
111 W.O. 33/1, pp. 5-9; copy also in R.A. E 45/53.
112 R.A. E 45/49, Hardinge to Albert, 26 August 1853.
113 N.L.S. mss 1848, f. 119, Hardinge to Brown, 28 September 1853.
114 Hardinge papers, Prince Albert to Hardinge, 26, and 27 September 1853.
115 R.A. E 3/8; see also Hardinge papers, Prince Albert to Hardinge, 7 December 1853.
116 Hardinge papers, memo by Hardinge, 22 May 1854.
117 Howard N. Cole, *The story of Aldershot*, p. 29.
118 Ibid., p. 31.
119 Hardinge papers, memo to *Ministère des affaires étrangères* [of Belgium], 26 March 1853; H. B. Harvey, *A visit to the camp of Beverloo*.
120 Bodleian Ms Clarendon Deposit c 4, f. 331, and c 6, ff. 480-1, Hardinge to Clarendon, 31 August and 14 September 1853.
121 Ibid., c 1, ff. 571, 577, Raglan to Clarendon, 10 and 15 August 1853.
122 Hardinge papers, memo by Hardinge, 22 May 1854.
123 Ibid., Hardinge to Prince Albert, 8 July 1854; Newcastle papers, NeC 10701, Smith to Newcastle, 18 October 1854.
124 R.A. G 21/98.
125 *N. & M.G.*, 2 December 1854, p. 77.
126 Newcastle papers, NeC 10058, 10059a, 10060, Hardinge to Newcastle, 8 and 10 February 1854.
127 B.M. Add. Mss 40475, ff. 85, 87, 90, Hardinge to Peel, 30 December 1845.
128 N.L.S. mss 1847, f. 111, Macdonald to Brown, [? April 1844].
129 B.M. Add. Mss 49130, f. 61, C. Napier to G. Arthur, 11 May 1844; for Harry Smith's comparable view, see B.M. Add. Mss 54555, f. 14.
130 Hereford C.R.O., G/IV/A/399, Hardinge to Airey, 8 December 1854.
131 Raglan private papers, 7/196, Raglan to Katherine Somerset, 9 June 1854.

132 Rait, *Life of Gough*, II, p. 222; J. G. A. Baird (ed.), *Private letters of the Marquess of Dalhousie*, pp. 203, 207, 340.
133 George Douglas and George Dalhousie Ramsay (ed.), *The Panmure papers*, I, pp. 321, 432; see also R. J. Lindsay to Colonel Moncrieff, 3 July 1855, quoted in Sotheby catalogue, sale of 3 December 1974, lot 100; Newcastle papers NeC 9940a, Raglan to Newcastle, 23 December 1854; N.A.M. 6210/9415, Claremont to Wetherall, 16 February 1855.
134 Douglas and Ramsay (ed.), *Panmure papers*, I, pp. 265, 282, 287, 297, 391, 406, 412, 418, 438-9,472.
135 Marquess of Anglesey, *History of British cavalry*, II, pp. 68, 94, 96-7, 99-100.

CHAPTER 6
MATCHING MANPOWER TO COMMITMENTS

1. *Imperial defence*

If imperial defence had not been the army's main strategic role in the nineteenth century, the regiment would never have occupied so central a position in military reform. For a colonial power, the battalion was a convenient administrative unit: it could be contained in a troopship and it was neither too large for local policing nor too small for independent operations against dissident natives. The professional soldier, isolated for long periods from his homeland, made it the focus of his life. It conferred security, discipline and, as we have seen, benefits and rewards. It directed the careers of its officers: despite the impressions created by slow promotion or by leapfrogging through purchase, in 1871 half the regimental commanding officers had spent all their military lives in the regiments they were then commanding.[1] Regimental soldiering and imperial defence moulded the attitudes of these officers and therefore conditioned their units. Indeed it is a tribute to the Horse Guards' system of half-yearly inspections, and their accompanying confidential reports and returns, that relative uniformity was maintained in an army so widely scattered.[2] The outposts were not bonded by efficient communications or by a well developed staff system. The army's excellence lay in its parts. The nature of its service fitted it for regimental duty in the empire. It did not prepare it for European war.

The extent of the empire presented the army with the need to match commitments to resources. The difficulty of this intensified the focus on imperial defence. In 1792 Britain's overseas territories tied down 15,100 men, and in 1853 the same area held 15,030 (although the distribution was different). But between these years Trinidad, Tobago, St. Lucia, Demerara and Berbice, Malta, the Ionian islands, the west coast of Africa, the Cape, Mauritius, Ceylon, Van Diemen's Land, the west coast of Australia, New Zealand, St. Helena and Hong Kong were added, although only 23,172 men were allocated for their protection. In 1792 India employed 9,513 of the Queen's troops but in 1853, largely owing to the conquests of Gwalior, Scinde and the Punjab, this figure stood at 26,693.[3]

Nonetheless, Joseph Hume monotonously proposed a reduction on the estimates each year, taking the army's 1792 strength, a total of 48,849 men, as his target. Although his motions were never in danger of being passed, they did contribute to a consensus within the Commons that the army was, in Burgoyne's summing up, no more than 'a reserved police for the preservation of internal tranquillity at home and abroad'.[4] By 1823, 147,080 men had been lopped from a wartime strength of 247,113.[5] Wellington told the Prime Minister, Lord Liverpool, that 'we have not even one post throughout the empire sufficiently garrisoned'. He then added, 'The fact is that the British empire is now extended in separate parts to all quarters of the globe; and troops are required in each separate part either to perform the legitimate service of troops, that of defence against the attacks of a foreign enemy, or to preserve the lives and properties of his Majesty's subjects against domestic insurrection and disturbance.'[6] In this context it was wrong, as Palmerston pointed out to the Commons in 1839, to frame an army with reference to peace, when the empire faced it with 'an immediate probability of war'.[7]

The numerical weakness of the army was the single reform most urgently in need of attention. Wellington himself was in the van of the assault, telling Peel in 1839 that an increase in establishment was the basic preliminary without which there was little point in attempting anything else.[8] As Commander-in-Chief he pleaded each year, on the occasion of the estimates being presented in the Commons, with the Secretary of State. Lord Stanley was warned that invasion by France was imminent, that the whole empire was exposed, that even without war colonial reliefs were almost impossible to contrive, and that, in the face of continued indifference by Parliament, Wellington could do little else than wash his hands of responsibility for the disasters that would overtake Britain.[9] Grey, Stanley's successor, was similarly berated. In 1848 the army was 'the minimum of the lowest Peace Establishment, and provides ... in no case for the purpose of defence': Grey's response to this particular appeal was to propose a reduction of 7,000.[10]

Of course the government's position had to be tempered by economic and political considerations. The result of this annual tug-of-war was a fluctuation in strengths that seemed superficial but which in the context of the tight margins imposed by the small size of the available force made contingency planning impossible. A difference of even 200, as between 1846 and 1847, was enough to disturb the rhythm the Horse Guards wished to impose. Nor did an average of about 100,000 men (excluding India) compare favourably with the European armies of the time. In 1854 the French, with only Algeria as a colony, were reckoned to have about 570,000 men under arms. Austria had 350,000, Prussia 200,000 and Russia 820,000.[11] The British total was even more paltry if the non-effectives are deducted — deserters, prisoners, invalids, and recruiting parties sent out by regiments. In 1846 as many as 819 parties were out, each formed on average of five other ranks[12] and in the same year 2,417 men deserted.[13] Admittedly the number of parties was abnormally high but the total of deserters is on the low side, and between them, without even considering the ravages of sickness, drink or active service, they account for 6,512 men for the year.

The strength of the army, 1830-54

1835	109,285	(18,948)
1836	109,369	(18,948)
1837	109,405	(18,948)
1838	120,961	(18,949)
1839	124,838	(19,751)
1840	131,112	(26,855)
1841	130,277	(28,217)
1842	141,089	(29,583)
1843	118,628	(27,794)
1844	138,680	(28,538)
1845	138,461	(28,538)
1846	148,760	(28,617)
1847	150,486	(28,617)
1848	152,870	(24,198)
1849	148,704	(27,459)
1850	143,850	(29,617)
1851	143,751	(30,915)
1852	145,522	(31,105)
1853	149,089	(29,706)
1854	152,780	(28,955)

Note: These figures include Ordnance troops, which were taken separately from the Army Estimates. The totals in parentheses, which are included in the main figures, are the Queen's troops in India, whose cost was borne by the East India Company, and which were not voted by Parliament.
Source: P.P. 1859, session 2, vol. XVII, pp. 8-25; see also P.P. 1851, VII, p. 6.

1841 was a crisis year that highlighted the hand-to-mouth expedients dictated by undermanning. Hardinge, then Secretary at War, had as his ideal thirty-two battalions of infantry at home and seventy-one abroad. But the Papineau rebellion of 1838 and the threat of its support from the United States meant that the customary nine battalions in Canada had to be supplemented by ten more of the line and two of Foot Guards. In 1839 additional battalions were required over and above the normal twenty stationed in India, since there were expeditions to China and Afghanistan. Between 1838 and December 1840 the East India Company's requirement of British troops increased from an abnormal low of 14,780 to 21,362, or twenty-two battalions of 971 men each.[14] The result was that, whereas in 1828 33,556 men had been at home and 27,864 in colonies other than India, in 1839 the proportion was reversed, with 32,321 abroad and 28,277 in the United Kingdom.[15] In all, therefore, a mere nineteen battalions were at home in 1841, of which only eleven had been back for more than a year and none for more than four.[16]

This situation was intolerable because it not only left Britain herself exposed to attack but also allowed her no disposable force in case of fresh crises. A regiment on return from abroad was often deprived of its veterans, who had either died or had 'volunteered' into other units staying in the colony. To absorb its vast intake of recruits and recover its health took a year. Eight of the nineteen battalions in Britain in 1841 could not, therefore, be considered as fit for service.

Numerically during the 1840s the situation improved. At the end of the decade 39,820 men were to be found at home and 26,680 in colonies other than India. Since 1828 the garrison in Jamaica had been reduced by four-fifths, those in the Ionian Islands, Nova Scotia and the Windward and Leeward Islands halved and that in St. Helena ended. Part of the reductions in the West Indies was attributable to a concentration of troops in Bermuda and Barbados, so as to improve both training and health. This was a measure proposed by Whittingham in 1837 but, since it was dependent on the constant availability of a steam vessel (to allow rapid deployment in the adjacent islands) for its implementation, it was not fully carried through until 1853.[17] In addition, not least because of improving relations with the United States, there had been a swing away from the Atlantic and the western hemisphere, in itself a relic of Pittite strategy. But the army's colonial burden was thereby only partly reduced. Expansion to the Indus meant that 24,000 Queen's troops were in India, the Kaffir wars had doubled the garrison at the Cape, Australia and New Zealand had absorbed a further 1,000, and Hong Kong had been acquired. In addition these stations were much further removed from Britain than the western colonies, and the time spent confined in a ship on the long haul round the Cape added to the number of ineffectives. In 1841, at any one time, 600 men were on passage: in 1845, 3,140.[18]

The expense in transport, in terms of man-hours as well as money, helps explain the length of time spent by any one regiment in the same station in the 1820s and '30s. Although the Quarter Master General tried to keep the period in a colony to ten years, in the case of India it was nearer twenty, and thus a battalion probably spent four out of thirty-four years at home.[19] Furthermore, some battalions moved from one tropical climate to another. In 1836 seventeen regiments went (via Britain) from the East to the West Indies, or vice versa. There was no necessity for the two postings to be successive — of the 2,024 years of service by the 103 battalions between 1818 and 1837, 1,404 were passed in the colonies, of which 770 were in those classified as tropical.[20] But the rotation was based on the dates of arriving and leaving Britain rather than on the category of colony to which the regiment was dispatched. In addition the military press was probably correct in detecting favouritism in the movements of the more fashionable battalions.

Over a hundred years such inequities might be balanced out, but in the immediate run they had a harsh effect on a battalion's efficiency for the field. Between 1819 and 1827 the 92nd Highlanders in Jamaica lost 860 men, women and children, including seventeen officers — 'more by fever than were killed in action during all the war with France'.[21] The unaccustomed climes of China proved as deadly: between July 1842 and February 1844, 432 of 766 other ranks in the 98th succumbed.[22] The 78th Highlanders lost three officers, 532 other ranks, 68 women and 134 children in eight months in Scinde.[23] The demands for troops posed by the East India Company in 1836 made it seem likely that the 9th Foot would serve in the subcontinent from 1832 to 1856 and the 4th Foot until 1858.[24] Consequently, if a carefully nurtured regimental system was not smashed by disease, it would instead be forfeit to the veterans who would volunteer to stay in their country of adoption when the regiment went home.

Until 1835 the impressions gained of a colony were based more on isolated epidemics rather than on a balanced, long-term picture. Sir James McGrigor, on his appointment after Waterloo as Director General of the Army Medical Department, had instituted a system of half-yearly returns of the sickness of troops at home and abroad, so that an empirical basis could be established for preventive medicine in garrisons. At the same time, Dr. Henry Marshall began to amass similar, if incomplete, statistics. As a result of their publication in 1835,[25] Howick commissioned Marshall and Lieutenant A. M. Tulloch to collate the evidence amassed since 1817.[26] The results for the West Indies were published in 1837.[27]

The report's impact on diet, barrack construction and other living conditions has already been noted, but its implications spread even to the regimental system itself. In many cases suspicions were confirmed: mortality in Gibraltar was 21·4 per 1,000 but only 13 (less than Britain) if epidemics in 1828 and 1834 were discounted. In Malta venereal disease ran at 20 per cent a year, but in other respects the rate of sickness there and in the Ionian islands was similar to the Rock. By contrast Sierra Leone had a death rate of 483 per 1,000, and in 1825 deaths had reached 783 per 1,000. The West Indies, for so long the white soldier's dread, ceased to be an amorphous mass. Antigua and Montserrat (40·6 per 1,000), Barbados (58·8), Grenada (61·8) and St. Vincent (54·9) were distinguished as relatively healthy. Tobago (152·8), St. Lucia (122·8), Dominica (137·4), the Bahamas (200) and Jamaica (128, but as high as 140·6 in the main barracks at Up Park) pointed the contrast. The withdrawal of garrisons from certain West Indian stations and their concentration in the healthy locations was a direct result of the report. The overall figures showed an average annual mortality of 15·9 per 1,000 in Britain, 21·1 in the temperate colonies (America and the Mediterranean), and 63·4 in the tropics. Furthermore it was clearly demonstrated that in the Windward and Leeward Islands troops did not profit from acclimatisation but on occasion were more prone to disease. This was perhaps attributable to boredom and drink, and two main conclusions about foreign service were clear: that it was in the best interests of the men's health and therefore of the regiment's integrity that postings to tropical climates be kept short, and secondly that they be alternated with service in temperate stations, thus equalising the burden of duty.

As soon as Howick had the section of the report devoted to the West Indies, he despatched memoranda to the Secretary of State on reducing the force in that area, to the Board of Ordnance on barracks, to the Treasury on diet and to the Commander-in-Chief on exercise and amusement.[28] Vivian at the Ordnance agreed with the need to address the problem but, in spite of the statistical evidence, maintained that long exposure to tropical climates encouraged resistance to disease. He suggested that regiments stay in one place but that a constant flow of men be maintained between it and its depot.[29] At the Horse Guards, Hill was as anxious as Howick that the ten years spent in the West Indies should be reduced to five, but was at a loss as to how to effect it.

Tulloch himself came to the rescue with an article in the *United Service Journal*. Thirty-seven infantry regiments were, he calculated, at healthy stations, the same number at unhealthy, twenty-six at home and three at sea. Eighteen of these had gone from one unhealthy station to another via four years' home duty, whereas sixteen had been totally exempt from tropical service. Double tours of the latter wore men out sooner and made for an unfit regiment and, in the long term, a higher pension bill. Over twenty-five years, only 136 out of 1,000 could reckon to survive such treatment, whereas in a favoured battalion 691 did. Tulloch therefore urged three separate foreign tours, each totalling ten years abroad. The Atlantic circuit should be made up of four years in the Mediterranean, three in the West Indies and three in America. To the east, India should count as a complete ten-year tour in itself, and the remaining stations be divided into New South Wales three years, Ceylon or Mauritius four, the Cape or St. Helena three.[30]

Howick proposed Tulloch's Atlantic circuit in exactly its author's form and Hill expressed his 'entire concurrence'.[31] Although put into operation immediately, its implementation was threatened by two short-term problems. The Papineau rebellion drew a disproportionate number of battalions to America and the end of the circuit, while others, recently sent to the Mediterranean after long bouts of tropical service, found themselves at the beginning. Fortunately Howick rode roughshod over the temporary sufferings thereby caused to individual regiments. His intentions were aided by the augmentations of the early 1840s, which created more battalions, and thus meant that home service could be kept at five years and foreign at ten.

A formalised system of rotation was not introduced for the eastern hemisphere. Hill had opposed Howick's suggestion of service in the Cape leading on to time in India, as it had already been found to break men's healths before they even reached the subcontinent. The same proved to be true of transferring from Australia to India. However, the press repeatedly urged the virtues of evolving some sort of scheme, and on Grey's appointment as Secretary of State the issue was revived, Tulloch in 1846 suggesting a rotation from India to Australia or South

Africa.[32] In 1848 Fox Maule pressed that two tours be adopted, one taking in the East Indies (ten years) and then Australia (three to five years) and the other Ceylon and Hong Kong (three or four years), Mauritius (three years) and the Cape (a final three years).[33] In May 1849 Grey proposed to Willoughby Gordon that regiments serving in India should go on to Australia, New Zealand or the Cape, but the Quarter Master General anticipated the greater likelihood of active service in the subcontinent disturbing such an arrangement.[34] An inclusive rotation of Australia, India and the Cape, giving a total of fourteen years, was viewed as too long by Tulloch.[35] However, in July, Grey put to Wellington his idea of an eastern hemisphere rotation, whereby regiments would go on to Australia, the Cape or New Zealand, with a view to encouraging men to take their discharges and settle in those colonies. As with limited enlistment, Wellington was naturally frightened of losing old soldiers by such a scheme, but he also envisaged that exception would be taken to further foreign service after the demands of India, especially when it would probably make the target of a maximum of ten years abroad unattainable.[36]

However, although the eastern hemisphere did not have a rotation system as such, it did profit from the general trend. The Duke always maintained the ideal of a ten-year maximum whatever a regiment's station. Although not uniformly achieved, by 1848 no regiment had been abroad for more than twelve years[37] and a proportion of ten years abroad and five at home for the 'inner service' was matched by fifteen and seven and a half for India and the more distant colonies.[38] The results could be seen in the dramatically improved health of the army. For the year 1851-2, mortality in Jamaica stood at 44 per 1,000 and for the rest of the West Indies at 22·1. The average in India for the previous thirty years had been 74·2, but had now sunk to 48·5. Even the temperate zones had registered an improvement, the American colonies falling from 21·2 in the Marshall and Tulloch report to 14, and the Mediterranean stations from 23·5 to 12·7.[39] On a world-wide aggregate, this was equivalent to the saving of a whole battalion a year.

The declining rate of mortality among British soldiers in tropical colonies sprang also from the fact that there were fewer stationed in them. Marshall's and Tulloch's statistics had confirmed the greater resistance of the indigenous population to disease. Sepoys in India died at a rate of thirteen per 1,000, lower even than British soldiers at home, and in the West Indies mortality in negro regiments ran at between 46·3 (St. Kitts) and 28·4 (Grenada). These figures were high but infinitely better than totals in the hundreds suffered by European regiments. Howick therefore stressed to Glenelg 'the importance of substituting as far as it may be practicable a force composed of Natives of a Tropical Climate for British Regiments in these stations'.[40]

Two West India Regiments had emerged after 1815, the First scattered in nine detachments over the Leeward islands, the Second in the Bahamas and Honduras, and a joint depot company was maintained at Sierra Leone for recruiting. Although negroes were found to be efficient and well disciplined soldiers, the West India Regiments were little more than garrison troops. If real trouble developed, the European troops concentrated on Barbados were to be employed.

The desire to economise in British lives was also applied to West Africa. Of 1,658 Europeans sent to serve in the Royal African Corps between 1822 and 1830, 1,298 perished.[41] The corps was therefore filled with negroes, who succumbed at the lower rate of thirty per thousand. However, in this case, the soldiers were so close to the indigenous population, the officers so reluctant to serve in the climate and the force of example of European regiments so utterly lacking that the corps' commanding officer recommended it rotate with the West India Regiments across the Atlantic. In the light of the Marshall and Tulloch report, the War Office and Horse Guards were already keen to expand the West India Regiments, and therefore in 1842 the Royal African Corps became the Third West India Regiment, six companies from the three regiments serving in turn in Africa for a three to four year spell.[42] However, the officers were only obliged to serve a year at a time, and were granted leave in England on the way back. Therefore the West India Regiments lost the services of six captains and eighteen subalterns, divided equally between the sea, England and Africa. Even without this problem officers tended to use the cheaper commissions of the West India Regiments as vehicles for promotion, and the regiments were therefore in large measure deprived of the services of the one body that might have brought them to the standard of the line. Consequently, in 1849, the Gold Coast Corps was established;[43] officering it proved to be as difficult as its predecessor but at least the efficiency of the West India Regiments was no longer jeopardised.

A similar rotation was evolved to cover the enormous casualties suffered by British troops stationed in China. In 1847 the Ceylon Rifles, formed in 1796 and recruited from Malays, sent a detachment to Hong Kong.[44] The Malays took exception to being uprooted. The three-year rotation introduced in consequence[45] meant that, like the West India

Regiments, the united capabilities of the corps never had any chance of being developed, detached duty being the norm and being exacerbated by frequent sea voyages.

A similar corps, which could also be considered fit only for garrison duties, was the Royal Malta Fencibles. It was formed as a police force but the fact that its mortality was only nine per 1,000, as against 18·7 for British regiments, encouraged its adoption in 1839 for more military purposes.[46] However, the government refused to augment it,[47] and its soldierly pretensions do not seem to have been very serious. Unlike the West India Regiments, its officers were local Maltese and did not exchange into other units.

The condemnation of the military capabilities of these regiments must not be allowed to obscure the fact that, owing to their knowledge of the country and their hardiness when exposed to its elements, native troops could have a tactical role outwith the garrison. Those who knew the West India Regiments best frequently pointed out that the jungle was the negro's *métier*, and that therefore he should be trained and equipped to that end and not to fighting in the serried ranks adapted to the European line. Similarly in New Zealand the fighting virtues of the Maori, if they could only be harnessed, suggested a solution to the problems of bush warfare. Tribal loyalties and traditional enmities might be the basis for enlisting the aid of at least part of the local population.

The best example of this was to be found at the Cape. Sir Harry Smith, mindful of the role played by native troops in the conquest of the Sikhs, anticipated that the Kaffirs who elected to side with the British would be 'formed on the Principles of the Sepoy army'.[48] The principal permanent local forces in South Africa were the Hottentots of the Cape Mounted Rifles. They were said to be tough, good-humoured, keen-eyed, tolerant of fatigue, hunger and thirst, good trackers and possessed — naturally enough — of a sound knowledge of the country. In 1833 Sir Lowry Cole reported on the value of the Cape Mounted Rifles' contribution and urged an increase in their strength.[49] His successors in the governorship echoed him, and in 1847, on Sir Henry Pottinger's request, Grey approved a second regiment.[50] In the event it was never formed.

Grey's enthusiasm for the Cape Mounted Rifles sprang from his faith in local regiments as part of a co-ordinated strategy of imperial defence. He alone seems to have been trying to formulate a pattern for future development, so that budgetary and manpower problems could be overcome and at the same time colonial crises met and absorbed.[51] At its roots lay the Royal Navy. British sea power was used to justify the withdrawal of troops so as to create a larger disposable force in the United Kingdom: 'The policy upon which we ought to proceed in these days of easy communication by steam between different parts of the Empire, is not to scatter our force more than can possibly be avoided, but to keep a larger reserve in this country (our citadel, as it is well termed by Sir J. Graham), ready to be sent at a short notice wherever danger may threaten.'[52] It was a theory to which Stanley also subscribed.[53] Wellington was not slow to point out the investment in steamships that such a policy demanded,[54] but Burgoyne was to emerge as its really vociferous opponent. Overlooking possible technological developments, the Inspector General of Fortifications saw land defences as not merely cheaper to maintain but also safer, since an enemy fleet need only have the initiative for a brief period in order to effect a landing.[55]

Grey did not go so far as to propose the removal of all land forces from the colonies. A striking force from Britain might be unacclimatised and would certainly need a base. However, the normal daily benefits of a continued military presence — protection against insurgents and the execution of police duties — were conferred on the local population alone. The advance of free trade and the advocacy of colonial self-government carried the corollary that the colonies should be responsible for a share of imperial defence. Grey, as an imperialist and free-trader, was anxious to progress the idea. However, he feared that, in the case of Canada in particular, an over-insistence on the point would drive the colonists to rebellion. These worries were perhaps exaggerated: European settlers were much more aware of the values of military protection than their cousins at home.

In 1846 Russell proposed that the colonies should organise their own militia, erect their own fortifications and maintain the British troops sent to defend them: they might be allowed M.P.s in proportion to their contribution to defence.[56] By 1849 Malta, Mauritius, Ceylon, British Guiana, the Ionian Islands and Gibraltar were all contributing to the cost of military expenditure. But specific problems in each outpost moderated the general principle. Only in Australia was a real attempt made to implement the model, and even there it was argued that, as the home government established it as a convict settlement, it retained an obligation to defend it. Nevertheless the fortifications were handed over, and in return for their upkeep a fixed number of imperial troops were provided, with additional ones available at the colony's expense. In Canada, Grey planned to concentrate the Queen's troops on Quebec and Kingston, and leave the rest to auxiliaries, but fears of separatism and

American aggression made progress slow.⁵⁷ Frequent frontier problems at the Cape might have been expected to justify that colony's continuance on the imperial exchequer. But the Kaffirs wars, particularly in 1851-2, coincided with fears of French invasion, and, by concentrating troops in one colony, the empire's overall capability was weakened. Furthermore the behaviour of the Boers encouraged the conclusion that, since they did not have to meet the cost of war, they were in consequence more reckless in incurring its risks. Both Grey and Newcastle urged self-protection on the Cape farmer, thus ironically fostering those military qualities which were to be turned against the imperial troops at the end of the century.⁵⁸

As an advocate both of colonial self-government and of the creation of a disposable reserve, Grey favoured a specific application of colonial funds in the maintenance of local regiments. 'The only practicable mode of reducing the expenditure of the Army,' he wrote in 1837, 'is to increase the use made of local corps for the defence of the colonies.'⁵⁹ By 1846 he seemed to envisage not so much an overall decline in numbers in colonial garrisons as a change in composition. More colonial corps were required. They should be of two kinds: 'those in which both men and officers are of British origin, and those of which the officers only, and sometimes not even the officers, are British'.⁶⁰ But Wellington was opposed to either category: he told Lord John Russell in 1846, 'I feel great jealousy of Local Armies,' citing the American rebellion and correctly sensing a similar danger in India.⁶¹ Most brittle were the tribal enmities on which the South African forces were based. The expansion of the Cape Mounted Rifles in 1837 introduced unreliable elements into the regiment, which the officers were not equal to controlling. However, mutiny the following year was not interpreted as a warning. In 1851 desertions from the corps reached epidemic proportions, and, on Smith's advice, 'these volatile, fickle, and credulous Hottentots'⁶² were replaced by Europeans.

The Horse Guards were as dubious of the value of white local regiments. Although their loyalty was less suspect, they were not available to reinforce other parts of the empire and could therefore only be viewed as an addition to the line rather than a replacement. Because they were sedentary, they were more likely to lapse into inefficiency. Moreover, the homogeneity of the army suffered. Where climatic conditions demanded that for health reasons native troops be employed, the Horse Guards accepted it. But European regiments in moderate climates should be regular troops. Grey acknowledged both criticisms of his two categories of colonial corps — that natives were unfaithful and

Europeans inefficient — to the extent that he conceded that local regiments should not be in a majority on any one station.[63]

However, garrison duties often only served to warp the qualities of even the best line units. Detached service, an inhospitable climate or limited manoeuvring space were each of them sufficient reason for accepting that second-class troops had an effective role to play, not only in themselves but also to protect the efficiency of the regulars.

When Howick arrived at the War Office, the only European troops employed in colonial garrisons and not for general service were the Newfoundland Veteran Companies. These were distinguished by their general inefficiency and in particular by the incompetence of their officers. Thus, in terms of cost effectiveness, Veteran Companies did not please the Secretary at War, and he opposed Hill's suggestion that the principle be extended to St. Helena.[64] In consequence, when a corps was raised for St. Helena in 1841-2, it was formed from recruits enlisted for general service. However, it confirmed the doubts of the Horse Guards about European colonial regiments: discipline was bad and the principle of recruiting in competition with the line and the East India Company undesirable. In 1849 the terms of service were altered to embrace only the island itself, and thus the anomaly which in practice existed was confirmed. If extended, European colonial corps on this basis would destroy the homogeneity of the line and undermine the supply of men to the regular army.

A solution to Howick's quandary was presented by the examples of Russia and Austria. They had formed 'military colonies' on their disputed frontiers, in order to create an indigenous militia to meet any incursions. In 1837 Gordon sent Howick a book on the subject, suggesting its application to Canada.[65] The ground was fertile. In December 1835 Howick 'had ... a long conversation with George Grey about the possibility of forming colonial corps, & agreed with him that my favourite scheme of a militia settled on allotments of land and serving one or two days in the week might be tried with advantage in Canada'.[66] In addition to its specific military functions, such a force could develop land which had previously been neglected by settlers, and so, by conferring the economic benefits of stability and civilisation, curb the activities of marauders or semi-feudal societies.

Although Howick saw it as a general scheme, applicable to much of the empire, special circumstances favoured North America as the point of departure. The frontier with the United States was not settled in the extreme west and could only be regarded as fluid in the centre. War between the two countries seemed possible. The permanent maintenance of a large number of regular battalions in North America could not itself cover such a large front, and at the same time higher wages and promises of unlimited opportunities drew deserters across the St. Lawrence in increasing numbers. A buffer of military settlers would therefore help solve several problems.

In 1836 Howick proposed the organisation of a battalion, service in which would be a reward for at least fourteen years completed in the line. Its members were to be encouraged to farm, and were to be quartered by companies in villages, within a small enough radius to allow the battalion to assemble once a week. The pay proposed was 15d. a day, so that membership would be a reward for good conduct. Hill agreed on the need for some check to the desertion rate in Canada but had his doubts about this scheme. Militarily it did not augur well for soldiers to be so dispersed, a problem that would be exacerbated as men were discharged and their replacements have to be put on land further out. If Howick's hope of it being attractive to well conducted men was realised, the line battalions would suffer. Sir John Colborne, then Lieutenant Governor of Upper Canada, agreed with Hill: the example of the commuted pensioners was too vivid to suggest that senior soldiers would be any better at settling. Both he and the Commander-in-Chief preferred that those discharged soldiers who settled in Canada be attached as supernumeraries to a regular regiment.[67]

By the following year, however, Colborne had undergone a change of heart. Furthermore, Charles Grey wrote as a regimental commander in Montreal to support his brother. He doubted the possibility of procuring enough men of fourteen years' service, and therefore suggested that married men of seven years' service be acceptable.[68] By now, however, Howick himself had taken fright. The original scheme was designed to create a force that would not only be efficient but also cheap. The consequences of his brother's and Colborne's modifications were that rations would be given to families and the troops would have to be paid all the time, whether serving or not. The spectre of the Veteran Companies arose, and the scheme was postponed on the grounds of expense.[69]

As the example of the St. Helena Corps suggests, the essence of Howick's scheme, for military settlers rather than for regular soldiers with limited obligations, was lost on his resignation. Lord John Russell drove the project on but the pay was kept at 13d. per day, so that the surplus could go towards the purchase of land on the soldier's discharge.[70] Although a man was to be encouraged in his trade and fifteen years' good character was still required for admission, the regulations promulgated for the formation of the Royal Canadian Rifles in 1841 smacked of a regular corps rather than of a framework for a military colony. Only twelve women per 100 men were allowed, the officers formed part of the line and the men were liable for service anywhere in North America. Howick had regarded the award of land as an essential incentive to good conduct and as a means to the creation of a reserve. The unit as formed had no permanent home, the reward was therefore minimal and in consequence a second-rate line regiment had been created with no balancing compensations.

Gloomy prognostications about the regiment proved amply justified. The officers were too old, and the men given to drink. In 1848, 108 — about a tenth of the strength — were discharged as unfit before their full ten years' service was completed.[71] The benefits the regiment offered were too few to attract sufficient volunteers. Commanding officers may have been reluctant to part with their best men and therefore discouraged the idea, but it required little intelligence for the soldier to see that there was a good chance that his wife would not receive rations, and that, if an n.c.o., he would lose his rank and its pension. Opening recruiting to the United Kingdom as well as Canada, and allowing men to volunteer after twelve years' service[72] could not therefore save the situation, and in 1852 the establishment was reduced from ten to six companies.[73]

Grey's return to power as Secretary of State in 1846 enabled a fresh approach to be made on the subject of military colonies. In April that year Edward Gibbon Wakefield had written to Sidney Herbert suggesting the military colonisation of the Cape, Australia and New Zealand by regiments of married men, on the lines of the military cordon established between Austria-Hungary and Turkey. Grey's known interest in the subject ensured that the letter was forwarded to him, and he duly commended Wakefield's suggestion.[74]

In September Grey lighted on the idea of two to three thousand pensioners each being sent to New Zealand, the Cape, Jamaica, Canada and the North American provinces.[75] The indefatigable Tulloch was commissioned to produce a memorandum, in which he urged that the continued burden of the non-effective list could be diminished by using the pensioners as military colonists. At home, the pensioner was the first to lose his job, as he was unskilled, not eligible for poor relief, and old, and therefore tended to wander destitute round the country, a bad advertisement for the army, open to incitement and unavailable for reserved service. A body of men was thus ready to go out, and could be supplemented by a rotation system which brought a regiment to a suitable colony last before returning home and where free discharges might be given to those desirous to settle.[76]

In his cabinet memorandum on the army of October 1846, Grey proposed two distinct European colonial forces. Pensioners on the lines advocated by Tulloch should be quartered 'in some of the more healthy colonies'. Secondly he reverted to the original scheme, 'unfortunately lost sight of', for the Canadian corps. The objects of this regiment and others like it 'were to make admission to such corps a reward to good soldiers of the line, and at the same time to make them the means of increasing in the colonies the population of British origin, closely connected with the mother country by the ties of family and kindred'.

In the event Wellington's opposition to colonial regiments and his fear of the loss of his veterans manifested in the debate on limited enlistment meant that Grey's two categories became suffused in one, that of the pensioners. He did, however, continue to incorporate with it the schemes of rotation and limited enlistment. Soldiers should be encouraged to take their discharges in the colonies, with a claim to a deferred pension if they enrolled. The last colony of foreign service must therefore be Canada, the Cape or the Antipodes; the returning regiment would be but a skeleton and consequently cheaper to bring home. Especially after 1847 and the introduction of limited enlistment, Wellington had no desire to encourage premature retirement from the army, but, although he checked Grey's idea as a general principle, the Secretary of State implemented it with regard to New Zealand and Australia.[77]

The former of these two colonies was the first to benefit from Grey's imagination. He proposed that the pensioner be employed on public works for the first year, after which the pensioner's acre of land should be productive, and his family established in the cottage provided. The pensioner would have an absolute right to the property after seven years if he drilled twelve days a year.[78] In October 1846 Russell and Wellington both approved the scheme in outline. Six hundred were required and the offers of service proved so numerous that the upper age limit was reduced from forty-eight to forty-five.[79] Before their departure, some elementary instruction in Maori warfare was provided. However, newspaper reports suggested that the scheme had its imperfections: discipline was already waning by 1850, with the result that the scattered forces were hard to assemble, and old soldiers lacked the resource or the skills required of good farming settlers.

Nonetheless Grey received sufficiently favourable comments to confirm him in his, no doubt, preconceived notions. By March 1850 thirty pensioners had been settled in the Falkland islands, 150 in Van Diemen's Land, eighty at Hudson's Bay and 140 in western Australia.[80] By November 1851 there were 1,180 pensioners in New Zealand and 480 in Canada.[81] In 1850 pensioners from the West India regiments were enrolled in Gambia[82] and in 1853 were actually engaged in operations against the king of Keenung.

However, South Africa was to point the limitations to Grey's hopes. In 1848 he proposed to Smith that a corps of pioneers serve at the Cape on a similar basis to the pensioners, but to do three months on public works for every one month's soldiering.[83] Officer procurement had proved the great stumbling block to the pensioners' efficiency, and Smith correctly foresaw that a body such as Grey proposed would be useless. 'Example, precept, honour, good officers and non-commissioned officers' were the binding forces in a regiment, and Smith felt that pensioners alone might be so imbued with these qualities as to remain of some use in an extended colony if attacked.[84] Grey agreed. Thus in 1848 all men whose regiments were due to leave the colony were allowed to take their discharge and settle. Sixty of the 91st did so, and most of these old soldiers were established in four villages on the Cape eastern frontier. On Christmas Day 1850 they were surprised and massacred, almost to a man.

In essence, because of their own failings and the lack of officer-settlers, pensioners could never be a front line against a native uprising. However, they could perhaps form a reserve for a regular force. The 522 pensioners in Van Diemen's Land were a valuable barrier between the convicts and the recently discovered gold; those in New Zealand had relieved 800 regular troops; the 600 enrolled in Canada had enabled the reduction of the Royal Canadian Rifles by four companies. Administratively the pensioners made sense, if not militarily. They were, however, more than an interesting symptom of a desire to evolve an integrated system of colonial defence: they were also in a sense the forerunners of the Australian, New Zealand and Canadian forces of the two world wars.

2. *Home defence*

The attempt to construct a rationalised system of imperial defence was not simply an end in itself. The underlying purpose was to release as many troops as possible for service in the United Kingdom, not only so as to have a disposable force for the colonies but also — and more important — to be able to counter the French invasion which steamships seemed to have made more likely. In 1828 33,556 soldiers had been at home but at the height of the garrisoning crisis in 1839 only 28,277 men remained to deal with any threat from Europe. In the ensuing decade the forces in the colonies (including India) declined from 52,680 to 46,940, while those in Britain sprang from 28,277 to 52,460.[85]

Grey's imaginative schemes must bear responsibility for much of this achievement, but just as important was Wellington's constant pressure. As early as 1824, when Master General of the Ordnance, the Duke had envisaged 10,000 French crossing to attack unopposed the arsenals of Portsmouth, Sheerness and Pembroke.[86] The decline in Anglo-French relations in 1844 after the Tahiti incident was rapidly followed by the publication of the Prince de Joinville's proposed plan for an invasion of Britain. Wellington told Peel that he took de Joinville's pamphlet seriously,[87] and he was supported by Gordon, who after consultation with the Admiralty reported that 8,000 French infantry could steam from Cherbourg alone.[88]

Britain's coastal defences had been inspected in 1838, on Hussey Vivian's initiative, but Vivian himself was inclined to pooh-pooh the danger. In his view the main point was that Britain's coasts would be safe if the Royal Navy continued to control the Channel. This in turn might be dependent on the security of the Channel Islands and he therefore thought that they alone should be the focus of serious attention.[89] His successor at the Ordnance, Sir George Murray, set up a secret committee on coastal defences and devoted considerable attention not only to the fortifications of the Channel Islands but also to those of the United Kingdom, asking for reports on their battle worthiness and consulting the Admiralty on their use.[90] The Duke therefore opened a lengthy correspondence with his Peninsular colleague, each of them sending copies of their memoranda to Peel. In late September 1845 Wellington went on a personal tour of the south coast, which only served to confirm him in his gloomy prognosis. Both he and Murray were old, and the latter felt that, although their expertise was unlikely to be available against the French, they could at least leave behind 'a well considered plan for the organization and prompt augmentation of a sufficient army — and substantial military works to aid the endeavours of the troops, and give solidity to the system of defence'.[91]

However, Peel thought war with France extremely unlikely.[92] Furthermore he was anxious to balance the budget, and, although agreeing on the need for some improvement, was not disposed to panic. What the government envisaged was a process of improvement to the dilapidated south-coast fortifications, albeit gradually done to avoid alarming the French.

The change of ministry in 1846 brought a quickening of tempo. Murray's replacement by Anglesey left Wellington with as strong a supporter at the Ordnance; Palmerston, the new Home Secretary, had likened the advent of steam to a bridge across the Channel; all three felt that in Russell, the Prime Minister, they had an ally. In November 1846 Sir John Burgoyne, independently of Wellington, wrote a memorandum on a possible war with France, and called immediately for a disposable force at home of 30,000 men, expandable to 60,000 in war, together with a militia and forts on the vital coastal points. Palmerston and Anglesey presented Burgoyne's case to the cabinet.[93] A copy went to the Commander-in-Chief, who replied in his most famous statement of the problem, expressing his entire concurrence with Burgoyne's views and reiterating his earlier arguments. He concluded with the emotional sentences: 'I am bordering on seventy seven years of age passed in honor! I hope that the Almighty may protect me from being the witness of a tragedy which I cannot persuade my contemporaries to take measures to avert.'[94]

Throughout 1847 the administration focused — at least for peacetime — an almost unprecedented amount of attention on the army. Grey's cabinet memorandum of 1846, the limited enlistment debate and the fear of invasion, all heightened the tension. Russell himself acknowledged the need for 60,000–70,000 regulars at home and for the creation of an army reserve.[95] A French observer, commenting on the debate on the army estimates, spoke of 'ces manifestations, d'un ordre tout nouveau', which augured 'une révolution complète du système militaire anglais': *pace* Peel's worries of 1845, he even considered possible a British invasion of France.[96] In October, Grey feared that on the question of home defence the majority of the cabinet were prepared 'to plunge into very ruinous expense'.[97]

Then the bubble burst. In January 1848 *The Morning Chronicle* published Wellington's letter to Burgoyne of the previous year. Although he had at last awoken his contemporaries to the dangers which had so preoccupied him, the Duke was offended by the accusations of alarmism and denied that he had sought its publication.[98] In the Commons, Russell found that his request for an increase in income tax to cover defence expenditure mustered little support. The government was released from its quandary by Louis Philippe's fall and the removal of the immediate danger. At the same time, in his dudgeon, Wellington's pronouncements of impending catastrophe suddenly ceased. The only tangible product was the organisation of the dockyard workers into battalions, giving a force of 9,800 men. By 1850 even the *United Service Magazine* could criticise Sir Francis Head's book, *The Defenceless State of Great Britain*, as appealing too much to ridicule by overstating its case.[99] A second memorandum by Burgoyne, written in May 1850, which anticipated a French invading force of 100,000 men, caused scarcely a frisson.[100]

The accession to power of Louis Napoleon revived the question of home defence. The new emperor might be anxious to succeed in the one area where his famous forbear had not. A French parliamentary report on the navy in January 1852 was said to include plans for amphibious operations against Britain.[101] A Swiss officer, Baron Maurice de Sellon, reckoned that France had the means, including the ships, to land 151,800 men, 22,000 cavalry, 450 field guns and 86 siege guns at three points in Britain.[102] Fuel was added to the flames by numerous pamphlets, and in particular by James Fergusson's widely read *Perils of Portsmouth*.

Hardinge himself was as impressed as his predecessor had once been with the imminence of the danger. He revived the committee on coast defences, and personally toured the fortifications on the south coast and in the Channel Islands.[103] At the end of 1852, apparently on Hardinge's instigation,[104] monthly meetings were begun between the Horse Guards, the Home Office and the Ordnance. Although not as regularly constituted as the term would apply, the Council for National Defence[105] also embraced the Secretary at War, the Inspector General of Fortifications, the First Lord of the Admiralty and on occasions the Chancellor of the Exchequer and the Secretary of State for War and the Colonies.[106] The work of the departments was thereby co-ordinated in a way that the divided administration of the armed forces had hitherto precluded, and a united front was presented to the cabinet.

Hardinge certainly made considerable headway, particularly when he was at the Ordnance. But contingency planning for the army was still in its infancy. The navy was indisputably the first line of Britain's security. The importance of the debate on national defence was that it suggested that sea power in itself might provide insufficient insurance; and yet the long-term drain on resources that a large standing army at home would involve did not seem compatible with a peaceful posture or with the wishes of the constitutionalists. Fortifications therefore presented a beguiling alternative to manpower. They would constitute a once-and-for-all investment — a show of militarism sufficient to satiate economists, constitutionalists and free-traders.

Thanks to the Board of Ordnance's involvement, many of the reports on Britain's defences were compiled by the Royal Engineers. They naturally preferred fortifications as the principal means of repelling the French attack. In 1846 Colonel Lewis proposed that south-east England, as lying on the most direct route from France to London, should be fortified by two lines concentric with the coast. The first would run from Chatham to Portsmouth, and have three 'strategical' fortresses between the two flanks; the second inner line would be formed of field fortresses between Canterbury and Chichester, together with larger works at Tunbridge Wells, Cuckfield and Pulborough. The entire proposal was estimated as costing £7 million.[107] In 1852 the memorandum of another sapper, Colonel Jebb, was printed for the attention of the cabinet. He referred with approval to Lewis's report, but advocated three interior lines, the last running from Woolwich to Windsor in order to cover London.[108] Not even the heads of departments were immune from the mania: Murray wanted to construct a ring of works round London,[109] and Wellington's proposals for the defence of the Channel Islands would have cost £5 million to £6 million.[110]

Although born of a limited appreciation of the speed with which developments in technology would outdate any permanent systems, fortification pleased the politicians. Since the country would not tolerate a large standing army, Peel approved the gradual implementation of the proposals of the 1844 committee on coast defences. Between 1843 and 1847 annual expenditure on Ordnance works for home defence rose from £87,210 to £294,842.[111]

However, Murray and, to a greater extent, Wellington viewed fortifications as simply a part of the solution. Their policy was to make effective those works that were absolutely necessary. But the Duke's south-coast tour had shown him that 'Infantry can be landed at any time, whatever the state of the wind or tide on any part of the coast from the North Foreland to the Land's End'.[112] Therefore, permanent defences on a practicable scale would only deny the enemy the use of the best facilities: they would not necessarily forestall invasion itself.

The Duke's strategy was to establish a disposable force, which, by its speed of concentration on the decisive point, would compensate for its numerical weakness. Half should be centred on London and half on Dublin.[113] In November 1847, on the Prince Consort's prompting,[114] the Duke brought into play the logistical mastery that had served so well in the Peninsula. The Horse Guards should liaise with the railway companies to prepare rolling stock to carry 10,000 men, 1,000 horses and twelve guns each from Dublin, London and Edinburgh. 'There must be no doubt as to ... the length of time required to move the whole a given space by the Rail Road measurement! The exact place at which the whole can be taken off the carriages, and the length of time which would be required to place each description of arm on the ground from which it would commence its operation.'[115] The South Eastern Railway, in reply to the Duke's questions, calculated that by halving existing services 30,000 men could be moved forty miles in three days.[116]

Hardinge carried on the Duke's strategy. His concern to concentrate troops at Chobham, and later at Aldershot, shows his desire to keep his options open by having a mobile reserve. In particular an adequate force of field artillery would be much more effective than tying up great quantities of garrison artillery in coastal defences that might never be attacked. Hardinge had been impressed by the efficacy of large calibre field artillery in the first Sikh war. He saw a powerful artillery as the best means to check invasion, not least because it would be the arm that the attacking force would lack on first landing. However, the increase in the strength of the Royal Artillery between 1846 and 1848 embraced men, not horses. Thus in 1851, the total disposable strength of the field artillery in the United Kingdom was still a mere forty guns, together with the additional twenty-eight of the Royal Horse Artillery.[117] In 1852, as Master General, Hardinge called — and more surprisingly secured approval — for a target of 244 field guns by the end of 1853 and of 300 by 1854.[118]

Furthermore, large numbers of troops would need to be moved simultaneously, and Hardinge therefore urged the completion of a united railway link for the south coast.[119] He held discussions with the Railway Department of the Board of Trade, and in January 1853 Captain Simmons, R. E., was sent to France and Belgium 'to ascertain their system of conveying troops by Railway'. On Simmons' return in February Hardinge established an Army Transport Committee in an endeavour to secure 'for Army conveyances, ... a direct narrow gauge communication from all the Northern Counties from Birmingham to Guildford & thence to Portsmouth, Dover & the whole of the South-Eastern coast'.[120] He also lobbied for a narrow-gauge connection between Oxford, Reading and Basingstoke so that troops could go straight from Ireland to Birkenhead and thence to the south coast.

Modern thinking favours Wellington's and Hardinge's preference for a mobile reserve. However, it is to be suspected that not unnaturally they had failed to grasp fully the implications of rapid, massive troop movements of this sort. Prince Albert glibly supposed that an army could be moved to the south coast in twelve hours.[121] The transport of isolated regiments in the 1840s and a trial movement of artillery in 1853[122] did not themselves reveal the compounding effect that slight delays would have if the movement were large. The complications foreseen by Maurice de Sellon lacked the force of experience. To move 21,477 men and eighty-four guns would require 152 trains (each drawing eighty tons). A thirty-minute gap would be necessary between each train to allow water and coal to be taken on board, and therefore a seventy-six-hour delay would occur in the force setting off. He calculated that it would be over 100 hours before the relieving force could arrive at the point of invasion, by which time a bridgehead would have been established.

These, however, were qualifications which could only serve to underline the priorities in thinking on British home defence. In 1845 Burgoyne, still fresh from his own appointment with the Railway Department, stated to the Commissioners on the Gauge of Railways that he looked upon 'the whole safety of the Kingdom to depend upon railways ... The whole question of war depends upon the general who can concentrate his troops with the greatest rapidity, and in the greatest numbers, upon a given point of importance.'[123] The apparent worth of fortifications shown by Sebastopol was to deflect British thinking — and Burgoyne's in particular — from so admirable a policy.

Both the fortification and the mobile reserve schools were vitally dependent on more men to implement either of their strategies. When Wellington formulated his scheme of defence in 1845, he found that, after allocating troops to guard existing defences, 'we have not one disposable soldier'.[124] On completing his south-coast tour, he calculated on 65,000 being absorbed in coastal defences, and wanted his London/Dublin disposable force to total 170,000.[125] Therefore, throughout 1847, he lobbied the Russell administration for 20,000 men to be added to the regular troops — the maximum he thought the country would stand — and for a militia of 150,000, thus giving the 170,000 total that he had urged on Peel.[126] On 27 December, Wellington calculated that 75,000 were required to man the principal garrisons, whereas there only were 55,000–58,000 in the United Kingdom and most would be required in the colonies in the event of war. To avoid 'the indelible disgrace and destruction' that this situation foreboded, only an increase of 10,000 regulars a year for the next three years and a militia of 150,000 would be sufficient.[127]

However, the passing of the crisis in 1848 meant that by 1850 the United Kingdom garrison had dwindled to 39,820, a fall of 12,540 in two years.[128] Hardinge summarised the position in a letter to Newcastle on the 1853-4 estimates. If war with France broke out, 5,000 troops would have to go to the Channel Islands. Assuming also that one fifth of the force was unfit or untrained, 14,123 soldiers would be available in England. The south-coast dockyards had an immediate requirement for 11,600 of the remainder, although this rested on the assumption that 30,000 auxiliaries would man the less important defences. Therefore, a field force of 10,000 men could be formed only by entrusting Britain's vital arsenals to the militia.[129] Hardinge's private wish was to have 80,000 line troops in the United Kingdom,[130] but his request for an increase of 10,000 infantry was rejected by Newcastle.

Thus it could be said that, on the only army issue on which the Great Duke had staked his reputation while Commander-in-Chief, neither he nor his successor found satisfaction. The strategy round which they both planned the defence of the United Kingdom was inoperable without a considerable augmentation to the regular army. When increases in manpower were proposed, radical M.P.s would conjure up myriads of men, drawing on every description of auxiliary force, without regard to their quality or fitness — W. Williams in 1844, by including half-pay officers, pensioners, police and shore-based marines, claimed a total of 266,078.[131] On the principle of getting something for nothing, the temptation to cover up the inadequacies of the regular forces by large numbers of part-time soldiers, impressive only on paper, was irresistible to Parliament.

Of the three categories of reserve force employed in the Napoleonic wars — militia, fencibles and volunteers — only the cavalry part of the volunteers, normally called yeomanry, had survived. In 1828 all those regiments which had not been called out in the past ten years were disbanded and, despite the yeomanry's employment in the Reform Bill riots, further reductions took place in 1838. In the early 1840s the yeomanry were frequently called out to aid the civil power against the Chartists and a small augmentation took place in the disturbed counties. However, reductions elsewhere meant little overall change and by 1851 there were fifty-two corps of yeomanry making a total of only 13,672 men.[132]

The principal reasons for not encouraging the yeomanry were political.

Although Charles Napier praised its use as an aid to the civil power, since it showed society defending itself rather than the army defending society,[133] the more common sentiment — founded on the examples of Peterloo and Bristol — was that it represented the higher classes riding down the lower. The radicals had every reason for suspicion: the yeomanry had not remained above politics in the early 1830s, and, through his personal investment in the corps, a regiment served to strengthen the power and patronage of the local grandee. Its value as an aid to the civil power was further diminished by the tendency for riots to occur during the harvest when the farmers of the yeomanry were already fully occupied. The men provided their own horses and they were therefore poorly disciplined in the confined movements of cavalry drill. To all this was added financial expediency; regular troops were paid whether called out or not, yeomary were not.[134] Therefore for a government to fly in the face of radical views by expanding the yeomanry seemed to be militarily unnecessary and politically undesirable.

Much more attractive to all parties was the idea of employing pensioners. This was canvassed in the late 1830s: it pleased the Commons, since it gave some return on their money, and satisfied the Horse Guards, as the men were already trained soldiers. Between 1839 and 1842 some were employed as special constables, although only on a temporary basis.[135] In August 1842, on Wellington's advice, Sir James Graham asked Hardinge 'to mature a Plan which will render the most effective of the Pensioners at all Times available in large Towns and the Manufacturing districts', so that they might form 'a Corps of Reserve between Garrison Battalions and Special Constables'.[136] An act of 1843 allowed 10,000 to be enrolled and armed in Britain, and a warrant of 12 April 1844 established that they would be liable for eight days' training in the year and to be called out to aid the civil power. Only those under fifty-five were eligible, £1 was to be granted per annum for their equipment, and they were to be organised into local companies, under half-pay officers called Staff Officers of Pensioners. By February 1844 Hardinge had established thirty-two headquarter stations and thirty-eight out-stations in England and Scotland, to give a total of 5,200 men, and twenty-five headquarter stations in Ireland to enrol up to 4,200 men.[137]

The Horse Guards' sole purpose in enrolling the pensioners was to enlist their services for the civil power (and thus also to deny them to the Chartists). The memorandum sent round in 1844 affirmed that they were only liable to be called out in times of riot and tumult, and that they were not to form garrison or veteran battalions. But, with the invasion scare of

1845, Peel suggested that, of the 74,000 pensioners in the United Kingdom, 25,000 be enrolled in local companies and 19,000 in reserve companies.[138] Wellington was averse to the use of pensioners for home defence, but told the Prime Minister that 30,220 were totally unfit for further service, 19,112 were fit to occupy buildings and 24,937 were capable of service in local companies — although only 17,790 had served in the infantry.[139] Thus, when in 1846 Grey called for a force of 100,000 pensioners,[140] he could only have come anywhere near achieving it had his limited enlistment bill of 1847 embodied its original clause, that soldiers discharged after ten years' service could qualify for a deferred pension by eleven years with the enrolled pensioners.

Nonetheless some attempts were made to expand the force. In 1847 a fresh warrant incorporating naval pensioners gave a total establishment of 13,616 pensioners, although only 13,000 could be procured.[141] In 1848 East India Company pensioners became eligible for enrolment. By 1850 there were ninety-seven headquarter stations, and twenty-one outstations in the United Kingdom embracing 15,000 pensioners, all maintained for the price of one regular battalion.[142] Reports suggested that they were efficient and well disciplined, and in 1850 they received percussion muskets. The 1852 invasion threat produced a fresh cry for more to be enrolled, but with the existing structure of the army a substantial increase was impossible. In 1853, of 70,616 pensioners, only 21,800 were aged under fifty-five and eligible, of whom 16,857 were enrolled, the remainder being exempted by virtue of their occupation or geographical location.[143]

A much more numerous second line was required if the regular army was to be adequately supported in home defence or released as a disposable force for employment elsewhere. The militia, proudly called the 'constitutional force' in implicit derogation of the dubious legality of a standing army, had been the favourite resort of previous Parliaments. It survived the peacetime reductions and was even called out in 1820, 1821 and 1825. However, it was in decline, its system abused and its training inadequate. It existed under legislation that was increasingly out of step with the aspirations of an industrialised society. In 1829 Wellington himself suspended the ballot by which the force was conscripted, and, although the services of the militia were required in the Reform Bill riots, Whig policy was to let it wither. In 1835 Howick spoke with contempt of the unfair burden it placed on the lower classes, who could not afford to purchase substitutes if balloted, and of the £100,000 and more it cost each time it was called out.[144] However, the *coup de grâce* was not administered. In 1836 Russell drew up a fresh militia bill. Its primary purpose was to allow the appointment of pensioners from the regular army to the militia staff. The argument was that this leavening of professionals would reduce the cost of an independent staff and would justify the paltry training of one day a year.[145] Russell proposed to continue the ballot, but in 1837 Howick suggested that the militia be voluntarily enlisted. In addition he wanted it to be employed only in its own locality, thus making the period of ten years' service less harsh. In the event, only in the Channel Islands, where all men aged sixteen to sixty were liable to serve, was the militia enrolled and in 1842-3 to a certain extent reformed — thanks largely to William Napier, the Lieutenant Governor of Guernsey.[146]

Therefore, an increasingly inefficient militia staff was retained to provide for units whose personnel no longer existed even on paper. As Harding pointed out to the Duke in 1843, the government either needed a return for its money or it should abolish root and branch.[147] The following year, Sir James Graham described the militia as the national reserve, and called for it to be rendered efficient.[148]

The 1845 home defence crisis prodded Peel into resolving these criticisms. In July, Palmerston demanded that the militia be balloted and trained for a month.[149] Wellington proposed that the annual bill for the suspension of the ballot should not be introduced.[150] The Prime Minister, however, was not prepared to court the unpopularity implicit in conscription,[151] and instead favoured voluntary enlistment. In September the militia staffs were ordered to be inspected with a view to the militia being called out, and Sir George Murray put in hand the preparation of clothing, arms and equipment. On 30 October, Herbert told Murray that he and Graham had taken measures 'to enable the Government to proceed at any moment it may be necessary to ballot for, and train the Militia, and at all events to call them out next Spring'.[152] Only at the end of the year does it seem to have been borne in upon the Secretary at War and the Home Secretary that the inefficiencies of the militia required to be eradicated by revised legislation.

A bill was therefore drafted, proposing to preserve the ballot mechanism, but giving counties the option to raise their quotas by volunteering. Lists were to be prepared every five years, and were to incorporate a maximum of 100,000 men aged between eighteen and forty, who could be trained for up to three months a year and who were to serve seven years. The bill would have given the government the power to make the militia efficient only if it wished to implement it: for example, it was probably planned to embody no more than 40,000 for a month in 1846.[153] No statutory obligations would have ensured the permanent provision of a fully trained and adequately sized reserve.

The 1845-6 proposals were shelved by the corn law crisis and the fall of Peel's administration. Its successor grandly dismissed as inadequate the provision for 100,000 men, 150,000 being put as a desirable target for England and 250,000 for the United Kingdom. These totals were to be doubled in wartime.[154] However, although faithfully reflecting Wellington's advice in respect of numbers, Russell spurned the Duke's suggestion of a voluntarily enlisted militia, with the ballot in reserve, and a training period of four months every two or three years.[155] The liberal wing of the party (including Grey) was frightened of the disruption to industry which a regular militia would cause. Russell therefore proposed to enlist only local militia, confined to service within the county.[156]

To meet the criticism that local militia would be less effective than regular militia, Fox Maule formulated a hybrid scheme that pleased nobody. A regular militia of 50,000, all unmarried and under thirty, was proposed 'as a kind of war force'. It could be exercised for up to sixty days at a time, but was only to be balloted, enrolled and embodied when 'there is a likelihood of war'. Secondly Maule envisaged 'an army of reserve' formed of volunteer corps and balloted men, to total for England alone 150,000 in peace and 300,000 in war. Its services were to be confined to the counties, and, after a month's training in the first year, two weeks was to be the maximum commitment in subsequent years. The only merit of Maule's scheme was that it acknowledged the distinction between a force to repel invasion (the regular militia) and an organisation to supply men to the regular army (the army of reserve).

Palmerston and Sir Charles Wood both attacked the duplication in two separate forces. It was a complex proposal, full of special provisions, that had all the vices of subdividing the army and its terms of enlistment, and none of the advantages that a properly integrated line and reserve would bring.[157] Palmerston pointed out that the local militia would not be available at the moment of invasion; he consequently advocated a regular militia, able to serve throughout the United Kingdom and 'in a shape and character as nearly as possible resembling a regular army'. Wood, although equally disenchanted with Maule's proposal, put the reverse case: a seven-year commitment to serve in peacetime anywhere in the United Kingdom would disrupt trade and prevent marriage.[158] Russell tried to compromise: a fifth of the proposed force of 200,000 was to be balloted and raised each year from men aged eighteen to twenty-five;

their commitment was to be five years, but the length of training was to be reduced in each of the years and in the last two they were only to leave their counties in the face of imminent invasion.[159] Russell's proposal was a political solution that made military nonsense. An effective battalion could not be forged from men whose obligations and terms of service were so varied. Furthermore, it would be five years before the force was up to strength and two more years before it would be efficient. Fortunately France's domestic crisis presented a perfect pretext for postponement.

Although Russell's immediate ambitions were foiled at the beginning of 1848, his administration's predilection for local militia as a means to soften the personal and commercial inconvenience caused by the ballot did not die. In response to the alarms of 1851–2, he introduced a scheme very close to that proposed by Maule for his 'army of reserve', but without the regular militia to supplement it. Volunteers would be accepted, but the balance would be made up by balloting those aged twenty and twenty-three in the first year, and twenty to twenty-one subsequently. Thus the chance of disturbing married men in settled occupations was minimal, and even for those taken only a fortnight's service each year for four years was envisaged. For an outlay of £200,000 in the first year of the scheme, Russell hoped to have 70,000 men, rising to 100,000 in the second year and 12,000 in the third.

Palmerston did not like Russell's bill. The local militia would not take substitutes, it would train in squads and not in battalions, its services would be confined to individual counties, and it could only be called out in the event of invasion rather than in anticipation of it. The local militia of the Napoleonic wars had been designed as a reserve for the regular militia and not as a substantive or permanent force in itself. Palmerston's arguments were cogent and long-standing: his amendment to Russell's bill — that it be based on existing acts and that the word 'local' be omitted — was not solely the product of pique at his dismissal from the Foreign Office. The amendment was carried by 125 votes to 136, and Russell's government resigned.[160]

The new administration, headed by Derby, had the introduction of a militia bill as its first commitment. On 29 March 1852 Walpole proposed a measure to raise 80,000 men (50,000 in the first year and the remainder in the second) by voluntary enlistment, with recourse to the ballot only if quotas were not met. The age limits were eighteen to thirty-five, so that by taking those over twenty-five army recruiting would not be affected. The justification for the higher cost of the scheme (up to £400,000 in the first year and £250,000 thereafter) lay in the fact that the force was designed to be constantly ready for service. A man would train for twenty-one days (extendable to fifty-six days) in each of his five years' service, his officers would as far as possible be half-pay regulars and the force could be embodied in case of imminent danger.[161] The purists wanted a smaller force that would train for longer periods, but, as Wellington pointed out in his last major speech in the Lords, the provision made was at least a basis for expansion: 'I recommend you to adopt this measure as the commencement of a completion of a peace establishment.'[162]

In the Commons, radical opposition ensured that a vote had to be taken on each of the major clauses. The principal prong of the attack rested on the potential disruption to industry. Areas of full employment and high wages — Yorkshire and Lancashire in particular — would be the most likely to have to resort to a ballot. Frederick Peel, in a reasoned argument for a proper division of labour in peacetime, condemned the militia as 'an uncalled-for interference with the industrial economy of the country'.[163] The fears of Chartism in 1848 had proved so ill-founded that nobody rested his opposition solely on the danger of arming the urban masses.

Such a risk, even if it existed, was considerably reduced by the dependence on volunteers rather than conscripts. So strong was the military spirit of the nation, rooted in the fear of Louis Napoleon and fired by the military procession at Wellington's funeral, that by January 1854 66,280 of the 80,000 had been enrolled and, although counties with full employment were below their quotas, the ballot was dismissed as unnecessary.[164] Cobden's description of the militia bill as 'nothing but a measure for raising a volunteer corps under militia regulations'[165] was therefore proved remarkably apposite. In particular the proliferation of different categories of auxiliaries was rendered unnecessary by the bill. In the Napoleonic wars, militia, yeomanry, fencibles and volunteers had all competed with the regular army, offering different terms of service and serving only to complicate the system.

The government's delay in providing a reserve for home defence in the 1840s had produced a call for self-help in the shape of volunteer corps. At the beginning of 1852 the enthusiasm for volunteers was hardening into positive action, with the radicals in particular pressing the advantages of middle-class organisations founded (and funded) by the big towns. Grey saw no objection to the volunteers existing side by side with a voluntarily recruited militia, since the former drew their recruits from the middle class and the latter from the lower class.[166] Russell, perhaps to appease his radical wing, was consequently prepared to accept the services of volunteer corps as alternatives to the local militia provided they were recommended by their Lords Lieutenant and were self-sufficient.[167] His successors in office, with their greater commitment to a voluntary and efficient militia, could not afford to test Grey's distinction. Walpole, whatever lip service he might have paid to the offers of volunteers in Parliament,[168] had no intention of accepting them unless the militia failed.[169] Militarily they were unsatisfactory as they were entitled to leave the service whenever it suited them, and socially their middle-class basis made them a divisive influence in an issue which ideally should have been of universal concern. Although men of property had a vested interest in defence, their very commitments and their power in Parliament would enable them to place demands on the budget which their military efficiency would not warrant.

The merit of the 1852 bill, therefore, was that it secured the enthusiasm of the volunteers without at the same time forfeiting the government's initiative in their employment and organisation. The attendance at training proved to be good. Of fifty-two regiments inspected in 1853, 5,175 of 38,585 enrolled were absent without leave: 3,924 of these were from fourteen regiments, principally those based on the metropolitan and manufacturing districts, while the remaining thirty-eight regiments had an average of thirty-three each. The principal problem lay in the procurement of officers: only 225 former regulars were forthcoming, the deficiency in subalterns and captains was not made up and those that did join were not very efficient.[170]

The better class of the militiamen brought with it greater intelligence and self-reliance than was found in the regular army. These virtues had to be maximised in order to allay the critics' doubts as to the militia's military competence. Some were employed as artillery, and by September 1853 there were eleven militia artillery regiments, comprising 3,500 gunners.[171] Others were used as light infantry, on the grounds that their ignorance of drill made them ill-suited to stand in line in the open field. Yet more — in deference to the argument that light infantry work was the acme of military skill — were instead employed behind walls, as garrison troops and a further aid to the fortification lobby.

Doubts about the application of militia battalions in battle led some to the conclusion that they had no independent military role. Instead their function was to provide a reserve of manpower, wherein a recruit could be gradually weaned from civil life before being passed on to the regulars. This was certainly the principal application Maule envisaged for his local militia, and Hardinge too thought the militia constituted a reliable source for recruits if others became exhausted.[172] The problem with this level of administrative subordination to the regulars was twofold. It would undermine the morale and unity of the militia battalions, and it would rob them of their separate, 'constitutional' status. In practice, as we shall see, in 1854 the answer lay in a middle way.

3. Regimental organisation

What the militia certainly did not become was a fully integrated reserve. Moreover, although a reserve did exist, it was a peacetime system, founded on the regiment, and adapted to colonial service. It was not planned as a basis for the army as a whole in the event of major wartime expansion.

Conceived by Wellington in 1825,[173] the arrangement was for a regiment going to any foreign station other than India to divide into six service companies and four depot companies. The depot remained at home in order to supply the regiment abroad with trained recruits and officers, and at the same time to offer a haven for soldiers incapacitated by disease, climate or wounds. By meeting the casualties and contingencies of colonial service, Hill reckoned that 'the whole efficiency of our Military system has unquestionably been hitherto mainly preserved through the instrumentality of these Depots'.[174]

The 1837 establishment of the six service companies was eighty-six rank and file each (or 582 all ranks) and that of the four at the depot was fifty-six (253 total).[175] Sir Willoughby Gordon concluded that such massive roots could well support a larger tree, which in turn would mean that fewer battalions would be needed in each station abroad.[176] Palmerston too had reckoned that seventy-six battalions of 1,000 men each would have been almost £100,000 per annum cheaper to run than 103 battalions of 739 men.[177] But while administrative demands pushed for larger units, tactical arguments made for smaller ones. George Cathcart thought that a battalion of 800 gave 600 effective in the field. Formed in two lines, it covered 200 paces, and could be commanded by a single officer. A larger body would have to act by wings, and thus be 'no better than two small imperfect battalions'.[178] Wellington agreed, and argued that a battalion of 800 or 1,000 should on service be divided into two bodies.[179]

The depot system seemed to give the Duke his two weak battalions. Many colonies, he argued, were better adapted to a small regiment, particularly the islands of the Mediterranean and the West Indies. More important, however, at home the disproportionate depot gave a large number (fifty-six in 1839) of independent, small, disposable units, to aid the civil power.

The underlying theme, therefore, of Wellington's scheme was the preservation of cadres that could be rapidly expanded into second battalions. However, until 1842, of the hundred infantry regiments, only three had second battalions. Furthermore none of these battalions was an expanded depot. Since 1825 new colonies and shifting balances had required the services of fourteen additional battalions, which had been procured by delaying reliefs and reducing the force at home. In 1842, rather than accept Gordon's proposal of larger battalions, Hardinge, as Secretary at War, suggested the creation of more battalions. Six regiments should be increased to twelve companies or 1,200 rank and file, divisible into two parts of six companies each. The cost would be borne by reducing fifty regiments from an establishment of 800 to 740.[180] In the event, nine regiments were chosen, and were split into a first battalion, based on the existing service companies (540 rank and file), a reserve battalion, formed from the depot (540), and a recruiting depot (120). Augmentations in 1846 allowed eight more regiments to be increased to 1,200 men, to be formed into first and reserve battalions or into large regiments of ten companies each.

The scheme must not be taken as a precursor of Cardwell's linked battalions. There was no home and abroad rotation of the two, nor was the so-called 'reserve' battalion a reserve in the strict sense of the word. It was merely an expedient to give more single battalions, and was regarded as simpler than raising additional regiments and then disbanding them. Both first and reserve battalions were regarded as equally ready for foreign service.

The logic of the expansion of depots into reserve battalions was that they could as simply be reduced. When the army was contracted again in 1849, Grey found that eleven of the seventeen reserve battalions were at the time stationed with their first battalions, and thus they were relatively painlessly compressed into one battalion of ten companies or 1,000 men.[181] Right up to the Crimean war, the expansion of the four-company depots into six-company battalions remained the Horse Guards orthodoxy in the creation of a regular reserve. Hardinge proposed to add thirty-one new battalions in this fashion in 1853.[182]

Hardinge's continued preference for the depot system was surprising, because he had by 1853 recognised its military inefficiency. Four small companies had a value as police but they were totally unsuited for defence against invasion. They could not be brigaded and were therefore unfit to enter the line. Their qualities as fighting troops were extremely suspect. As far as possible the men left at home by the regiment were those over-age or unfit for foreign service. The 71st, on going to Canada in 1838, did not leave a single fully fit man.[183] The justification for retaining these old soldiers was the experience which they passed on to the recruits. But the employment of the depots in policing and guard duties interrupted the recruits' already inadequate instruction. If training was conducted, it was in the hands of the acting adjutant, very often a young officer, the person best qualified for the job being with the service companies. Nor was it only the recruits who suffered: newly commissioned officers also received their basic instruction at the depot but were frequently encouraged 'in idleness and restlessness, and in skulking foreign service'.[184]

Harmony between depot and service companies was rare. Although theoretically the officers and n.c.o.s at the depot exchanged their positions every two years, in practice a separate set of interests was created. Officers only had their passage paid if they accompanied a draft of other ranks,[185] and thus the legitimate excuse of impoverishment could be used to forestall an exchange. They therefore tended to be drawn homewards, away from the service companies: in 1841, only five subalterns of the 85th were with the regiment, three of the remainder being on leave and twelve at the depot.[186] Furthermore, it could be difficult for the depot to perform its main duty to the regiment, which was to maintain the strength of the service companies. The distance between the two meant that casualties could not be readily replaced. The size of the battalion abroad might therefore be very low — at the Cape in 1852, each regiment's effective strength averaged between 300 and 350 rank and file, with the 73rd down to 250.[187] And there were occasions when the establishment of the depot was kept up at the expense of the service companies.[188]

Nor apparently was this bane to individual or regimental excellence the most efficient method of garrisoning the colonies. In terms of men, 60·3 per cent of the infantry of the line was abroad in 1820 and 61·9 per cent in 1839. But, owing to the low service strength of the regiment after the introduction of the depots in 1825, 56·7 per cent (fifty-five of the ninety-seven infantry battalions) abroad in 1820 had grown to 75·7 per cent (seventy-eight of the 103) in 1839.[189] In 1853 it was calculated that if entire regiments served together only twenty-five need be abroad at any time as opposed to the forty-nine then in colonies other than India. Furthermore a rotation of six years at home to four away would be possible.[190]

The alternative to the four-company depots favoured by the military press was their reduction to one or two companies and their incorporation into so-called provisional battalions. These would have a permanent staff, be organised according to the areas in which the service companies were stationed, would permit a much fuller scheme of instruction for recruits and would create stronger battalions abroad. The model was derived from Chatham, where since 1830 the depot companies of the East India Company's European regiments and of the Queen's troops in India and New South Wales had functioned on just this system. Not dissimilar was the procedure adopted in relation to the cavalry, who on going to India left behind three officers and forty-one other ranks to recruit. These men were based on the Cavalry Depot, moved from St. John's Wood to Maidstone in 1832. All recruits for the regiments in India were trained at Maidstone and each cavalry regiment at home sent two men at a time for instruction in equitation.

From 1836 the *Naval and Military Gazette* repeated rumours of the extension of provisional battalions to regiments in the West Indies (to be at Cork), the Mediterranean (at Plymouth), and to Ceylon, the Cape and Mauritius (at Portsmouth). Howick, supported by the reports of his commanding officer brother, and no doubt impressed by the potential economies in the scheme, suggested that battalions be formed of ten companies, eight of which would be for foreign service and two (totalling 139 men) should form part of a provisional battalion of five or six regimental depots. In consequence, forty-nine battalions would be abroad for ten years at a time, and thirty at home for four years, eight months.[191] The provisional battalions, he suggested to Wellington, might be formed of regiments recruited in the same part of the kingdom and stationed accordingly, for example that for the Scottish regiments being in Edinburgh.[192]

Hill and Wellington opposed on the grounds that provisional battalions would run counter to the regimental system. They would not discipline a recruit in a regimental way, and he would therefore still have much to learn on joining the service companies.[193] Neither officer seems to have envisaged provisional battalions as a means for the Horse Guards to secure greater uniformity amongst its scattered battalions, so sacrosanct had the regiment become. The only result of this sally was a redistribution in favour of the service companies (200 to 600), but in other respects Russell agreed to retire the government defeated.[194]

The transformation of some depots into reserve battalions in 1842 left those regiments with depots of only 120 rank and file. In this instance so small was the unit that the Horse Guards had little choice but to accept the provisional battalion organisation. All the depots of the enlarged regiments were concentrated at Parkhurst, in the Isle of Wight.[195] The reduced establishment of each and the collective capability of the whole meant too that all those unfit for foreign service were weeded out, so that the battalion was as effective as possible. By 1848, partly owing to the withdrawal of troops from the colonies, only thirteen four-company depots were left as opposed to sixty a few years before.[196] The reduction of the reserve battalions in 1849 led in turn to the disappearance of the depot battalion (as it was called), but apparently Wellington was so converted to the idea that at his request its execution was stayed until 1851.[197]

Apart from impressing the Duke himself, the example of the Isle of Wight depot battalion reinforced the convictions of other more inventive minds. Charles Grey's hatred of the depot system caused him to take his brother's proposals to heart. By 1848 he had redrafted them into a far more comprehensive scheme of infantry organisation. The four-company depots, the recruiting districts and the militia staff should all be abolished, and in their stead provisional battalions of reserve companies (100 rank and file each) established. Permanent barracks should be built for each battalion, in areas chosen with reference to the counties in which the regiments were originally raised and to which they should in future confine their recruiting. The militia and pensioners of the area could be grafted on to the provisional battalion and so integrated with the line. The depot would become an effective organ of administration and instruction.[198] Moreover such an organisation dovetailed neatly with Lord Grey's preference for local militia, which he envisaged as feeding a second home-service battalion for each regular regiment, officered by the first battalion and from which voluntering into the first or foreign service battalion would be encouraged.[199] Although Tulloch doubted whether in peacetime sufficient volunteers would be forthcoming,[200] there was no reason for the other end of Grey's scheme not to work. He proposed that, after serving the ten years of limited enlistment, a soldier could qualify for a deferred pension by signing on for eleven more years of regular service or enlisting in the reserve.

Taken as a whole, here in germination was a plan which embodied two important principles. The first was that of encouraging local connections, which with the example of the Highland regiments most commentators look to encourage better discipline. Since 1782 each regiment of the line had had a county title but in practice the links had been little better than nominal. The second great principle, and the one towards which Maule had been faltering in his 'army of reserve' proposals of 1847, was an integration of the militia with the line. This, as several military observers noted, was the natural extension of giving battalions local links, with the reserve acting as the funnel through which willing and well conducted recruits would pass. Whether the second battalion was a part-time body or formed of regulars for home service only, the point was that the depot should be a permanent centre for the regiment, a good school for recruits and, in Lord Seaton's words, 'a kind of home'.[201]

Thus a strong body of military opinion supported the principles of the Grey brothers' ideas. However, the most important convert was Prince Albert. Charles Grey was the prince's private secretary from 1849 but, as a soldier, he was diffident about trumpeting his scheme abroad, particularly as it might involve collision with the Commander-in-Chief. Therefore, with the inefficiencies of the local militia bill as impetus, the Prince Consort took Grey's ideas in hand. He emphasised the creation of a trained reserve through the offer of deferred pensions and in February 1852 sent Grey's and his own proposals to Russell and Hardinge.[202] The Prime Minister duly passed it on, with his blessing, to Wellington.[203] The consequences were predictable. The Duke asked Fitzroy Somerset and Brown for their views. The former rehearsed the familiar arguments in favour of the four-company depot as essential to the preservation of the regimental system.[204] The Adjutant General pointed out that the provisional battalions would cost £$2\frac{1}{2}$ million; of the suggested training depots, he asked, 'If the infantry is all to be converted into Sappers and Gunners, the question occurs who is to carry our muskets'; the system would destroy regimental pride; and in conclusion 'it may be confidently asserted that the proposed system would not render the Army in any respect more efficient, but probably less so'.[205] Sir George was hoping that if he shut his eyes tight enough the problems would disappear. What he and the Military Secretary said was what the Duke wanted the hear. Above all else, Wellington disliked the proposals as enshrining the 1847 enlistment act. Charles Grey had realised that the only really efficient way to form a reserve was to make discharge after ten years service obligatory, except for n.c.o.s.[206] The Duke's worst fears would be realised, and the line would be deprived of its most experienced men. This objection was enough to destroy the entire edifice.

The fall of Russell's government and the departure of Lord Grey made reform less provocative. Prince Albert drew up a proposal which rested on the assumption that, since Parliament had rejected Russell's militia bill, it would not accept any militia. This could be an advantage. Instead of a semi-disciplined militia, 25,000 men should be added to the regular army, and the equivalent number of over seven years' service discharged into a reserve to qualify for a deferred pension. Thereafter, those of ten years' service would be eligible, and in three years a reserve of 50,000 trained men would be created, with the existing enrolled pensioners forming a second-line reserve for men over fifty. Permanent depots, which would be the headquarters for the reserve companies, would replace the four-company depots, the reserve would form second battalions and would recruit in that county whose name the regiment bore.[207] This proposal — 'Prince Albert on Grey' — was put to Derby, who promised to consider it if Parliament threw out his government's militia bill.[208] However, the bill was passed.

The Duke's demise, as with so many other reforms, presented an opportunity to test the Horse Guards again. Panmure, in a letter of advice to the new Commander-in-Chief, had prepared the ground by urging the creation of an army of reserve based on the offer of a deferred pension to those of ten years' service.[209] Hardinge had already been thinking along these lines in November 1851: the model of Pitt's 1803 army of reserve suggested to him the formation of second battalions based on volunteers from the militia.[210] However, although the reserve aspects of Grey's proposals appealed to him, Hardinge still remained unconvinced of the defects of the four-company depot.[211] Charles Grey reiterated these in a letter to Airey, the new Military Secretary. He stressed the advantage to recruiting and to training that a provisional battalion with a permanent headquarters would offer.[212] At the same time Russell commended Grey's proposals to Sidney Herbert, with the encouraging note that he felt Hardinge would prove more amenable than the Duke had been.[213]

Further fuel was added to the debate by a paper penned by the Duke of Cambridge in January 1853. Although an attempt to regularise the establishment of individual battalions had been made the previous year, the shifting manpower policies of the 1840s, and the creation and withdrawal of the reserve battalions, meant that, of the eighty-three infantry battalions not in India, fifty-nine were 850 strong, nine 900, eight 1,000 and four 1,200. The situation was complicated by the useless four-company depots. Cambridge therefore favoured battalions of 1,000 men (which meant that twelve more regiments could be at home), with two-company depots grouped into provisional battalions.[214] Charles Grey endorsed the scheme, and in particular urged that 'Permanently established Places for instruction, & well selected instructors wd go far to remove the objection to our present system'.[215] Cambridge, however, had favoured the skeleton depot only for recruiting and not for training: for him 'All Depots are conceived to be objectionable for Officers & men, & the sooner both are ordered to join their respective regiments the better'.[216] The correspondence was sent to Airey, who stated his preference for regimental depots over provisional battalions,[217] and therefore implied that training should be done at home and not with the regiment.

Progress towards an integrated scheme was therefore slow, and events were soon to overtake the exchange of memoranda. Hardinge and Herbert were agreed in favour of a reserve army to be created by offering a pension to those who, having served their initial ten years in the regulars, opted either for eleven more years or twenty-two in a reserve battalion. Herbert, however, was fearful of the damage this might do to the militia and of the cries that regiments would lose their best soldiers. His proposed warrant of 1853 therefore never appeared,[218] but its seeds are to be found in his abortive attempt to establish a reserve in 1859.

At the outbreak of the Crimean war, Hardinge's worries over manpower and concerning the difficulty of administering the depots, shorn of their officers but swelled by recruits, led him to produce proposals for a reorganisation of the infantry. He suggested twelve-company battalions, with two four-company depots to form provisional battalions at home. An addition of four captains and eight subalterns would be required to officer the depot and this should be regarded as permanent when peace came.[219] Charles Grey bitterly opposed the four-company depots, because they would be over-staffed when peacetime reductions were imposed: he was more realistic than either the Commander-in-Chief or the Prince Consort in realising that no long-term commitment as to officer employment could be made by any government.[220] The prince himself steered a middle course. While embracing Hardinge's twelve-company battalion, he revamped aspects of Grey's plans. Provisional battalions should have the local links implicit in the 1782 county titles, and their staffs could also administer the militia.[221] In July information on the Prussian *Landwehr* was actually requested.[222] Out of the *ad hoc* wartime expedients, both the Prince

Consort and the Commander-in-Chief hoped to fashion something more durable.

The demands, however, were too immediate for a long-term reconstruction. Moreover, theories on the organisation of a reserve were to need much more than just the shock of the Crimea to secure their implementation. Before Cardwell's arrival at the War Office, the army was to suffer similar strains during the Indian Mutiny, was briefly to become the front line of British defence in Europe when the French led in the construction of ironclad warships, and was to be provided with practical examples of the value of trained reserves by the continental armies.

The pre-1854 schemes started too from a series of preconceptions which throw into greater relief Cardwell's work. Although Charles Grey, Herbert and others were moving towards the idea of a trained reserve of ex-regulars, the core of their contemporaries' plans was to integrate a reserve of second-line troops so that it could feed the regulars. This was natural, since colonial service implied long-term enlistment. As Cardwell's work itself was to prove, a short-service army on the continental model, which trained men as fast as possible with a view to their discharge into the reserve, made the reserve the true war-force. British colonial commitments meant that the regular army could not afford to be so preoccupied with the formation of troops but needed to be capable of acting immediately with efficiency. The numerical weakness of its battalions and the lack of physical maturity among their members provide evidence of this defect in Cardwell's conception. Cardwell hoped to attract sufficient good recruits by a reform in the conditions of service in the army, but this, Hardinge's generation could have told him, had been tried in the 1840s without any noticeable upturn in recruiting.

The initiative displayed by Cardwell in switching to short service shows commendable courage, not least in that it overthrew the assumption in favour of veteran soldiers which the pre-Crimean generation had — despite the 1847 limited enlistment act (which in this context cannot be construed as short service) — inherited from the Duke of Wellington. Cardwell was to give to Britain the military organisation which both Greys had so energetically sought, whereby colonial commitments were covered by more than annual expedients. It was nonetheless a system which enshrined the regiment as the focus of the British army. This may have been a sound principle in view of the empire's peculiar administrative problems, but its implicit derogation of the brigade and division was a bad preparation for the field.

4. The Crimea

All the plans for maximising manpower and for reorganising regiments revolved around the demands of home and imperial defence. They did not give any serious consideration to the possibility of a major war overseas against a European opponent. Indeed, without the fears of French invasion and the reforms that they prompted, the home army might well have been unable to mount an expeditionary force. As it was, the best troops were already committed to the colonies, with the result that new levies had to form the field army to meet a European enemy.

The depots proved unequal to the task of training large intakes. In March 1854, with thirty infantry battalions preparing for foreign service, Hardinge found that he had a rump shorn of its officers and scattered in sixty-two depots.[223]

The militia was of some assistance. It enabled certain regular regiments to be released and — in the short term — formed a reservoir of men. In May 1854 it was embodied for home service. In July it took over garrison and guard duties at home and early the following year ten battalions were dispatched to the Ionian Islands and Malta. In the course of 1854 12,265 militiamen entered the regular army.[224] This traffic was controlled by a circular of November 1854, which allowed a maximum of 25 per cent to volunteer for the regulars. Herbert argued — with Hardinge's, Raglan's, Russell's and Prince Albert's support — that the militia should be the chief source of recruits for the army. Not only had their training been commenced, but also the excessive youth of those recruited directly into the ranks was balanced by more mature men. His opponents — Newcastle, the Grey brothers, and the Duke of Cambridge — rested their case on the cost of this method of indirect recruiting for men who would probably join in any case.[225] But the crisis in manpower crushed such scruples. By the end, the militia had provided the army with 33,000 men.[226] Not only did this imperil 'the constitutional force' itself, it was also plainly anomalous to have both the regulars and the militia recruiting for the same ends, particularly as it made direct enlistment to the regulars a less palatable alternative.

But it was in the Crimea itself that Britain reaped the most grievous consequences of maintaining an undersized army. In April 1854 Hardinge was already concerned as to how Britain was to meet the demands for officers and trained men that two battles and a period in a tough climate would impose.[227] He anticipated 100 casualties a month per battalion of 800 men from disease alone.[228] The nominated reserve,

Cathcart's division, was sent out in July, before the expedition had even reached the Crimea. It had been reckoned, before the war, that, to allow sufficient time for recuperation, the men of a besieging force should be in the trenches every fourth day at the most.[229] At Sebastopol two out of three nights was a more common average, and de Lacy Evans concluded that 'the work cut out for us was entirely beyond our numerical strength' and a prime cause of the army's sufferings.[230]

'The army of the East,' Herbert wrote in November, 'has been created by discounting the future. Every regiment at home, or within reach, and not forming a part of that army, has been robbed to complete it.'[231] The system permitted an efficient force to be rapidly created, but left no means of renewal. Not even sapping the Indian garrison and raising foreign mercenaries could relieve the overwork that was the chief cause of the disease and suffering in the Crimea. In the years of the 'long peace' the army had not been prepared for a third tier to be added to its already onerous responsibilities.

Notes

1. John Wheaton, 'The effect and impact of the administrative reform movement upon the army in the mid-Victorian period', pp. 203-4.
2. On the value of the inspection system, Portland papers, Pw Jf 2299, Whittingham to Bentinck, 29 June 1834; C. T. Atkinson, *Regimental history, The Royal Hampshire Regiment*, I, p. 174.
3. S.R.O., GD 45/8/155; P.P. 1859. sess. 2, XVII, pp. 8-25, gives 29,706.
4. Grey papers, memo by Burgoyne, 29 May 1850, p. 1.
5. P.P. 1859, sess. 2, XVII, pp. 8-25; P.P. 1854, XIX, 833, p. 6, gives 128,096 from 219, 852, a discrepancy which is only in part explained by the fact that it excludes troops on the Indian establishment.
6. *Wellington despatches*, II, pp. 173, 174.
7. Hansard, 3rd series, XLVI, c 1164.
8. B.M. Add. Mss 40310, f. 310, Wellington to Peel, 18 December 1839.
9. Wellington papers, Wellington to Stanley, 3 June 1843, 11 June, 15 and 19 July, 1 August 1845; W.O. 1/597, p. 378.
10. W.O. 1/599, pp. 243-9.
11. J. S. Curtiss, *The Russian army under Nicholas I*, p. 108.
12. P.P. 1850, X, pp. 186-7.
13. N.L.S. mss 2849, f. 213, casualties of the army 1841-50.
14. W.O. 6/127, p. 119.
15. P.P. 1850, X, pp. 770-3.
16. B.M. Add. Mss 40474, ff. 42-7, memo by Hardinge, 24 January 1842. The total of 18,277 includes the regimental depots, which were not formed into disposable battalions.

17 Portland papers, PwJg 382, memo by Whittingham, 1837; W. P. Morrell, *British colonial policy in the mid-Victorian age*, pp. 381-2.
18 B.M. Add. Mss 40461, ff. 185-6, Wellington to Peel, 12 August 1845.
19 P.P. 1836, XXII, p. 7; N.L.S. mss 2839, f. 124, Gordon to Brown, 29 August 1834.
20 P.P. 1840, XXII, p. xxi.
21 C. Greenhill Gardyne, *Life of a regiment*, II, p. 10.
22 Lt.-Gen. Shadwell, *Life of Lord Clyde*, I, p. 123.
23 H. Davidson, *History of the 78th Highlanders*, I, p. 144.
24 *N. & M.G.*, 30 April 1836, p. 280; 27 April 1837, p. 330.
25 *U.S.J.*, 1835, I. p. 145.
26 W.O. 43/688, f. 128.
27 P.P. 1837-8, XL, p. 417; later reports are P.P. 1840, XXXIV, p. 1; 1840, XXX, p. 135; 1839, XVI, p. 129; 1842, XXVII, p. 147.
28 W.O. 43/656, ff. 204-19.
29 N.A.M. 7709-6-11, p. 73, Vivian to Melbourne, 18 April 1838; pp. 80-6, 88-93, Vivian to Secretary at War, 22 and 23 March 1841.
30 *U.S.J.*, 1836, III, p. 289; attributed to Tulloch in *N. & M.G.*, 22 December 1838, p. 816, and 23 November 1839, p. 752.
31 W.O. 43/656, ff. 237-9, 242-3.
32 Grey papers, Tulloch to Grey, 25 September 1846.
33 S.R.O. GD 45/8/20, memo by Maule, 23 January 1848.
34 Grey papers, Gordon to Grey, 28 May 1849.
35 Grey papers, Dalhousie (i.e. Fox Maule) to Grey, 26 June 1849.
36 W.O. 43/876; W.O. 30/112, memo of 11 July 1849.
37 *N. & M.G.*, 30 September 1848, p. 633; Hansard, 3rd series, XCVII, c 1156.
38 Hansard, 3rd series, CXV, c 749; P.P. 1851, VII, p. 9.
39 Hansard, 3rd series, XCI, cc 1326-7; CIII, c 976; CXXIV, c 677.
40 W.O. 43/656, ff. 172-89; see also Grey papers, Howick to Glenelg, 18 January 1836.
41 Neil Cantlie, *History of the Army Medical Services*, I, p. 642; W.O. 43/183 and 463.
42 W.O. 3/95, p. 371; W.O. 6/127, pp. 44, 53, 66, 164; W.O. 43/744; Wellington papers, memo of 18 September 1841; *U.S.M.*, 1849, I, pp. 548-58.
43 W.O. 6/128, p. 58; P.P. 1850, X, pp. 69-71, 653-4; W.O. 43/861 and 924.
44 W.O. 3/104, p. 460.
45 W.O. 43/830.
46 S.R.O., GD 45/8/37, memos by R. More O'Ferrall, 1848; A. Samut-Tagliaferro, *History of Royal Malta Artillery*, I, pp. 99-106.
47 W.O. 6/127, p. 53.
48 Grey papers, Smith to Grey, 28 June 1848.
49 W.O. 43/630.
50 Grey papers, Grey to Wellington, 21 July 1846; W.O. 1/597, p. 339; W.O. 43/831.

51 See Hew Strachan, 'Lord Grey and imperial defence', in Ian Beckett and John Gooch (eds.), *Politicians and defence*, pp. 1-23.
52 S.R.O., GD 45/8/21, Grey's cabinet memo, 17 October 1846, p. 3.
53 Wellington papers, Stanley to Wellington, 22 January 1844.
54 W.O. 1/599, pp. 539-47.
55 Grey papers, Burgoyne to Grey, 21 November 1846; Anglesey to Grey, 20 September 1849, enclosing memo by Burgoyne.
56 Grey papers, Russell to Grey, 27 September and 13 November 1846, 27 December 1848, 19 August 1849.
57 C. P. Stacey, *Canada and the British army*, pp. 69-84; Newcastle papers NeC 9647 and 9650.
58 W. P. Morrell, *British colonial policy in the age of Peel and Russell*, pp. 286, 472; *British colonial policy in the mid-Victorian age*, p. 49.
59 W.O. 43/485, f. 177.
60 S.R.O., GD 45/8/21, Grey's cabinet memo, 17 October 1846, p. 4.
61 Grey papers, Wellington to Russell, 11 November 1846.
62 Grey papers, Smith to Grey, 18 and 19 August 1851.
63 W.O. 43/715, f. 122.
64 W.O. 6/127, pp. 44, 53; W.O. 43/693, f. 335; W.O. 43/713, ff. 2-16.
65 Grey papers, Gordon to Howick, 7 August 1837.
66 Grey papers, C 3/1B, journal entry for 21 December 1835.
67 W.O. 43/745, ff. 63-156.
68 Grey papers, Charles Grey to Howick, 27 August 1838; see also W.O. 43/745, ff. 158-62.
69 Grey papers, Howick to Charles Grey, 13 December 1838 and 5 February 1839.
70 W.O. 43/745, ff. 207-46.
71 W.O. 3/309, p. 372.
72 W.O. 3/112, p. 194; W.O. 4/270, p. 155.
73 W.O. 1/601, p. 107; W.O. 6/128, p. 171.
74 W.O. 1/598, ff. 747-50; W.O. 4/268, p. 332.
75 S.R.O., GD 45/8/21, Grey to Maule, 13 September 1846.
76 Grey papers, Tulloch to Grey, 25 September 1846; S.R.O., GD 45/8/21, pp. 17-19, Grey's memo, 17 October 1846.
77 P.P. 1849, IX, pp. 522-3; W.O. 43/876, ff. 265-367.
78 S.R.O., GD 45/8/115.
79 W.O. 43/853.
80 P.P. 1850, X, pp. 173-4.
81 N.L.S. mss 2849, f. 212, distribution of army, 27 November 1851.
82 W.O. 43/925.
83 Grey papers, Grey to Smith, 20 April 1848.
84 Grey papers, Smith to Grey, 28 June and 7 November 1848.
85 P.P. 1850, X, pp. 770-3.
86 W.O. 44/122, memo by Wellington, 18 August 1824.
87 Wellington papers, Wellington to Peel, 20 December 1844.
88 Ibid., Gordon to Wellington, 10 September 1844.

89 N.A.M. 7709-6-14, p. 86, Vivian to Wellington, 18 July 1838; 7709-6-15, pp. 1-21, Vivian to Palmerston, Dundas, Russell, August 1840; pp. 45, 58-62, Vivian to Melbourne, Normanby, October 1840.
90 W.O. 55/1409; N.L.S. Adv. Mss 46.9.13, ff. 201-2, 203; 46.9.14, ff. 44-6, Murray to Inspector General of Fortifications and Director General of Artillery, 30 and 31 May, 1 August 1842.
91 Wellington papers, Murray to Wellington, 19 October 1845.
92 Wellington papers, Peel to Wellington, 4 January 1845.
93 Wrottesley, *Life of Burgoyne*, I, pp. 434-6; Marquess of Anglesey, *One leg*, p. 324.
94 Draft in Wellington papers, Wellington to Burgoyne, 4 (in the event sent on 9) January 1847.
95 Wellington papers, Russell to Wellington, 3 September 1847.
96 *Journal des sciences militaires*, 4th series, II, 1847, pp. 35, 47.
97 Grey papers, c 3/13, journal for 18 October 1847.
98 Wrottesley, *Life of Burgoyne*, I, pp. 476-81.
99 *U.S.M.*, 1850, III, p. 496.
100 George Wrottesley, *Military opinions of General Sir J. F. Burgoyne*, pp. 24-59.
101 H. Sandham, memo book for 1847 [-52], p. 166.
102 P. E. Maurice [de Sellon], *On national defence in England*, trans. J. E. Addison.
103 Hardinge papers, Hardinge to Derby, 19 August 1852; Archives Historiques de Guerre, MR 1430/26, 28, 31, 33.
104 Hardinge papers, Hardinge to Palmerston, 9 January 1853, and reply, 15 January 1853.
105 The title was used by Hardinge, Seaton papers, Hardinge to Seaton, 13 May [1853].
106 Hansard, 3rd series, CXXXI, cc 242-3; CXXXII, c 655.
107 *Royal Engineers Professional Papers*, IX, 1847, pp. 1-23, and X, 1849, pp. 37-47.
108 S.R.O., GD 45/8/110.
109 B.M. Add. Mss 40461, ff. 344-6, Murray to Wellington, 8 November 1845.
110 Wellington papers, Anglesey to Wellington, 18 September 1847.
111 P.P. 1849, IX, pp. xlviii-lii.
112 B.M. Add. Mss 40461, f. 265, memo by Wellington, 5 October 1845.
113 Ibid., ff. 89-91, Wellington to Peel, 2 April 1845; Wellington papers, memo of 10 September 1845.
114 Wellington papers, Prince Albert to Wellington, 5 November 1847.
115 R.A. E 42/13, Horse Guards memo, 17 November 1847.
116 R.A. E 42/15, 16, 19, 20, Wellington's correspondence with railway companies, 22 November-2 December 1847.
117 *U.S.G.*, 25 January 1851, p. 3; *N. & M.G.*, 25 January 1851, p. 52.
118 R.A. E 44/15, pp. 29-33, memo by Hardinge, 23 September 1852.
119 Hardinge papers, Hardinge to [London &] South Western Railway, 25 May 1853.

120 R.A. E 44/89, Hardinge to Albert, 31 January 1853; see also Herbert papers, III A 45.
121 R.A. E 44/23a, memo by Albert, 10 November 1852.
122 W.O. 46/87, p. 325; *Military Review*, I, 1853, p. 176; *British Army Despatch*, 18 March 1853, p. 180.
123 P.P. 1846, XVI, p. 328.
124 B.M. Add. Mss 40461, f. 155, Wellington to Peel, 7 August 1845.
125 B.M. Add. Mss 40461, f. 288.
126 Wellington papers, Wellington to Anglesey, [8] February 1847, 9 March 1847; Wellington to Russell, 4 September 1847.
127 Wellington papers, Wellington to Maule, 29 December 1847; S.R.O., GD 45/8/34, memo by Wellington, 27 December 1847.
128 P.P. 1850, X, pp. 770-3.
129 W.O. 1/601, ff. 221-35; Newcastle papers, NeC 10055, Hardinge to Newcastle, 28 January 1853.
130 Hardinge papers, Hardinge to Prince Albert, 5 November 1852.
131 Hansard, 3rd series, LXXIII, c 534.
132 N.L.S. mss 2849, f. 213, distribution of army, 27 November 1851.
133 W. Napier, *Life of C. J. Napier*, II, p. 30.
134 W.O. 80/3, Murray to Peel, 9 August 1845; N.L.S. Adv. Mss 46.9.19, f. 12, memo by Murray, n.d; F. C. Mather, *Public order in the age of the Chartists*, pp. 146-7.
135 F. C. Mather, *Journal of the Society for Army Historical Research*, XXXVI, 1956, pp. 110-24; Wellington papers, E. Macarthur to Somerset, 16 August 1842, and Wellington to Graham, 19 August 1842.
136 Wellington papers, Graham to Wellington, 22 August 1842.
137 S.R.O., GD 45/8/21, Grey's memorandum, 17 October 1846, p. 7; W.O. 43/844; W.O. 44/539.
138 B.M. Add. Mss 40461, f. 176, Peel to Wellington, 9 August 1845.
139 B.M. Add. Mss 40461, f. 184, Wellington to Peel, 12 August 1845.
140 S.R.O., GD 45/8/21, Grey's memo, 17 October 1846, p. 7.
141 W.O. 43/844, ff. 481, 487.
142 P.P. 1850, X, pp. 163, 168, 1014.
143 Herbert papers, III A (77) (b).
144 Hansard, 3rd series, XXVII, c 1155; J. W. Fortescue, *History of the British army*, XI, pp. 99-104, 448.
145 Rollo Russell (ed.), *Early correspondence of Lord John Russell*, II, pp. 117-19, 126-31, 176, 179-82.
146 W.O. 43/729; P. P. 1850, X, pp. 911-12; H. A. Bruce (ed.), *Life of William Napier*, II, p. 83.
147 Wellington papers, Hardinge to Wellington, 11 October 1843.
148 Herbert papers, I L (8), Graham to Fremantle, 11 October 1844.
149 Hansard, 3rd series, LXXXII, c 1226.
150 Wellington papers, Wellington to Stanley, 15 July 1845.
151 B.M. Add. Mss 40461, f. 176, Peel to Wellington, 9 August 1845.
152 Herbert papers, I M (26), Herbert to Murray, 3 October 1845.
153 Herbert papers, I M (47), I O (8), II A (1).

154 R.A. E 42/26, memo, 22 December 1847.
155 Wellington papers, Wellington to Russell, 6 September 1847.
156 R.A. E 42/26.
157 S.R.O., GD 45/8/36; see also GD 45/8/21, Grey to Maule, 17 January 1848.
158 G. P. Gooch (ed.), *Later correspondence of Lord John Russell*, I, pp. 245-66.
159 Spencer Walpole, *Life of Lord John Russell*, II, pp. 19-22.
160 Hansard, 3rd series, CXIX, cc 551-8, 578-80, 842-9, 874-6.
161 Ibid., CXX, cc 275-9.
162 Ibid., CXXII, cc 729-31.
163 Ibid., CXX, c 1063.
164 Ibid., CXXXI, c 182; see also CXXIV, c 689.
165 Ibid., CXXI, c 336.
166 *Speech of the Rt. Hon. Earl Grey on the second reading of the militia Bill ...*, p. 33.
167 Hansard, 3rd series, CXIX, cc 58-9; R.A. E 43/14, memo 7 February 1852.
168 Ibid., CXIX, c 1426.
169 Wellington papers, Walpole to Wellington, 15 April 1852.
170 Herbert papers, II G (4); R.A. E 45/38, Herbert to Albert, 29 July 1853.
171 *British Army Despatch*, 2 September 1853, p. 564.
172 Hardinge papers, Hardinge to Prince Albert, 5 November 1852.
173 *Wellington despatches*, II, pp. 378-9, B.M. Add. Mss 40474, f. 42, memo by Hardinge, 24 January 1842.
174 W.O. 43/693, f. 311; W.O. 1/595, p. 54.
175 *King's Regulations*, 1837, p. 165.
176 Wellington papers, Somerset to Wellington, 7 July 1839, enclosing Gordon's memorandum.
177 P.P. 1833, VII, p. 228.
178 Sir George Cathcart papers, 'Essay on the organization of an army', May 1831.
179 B.M. Add. Mss 37415, f. 136, Wellington to Fitzgerald, 26 March 1842.
180 W.O. 1/596, pp. 515-43; also pp. 561-75, where Lt. Black puts the idea forward, 1841; Wellington papers, Wellington to Stanley, 5 February 1842.
181 W.O. 6/128, p. 58, S.R.O., GD 45/8/64, Grey to Wellington, 7 December 1849.
182 W.O. 1/601, pp. 232-3.
183 Grey papers, Charles Grey to Howick, 23 April 1838.
184 *N. & M.G.*, 24 August 1850, p. 538.
185 Grey papers, Charles Grey to Howick, 23 April 1838.
186 W.O. 3/97, p. 323.
187 Hugh Robinson, letter of 15 April 1852.
188 W.O. 3/95, p. 122.
189 W.O. 1/595, pp. 74-81.
190 *U.S.M.*, 1853, I, pp. 608-11.
191 W.O. 1/595, pp. 82-94; W.O. 43/693, ff. 329-30.

192 Wellington papers, Howick to Wellington, 28 June 1839.
193 Wellington papers, Normanby to Wellington, 17 June 1839, and reply; Wellington to Howick, 30 June 1839; W.O. 1/595, pp. 97-114, 195-207, 227-55.
194 W.O. 6/127, pp. 55, 58; W.O. 1/595, p. 221.
195 W.O. 3/296, p. 157.
196 *N. & M.G.*, 30 September 1848, p. 633.
197 W.O. 6/128, pp. 58, 67; W.O. 1/600, p. 203; W.O. 3/112, pp. 94, 104.
198 Grey papers, Charles Grey to Howick, 24 January 1848.
199 Grey papers, Grey to Tulloch, 11 November 1847.
200 Grey papers, Tulloch to Grey, 14 January 1848.
201 Seaton papers, unsigned and undated memorandum, [?1853].
202 Grey papers, Charles Grey to Grey, 10 February 1852; R.A. E 43/24, Albert to Russell, 14 February 1852; Theodore Martin, *Life of Prince Consort*, II, pp. 433-7.
203 R.A. E 43/27, Russell to Albert, 15 February 1852.
204 Wellington papers, memorandum by Somerset, 17 February 1852.
205 Wellington papers, memorandum by Brown, 17 February 1852.
206 Grey papers, Charles Grey to Grey, 10 February 1852.
207 R.A. E 36/1, memo by Albert, 14 April 1852; Grey papers, Charles Grey to Howick, 1 May 1852.
208 Theodore Martin, *Life of Prince Consort*, II, p. 444; Grey's journal, C 3/16, 24 April 1852.
209 Hardinge papers, Panmure to Hardinge, 26 September 1852.
210 N.L.S. mss 2849, ff. 208-9, Hardinge to Brown, 24 November 1851.
211 Hardinge papers, Hardinge to Prince Albert, 27 March 1856.
212 R.A. E 2/55, C. Grey to Airey, 31 January 1853.
213 Hardinge papers, Russell to Herbert, 15 January 1853; also Herbert papers, III A (53), C. Grey to Herbert, 7 February 1853.
214 R.A. E 2/54, memo by Cambridge, January 1853, quoted in Willoughby Verner, *Military life of Duke of Cambridge*, I, pp. 44-53.
215 R.A. E 2/58, C. Grey to Cambridge, 7 February 1853.
216 R.A. E 2/59, Cambridge to C. Grey, [February 1853].
217 R.A. Add. E/1 no. 149, Airey to Cambridge, 6 May 1853.
218 Herbert papers, III A (54), Herbert to C. Grey, 26 July 1853.
219 Newcastle papers, NeC 10591 and 10595b, memo by Hardinge, 21 March and 29 April 1854; Hardinge papers, Hardinge to Prince Albert, 22 March, 5 and 10 May 1854.
220 Newcastle papers, NeC 9688, Albert to Newcastle, 25 March 1854; 10593b, C. Grey to Newcastle, 29 March 1854, and 10605b, memo by [?] C. Grey, n. d.
221 Herbert papers, Prince Albert to Hardinge, 17 April 1854, and undated memorandum; Newcastle papers, NeC 9688, Albert to Newcastle, 25 March 1854; 98785, f. 52, Newcastle to Albert, 25 March 1854; 10592, C. Grey to Newcastle, 29 March 1854.
222 W.O. 6/128, p. 277; Newcastle papers, NeC 10648, Manteuffel to Bloomfield, 6 March 1854.

223 R.A. E 3/52, Hardinge to Newcastle, 22 March 1854.
224 P.P. 1854-5, XXXII, p. 483.
225 Olive Anderson, 'Early experience of manpower problems', *Political Science Quarterly*, LXXXII, 1967, pp. 530-1.
226 J. W. Fortescue, *History of the British army*, XIII, p. 525.
227 Hardinge papers, Prince Albert to Hardinge, 19 April 1854.
228 R.A. E 3/53, memo by Hardinge, 21 March 1854.
229 *Aide-mémoire to the military sciences*, I, pp. 2-3.
230 P.P. 1854-5, IX, part I, *2nd report*, p. 48.
231 Herbert papers, III B (216), memo by Herbert, 27 November 1854.

CHAPTER 7
THE ADMINISTRATION OF THE ARMY

1. *The system*

The division of the army's strategic responsibilities into three possible areas — the defence of Britain, the protection of the colonies, and the launching of an overseas expedition — was reflected in a three-way split in cabinet administration. The supreme political officer was the Secretary of State for War and the Colonies, and his combination of duties in part explains the increasingly imperial orientation of the army's priorities. Grey demonstrated that his powers were sufficient to overcome much of the incubus of bureaucratic lethargy but his frustration bears witness to the limitations imposed on some of the directions in which his reforming zeal pointed him.

The Home Secretary was answerable for the defence of the United Kingdom and its civil order. He controlled the reserve forces, the movements of regular troops in Britain and appointments to the commands of home districts. As with the Secretary of State for War, these powers in practice extended little beyond formal approval for the actions of the Horse Guards or the War Office, but they deprived these latter two of initiative and overall responsibility in key areas.

The third Secretary of State, that for foreign affairs, had no fixed responsibility in defence matters, and this was even more dangerous, for he was in consequence not kept fully informed of military developments. As the *United Service Magazine* caustically commented, 'Though he may exercise no executive control over details, it is chiefly to the blunders and intriguing of such functionaries that our participation in European wars is owing.'[1] Thus the Foreign Office was central to British strategy. However, formal contact extended little beyond occasional requests for intelligence on military affairs abroad. The lack of an administrative machinery for the ready exchange of information in peacetime implied a divergence between foreign policy and military planning in wartime.

A fourth senior cabinet minister also exercised power over the army, and, as in the case of the Foreign Office, it was no less real for being on the whole implicit. This was the Chancellor of the Exchequer. He had direct responsibility in one vital area — that of the Commissariat — since, in addition to its duties of transport and supply in the field, the Commissariat disbursed from the government chest overseas. Beyond this, the Treasury had a nominal interest in all military affairs by virtue of its comprehensive financial control. Furthermore, in the Treasury the growth of a professional civil service was more pronounced than in other departments, and consequently its supervision of expenditure was tighter and even pettifogging. De Lacy Evans expressed the exasperation which many soldiers felt after dealings with the fount of their livelihood: 'It appeared to me almost that the regulations of the Treasury, or the technical regulations, were adopted in a sort of antagonistic spirit, rather than one of cordial concurrence with us'.[2]

Those who became inured to the tight purse-strings of Victorian administration had to contend with a different but as confounding a problem. Penny-pinching rather than good management became the hallmark of the head of a department. Dr. Andrew Smith, Director General of the Army Medical Department in 1854, succintly expounded the consequences: 'Until the war broke out, I had for forty years been nursed to save money, and not to spend it; and when I found on this war coming on that the country was liberal, and that I dared to spend money, I felt that the screw had been so tightly applied to me, that I could not believe myself when I knew that I could spend money without going through the regular forms'.[3]

All the four ministers mentioned above were of cabinet rank: less frequently included in this cachet was the Secretary at War. Nominally, his ministerial superiors could control his every action. Even in the realm of army finance, for which he was responsible to Parliament, Howick was infuriated to discover that the Treasury could act on all questions of military expenses which had to be defrayed out of the grant for army extraordinaries without consulting the Secretary at War. Strictly speaking, his responsibility was only 'that of administering in detail and on fixed and previously sanctioned rules and principles those grants which are made by Parliament upon the annual estimates which have been framed by him in strict conformity with the principles to which my Lords of the Treasury have given their approval'.[4]

In practice, however, the daily management of military expenditure gave the Secretary at War considerable discretionary power. One of

Howick's successors, Fox Maule, revealed the range of War Office involvement. Although the Ordnance administered the army's buildings, the Secretary at War distributed the allowances arising from them; although the Ordnance contracted for provisions at home, the Commissariat for those abroad, and the Admiralty for those on board ship, the Secretary at War paid the regulated stoppages; although the Horse Guards commanded the army, the Secretary at War supervised divine service, was in charge of military prisons, prepared the Mutiny Act and Articles of War, and ran the army's schools and libraries.[5] In the jungle of military administration, the astute Secretary at War could therefore achieve much without making an issue of consolidation. What Howick objected to was in part no more than form.

The scale of his achievement depended to a considerable degree on his relationship with the Commander-in-Chief — as Howick's and Hill's uneasy truce, and Herbert's and Hardinge's more enthusiastic collaboration, testify. The Horse Guards gave executive authority but could not act without the War Office's financial support; in its turn the War Office was the weaker if it lacked the sympathy of the Horse Guards. The balance of the relationship was, in Palmerston's reckoning, of recent origin.[6] There had been no effective Commander-in-Chief before the Duke of York's appointment in 1795. His royal status, combined with the crisis of the Napoleonic wars and a succession of weak Secretaries at War, created a powerful basis for the Horse Guards. But, although the close link between the throne and the Horse Guards might give the Commander-in-Chief occasional illusions as to his powers, in terms of policy he was simply the executive officer of the Secretary of State for War and the Home Secretary. His department consisted of the Adjutant General, responsible for discipline, dress, recruiting and similar matters, and the Quarter Master General, in charge of quarters, routes and orders of march. He was aided in the performance of his duties by the Military Secretary, who busied himself in particular with promotion and the allied problems of army officers. The Adjutant General worked closely with the Judge Advocate General, a political appointee answerable to the sovereign, who scanned the proceedings of courts-martial and supervised the correct interpretation of military law.

All these Horse Guards officers, their departments, assistants and deputies, were preoccupied — not unnaturally — with the daily problems of administering an army scattered over much of the globe. Their task was to follow the broad principles on which the army was run, to read the reports and returns — which grew in number throughout the 1830s and

'40s and to which the reforms of this period and of the Duke of York's command had given rise. The initiation of change and broad policy discussion did not lie within the confines of their jobs. True, the Horse Guards had its own deliberative council, the Board of General Officers. From the Board, an acting committee of a lieutenant-general, four major-generals and a secretary was nominated by the Commander-in-Chief.[7] But its business, aside from the consideration of the future of Sandhurst in 1832, was almost entirely confined to matters of dress and lesser items of equipment; firearms did not normally come under its scrutiny, as they constituted a province of the Board of Ordnance. Even in those matters constituting its normal currency it could only consider such business as the Commander-in-Chief put before it, and tended to follow the Commander-in-Chief's own opinion.

The final branch of the military administration of Britain was in many ways uncluttered with the conflicting responsibilities, the lacunae and overlaps encountered by the rest. This was the Ordnance department, comprising at its apex the Master General of the Ordnance and the Board of Ordnance. J. H. Stocqueler defined the department's duties as 'The provision, custody and supply of every description of warlike stores, whether for sea or land service; ordnance, carriages, small arms, ammunition, pontoons, tents, and camp-equipage, entrenching tools: everything, in short, which is required to arm a fleet or fortress, or to equip an army for the field'.[8] Many of these items were developed and manufactured by the department itself, whether for the army or navy. On to its responsibility for the fortresses of the empire had been added in 1822 the care of barracks, previously a department within the Horse Guards. The Royal Engineers, who, together with the Royal Artillery and the Royal Military Academy, also came under the aegis of the Ordnance, were thus as concerned with civilian architecture as with military. Owing to the need for adequate maps for home defence, the survey of the United Kingdom was in the Ordnance's hands. The maintenance of permanent stores at home and in the colonies, which the issue of arms and accoutrements necessitated, meant responsibility for the clothing of those regiments not provided for by their colonels, the issue of greatcoats and the equipping of the militia. The Commissariat was relieved by the Ordnance of the necessity to keep stores of its own, and bread, meat and forage at home, and oats, fuel and light abroad came from within the latter's portals. To administer all this, each station had so-called 'respective officers': these were the principal storekeeper and the local commanders of the Royal Artillery and Royal Engineers, who were jointly answerable to the Board of Ordnance for the equipment and buildings in their charge.

This association of civil and military duties in one functionary was what marked the Ordnance as so clearly independent of the traditions and developments of the other departments. The latter had been conceived after 1688 and were hedged around by constitutional trammels, but the ancient Ordnance breathed the simpler, monarchical air of the Tudors. Supervision of its activities was minimal. The Master General was a soldier and yet his appointment was political, carrying with it until the Napoleonic wars cabinet rank. The Treasury made a block grant, but its ratification was not required for any alteration in the use of the money, provided the overall total was not exceeded.[9] Although the department's concern for barracks brought it into regular dealings with the Quarter Master General and for arms and equipment with the Adjutant General, its contact with the Secretary at War was only occasional. Thus it embodied within itself its own departments of expenditure and account, its own deliberations and resolutions.

While the Master General was supreme in all this, in practice much was delegated. The civil business was the affair of the Board of Ordnance, whose meetings the Master General rarely attended. The Board was formed of the Surveyor General, the Clerk of the Ordnance, and the Principal Storekeeper: in 1854 the first two of these appointments were political, and, although one of the two was often a soldier and the storekeeper a sailor, no room was found for gunners or sappers. These two corps had their own effective heads, the Deputy Adjutant General of the Artillery and the Inspector General of Fortifications for the Engineers. Both dealt directly with the Master General or his secretary. Also directly answerable to the Master General was the Ordnance Select Committee, formed of the heads of the artillery departments, for the purpose of examining new inventions, particularly firearms and other weapons. Although often accused of obscurantism, owing to the frequency with which it had to reject fantastic submissions conceived by Heath Robinson minds, in fact the Select Committee, particularly under Sir George Murray's guidance, consulted a wide body of opinion, including line and naval officers, sappers and scientists. Like the Board of General Officers, it was 'a committee of opinion, not a committee of decision',[10] but unlike the former it was readily consulted and it spawned a number of imitators, including the Small Arms Committee (set up in 1848)[11] and the Coast Defence Committee. Thus, in theory at any rate, the Ordnance was a model to the other departments of rational organisation, of responsibility centred on one man but balanced by delegation, of a board of account held from too much pruning by the experience of a senior officer.

In practice, of course, the Ordnance, although so beautifully balanced and self-contained, only added to the proliferation of departments within the army's administration. It had survived because in the overall management of defence it was offset by the departments of economy and of rigid accounting. This division of authority, part answerable to Parliament, part (in theory) falling within the royal prerogative, was a direct result of the 1689 settlement. It had managed to survive in an age when the maturity of constitutional government had made such a division an unnecessary precaution and when the complexity and size of armies meant that so many splits at ministerial level confounded the running of the army. Those who clung to the constitutional argument in defence of the *status quo* did so less to protect the royal prerogative, which parliamentary financial control had effectively already eliminated, than in the fear of total subordination to the cheeseparing parsimony of the Treasury.

The administration of the army therefore embodied in its structure the mutual animosity of soldiers and politicians. In many instances both desired the same ends, and certainly both were interested in overall military efficiency. Furthermore, Grey's work would have been considerably easier had he enlisted the wholehearted support of the military fraternity. But, while much of the blame can be attached to his abrasive personality, a due measure should be heaped on the institutional difficulties. The fixation afforded by an external threat could allow one personality to dominate for a sufficient period for something to be done — fear of invasion gave both the Duke of York and Lord Hardinge sufficient importance in counsel to achieve much reform, and Grey's colonial interests were a key to his successes in military administration. But the norm was an impasse, made more insurmountable by parliamentary indifference. Schemes could thus disappear in the no man's land between the military and civil camps.

The atmosphere of rancour and distrust between the two sides, which the Crimean war did nothing to alleviate, gave the military a sense of corporate identity. It was perhaps a false professionalism, born not of achievement but of the sufferings of military service, and of a 'them and us' mentality in the institutions of government. Its products in terms of military policy were unreservedly evil. Many minor reforms discussed in this book foundered on the route from one desk to another, from a rigidity in the proper channels of communication, from a deliberately narrow interpretation of a certain office's duties. In this, of course, Wellington was a past-master. It meant that, assuming relative parliamentary indifference, a cohesive reform programme and its adaptation to a broad national strategy were physically, quite apart from psychologically, impossible.

The reluctance to initiate sprang not simply from inertia or conservatism. Many officers and civilian administrators had positive suggestions and ideas for the army. The rudiments existed for their examination and development — the Quarter Master General's office, the Ordnance committees, the Board of General Officers, the Senior Department at Sandhurst, and the *ad hoc* meetings of departmental heads in 1852-4. But increasingly the plethora of departments created a bureaucracy that drowned itself in the very forms, returns and reports which reform threw up. Between 1835 and 1852 the War Office's workload increased by 101 per cent (it dealt with 34,528 letters in 1836 and 1,069,371 in 1852) but its staff rose by only 60 per cent, and it needed eight more clerks than it had.[12] Nor were the other departments any better off: in 1825 831 cases were referred to the Master General of the Ordnance and 32,586 matters put to the Board for decision; in 1848 these figures were 1,356 and 45,163.[13] At the Horse Guards the consequences of the revised articles of war and of the proposals of the punishment commission were to unleash a flow of periodic returns on matters that the commanding officer had previously been left to deal with himself. Minor reforms without a major reshaping of the overall administration only added to the burden of a badly designed machine: the Director General of the Army Medical Department ruefully pointed out that a considerable diminution in his work-load would have been possible if he had been answerable to one man alone.[14]

The problems of good command were therefore multiplied in accordance with the number of authorities to be dealt with. The army felt angry about the barracks, which, it argued, the Ordnance constructed but it had to live in. Sir Charles Napier expressed the difficulties of grappling with these coils while in command of the Northern District in 1839. In trying to settle the accommodation of the gunners in his command he was an intermediary from another department placed between two sections of the Ordnance. He wrote: 'This, and other difficulties and irregularities proceed from the monstrous absurdity of giving the army half a dozen instead of one. The Ordnance alter your barracks, yet I know nothing of it, because we belong to separate armies: — one commanded by the Master-General of the Ordnance, the other by the Master-General of the Infantry and Cavalry. Then comes a third: — the Master-General of Finance. Last, not least, the Master-General of the Home Office, more potent than all ... God help the poor English army among so many cooks.'[15] The Ordnance officers, from their side, could bemoan that the sizes of their corps were fixed not as a proportion of the size of the army with which they would serve but as an element in the Ordnance estimates: the number of gunners was affected more by the numbers of storekeepers to be paid, forts to be built, barracks renovated, than the numbers of infantry or cavalry they would have to support in battle.

The most vulnerable administrative areas were those that lay beyond the range of an energetic minister, or were peripheral to his own or another's department. Above all, as the Crimea was amply to demonstrate, this was true of the Commissariat. Herein was the principle of balanced interests finely honed — administered by the Treasury, it worked for the army; responsible for the provision of stores, it was itself not a storekeeper's department but only contracted for stores from others; a department of account, expenditure lay with the fighting branches. The equipoise was however taken further by the progress of colonial administration. The commissaries serving in colonies reported to the Treasury only the details of the contracts for provisions, forage, fuel and light that they had made: the actual administration of the government chest was done by the commissaries themselves, and thus their principal function became banking.[16] In 1851 therefore their duties were defined as:

1. To raise, keep and disburse funds for the foreign expenditure of Britain.
2. To get provisions, forage, fuel and light for the army and navy.
3. To purchase or contract for all stores, except buildings and barrack supply.
4. To provide all land and inland water transport.[17]

The contrast with the duties of a commissary-general as defined by one who had had field experience at Walcheren and in the Peninsula, in Canada and the West Indies, Sir R. I. Routh, is self-evident: 'The Commissary-General is responsible, in all its extensive meaning, for the supply of the army. He is to provide the money, he is to pay the troops, he is to victual them, and he is to furnish all the Transport, — of which the prominent details are the conveyance of all kind of stores, the heavy guns and materials for siege, the ammunition, the field equipment, the supplies of provisions and forage corn, the removal of the sick, and bringing up from the rear the clothing and other necessaries as required ... Much, therefore, must every military operation depend on his judgment and ability.'[18] The total neglect in practical terms of this definition of the Commissariat's duties put all the weight on the other end of the balance, which came crashing down in favour of routine, form-filling and sterility.

Surprise is justifiable, for was not the army at Waterloo in so many respects an eighteenth-century one? Should it not therefore have been as enamoured of its magazines and transport arrangements as had been Frederick the Great? Wellington indeed had clearly grasped the fundamental importance of the Commissariat in the Peninsula. Successive sieges and continued campaigning over the same area, particularly in a country as backward as Spain, gave the war in regards to supply an appearance very different from that of Napoleon's early campaigns. Requisitioning remained the crux, but it was supplemented by lengthy supply lines fed from the sea. These factors, and the need to maintain the friendship of the indigenous population, forced Sir Robert Kennedy to establish a highly organised system of accumulation and distribution. Nor did the Duke forget in later life the crucial position that supply occupied in the maintenance of an army. For him and for all his pupils, the Kabul disaster was a salutary reminder. Sir Harry Smith thought the supply question central to an understanding of the failures in Afghanistan, since 'The success of all military operations depend upon Food and Transport'.[19] Not surprisingly Smith was a keen supporter of Charles Napier's baggage train,[20] formed for service in Scinde.

Little followed from these insights primarily because, beyond the protection or plundering of convoys, transport and supply did not constitute part of a British soldier's duties. The details of their management were the province of the Commissariat department. Even in the Crimea, Raglan, according to Airey, thought that they had no claims on the attentions of the Adjutant General or of the Quarter Master General.[21] In 1852, in an otherwise breathtakingly panoramic view of the problems of creating an army for home defence, Hardinge skated over the entire question. From precise details of ammunition waggons he passed to a brief reference to common carts for the conveyance of provisions. 'I do not enter,' he added, 'upon the subject of the stores required by the Army Medical Board nor the Waggon Train for sick; nor upon the Commissariat Department, a very large subject. These are arrangements made under the authority from the Treasury, and for which preparations, the Ordnance Department is not responsible.'[22]

Furthermore, such military thought as was devoted to transport and supply rested on the premise that Britain would be fighting a defensive war in friendly territory. Local resources would therefore be available to supplement supplies arriving by sea. The army would not be tied down by siege operations, but would move rapidly over well cultivated land. J. W. Jervis calculated that an army of 100,000 men would cover 270 square miles in a day's march, or in a wheat-producing area enough for twelve days' rations.[23]

More realistic were the comments of Sir John Bisset. By invading from the sea, the British army was forced to act without its supply train and, particularly if the enemy removed all livestock and forage from the littoral areas, any movement could be effectively hamstrung.[24] Tied powerlessly to the coast and precluded (by its desire for friendly relations with the inhabitants) from the customary methods of military supply, those of requisitioning and plundering, the British were more truly dependent on the umbilical cord of the sea than any mainland European power. The fact that in 1854-5 the army also undertook the sedentary operations of a siege simply confirmed the strategic shackles within which it was destined to operate.

But the cautionary wisdom of Bisset ran counter not only to the prevailing notions of likely British military involvement but also to the wishful thinking of the Treasury. Although he had commissioned Bisset's book, Sir Charles Trevelyan, appearing before the Roebuck commission, argued that no amount of transport from outside the theatre of operations could enable an army to take the field. It simply had to rely on the resources locally available. Therefore, although an expeditionary army would be mounted from the United Kingdom, it was here alone that the Commissariat did not supply the army, nor possess any contingency plans should it have to do so. By relying on local transport, the Commissariat was even more subject to the vagaries of British strategy than any other military department. Trevelyan maintained that not even provisional supply arrangements could be planned before the theatre of operations was decided upon.[25]

The lack of a system of transport and supply fit for the field had not entirely escaped the attention of soldiers, even if the ease with which responsibility could be passed on to the Treasury allowed them to wash their hands. The disbandment of the Royal Waggon Train in 1833 prompted unfavourable comment. The 1838 rebellion in Canada showed that Routh, although later the author of the nearest thing to a manual on the Commissariat (*Observations on Commissariat Field Service*, 1846 and 1852), in fact had little notion on the organisation of arrangements for a campaign. In fairness, the notice given him was short, but Sir George Cathcart's observations were to find later echoes. The men who staffed the Commissariat were unfit for the task. The system of ration returns conceived by the Treasury for office use was so complicated for the field that a unit as small as a sergeant's party was requested to fill in its returns in quintuplicate. Eventually Sir John Colborne sanctioned virtual plunder as the Commissariat broke down altogether.[26]

The fighting in South Africa in 1846-7 revealed a similar tale. 'Our Commissariat Department,' one officer wrote, 'is still the complicated piece of mechanism it was in former days — at all times a source of annoyance and perplexity to military commanders.'[27] Thereafter the military press reflected increasing concern, and several of the soldiers later involved in the Crimean expedition shared its scepticism. Burgoyne, Raglan's strategic adviser, who had sounded off on the subject of the Commissariat in his memorandum on home defences of 1846,[28] referred again to its deficiencies in 1853, urging the establishment in Britain of a complete system of transport and supply for a division.[29] Lord De Ros, the expedition's first Quarter Master General, in a book of 1851, averred that Wellington's field train had been sacrificed to the peacetime duties of 'government accountants'. 'From our Commissariat being under civil organization in peace time,' he concluded, 'whenever a British army takes the field again in Europe, the Commander of it will have to go through, all over again, the training and formation of his field commissaries.'[30] Sir George Brown, who commanded a division in the Crimea, told the 1850 committee on army and ordnance expenditure that a commissary's current peacetime duties were not the slightest training for the field. His opinion was shared by the future Lord Raglan himself.[31]

Any analysis of the training, appointment and promotion of the Commissariat department reinforced this conclusion. Candidates for clerkships were required to know the arithmetical rules of practice, interest, the rule of three and vulgar fractions, the principles of book-keeping by double entry, and had to be able to write English fairly and grammatically.[32] In 1839 the forty clerks thus recruited were employed purely as accountants, and, since the promotion blockage was as great as in the army itself, they had no prospect of becoming officers for a minimum of ten years. Thus the fitness of their youth was passed in an atmosphere far removed from the exigencies of field service.

The commissaries who had been forged in the Peninsular school confirmed these criticisms, even if they tempered them out of deference to their own department. Sir Robert Kennedy's own doubts, expressed in 1840,[33] were supplemented by those of Routh, whose main concern was for home defence but who pointed out to Fitzroy Somerset in 1845 that no experienced Commissariat existed for any force starting out from the United Kingdom. He urged the maintenance of depots, and of detailed plans for their mobilisation, including the possible employment of railways.[34] Sir John Bisset argued for the formation of the nucleus of a supply train at home and pointed out that the commissary general on service could not possibly cope with both the financial and military duties. If an expedition was despatched without attention having been paid to the likely problems, the backlog could only accumulate, with terrible consequences.[35] Finally the vacillating evidence of William Filder, the Commissary General in the Crimea, in addressing the 1850 committee, could only have reinforced the doubts raised by Brown and Somerset before the same body.

The defence presented to the committee by Sir Charles Trevelyan, rather feebly seconded by the Chancellor of the Exchequer, was in hindsight sinisterly double-edged: 'Should events require a British army again to take the field, a body of well-trained commissariat officers, animated by the best spirit, would be ready to perform all the necessary services, and to keep in check the lavish expenditure which has generally been incurred at the commencement of a campaign.'[36] This statement, tantamount to a full acceptance of responsibility for 1854, flew in the face of all informed opinion. However, the suggestion the committee adopted was that of William Booth, a commisary in the Peninsula. He concluded that, since in peacetime the men intended for the field were only employed in offices and were not fit for service, it was pointless to keep up the establishment 'with a view to the remote contingency of having a corps applicable to the purposes of war'.[37] The committee's recommendation along these lines[38] is an excellent illustration of the consequences of divided administration: the soldiers had lacked the political muscle to get what they wanted, but had nonetheless divested themselves of responsibility. The commissioners had read the expert evidence aright, but since no plan for the use of an expeditionary force existed had opted for a false economy. Even Sidney Herbert, as Secretary at War in 1853, reflected the same attitude: he knew that 'the machinery fit for larger operations, or capable of sudden expansion, is not being maintained', but nonetheless accepted the Treasury's avowal that the Commissariat would be fit for the task.[39] Even for those who realised the likely consequences, the cosy cocoon of self-delusion was too attractive. After all, nobody really knew what they were planning for.

The argument that a stronger internal organisation of the Commissariat might have mitigated the effects of divided higher control is not borne out by the example of the Army Medical Department. In 1810 the independent functioning of the Physician General, Surgeon General and Inspector General of Hospitals, who together made up the Army Medical Board, was brought to an end. In its stead a consolidated Army Medical Department under a Director General was established. In 1815 this appointment was given to Sir James McGrigor, who had already carried through with considerable success a programme of reform in the Peninsular army. The department was to have the benefit of his care until he was succeeded by Dr. Andrew Smith in 1851.

McGrigor's achievement was twofold. Of the first aspect, the role of the medical officer in army reform, and in particular the accumulation of statistics relating to mortality and disease and their application to the improvement of the soldier's conditions of service, much has already been said. It was the essential preliminary to an adaptation of the army to the requirements of colonial garrisoning.

The second aspect of his work was to make military medicine a profession in its own right. In 1816 educational standards for a first commission were set, and from 1826 a diploma from one of the Royal Colleges of Surgeons was required.[40] A museum and library devoted to military surgery and hygiene were set up in Fort Pitt, at Chatham. It was here that the novice underwent the training designed to turn him from a civilian doctor into a medical officer. Foreign diseases, gunshot wounds and other subjects of which he had as yet no practical experience were studied. In 1844, the course, one future surgeon-general recalled, was 'more extensive and comprehensive than that required by the different universities and schools of medicine and surgery'.[41]

Peacetime contraction adversely affected the medical officers' morale as much as any others'. Not only was promotion slow: it was also irregular. Regimental surgeons were on the regiment's establishment rather than that of the Army Medical Department. The gap between the two was widened by the fact that the latter could recruit its lowest grade, assistant inspector general of hospitals, direct from civilian life. For his part the regimental surgeon might be ambivalent about seeking promotion into the Army Medical Department. On the one hand there was the danger that from there he would be put on half pay; but, on the other hand, if he had a private practice, this relegation could prove highly lucrative, and therefore even while on full pay the attractions of building up a practice would distract him from giving full attention to his military patients.[42] Finally, although primarily administrative in its duties, the department's appointments reflected the medical division between physic and surgery which the omnicompetent regimental surgeon could not afford to recognise.

In 1830 McGrigor, with Hardinge's aid, carried through a reform of the rank and promotion organisation, which integrated the regimental and staff systems and gave the profession a regulated career structure. All had to enter as assistant surgeons: the rest of the ladder went through the ranks of regimental surgeon, staff surgeon (on the departmental establishment) and then on to three grades of inspector of hospitals. A minimum period of service in each rank was stipulated, and pay was increased according to service. Thus promotion for merit was retained at the same time as the burden of peacetime contraction was shouldered: the long-serving surgeon had at least a pecuniary reward if no elevation in rank. The right to retire on half pay was limited to those of more than twenty-five years' service. Physician's rank was ended, as, for reasons and with consequences that will be discussed below, were those of apothecary and purveyor. The work was completed in 1841, when, on the recommendation of the 1840 promotion commission, the rank of assistant inspector of hospitals was abolished and that of staff surgeon split into two classes, the lower ranking with regimental surgeon and the senior with the old assistant inspector: the intention was simply to stress that staff surgeons in certain appointments were senior to regimental surgeons. At the same time, the rates of pay were again improved, thus providing some compensation for McGrigor's continued concern for the inevitably slow rate of promotion.[43]

Two criticisms of the Army Medical Department remained. The first was that it was insufficiently military. The surgeon received his professional education in the same establishment and in the same manner as any civilian surgeon, without any specific attention until later to the types of wound, the variety of tropical diseases or the rules of military hygiene. All this was picked up, after qualifying, at Fort Pitt or with his regiment. A manifestation of this civilian status, minor but one which rankled, was that although medical officers were as much under fire as combatants they were not eligible for the military division of the Order of the Bath. G. J. Guthrie, the distinguished military surgeon and author of *Commentaries on the Surgery of War*, saw this as indicative of a whole process which was preventing surgeons identifying with the military profession. With pardonable hyperbole he used the issue to conclude that 'If a continental war should take place within the next ten years, I am quite satisfied, the same loss of life, the same state of inefficiency will occur in any British Army that may take the field in 1860 that took place in 1810 — Good Physicians, Surgeons and Administrative Officers are only made by encouragement'.[44] With the support of the military and medical press, and of de Lacy Evans in Parliament,[45] officers of the Medical Department and, significantly, of the Commissariat were made eligible for the military division of the Bath in 1850.

This minor issue was therefore a reflection of the major point concerning medical officers' professionalism. A Chair of military surgery, held from 1825 by Professor Sir George Ballingall, was established at Edinburgh University in 1807, and the size of his class reflected a steady growth in interest, expanding from four in 1824 to eighty-one in 1839.[46] Ballingall, with publicity from the *Naval and Military Gazette*, urged the establishment of further professorships, and the attacks on McGrigor for favouring medical officers of his own nationality were perhaps no more than a reflection of Edinburgh's primacy in the field. Lectures on military surgery were started in Dublin in 1846,[47] but not until February 1853 did Dr. Andrew Smith, with Evans' support in the Commons, successfully press on Sidney Herbert the establishment of two new Chairs at Dublin and London, and the transfer of the administration of the Edinburgh Chair from the Home Office to the War Office.[48]

The first criticism of the Army Medical Department was thus countered, but the second was both more controversial and further reaching in its results. In 1813 disease in Wellington's army had been checked by McGrigor's decentralisation of the hospitals. Not only did regimental rather than general hospitals restrict the danger of infection, but they also enabled the sick to have to travel less far for treatment and to be in the hands of those who knew them. The emphasis in favour of regimental hospitals was reinforced by the scattered colonial duties of the army after 1815, which meant that often a regiment would be serving in isolation and that a general hospital would be superfluous. The total absence of general hospitals abroad therefore suited McGrigor's adaptation of the Medical Department to colonial service, as much as it conformed to the War Office's financial restrictions. The only general hospitals in the British army were that at Fort Pitt and those long established at Dublin and Cork.[49]

However McGrigor's solution to the treatment of disease was less applicable to the care of casualties caused in combat. After the battle of Ferozeshah, the regimental surgeon of the 29th Foot and his assistant found that, although they had more than enough casualties to treat from their own regiment, they had to cope with the wounded of the whole division, since there was no medical chief for the army nor a properly organised ambulance service.[50] The advantages of a higher organisation in the field were shown at the battle of Boomplatz in 1848, when Dr. John Hall, as principal medical officer in Kaffraria, coped with three times the number of casualties Sir Harry Smith had warned him to expect.[51] Dr. Andrew Smith therefore proposed a predominance of staff over regimental medical officers, since they could then go to the regiments who had suffered most in action rather than — as was the case with the regimental surgeons — leave certain units over-staffed while others who had been in the centre of the fighting went short.[52]

Not only did Smith's proposal run counter to the Peninsular experience propounded in 1854 by Guthrie, but of course it also upset the whole balance in the army's organisation for imperial defence. Hardinge, when Master General of the Ordnance, vehemently argued for the preservation of the Royal Artillery's regimental medical system. He felt that a consolidated department would undermine the medical officers' zeal and their attachment to their regiment: for their part, the men would find themselves treated by strangers.[53] He was supported by commanding officers who preferred to keep their regimental surgeons answerable to themselves rather than to some higher medical authority. The consequence of this thinking was to produce an admirable system for the army's peacetime duties, but to create a body of officers totally unfamiliar with the administration of general hospitals.

In particular it was at this higher level that the transport of the sick and the supply of medicines operated. In 1854 the Army Medical Department formed an excellent advisory body, helping with the construction of barracks, the diet of the soldier, and other areas of preventive medicine; at the regimental level, the soldiers encountered doctors who were kind, competent and knowledgeable. But between the two extremes there was nothing. No ambulance corps existed for the field, since in peacetime there had been no rear hospital whither to take the sick. Medical supplies were in the hands of the purveyor and the preparation of medicines in those of the apothecary. Yet by 1830 only three purveyors remained on the strength, one for each general hospital. Colonial service meant that regimental surgeons were their own purveyors and apothecaries.

It was here, and above all owing to ignorance of the purveyor's duties, that McGrigor's carefully constructed edifice came crashing down in the winter of 1854–5. Furthermore the principal reason was not the unfamiliarity of the medical officers with the running of general hospitals — on the whole they had sufficient resourcefulness to come to terms with that — but the divided nature of the purveyor's responsibilities. As with the commissary, the purveyor was an officer of account and therefore he could not be answerable to the officers of expenditure. His funds were obtained from the Commissariat chest, and, although he was himself responsible for the purchase of medical comforts (such as sago pudding and port wine), the Board of Ordnance provided the more substantial items, like clothing and bedding. The central role of the purveyor in the smooth running of a general hospital is further emphasised by the fact that he was also responsible for the hospital servants and the general cleanliness of the wards. Although it was clear that ultimately the purveyor was answerable to the War Office, the precise chain of command had become obscured by the fact that the branch had been abolished in 1830 and not revived until April 1853.[54] The purveyor-in-chief in the east therefore concluded that he could only take orders from the Secretary at War himself. Neither the purveyors nor the apothecary had been trained in systems of accounting and thus food could not be issued nor prescriptions made up because nobody even knew what was in store. Although the situation was exacerbated by the recalcitrant personality of the purveyor-in-chief, the real criminal was once again the divided responsibility fostered by excessive regard for constitutional forms. As soon as it was made clear that the purveyor was immediately responsible to the local inspector general of hospitals all began to function more smoothly. But in the interim a fine department, coping manfully with a task for which it had not been designed, was befouled by the army's administrative system.[55]

Indeed, what is remarkable is that the department did not fare even worse. Dr Smith told the Roebuck committee that as Director General of the Army Medical Department he was answerable to the Commander-in-Chief, the Secretary at War, the Master General and the Board of Ordnance.[56] The Treasury provided the money for the medical supplies, the Ordnance the supplies themselves. But the real division was between the Horse Guards, to whom the Director General made his recommendations for promotion, and the War Office, who first had to approve the expense. Financial stringency meant that there were too few medical officers not only in 1854, but even in peacetime. In 1841-4 there were requests for more medical officers from Canada, the West Indies, the Windward and Leeward Islands, New South Wales, western Australia, Gambia and Jamaica.[57] Yet so jealous was he of the expense of a doctor that the Secretary at War's logic could at times be counter-productive: in 1847 he refused to allot more medical officers to the unhealthy climate of West Africa,[58] presumably for fear of losing such massive investments in education and training to the ravages of the disease they were required to check. Even should the War Office be prepared to shoulder the expense of appointing a doctor, there was a chance that his own capacity to help would be hamstrung by the limited resources available for the purchase of medicines and instruments: the resulting practice, according to Dr. David Dumbreck, was to cease to give medicine once a man was convalescent and to rely on diet to complete the cure.[59] Less surprising is it, therefore, that the Army Medical Department should have developed preventive medicine on empirical evidence to such a high degree.

Finally the department could not plan the medical arrangements for a campaign without knowing the strategic alternatives. In fact in the long term it made a greater commitment to colonial defence than other departments, but in the short it was just like the Commissariat in its difficulty in fixing precise details within a framework of the army's likely movements or of intelligence concerning an area of operations. Therefore the Medical Department was limited in the scope of its work by its size, was unprepared to administer a general hospital and could not make prior arrangements for a European campaign — all, on one interpretation, because of the divided control of the army. G. J. Guthrie, admittedly not an officer given to reticence, drew his conclusion in his otherwise strictly professional manual, *Commentaries on the Surgery of the War*. As there was a war minister in charge of the department's finance, so it should be he who headed the department as a whole.[60] Although Guthrie did not say so, what was true for one department was true for the others.

2. *Its reform*

The complexity of the administrative system did not escape the gaze of the army's reformers. It is true that many were so preoccupied with making it work that they could rarely raise their eyes sufficiently to gain an overall perspective, but soldiers as much as statesmen expressed their views on what was fundamentally a political issue. For to unify the control of the army would increase its potential power in the state, whether as an independent pressure group applied to Parliament or as a further subject of parliamentary sovereignty. In the division of the army's loyalties between Parliament and the Crown, Wellington claimed he recognised constitutional safety: the lessons of an army united under

Parliament had been imprinted on Britain in the seventeenth century. In fact what he was doing was preventing its subordination to a government which he saw as hell-bent on false economy.

He and his disciples were able to argue their case so effectively because the Whigs of the 1830s, who first broached the subject, did so on a false premise. They might well have approached the army in a spirit of enlightened detachment, anxious to achieve the rationalisation and logical administration for which the Benthamites and Utilitarians provided the vocabulary. The object would have been economy certainly, but also efficiency. In fact their arguments contained little or no reference to such theories. Their attitude was much more partisan, and sprang from the frustrations of successive Secretaries at War in the War Office and a belief — subscribed to not least by Russell — that in the hands of the Commander-in-Chief army patronage was used for Tory ends. Thus the desire for the consolidation of the military departments was enmeshed in the squabble between the War Office and the Horse Guards.

The Horse Guards had been on the *qui vive* since 1827. The vacancy in the Commander-in-Chief's office in that year had resulted in the temporary transfer of his duties to Palmerston, then Secretary at War. The gap in the succession was prolonged by the ambivalence of Wellington's position and by George IV's own desire to lead his army. This allowed the germination of a number of schemes potentially challenging to the status bequeathed to the command by the Duke of York. Among others, Canning had planned the abolition of the post and the move of the Horse Guards staff to the War Office, with Palmerston elevated to the status of minister of war.[61] Canning's death pre-empted the proposal.

The next attempt at consolidation made little show of disguising the animosity for the Horse Guards in which it was grounded. Sir John Cam Hobhouse, Secretary at War from February 1832, felt that after the Reform Bill was carried the next priority was 'a thorough reform ... in the management of the army'. This conviction derived very largely from his opposition to Hill and his belief that further reductions in the army were essential. In January 1833 he proposed a plan for defining and raising the character of the Secretary at War, so that Hill's powers should be curtailed and his own become those of 'a great state officer'.[62]

Hill's opposition checked the minute in council by which Hobhouse had hoped to carry through his changes. Instead, in March 1833, the Prime Minister, the second Earl Grey, asked Hobhouse, the Duke of Richmond and Lord John Russell to consider new arrangements. This *ad hoc* committee was then replaced by a royal commission, which had a larger membership but which under Richmond's influence produced a very similar draft report.

It proposed that the army be consolidated under a board. The 1828 Finance Committee had reported in very favourable terms on the administration of the Board of Ordnance, and on the balance of its duties with those of the Master General. The Ordnance had consequently acted as a model for the reorganisation of the Admiralty in 1831-2, when its semi-autonomous boards had been replaced by departments, each responsible to a Lord of the Admiralty: the Lords constituted a Board, in which civil and military adminstration was brought under one head. Furthermore, by the reforms of Sir James Graham, First Lord from 1830 to 1834, the Admiralty submitted annually to Parliament an audited account of its expenditure, resulting in a reduction of £1 million with only arguable loss to maritime effectiveness.[63] Therefore the 1833 proposals, although they included the effective abolition of the Board of Ordnance, were really an attempt to apply its blending of accounting and executive responsibilities, of civil and military duties, to the army as a whole. The broad conclusions of Richmond's committee were that the civil departments of the army and Ordnance should be united under the War Office, and the military under the Commander-in-Chief. The War Office would be administered by a board, with a chief commissioner, and further commissioners for the War Office itself, for the Ordnance and for the Paymaster's and Commissariat departments; the board would also have its own secretary, a secretary to the chief commissioner and an accountant general. The cost of this (£10,800) was more than outweighed by the saving of £21,080 calculated as accruing from the abolition of the Board and Master General of the Ordnance, and of the posts of the Paymaster General, the Comptrollers of Army Accounts and the Agent for Commissariat Supplies.[64]

Confusion hit the report at the very outset. Richmond, who had been the driving force but whose proposals were only in draft, resigned and entrusted the commission to Russell. Since Russell entirely concurred with Richmond's report, he did not reconvene the committee, but confined himself to mentioning the issue to the new Prime Minister, Melbourne. Although urging consolidation, Russell vacillated between a board and a single head. By now, however, Sir James Kempt, the Master General, had revealed doubts about the disappearance of his department,[65] and the military press, perhaps stung by Joseph Hume's espousal of the reform, opposed the changes, with the exception of the transfer of the Commissariat to the War Office or to the Quarter Master General's department.

The administration of the army

The whole issue was given fresh impetus by the appointment of Howick as Secretary at War in 1835. Howick soon came to sympathise with the frustrations and ambitions suffered by Hobhouse, and certainly did not share Russell's more dilatory approach. In May the government conceded that the commission should be renewed,[66] and further evidence taken to add to that of the 1833 report. This was provided by the heads of departments, many of them distinguished soldiers. Sir James Kempt, as a former Master General, and Sir Hussey Vivian, as the current incumbent, both opposed the division of the Ordnance's civil and military duties. Hardinge too produced a cogent argument for the *status quo*. The manufacturing departments of the Board were considered as civil, but their products were military, that is to say artillery and ammunition. The passing of the Commissariat to the Ordnance would add an extra burden to an already busy department, and although War Office control of the Commissariat was less objectionable, the same effect would be achieved by the employment of experienced commissaries within the existing structure. This indeed was Hardinge's central theme: the system as it stood met Howick's objections already. The Secretary of State was supreme; when Hardinge was Secretary at War he had not clashed with the Commander-in-Chief; and to all intents and purposes the Royal Artillery and Royal Engineers were subject to the same military discipline as the rest of the army. Hardinge's arguments were reinforced by Wellington, who, most damning of all, also contended that a revision would make for inefficiency. The Secretary at War and the other officials were already fully occupied: if, as members of a board, they also had to consider the work of other departments, the transaction of business would become inordinately slow.[67]

All this had of course no impact on the single-minded Howick. Palmerston and Russell (who now favoured a supreme Secretary of State for the War Office, with three subordinate departmental heads[68]) both gave their advice. However, Howick drafted the committee's report himself.[69] Published in February 1837, its starting point was the fact that the whole army was not under one financial view, but was scattered over different estimates. Here was support for those soldiers who feared that consolidation would be but the preliminary to further reductions. The Richmond proposals were rejected since they did not bring all military expenditure under one head, but instead divided it over two. The solution now proposed was to give the Secretary of State's authority over the army to the Secretary at War. The latter should always be in the cabinet, should advise the King on the army's establishment, liaise between the government and the Commander-in-Chief, and be responsible to Parliament for the army. The Board of Ordnance and the Commissariat should be transferred to his control, but the Master General should retain his authority over the military department and over forts and works. The Commander-in-Chief's powers were to be left nominally unchanged, but in practice were severely curtailed by the enhancement of the Secretary at War's authority. The consolidation proposed would give one account for all military expenditure, would end the duplication of Ordnance and Commissariat stores, would permit all contracts to be made by one department, and would relieve the Treasury of business that was not naturally its own.[70] The scheme had many attractive aspects, but was flawed by the simple fact that its principal author and advocate was the man who stood to gain most in kudos by its implementation.

The clearest statement in favour of the continuance of the 1688 tradition, and a fundamental one because it was cited repeatedly until 1854, came from the Duke of Wellington in a memorandum to Melbourne of 25 March 1837: 'I have always understood that it was a principle of the government of this country, that he who exercised the military command over the Army should have nothing to say to its payment — its movement — its equipment — or even the quartering thereof excepting under the sanction of a civil officer who has himself subordinates in the hierarchy of civil office, and could not take the King's pleasure excepting upon matters of account'. The Duke opposed the commission's proposals because the constitutional checks would be removed, and an all-powerful political officer would put control of the army with Parliament rather than with the King.[71]

But the most important objections came from the King himself. Already ruffled by not having been informed of the progress of a committee so likely to touch on the royal prerogative,[72] William seized on the evidence of the expert witnesses. Not only had they opposed the division of civil and military Ordnance business, but such a division also ran counter to the guiding principle of the recent Admiralty reforms. In conclusion, His Majesty agreed to the report being laid on the table of the House of Commons but could not approve its proposals.[73]

By the end of March 1837 Melbourne, Glenelg, Palmerston and Hobhouse were already backing down: they assured the King that either the report would not be adopted or that it would be so altered as to render it harmless.[74] Melbourne then stated that the report would not be introduced unless all the cabinet agreed to it.[75] This, it was already clear, was unlikely to happen. The two military ministers other than Howick,

Glenelg, the Secretary of State for War and the Colonies,[76] and Vivian, the Master General of the Ordnance, had expressed their doubts.

As a distinguished general and the repository of professional wisdom in the government, Vivian's position was crucial to the thinking of the more open-minded members of the cabinet. The fact that he himself was unclear gave Howick false expectations. Vivian was quite content with the system as it stood, and, if there was to be any change, preferred Richmond's plan for one great department to administer all military matters. In March 1837 he argued for a supreme Commander-in-Chief or Minister of War, to be assisted by an adjutant general, a quartermaster general, a commissary general, a civil secretary (responsible for pay), a military secretary, an inspector general of fortifications, and a principal storekeeper. The supreme head and the civil and military secretaries should all be members of the government, since the constitutional danger was no longer a reality. Vivian was worried that the report, if implemented, would either necessitate constant reference from the War Office to the Ordnance or would take from the Master General the control of those Royal Artillery and Royal Engineer officers engaged in civil duties. However, if it was really felt that the best interests of the public would be served by the report, then he was at this stage prepared to see the Royal Artillery and Royal Engineers go to the Horse Guards, and the comparable financial departments to the War Office, provided an independent Board of Ordnance should continue to administer *matériel*.[77]

This concession was pounced on by Howick, eagerly gathering what crumbs of support he could find. Wishful thinking on his part and an over-anxiety on Vivian's to conform with the wishes of the government were to produce confusion and bitterness. A month later Vivian was privately declaring to the King's secretary that the report bore no relation to the evidence and that he intended to oppose it. He saw that his own office was in truth the most vulnerable, for a strict division of military and civil duties between War Office and Horse Guards would to all intents and purposes abolish the Ordnance.[78]

Faced by this ambivalence, for the moment Howick could do no more than say it was too late in the session for a bill on the basis of the report.[79] However, the new session left him no nearer his goal. For, although the death of the King had removed one obstacle. Melbourne was now fearful of the accusation of pressurising the young Queen.[80] The pause gave Howick time for reflection and he concluded that, since an act would take up parliamentary time and ran the gauntlet of the Lords' opposition, as much as possible should be done without Parliament, through an order in council. Melbourne could always say that the measure was at least introduced in the old King's lifetime. Howick produced a modified scheme, which left the Ordnance estimates intact, but without the gunners and sappers, and with the Commissariat. The Master General was in other respects to stand in the same relation to the Secretary at War as the Commander-in-Chief and was to have the right of direct access to the King.[81]

Howick's plan was to placate Vivian. But instead the cavalryman became more intransigent. His belief in the good administration of the Ordnance department led him to resist the transfer even of accounting business to the War Office. He felt that Howick had taken his least favoured option, to which he did not feel bound, and round it had constructed an order in council that was bound to displease everybody — either because it did not go far enough or because it went too far. A Master General in the same position in relation to the War Office as the Commander-in-Chief would in all probability only add to the likely sources of conflict.[82] Vivian told Melbourne that if a disposition to act in concert had existed between the Horse Guards and War Office, no pressure for change would have emerged. Howick simply wanted to 'raise the Office to the Man & not humble the Man to the Office'. Eventually Vivian issued an ultimatum: if the scheme was to go through, either it would be with the support of Hill and Glenelg or he would resign.[83]

Melbourne was faced with a crisis in his government. Vivian had provided a rallying point for the soldiers. And yet five cabinet ministers felt themselves pledged to the introduction of some measure as they had signed the report. The Prime Minister took refuge in sending the proposed order in council to the Queen, and in asking Hill, as Commander-in-Chief, for his opinion.

Hill informed Melbourne that the Commander-in-Chief was already subordinate to parliamentary officers in such matters as the size of the army and the issue of weapons: all that would happen would be that an additional person would be involved and thus the executive process further delayed. However, the revocation of the 1812 memorandum (in which the Prince Regent had attempted to regulate the powers of the Secretary at War in relation to those of the Commander-in-Chief), when taken in conjunction with the other accretions to the Secretary at War's powers, would have a disastrous total effect: 'The Commander-in-Chief will be left certainly with the power of Commanding on the Parade, but he will no longer have anything to say to the clothing or equipment of the

Troops, their efficiency or general condition and while the responsibility of maintaining their discipline will still rest with him, his means of upholding it will be affected by the knowledge which the Troops will possess that he is without the power of improving their situation'.[84]

Hill had also asked Wellington for his views, and the Duke was thus given the opportunity to deliver a second broadside against the proposals. In fact this opportunity was timely, for in its metamorphosis from report to order in council the infringement on the Commander-in-Chief's powers proposed by the Secretary at War had been made more manifest. Wellington therefore opposed the recommendations on the grounds that they had not been investigated by the committee. As it was, 'The Comr. in Chief cannot move even a Corporal's Guard from one station to another without a route countersigned by the Secretary at War'. The interposition of the Secretary at War between the Home Secretary or the Colonial Secretary and the Commander-in-Chief could only add delay and confusion. The royal prerogative would be infringed by the concentration of military power in the hands of ministers accountable to the House of Commons. 'The British Army,' he concluded in a typical passage, 'however necessary, is an anomaly in our system. It has worked with safety to the Constitution as at present constituted ... Do not let us without reason make an alteration not necessary, which may render its working inconvenient and dangerous.'[85]

In the face of this opposition, Melbourne continued to stall, suggesting further deliberation. By overreaching himself in the order in council Howick had irredeemably weakened his case. He tried to point out that no attack on the Commander-in-Chief's power was intended: all that was to happen was that the Secretary of State's nominal powers (which he had no time to exercise) would be vested in the Secretary at War. The House of Commons, as it had shown in its enquiry in 1809 on the Duke of York's employment of his military patronage, already had an oversight of the Horse Guards.[86] His protestations sounded hollow both in the context of his own ambition and in the popular belief that here was an attempt to add to the already extensive scope of Grey and Whig patronage. Although the cabinet was broadly in favour of consolidation, it could not support a scheme so badly constructed and so naked in its pursuit of power for one man. A rift even opened between Howick and Russell, the former now favouring a board of professional men (like the Admiralty) under a civilian head,[87] the latter, having flirted once again with a board,[88] moving back to an all-powerful Secretary of State. Howick was prepared to agree to any plan that would be workable, but, by yielding to Melbourne's opposition to the order in council, he effectively lost the day.[89] In 1839 the issue was still nominally before the cabinet, but it could not agree, and by then the forceful Howick had gone and its advocacy rested with Russell's lethargy.

During the ensuing decade, the pressure for reform in military administration was taken up by army officers themselves. Sir Charles Napier's infuriation with the barrack system led him to advocate consolidation.[90] In 1841 Lord Seaton favoured the unification of military departments under the Commander-in-Chief and the civil under a minister of war.[91] The commanding officer of the 79th Highlanders, Lauderdale Maule, told his brother: 'The Administration of the British Land-service has for years stood still — the monstrous abuses, which dog all its machinery and impair its working efficiency are fresh and vigorous as they were years & years ago. The hindrances, the bungling and the lavish expenditure of the Ordnance Department are a disgrace to any service and to any nation; the nibbling and hermaphrodite Commissariat is a constant theme of wrangling and disgust; the Barrack-department is fraught with robbery and injustice — the Transport service is rotten to the core — grapple with these coils.'[92]

Although the failings in South Africa in 1846–7 had aroused concern for the Commissariat, the real object of vituperation was the Board of Ordnance. It was to advocate the breaking-up of this department between the War Office and the Horse Guards that much of the energy of the military press was bent. The clamour of frustrated inventors, more often than not blaming the Ordnance for the complexities of their own devices, coincided with the need to develop the new rifle-musket. At the same time the anxiety from 1848 for the state of the Royal Artillery, its equipment and training, led to the conclusion that it would be better under the Commander-in-Chief. Two gunners, Colonel F. R. Chesney and Sir Robert Gardiner, both favoured this solution, as, more surprisingly, did the Royal Engineers' professional journal.[93] But, although assailed from within as well as from without, the Ordnance seemed like 'an eyry in the fastnesses of the rock, which appears to defy all attempts at destruction'.[94]

In 1848 the Prince Consort was caught up in the general condemnation of the Board. Russell, while agreeing with Albert, showed a failing grasp of political sensitivity when he assured him that there was no 'strong wind' for change.[95] The 1849 committee on Ordnance expenditure, although confining itself rigidly to its terms of reference, could not disguise the fact that the department had fallen from the halcyon days of

1828. Ordnance expenditure had doubled between 1836 and 1848, from £1·5 million to £2·9 million. Despite the growth in business, there had been no proportionate increase in a staff which was further hampered by being geographically divided over a number of different offices.[96] In May 1849 Bernal Osborne proposed in the Commons that the 1837 proposals be implemented.[97] However, the year closed with another blistering memorandum from Wellington.

The Duke had sensed only too well the drift of opinion, even if it was well buried in the 1849 report. From an attempted rehabilitation of the Ordnance, he passed to his favourite theme of the Secretary at War's relationship with the Commander-in-Chief. He envisaged the implementation of the 1837 report, with resulting danger not only to the constitution but to the national safety. The superiority of the Secretary at War would prevent the Commander-in-Chief giving strategic advice to the Secretary of State. 'Let the consequences of such a system be considered! Look at them in the disgraceful consequences of such a system at Cabool!' MacNaughten was a political officer whose failure to consult Elphinstone, the military commander, was the principal cause of the disaster.[98]

As in 1837, the Duke had Hardinge's support. Although the 1849 report did not complete the deliberations of the committee, Hardinge realised as well as Wellington that consolidation would again be raised. The only concession he was prepared to make was for some internal improvement in the Ordnance.[99]

Wellington's paper drew a counterblast from Fox Maule, the Secretary at War, in which he showed the full range of his views. He rightly pointed out that the Duke had plunged 'at once into a subject not yet entertained by the present committee, but assuming that they are to arrive at the same conclusions with the Commission of 1837, he proceeds to denounce, while he at the same time misrepresents the suggestions of that Commission'. Maule's own view was that the Ordnance office 'is now notoriously a clog upon the military service'. Its cumbrous departments, complicated transaction of business and antiquated accounting system obstructed all its dealings. Reform was therefore inevitable, and Maule favoured the division of its civilian and military duties between the War Office and the Horse Guards. The Commander-in-Chief's powers would not be touched, but those of the Secretary at War would be increased by giving him the military duties then inadequately performed by the Secretary of State for War and the Colonies. One minister should be answerable to the House of Commons for all military matters, 'who shall be able not only to check expence, but to issue the orders of the Government to the Commander-in-Chief's Department from time to time, who shall direct the clothing, arming, lodging, medical attendance and recruiting of the Army, making it his duty to issue orders on all these points and to see that they are efficiently and economically conducted'. Whatever his protestations, Maule had now ventured into territory that the Horse Guards regarded as its own. Well might he conclude, 'I foresee great difficulty in carrying out these views so long as the Duke of Wellington or Lord Anglesea [then Master General] live.'[100]

The probable agenda of the 1850 session of the committee on army and Ordnance expenditure had thus become clear. In Parliament, Bernal Osborne and Joseph Hume called for consolidation, under a minister of war or in accordance with the 1837 proposals.[101] Hume submitted to the committee his proposal of a supreme minister advised by a board of the heads of departments.[102] But the main and familiar arguments were advanced by Grey. As usual he weakened his own case, but this time not so much through immoderation as through muddled thinking. First he maintained that the views of the 1837 report had been confirmed by experience. The Secretary at War should have the Secretary of State's powers of control over the army and thus be the only minister responsible to Parliament. He should have a board to advise him. But he did not consider the reorganisation of the civilian departments, though desirable, as a pressing reform; he felt the Commander-in-Chief's and Master General's military duties could be left intact, and all that needed to be done immediately was to create a minister of war without all the paraphenalia of ancillary support.[103] He was now in the position of advocating an inadequate change, that might come no nearer resolving the departmental conflicts.

The committee devoted most attention to the future of the Commissariat. Much of this discussion revolved round the question of handing over the Commissariat to the Board of Ordnance. It was therefore sterile, since it had already been demonstrated that the Ordnance's sufferings were largely due to being overburdened. In 1836 the Ordnance had offered to take on the supply branch of the Commissariat. But, as Trevelyan pointed out to the committee, the Ordnance was concerned with heavy and immobile stores, whereas the Commissariat was 'essentially locomotive'. The change had consequently been confined to Britain. What Trevelyan now wished to do was to make the Commissariat responsible for perishable supplies at home as well as abroad. He spoke with favour of a suggestion made in 1844 by Hardinge that all relating to the lodging, arming and clothing of the troops should be Ordnance business, their pay and allowances that of the War Office, and food, fuel, light and transport that of the Commissariat.[104]

Both Maule and Grey, however, had suggested to the committee that the Commissariat should be under the War Office. Trevelyan and Sir Charles Wood, the Chancellor of the Exchequer, opposed this, although without adducing any reasoned argument. The defence for the *status quo* was ably put by Routh, who saw that, if the financial duties alone of the Commissariat remained with the Treasury, the time gained on the military side would be lost by the department's inability to make a direct appeal on the pecuniary. Furthermore the War Office was no more concerned with field duties than the Treasury, and nobody was suggesting entrusting the responsibility of disbursement to the Horse Guards. Provisioning, transport and control of the government chest were indivisible duties in the field, and, since the latter was the Treasury's province, so were the former.[105]

Despite its comparative neglect of the administrative issue, the committee on army and Ordnance expenditure reported as Wellington and Hardinge feared it would. It favoured the 1837 report, and it 'would therefore urge the Government seriously and speedily to adopt measures to consolidate, economize, and simplify the Civil Administration of the Army in all its branches'.[106] However, since it refrained from making any specific proposals on the broad pattern of reform, the issue stood as it was.

The consequences that followed from the committee were confined to lesser matters. As a result of the suggestion that the Commissariat be reduced, a Treasury committee on Naval, Ordnance and Commissariat establishments in the colonies was convened in 1850. Its purpose was to bring the stores of all three under one head. The soldier on the Treasury's committee was George Cathcart. He favoured a reduced but still independent Commissariat; the financial and supply sections should be kept united and, since on occasion the Commissariat fed the navy as well as the army, the whole department should be civilian.[107] But Cathcart's views were modified by experience. An examination of the colonial stations and of the demands likely to be imposed on the Commissariat by fighting over trackless expanses led him to conclude that 'my doctrine is that *efficiency* is the first consideration — economy if not opposed to *efficiency* is desirable'.[108]

A second small measure of administrative consolidation accured from the weighty tomes of the report. The Ordnance Medical Department had tried to keep pace with the improvements in its sister service in the army. But the absence of any retirement allowance meant that, by 1848, the senior surgeons were all aged fifty-four to sixty and boasted thirty-five to forty-two years' service. In 1850 the department had no hospital that was exclusively its own. The Master General and Board therefore suggested that the two departments amalgamate their hospitals, but the Secretary at War and the Director General of the Army Medical Department would only agree if the Ordnance troops were also attended by line doctors. The importance attached to regimental surgeons was such that the matter was dropped.

However, the 1828 Finance Committee, the evidence put to Richmond's 1833 committee, and latterly the 1849 report on Ordnance expenditure had all urged the amalgamation of the Army and Ordnance Medical Departments. They had not envisaged touching the sacrosanct regimental hospital, but conceived of some economy by uniting duties in the higher echelons. In 1850 Sir John Webb, Director General of the Ordnance Medical Department, retired after fifty-six years' service. His office was deliberately kept vacant and, in March 1852, the 1849 recommendation was used to convene a committee on the amalgamation of the two Medical Departments. Hardinge, now Master General, emerged as the champion of the regimental hospital. He ensured that the two departments continued to be staffed separately sharing no more than a common Director General, who thus became answerable to the Master General as well as to the Commander-in-Chief. On 14 February 1853 the superintendence of the Ordnance Medical Department became the responsibility of the Director General of the Army Medical Department.[109]

Although experience was in one case at any rate to justify Hardinge's stand, his motives actually ran deeper. His official memorandum on the subject refused to be too explicit, since he was aware 'of other & more extensive consolidations affecting the Army & the Ordnance, to which I am entirely opposed'.[110] To Fitzroy Somerset he was prepared to be open. The object of the union of the Medical Departments 'goes much further — it is the insertion of the small end of the wedge, for the amalgamation of the army & ordnance into one great Dept; under a Secty of State, for which Lord Howick is still a determined advocate'.[111]

Clearly therefore Hardinge's concern for reform was not going to spill over into the army's administration. Like Wellington, he saw the only consequences as being further reductions in the military estimates and official subordination of professional advice in the army's affairs. Moreover his emphasis on the danger to the royal prerogative in Grey's scheme meant that in this area Prince Albert too was neutralised.[112] Grey asked how Hardinge distinguished between military authority and any other executive power of the Crown, for which the public held the government rather than the monarchy responsible. But by now Grey did not 'expect a change of system until some bad disaster has arisen from our present one which will happen as sure as fate if it is tried by real danger'.[113]

Before this test there was to be one more brief flurry of activity. In February 1853 Palmerston confided to Sidney Herbert that he wanted to see the unification of the offices of Secretary at War and Secretary of State,[114] and in the Commons Hume once again called for the enactment of the 1837 proposals. On this occasion it was Herbert who blocked the move, his own unanimity with the Commander-in-Chief obscuring from him the organisational pitfalls.[115]

Exactly a year later the outbreak of war showed just how much the erosion of twenty years had weakened the Wellingtonian fabric. *The Times* reopened the question of consolidation and on 17 February 1854 Lord Seymour, the chairman of the committee on army estimates, raised the matter in Parliament.[116] Russell, bridled by the Queen,[117] answered noncommittally. But within two weeks Hume had aired the subject again. Herbert replied that the 1837 report had arisen from a specific clash between the War Office and the Horse Guards; moreover the outbreak of war was a bad time for reorganisation and would swamp an enhanced Secretary at War with work. He did, however, favour the grouping of personnel under the Commander-in-Chief and *matériel* under the Master General. Hume and Seymour, Sir John Pakington (Secretary of State for War in Derby's government of 1852), Edward Ellice (Secretary at War 1833–4) and Russell ranged on his side.[118] In the Lords, Grey urged the formation of a board, thus uniting professional and civilian elements, all under a minister of war. Although Grey was opposed by Hardinge and Newcastle, he was supported by Panmure and Ellenborough.[119]

The Queen's concern for the royal prerogative meant that some change was necessary, if only to silence Grey. Therefore Russell's proposal that the Secretary of State for War and the Colonies simply be divested of his colonial responsibilities, which should henceforth form an independent office, found a measure of support within the cabinet. His attempt to graft on the military responsibilities of the Home Secretary was for the moment checked by the holder of that office, Palmerston. And so, in June

1854, Russell was able to announce the division of the War and Colonial Departments, and that this would be effected by an order in council.[120]

In fact, as Hume and Pakington observed at the time,[121] nothing was very much clearer. Newcastle's responsibilites were fewer in overall terms, but the same within the military orbit. No definition of his duties was provided and no fundamental reorganisation of the departments attempted. Furthermore he was not given the board that Grey had seen as an essential concomitant and he was thus in no better position to take professional advice. The government gave itself a ministerial scapegoat, with very little opportunity for him to save himself.

In the long run, Russell expected a division of military and civil departments between the Horse Guards and the War Office, such as had first been proposed in 1833.[122] The position of the militia, under the Home Secretary, and of certain of the Master General's duties came under consideration. But the only immediate departmental change proposed was the transfer of the Commissariat. Evidence of the collapse of this department in the field was already available. Under Filder, described by Sir George Cathcart in 1851 as 'a man of detail but not enlarged ideas',[123] whatever chances it had had of operating efficiently were finally killed by the addition to its responsibilities of the stores of the Quarter Master General's and Ordnance departments. These included not only tents and feed bags, but even the siege equipment of the artillery and engineers, since neither corps had depots in the field. Thus although not primarily a storekeeping department in peace, the Commissariat became one in the war.[124]

Newcastle was himself keen for the Commissariat to be transferred to his jurisdiction, and justification was somewhat spuriously given to his claim by the fact that all the military departments were now under a civilian head.[125] The Treasury's main military ally had changed his attitude after serving in South Africa. Sir George Cathcart, now with the authority of being Adjutant General, felt that the field Commissariat should be under the minister of war and its officers answerable to military discipline: if that meant hiving off their financial duties, so be it.[126] His conclusions were reinforced by the report of Lord de Ros, Quarter Master General in the east.[127] The Treasury predictably put up a stiff rearguard action, and it was not until December that the Commissariat was finally transferred to the War Office. Newcastle disclaimed responsibility for the move, saying altruistically that it had long been planned. However, there is a distinction between considering a change and actually arranging its implementation: for all that had happened was that the Secretary of State's duties had been increased by his running the department direct, rather than by having a head responsible to him. At such a stage in the war, consolidation was confounding not simplifying.

In the case of the Commissariat the decision was relatively clear-cut. Although Russell had placed a very large question mark over the future of the Board of Ordnance, no decisive action had been taken. The 1849 committee had already found that the department was overworked and under-staffed, and the onset of war clearly would not help it. Furthermore the Master General of the Ordnance had ceased to be a great political officer. He had not sat in the cabinet for many years and in 1852 Hardinge actually accepted the office under a ministry to which he was inimical, on the grounds that his interpretation of its responsibilities would be purely professional.[128] Thus, when Lord Raglan had gone to the Crimea, it had seemed possible for him to retain his office as Master General and for his duties to be carried on by the appointment of Sir Hew Ross as Lieutenant General of the Ordnance. Because no Lieutenant General had held office since 1831, it was mistakenly believed that Ross would take over the full position of the Master General. In fact, however, he was a member of the Board, with no powers to reverse its decisions or to approve its proceedings.[129] The Board itself was in a state of disarray: its authority was quoted when it had not been given and at times in 1854 only one of its members was active. Willam Monsell, the Clerk of the Ordnance, concluded that it would be better for the department to disappear gracefully and so put himself in direct communication with Newcastle.[130] As a result the Secretary of State bypassed the Board, which was in consequence ignorant as to the activities of its own department. Thus, rudderless, the Ordnance tried to cope with the demands of war. The branches began to rule themselves. The eccentric but brilliant Captain E. M. Boxer, at the head of the Royal Laboratory, took to dismissing Ordnance employees, 'in the spirit' moreover, 'of a foreman of mechanics in a manufacturing establishment' rather than that of a captain in the Royal Artillery.[131] More seriously, the Royal Laboratory on two occasions changed ammunition specifications without authority.[132]

The hasty division of his colonial and military duties had therefore pushed an even greater burden onto the Secretary of State. Departments either had chiefs who were not consulted, like Hardinge at the Horse Guards, or were without any chief except Newcastle. A board of heads of departments was vitally required to enable the Secretary of State to be properly informed of all the doings within the army and to allow each department to be properly administered.

Consequently, in December 1854, Palmerston and Herbert revived the meetings that had taken place the previous year to consider national defence. The first was held on 3 January 1855, and was composed of the Commander-in-Chief, the Secretary at War, the Lieutenant General and the Clerk of the Ordnance, and the Secretary of State. Thereafter they were held weekly until the collapse of the government. Herbert had in fact adopted Grey's plan for a board and had drafted an order in council to make its meetings compulsory.[133] What he envisaged was a War Office divided into three departments, financial, military and *matériel*, the three heads forming a board to advise the Secretary of War.[134] This was not to be achieved until Cardwell's War Office Act of 1870.

In 1855 the Ordnance and the militia were finally taken over by Newcastle's successor, Panmure. Only the Commander-in-Chief pursued a nominally independent existence, and the very power of the Secretary of War as well as constitutional practice made the independence tenuous indeed. But it was enough to continue the military/political split that had so hamstrung the pre-Crimean administration of the army and any attempts to reform it. Because the relationship between Commander-in-Chief and Secretary of War remained in a sense undefined, it was productive of jealousy and wrangling. Hardinge was not so far wrong then he told Raglan in June 1855, 'Of course the system will be worked indirectly for Political Objects — & as every Com. in Ch. will stand alone, having no political adhesion with the Govt. of the day, He & his Depts. will generally be found in the wrong.'[135]

The failure to reform the higher administration of the army by 1854 undermined much else that had been achieved. The first set of consequences were specific. The efforts of individual departments, and especially those concerned with transport, supply and medicine, were thwarted by disunited and proliferating bureaucratic responsibilities. The second set was more general. The agencies of army government were divided into civil and professional camps. This split prevented the formulation of a coherent military policy or a school of strategic thought. The Secretary of War did not have the full advantage of experienced advice when facing Parliament or the cabinet. Thus, while soldiers opposed a landing in the Crimea,[136] Newcastle followed popular pressure in advocating it. It was the Admiralty, where professional and civil opinion met on one board, which could dominate. The navy, not the army, wanted the seizure and destruction of Sebastopol. Nor were the tables turned until the creation of the General Staff and Army Council fifty years later.

Notes

1. *U.S.M.*, 1849, III, p. 198.
2. P.P. 1854-5, IX, part I, p. 48.
3. Ibid., p. 410
4. Grey papers, Howick to Melbourne, 10 January 1839.
5. P.P. 1850, X, pp. 435-6.
6. Kenneth Bourne, *Palmerston, the early years*, p. 180.
7. P.P. 1850, X, p. 322.
8. J. H. Stocqueler, *The British officer*, p. 119.
9. P.P. 1849, IX, p. 107.
10. W.O. 33/1, p. 106.
11. W.O. 3/309, p. 310.
12. Herbert papers, III A (1).
13. P.P. 1849, IX, p. 761. Of the 45,163, 35,163 were referred to the Board, and a further 10,000 passed straight to the departments concerned.
14. P.P. 1854-5, IX, part I, p. 419.
15. W. F. P. Napier, *Life of C. J. Napier*, II, p. 45.
16. P.P. 1837, XXXIV, p. 16.
17. P.P. 1851, VII, pp. 46-7.
18. R. I. Routh, *Observations on Commissariat field service*, p. 8.
19. W.O. 135/3, Smith to Kempt, 3 June 1842.
20. B.M. Add. Mss 54555, f. 52, Smith to C. Napier, 22 May 1846.
21. P.P. 1856, XXI, pp. 236-7.
22. R.A. E 44/15, pp. 47-8, memo by Hardinge, 23 September 1852.
23. J. W. Jervis, *Manual of field operations*, pp. 147-9.
24. John Bisset, *The Commissariat on field service abroad*, pp. 4-5.
25. P.P. 1854-5, IX, part II, pp. 15-17, 19, 82.
26. Sir George Cathcart papers, memoranda relative to Canada for Earl Cathcart, c 1845.
27. N.L.S. mss 2846, f. 106, A. Maidon [?] to Brown, [May-July 1847].
28. George Wrottesley (ed.), *Military opinions of Burgoyne*, p. 6.
29. Wrottesley, *Life of Burgoyne*, I, pp. 501-2.
30. Lord de Ros, *The young officer's companion*, pp. 331-2.
31. P.P. 1850, pp. 240, 605-7.
32. Minute of 7 May 1841, quoted in P.P. 1854-5, IX, part II, pp. 357-8.
33. P.P. 1840, XXII, pp. 205-6.
34. Wellington papers, Routh to Fitzroy Somerset, 21 November 1845.
35. John Bisset, *The Commissariat on field service abroad*, pp. 6-7, 11, 27.
36. P.P. 1850, X, p. 497; also pp. 568-9, 620-3.
37. Ibid., p. 588.
38. P.P. 1851, VII, p. 52.
39. W.O. 43/829, f. 338.
40. Neil Cantlie, *History of the Army Medical Department*, I, p. 430.
41. William Munro, *Records of service and campaigning in many lands*, I, pp. 5-6.

42 W.O. 43/342, f. 148.
43 Cantlie, *Army Medical Department*, I, pp. 432-3; P.P. 1840, pp. lxii, 191-2; W.O. 43/342.
44 S.R.O., GD 45/8/82, Guthrie to Maule, November 1850; see also P.P. 1840, XXII, p. 203.
45 Hansard, 3rd series, CVI, cc 639-40.
46 *N. & M.G.*, 30 January 1841, p. 73.
47 *British Army Despatch*, 22 November 1850, p. 1026; Cantlie, *Army Medical Department*, I, p. 435.
48 Herbert papers, III A (48); Hansard, 3rd series, CXXIV, c 686, and CXXX, c 1288.
49 P.P. 1854-5, IX, part 1, p. 393.
50 Herbert papers, I M (46), Surgeon of 29th Foot to Guthrie, 25 December [1845].
51 S. M. Mitra, *Life of Sir John Hall*, p. 254.
52 P.P. 1854-5, IX, part III, p. 164.
53 W.O. 44/542, memo of 29 July 1852.
54 W.O 43/531.
55 P.P. 1854-5, IX, part 1, pp. 282, 286, 289, 395, 402-3, 409, 435-6, 506-7, 664-70, 700; part III, p. 167.
56 Ibid., part I, p. 392.
57 W.O. 3/96, pp. 208, 422; 3/98, p. 346; 3/99, p. 129; 3/100, pp. 330, 501; 3/292, pp. 66, 363, 371; 3/294, p. 72; 3/295, pp. 113, 115, 287; 3/299, pp. 57, 79, 123.
58 W.O. 4/269, p. 201.
59 P.P. 1854-5, IX, part I, pp. 610-11.
60 G. J. Guthrie, *Commentaries on the surgery of the war*, 1853 (5th edition), pp. 2-3.
61 G. C. Moore Smith, *Life of Lord Seaton*, p. 251; W.O. 43/295; Kenneth Bourne, *Palmerston*, pp. 176-7.
62 Lord Broughton, *Recollections of a long life*, IV p. 196, 267, 270, 274, 276-7, 287.
63 C. J. Bartlett, *Great Britain and sea power 1815-1853*, pp. 10-11, 49-53.
64 P.P. 1837, XXXIV, 1833 report, pp. v-xii, 3-6, 63-4.
65 Rollo Russell (ed.), *Early correspondence of Lord John Russell 1805-40*, II, pp. 48-51, 125.
66 Hansard 3rd series, XXVII, cc 319-328, 1185.
67 P.P. 1837, XXXIV, evidence, pp. 1-40.
68 Grey papers, Russell to Howick, 6 October and 18 December 1836.
69 Grey papers, Howick to Charles Grey, 29 August 1836.
70 P.P. 1837, XXXIV, pp. 7-15.
71 S.R.O., GD 45/8/66/6, Wellington to Melbourne, 25 March 1837.
72 Grey papers, William IV to Melbourne, 18 February 1837 (copy).
73 R.A. C 37/24 and 26, William IV to Melbourne, 6 and 31 March 1837.
74 Wellington papers, Sir H. Taylor to Somerset, 27 March 1837.
75 R.A. C 37/27, Melbourne to William IV, 10 April 1837.
76 Grey papers, Glenelg to Howick, 3 March 1837.

The administration of the army

77 Ibid., Vivian to Howick, 2 March 1837.
78 N.A.M. 7709-6-14, pp. 273-8, Vivian to Taylor, 10 April 1837.
79 Hansard, 3rd series, XXXVII, cc 791-2.
80 Grey papers, Howick's journal, C 3/2, entry for 9 July 1837, by his wife.
81 Grey papers, Howick to Russell, 6 July 1837, and Howick to Melbourne, 15 July and 15 August 1837.
82 Grey papers, Vivian to Howick, and replies, 18-25 November 1837.
83 N.A.M. 7709-6-14, pp. 30-42, Vivian to Melbourne, 3-8 January 1838.
84 Grey papers, Hill to Melbourne, enclosed by Melbourne to Howick, 8 January 1838.
85 Wellington papers, Wellington to Melbourne, 4 January 1838.
86 Grey papers, Howick to Russell, 15 January 1838.
87 Ibid., Howick to Melbourne, 18 January 1838.
88 Russell to Melbourne, 8 October 1837, quoted in Gillespie, *Correspondence of Russell*, II, p. 205.
89 Grey papers, Russell to Melbourne, 22 January 1838.
90 C. J. Napier, *Remarks on military law*, p. 267; W. F. P. Napier, *Life of C. J. Napier*, II, p. 45.
91 Seaton papers, Seaton memo, 12 January 1841.
92 S.R.O., GD 45/8/18, L. Maule to Fox Maule, n.d.
93 F. R. Chesney, *Observations on the past and present state of fire-arms*, pp. 203-21, 234; Robert Gardiner, *Illustrations in questions and answers on the ... artillery of the British army*, p. 50; *Royal Engineers Professional Papers*, new series, I, 1851, p. 100.
94 *N. & M.G.*, 3 April 1847, p. 216.
95 R.A. E 42/55 and 57, Albert to Russell, 8 December 1848, and reply.
96 P.P. 1849, IX, pp. iv, xx-xxiii.
97 Hansard, 3rd series, CV, c 997.
98 S.R.O., GD 45/8/66/1, memo by Wellington, 30 November 1849.
99 Ibid., GD 45/8/66/5, memo by Hardinge, 12 January 1850.
100 Ibid., GD 45/8/66/7, memo by Maule, January 1850.
101 Hansard, 3rd series, CIX, c 682; CX, c 42; CXV, c 758.
102 P.P. 1850, X, pp. 1226-7.
103 Ibid., pp. 698-700, 715-24.
104 Ibid., pp. 489-97, 521, 1037-42.
105 R. I. Routh, *Observations on Commissariat field service*, 1852 (2nd edition), pp. 119-128.
106 P.P. 1851, VII, p. 57.
107 Sir George Cathcart papers, Cathcart to Earl Cathcart, 25 December 1850; Cathcart to Trevelyan, 28 January 1851.
108 Ibid., Cathcart to Earl Cathcart, 12 February 1851.
109 W.O. 43/877; W.O. 44/542; W.O. 3/312, p. 350.
110 W.O. 44/542, memo by Hardinge, 29 July 1852.
111 W.O. 46/89, p. 302.
112 R.A. C 17/68, memo by Albert, 25 May 1850; Hardinge papers, Hardinge to Prince Albert, 7 October 1852.
113 Grey papers, Grey to Charles Grey, 22 November 1852.

114 Herbert papers 20, Palmerston to Herbert, 6 February 1853.
115 Hansard, 3rd series, CXXIV, cc 741, 744.
116 Ibid., CXXX, c 817.
117 R.A. E 3/35 and 36, Albert to Russell, 17 February 1854, and reply.
118 Hansard, 3rd series, CXXXI, cc 223-5, 234-58.
119 Ibid., CXXXII, cc 606-37, 640-55, 662.
120 Olive Anderson, *A liberal state at war*, pp. 53-8; J. B. Conacher, *The Aberdeen coalition*, pp. 395-412.
121 Hansard, 3rd series, CXXXV, cc 327-41.
122 Hansard, 3rd series, CXXXV, cc 321-5; Newcastle papers, NeC 10291, Russell to Newcastle, 2 July 1854.
123 Sir George Cathcart papers, Cathcart to Earl Cathcart, 22 May 1851.
124 P.P. 1854-5, IX, part II, pp. 25-6, 226, 227-8; part III, *5th report*, p. 13.
125 Newcastle papers, NeC 12515, Newcastle to Aberdeen, 5 July 1854.
126 Newcastle papers, NeC 10568, memo by Cathcart, 25 July 1854.
127 Ibid., NeC 10387, de Ros to Newcastle, 28 November 1854.
128 Hardinge papers, Hardinge to Derby, 23 February 1852; Charles Grey's papers, D 5/2, p. 130, journal entry for 24 February 1852.
129 P.P. 1854-5, IX, part III, pp. 23, 199-200.
130 Newcastle papers, NeC 10331a, Monsell to Newcastle, 21 June 1854.
131 P.P. 1854-5, IX, part III, pp. 78-150; *5th report*, pp. 8-9.
132 W.O. 3/324, p. 441; 3/325, p. 99.
133 Newcastle papers, NeC 10044, Herbert to Newcastle, 4 December 1854; Herbert papers, Herbert to Newcastle, 8 January 1855, and III B (377), memo by Herbert, December 1854.
134 P.P. 1854-5, IX, part III, pp. 195-6.
135 N.A.M. 6807/289, Hardinge to Raglan, 7 June 1855.
136 Hew Strachan, 'Soldiers, strategy and Sebastopol', *Historical Journal*, XXI, 1978, pp. 303-25.

CONCLUSION

On many levels the British army was either being reformed or, more pertinently, reforming itself, in the period 1830 to 1854. And yet, even when allowance is made for press exaggeration and misrepresentation, all was not right with the expeditionary force of 1854.

The problems were not primarily due to lack of tactical ability or of fighting spirit. Indeed the Russian army, victorious over Charles XII and Napoleon, was defeated by a numerically inferior allied force fighting on the end of a long line of communications. Some would say that the immediate successes were those of the French army; in the long run they were the achievement of a liberal and industrialising state applying itself to war. Histories of the campaign tend to gloss over the collapse of the French in the winter of 1855–56 and to neglect the vigour of the British. But, if the honour of the British army was maintained in the preceding winter, it was thanks to the excellence of its parts, and in particular of its infantry battalions. Its shortcomings were primarily the product of wider considerations.

There are three specific areas where reform had failed. The first was manpower. The initial British contingent sent to the Crimea was 26,000 strong: it was made up disproportionately of fresh recruits (since it was formed from battalions at home) and it had no effective reserves. Battlefield casualties and cholera thrust an increasing burden on those that remained fit, and thus exhaustion rendered them in their turn more susceptible to disease. But, given its commitments in the empire, and especially in the potentially mutinous subcontinent of India, the army had no more men to spare. In any case additional troops would have proved a self-confounding solution. The barren uplands of the Crimea were inhospitable even for a small army: requisitioning, which remained a principal method of military supply into the twentieth century, depended on relative fertility. Small though the British army was, it was still inadequately fed. This was the second failure, the collapse of transport and supply. It exacerbated the problems posed by the first. In the winter of 1854–55, and particularly in November and December, the army could not cook for lack of firewood; its resistance to illness was undermined by malnutrition and, when sick, its powers of recovery were hampered by insufficient medical supplies. The chaotic Commissariat was itself the consequence of the third failure. Army administration was split over too many heads. Harassed and conscientious officials at Balaclava found their efforts nullified by competing bureaucracies and divided authorities.

Some reasons why these particular problems were not resolved before 1854 have been discussed in the foregoing chapters. But they must be set in the context of a more general and fundamental consideration. In the years after Waterloo military involvement against a European opponent seemed the least likely of a long list of possible contingencies. The army thought small because it fought small: the problems had been resolved to meet the demands of imperial garrisoning and home policing, and were therefore adapted to the level of the regiment.

After 1815 the empire became the army's *raison d'être*. Here lay the likelihood of immediate employment, and therefore here too lay the argument for attracting parliamentary funds. Furthermore, Cobden notwithstanding, military involvement in the empire had at least some popular appeal. Radicals were pleased to see the military forsake their aid to the domestic civil power. The colonial reformers, the advocates of emigration and systematic colonisation, gave the Whigs — and in particular Grey — a case for advocating military efficiency. And finally the soldier overseas became a Christian missionary and the harbinger of British civilisation. Lord Seaton provided a conceptual framework for such arguments: 'Essential benefit may be derived, if the opportunity is seized by our Country of combining and connecting more closely, our Military system with our Colonial interests. England with Colonies and Dependencies, extended over every part of the earth, may by improving on Military systems of Europe, and availing herself of a Military organization having wider views than mere Military protection, greatly accelerate the progress of her extensive Colonial dominions, and promote the welfare of neighbouring states.'[1]

Even more potent than the empire as a demand on the nation's budget was the protection of Britain. Fear of invasion was the cause of Hardinge's urgent preparations in 1852 and 1853: without it, the army would have been even more embarrassed in 1854 and 1855.

The reform that followed was at least in part the product of reconciling these two strategic obligations. Although it occurred in the so-called 'age of reform', the agencies associated with change in other areas — the radicals, the Utilitarians and the Benthamites — had little direct impact on the army.[2] For, what is remarkable about the reform of the British army between 1830 and 1854 was that it was largely self-generated.

Armies tend to be conservative institutions. They seek and respect tradition and continuity, because from them they can derive *esprit de corps*. They are saddled with the incubus of bureaucratic lethargy, which tends to judge matters from the perspective of what is rather than what might be. Generals, in the words of John Mitchell, 'have generally prospered by following established rules through the most active years of life, and [their] ideas, by the time they arrive at command, are thus too firmly fixed to be easily eradicated by the mere force of argument or demonstration'.[3] Aspiring soldiers tend not to criticise, and their superiors are deaf to outside commentary. In any case external pressure for root-and-branch reform has little inherent strength. It accepts the influences of received institutions and defers to professional wisdom until the latter is proved wrong.

Although the pre-Crimean army was beset with many of these problems, its great advantage was that it did have officers who were prepared to criticise and to innovate. The author of their professionalism was in large part regimental service in far-flung colonies. But it was also, in a very direct way, Napoleon Bonaparte. In British military history, the Peninsula and Waterloo were revolutionary. The army had engaged in a continental strategy, in which after Trafalgar the role of the Royal Navy was negligible. It had taken a considerable part in defeating the most formidable army, headed by the most outstanding general, that Europe had ever seen. Armies all over Europe set themselves to absorb and assess what had happened. France herself witnessed a proliferation of military journals and military societies in much the same way as did Britain. In the case of the United States, so dramatic was the flow of thought and writing that Samuel Huntington has dubbed it 'the American Military Enlightenment'.[4] Huntington traces the origins in part to the developing interest in science, and a consequent respect for technology and professional ability. The influence of the Royal Engineers and of gunners such as J. H. Lefroy would support this argument for Britain. But equally significant was the need to understand how Napoleon fitted into previous thinking on the conduct of war. The reduction of the armies of Europe during 'the long peace' meant that there were many half-pay and retired officers anxious to turn their talents to this analysis and to use the military press to publicise their conclusions.

Many of those conclusions were wrong. Much that was generated by the debate was reactionary. More important, by 1854 matters — particularly for the British army — were not very much clearer. Grey and Hardinge, among others, had attempted to draw the threads together, but the work had only just begun. Furthermore, the directions in which they were pointing army reform were not specifically aimed at fitting Britain to meet a European opponent. The more the army concentrated on the empire — or even on home defence — the less fitted it became for European war.

The army's despatch as part of an amphibious expedition against Russia could only have been, by Grey's and Hardinge's own lights, supreme folly. What followed was itself part of a recurring theme in the development of Britain's defence. The army had prepared itself for war as best it could by the standards of the day, but the shifts in foreign policy were more in accordance with popular pressures than with the army's capabilities. In modern parlance there arose a shortfall between strategy and policy implementation. The overall conduct of war in Britain was the responsibility of the cabinet. Relevant peacetime preparation was therefore hard to achieve, since the nature or timing of the war was not as susceptible of calculation as in absolute states. Equally, however, opposition from the field commander, or even the Commander-in-Chief, as to the ability of the troops to fulfil the allotted task was correspondingly harder to express. Raglan thought he was going to Turkey to fight a defensive war on behalf of the Sublime Porte. In his letter of appointment no more than vague reference was made to an attack on Russia itself, and only when the tools of democracy, particularly the press, ran away with the government was he positively ordered to capture Sebastopol. He replied that 'the descent on the Crimea is decided upon more in deference to the views of the British government than to any information in the possession of the naval and military authorities, either as to the extent of the enemy's forces, or to their state of preparation'. Deferential and mild though it was, this letter, by Raglan's own standards of self-effacement, was unambiguous. The British experience in 1854 supports those students of military involvement in politics who see professional soldiers as inherently cautious and pessimistic — certainly not warmongers.[5]

The navy was the fist in Britain's diplomacy, and it was to preserve her hegemony that the Russian naval installations at Sebastopol were to be destroyed. For the army it was a sudden storm in a century of continental disengagement. But the navy bound the empire, and therefore European problems, as soon as they impinged on maritime communications, could never be totally divorced from colonial security. Even in the matter of imperial policing, Britain depended on the forbearance of her European rivals. Any colonial disturbance, by distracting Britain, weakened her position in Europe. As Wellington advised Fitzroy Somerset on the occasion of the 1838 rebellion in Canada, 'There is no such thing as a *little war* for a great Nation.'[6]

In this context, then, the work of the pre-Crimean reformers could not avert the possibility of a Jena. They could, however — and did — achieve much more than the pre-1806 Prussian reformers in softening the blow and in preparing the ground for the subsequent debate. After all, Sebastopol was taken. The 1855 cry for army reform was sprung on Britain by the press *de novo*, but it had been conducted within the army itself for the previous twenty years. No clearly defined change in policy had been effected, but instead, in a Socratic fashion, the process of demolition and gradual replacement had been commenced. Nor, despite the flurry of 1855, the pontifications and the promises, was the tempo to change much after the Crimea. Instead the failings of certain regulations and systems were discovered when exposed to practice, and, after further inquiry, changed once more.

Notes

1. Seaton papers, memo by Seaton, p. 16, possibly that referred to in his letter to Hardinge, 15 September 1853.
2. Hew Strachan, 'The early Victorian army and the nineteenth-century revolution in government', *English Historical Review*, XCV, 1980, pp. 782-809.
3. *Monthly Chronicle*, I, 1838, p. 320.
4. Samuel P. Huntington, *The soldier and the State*, Cambridge Mass., 1957, p. 217.
5. Strachan, 'Soldiers, strategy and Sebastopol'.
6. Wellington papers, Wellington to Somerset, 5 January 1838.

BIBLIOGRAPHY

I. *Unpublished papers*

Archives Historiques de Guerre, Château de Vincennes, Paris, reports on the British army
Bodleian Library, Oxford
  Clarendon Deposit
  Napier papers (predominantly those of William)
  North Mss, papers of Colonel J. S. Doyle (later North)
British Museum
  Add. Mss 35060, Hill papers
  Add. Mss 37415, Wellesley papers
  Add. Mss 40310, 40313-4, 40459-61, 40474-5, 40575, 40581-5, Peel papers, especially correspondence with Hardinge and Wellington
  Add. Mss 41581, Col. Dansey papers
  Add. Mss 41964, Sir C. W. Pasley papers
  Add. Mss 49105-8, 49115-17, 49128-31, 49140, 49143, 49144, 49168, 54512-19, 54524-26, 54532, 54536, 54538, 54544-61, Napier papers (predominantly those of Charles)
  Add. Mss 49480, 49503, Sir J. W. Gordon papers
The Earl Cathcart
  Second Earl Cathcart papers
  Sir George Cathcart papers
Dr A. E. Clark-Kennedy
  Transcripts of Colonel John Clark-Kennedy's papers
Durham University, Department of Palaeography and Diplomatic
  Third Earl Grey papers
  Sir Charles Grey papers
Sir Fergus Graham, Bt
  Sir James Graham papers (microfilm in Cambridge University Library)
Hereford County Record Office
  Airey papers (see National Register of Archives report no. 10872)
R. E. Howard-Vyse, Esq.
  Hugh Robinson's letters, 1851-3
India Office Library
  L/MIL/3/64, 1752-4, 1905, 1907-10. Reports concerning Fitzclarence at Bombay

Bibliography

J. E. Colborne Mackrell, Esq.
  Seaton papers
McGill University Library
  Hardinge papers
Ministry of Defence Whitehall Library
  General Orders, Horse Guards Circulars and memoranda
National Army Museum
  A. S. H. Mountain papers
  Raglan military papers (relate to Crimea only)
  Sir Hussey Vivian papers
  Sir George Wetherall papers
National Library of Scotland
  mss 1847-50, 1855, 1857, 1859, 2839-54, 3259-62, Sir George Brown papers
  mss 3867, General Walter Scott papers
  mss 3870, G. R. Gleig papers
  mss 8105, journal of Captain C. H. Scott-Douglas
  mss 9319, 'Crimean Campaign 1854-1856', Scots Fusilier Guards
  mss 9869-74, 9880-2, Sir C. W. Pasley papers
  Adv mss 46.8.16-23, 46.9.1-19, Sir George Murray papers
Nottingham University Library
  Fifth Duke of Newcastle papers
  Portland Collection, letters to Lord William Bentinck from Lt Gen Sir S. F. Wittingham
Earl of Pembroke
  Sidney Herbert papers
Public Record Office
  P.R.O. 30/46, Sir William Eyre papers
  W.O. 1/595-601, in-letters, Colonial Department
  W.O. 3/90-119, 283-329, Adjutant General's out-letters
  W.O. 4/263-72, Secretary at War's out-letters
  W.O. 6/127-8, Secretary of State's out-letters
  W.O. 7/57-9, Reports of the Board of General Officers
  W.O. 30/112, 116, 118, miscellaneous papers (? Commander-in-Chief's)
  W.O. 33/1, War Office confidential papers
  W.O. 37, Sir George Scovell papers
  W.O. 43, Secretary at War, 'Very Old Series' and 'Old Series'
  W.O. 44, Board of Ordnance in-letters
  W.O. 46/86-92, Master General of the Ordnance out-letters
  W.O. 55/970 and 1931, Royal Engineers' instruction
  W.O. 55/1409 and 1563/7, coast defence
  W.O. 80, Sir George Murray papers
  W.O. 99, Royal Military College, Sandhurst
  W.O. 135, Sir Harry Smith papers
  W.O. 186/1, reports from Shoeburyness for Director General of Artillery
  W.O. 211, Hart papers on officers' biographies
Lord Raglan
  Raglan private papers

Royal Archives
  Queen Victoria papers
  Duke of Cambridge papers
Royal Engineers Museum, Chatham
  Sir John Burgoyne papers
  Colonel H. Sandham memorandum books
Scottish Record Office
  GD 24/1/936, Cornet Drummond papers
  GD 26/9/546, Ensign H. F. B. Maxse's memorandum book
  GD 45/8/1-124, Panmure papers
  GD 225/boxes 41-2, Leith Hay papers
Duke of Wellington
  First Duke of Wellington papers
East Yorkshire County Record Office
  DDCH 76-84, 118-19, Sir Charles Chichester papers
  DDCH 95-110, C. R. Chichester's diaries

II. *Parliamentary papers*

P.P. 1833, VII, Report from the select committee on the establishment of the garrisons and on the pay and emoluments of Army and Navy officers.
P.P. 1836, XXII, Report from His Majesty's commissioners for inquiring into the system of military punishments in the Army.
P.P. 1837, XXXIV, Report of the commissioners appointed to inquire into the practicability and expediency of consolidating the different departments connected with the civil administration of the Army.
P.P. 1840, XXII, Report of commissioners for inquiring into naval and military promotion and retirement.
P.P. 1846, XVI, Report from commissioners on the gauge of railways.
P.P. 1849, IX, P.P. 1850, X, and P.P. 1851, VII, p. 735, Report from the select committee on Army and Ordnance expenditure.
P.P. 1851, XVII, Report from the select committee on newspaper stamps.
P.P. 1854, XVIII, Report from the select committee on small arms.
P.P. 1854, XIX, 833, Report of commissioners on promotion in the Army.
P.P. 1854-5, IX, 1st-5th reports from the select committee on the Army before Sebastopol.
P.P. 1854-5, XII, 311, Report from the select committee on Sandhurst Royal Military College.
P.P. 1854-5, XXXII, 37, Report from an official committee on barrack accommodation for the army.
P.P. 1856, XX, Report of the commission of inquiry into the supplies of the British Army in the Crimea.
P.P. 1856, XXI, Report of board of general officers appointed to inquire into the statements contained in the reports of Sir John McNeill and Colonel Tulloch.
P.P. 1860, VII, Report from select committee on military organization.
Hansard's Parliamentary Debates, 3rd series, vols. XXVII-CXXXV.

Bibliography

III. *Periodicals*

The Army Reformer
Blackwood's Magazine
British Army Despatch
The Edinburgh Review
Fraser's Magazine
Journal des Sciences Militaires
The Military Annual for 1844
The Military Church Soldier's Temperance Magazine
The Military Magazine
The Military Review
Minutes of Proceedings of the Royal Artillery Institution
Naval and Military Gazette
Naval and Military Magazine (which became the *United Service Journal*)
Quarterly Review
Royal Engineers Professional Papers (or *Papers on subjects connected with the Duties of the Corps of Royal Engineers*)
The Royal Military Magazine (at first called *The British Soldier*)
Le Spectateur Militaire
United Service Gazette
United Service Journal, which became the *United Service Magazine*
Westminster Review

IV. *Contemporary published works*

(Official manuals are grouped under the headings 'Horse Guards', 'Ordnance' and 'War Office', according to the issuing authority. Anonymous works are listed under the first word of the title; pseudonymous under the pseudonym).

Aide-mémoire to the Military Sciences, 3 vols, London, 1846-52
Anderson, James, *System of National Defence*, Edinburgh, 1853
Armstrong, Maj. Gen., *Observations upon corporal punishments in the British Army*, London, 1834
The Army Reform Wanted — Maximum of Defence, with Minimum of Expence, London, 1851
An Artillery Officer, *Practical Hints for the Adoption of a Better System in the Government of the Royal Military Academy at Woolwich*, London, 1847
Bedford, Maj. W. D., *Some Suggestions for the Cheap Defence of the Kingdom*, London, 1853
Bennett, Maj. Richard, *Army Education Professionally Exemplified*, n.d. [?1848], no imprint
Bissett, Sir John, *Memoranda and observations regarding the duties of the Commissariat on field service abroad*, London, 1846
[Blane, Sir Gilbert], *Remarks on Military Punishments*, London, 1828
Boucher, John, *The Volunteer Rifleman, and the Rifle*, London, 1854
Bowles, Capt. W., R.N., *Suggestions for the Speedy and Sure Conveyance of Our*

Reinforcements to Canada, London, 1837
B[owles], W., *Thoughts on National Defence*, London, 1848
Bowring, John (ed.), *The Works of Jeremy Bentham*, vol. IX, Edinburgh, 1843
Bright, John, and Rogers, J. E. T. (ed.), *Speeches by Richard Cobden*, 2 vols., London, 1870
Burlton, Lt. Col. W., *A few brief comments on Sir Charles Napier's letter to Sir J. Hobhouse, 'On the baggage of the Indian Army'*, London, 1849
Burton, Capt. J. Ryder, R.N., *A Letter addressed to the Editor of the 'Morning Herald' on the National Defences*, London, 1848
Bustin, W. R., *A Militia: its relation to the Regular Army*, London, 1847
Campbell, Lt. Col. James, *A British Army, as it was, — is, — and ought to be*, London, 1840
Chesney, Col. F. R., *Observations on the re-construction of the Royal Regiment of Artillery*, London, 1849
   Observations on the Past and Present State of Fire-arms ... with a proposition for reorganising the Royal Regiment of Artillery, London, 1852
Cheyne, John, *A Letter to George Renny, Esq., M.D., on the feigned disease of soldiers*, Dublin, 1826
A Cidevant Cavalry Officer, *Army Reform: A Practical Method of reducing the Army estimates a million, without diminution of its numerical force*, London, 1833
A Civilian, *Hints for a Volunteer Coast Defence*, London, 1853
Clode, C. M., *The Military Forces of the Crown*, 2 vols., London, 1869
Cobden, Richard, *The Political Writings of Richard Cobden*, 2 vols., London, 1867
Connolly, T. W. J., *History of the Royal Sappers and Miners*, London, 1857
Crowe, J. W., *A Few Words on the Militia Question*, Edinburgh, 1852
Curling, Henry, *A Few Words in Recommendation of the Formation of Volunteer Rifle Corps*, London, 1850
D'Aguilar, Maj.-Gen., *Observations on the practice and the forms of district, regimental, and detachment courts martial*, Dublin, 1843
David, *Letters to the Editor of 'The Times', in answer to those of 'Emeritus'*, London, 1849
Delafield, Maj. Richard, *Report on the Art of War in Europe in 1854, 1855 and 1856*, Washington, 1860
de Ros, Lord, *The Young Officer's Companion*, London, 1851.
Downes, Alfred, *Manual of Information and Instruction of Candidates for Commissions*, London, 1852
Drummond, Henry, *A Letter to Captain Fitzroy on Rifle Corps*, London, 1852
Dupin, Charles, *View of the History and Actual State of the Military Force of Great Britain*, 2 vols., London, 1822
Eardley-Wilmot, Capt. F., *Soldierly Discipline*, Woolwich, [1852]
An Englishman and a Civilian, *The Invasion of England*, London, 1852
An Experienced Officer, *Complete Guide to the Senior and Junior Departments of the Royal Military College, Sandhurst*, London, 1849
Facts in refutation of some of the misstatements respecting the Board of Ordnance, in the ... 'Quarterly Review', London, 1848

Bibliography

Faddy, Lt. Col., *Essay on the Defence and Military System of Great Britain, at home and abroad*, London, 1848
Fergusson, James, *An Essay on a proposed new system of fortification: with hints for its application to our national defences*, London, 1849
  The Perils of Portsmouth, London, 1852
Fitzclarence, Lt. Gen. Lord Frederick, *A Manual of Out-Post Duties*, London, 1851
  Memoir on the Duty of Picquets, London, 1843
  Memoranda by Lieut.-General Lord Frederick Fitzclarence, for the use of Young Officers assembled in Poona during the Period of Exercise in December 1853, including instructions applicable to a combination of the Three Arms, London, 1854
  Suggestions for Brigade and Light Infantry Movements, London, 1851
[Fletcher, Quartermaster-Sergeant John], A Non-commissioned Officer, *Advice to the British Soldier*, London, 1839
Flood, Capt. Warden, *A Sketch of the Military and Political State of Prussia*, Portsmouth, 1833
Fyers, Capt., *Notes on the Defensive Resources of Great Britain*, London, 1852
Gardiner, Maj. Gen. Sir Robert, *Illustrations, in questions and answers, on the numerical deficiency, want of instruction, and inefficient equipment of the artillery of the British Army*, [London], 1849
  Report on the numerical deficiency, want of instruction, and inefficient equipment of the artillery of the British Army, [London], 1848
Gardner, John, *An Appeal to the British public, on the inhuman and disgraceful punishment of flogging, in the Army and Navy*, London, 1832
Gawler, Col. G., *Organised Special Constables*, London, 1848
Glover, R. Mortimer, *National Defence*, London, 1853
Gordon, Lt. Col. The Hon. A., *Remarks on National Defence, Volunteers, and Rifles*, London, 1853
Gore, Montague, *National Defences*, London, 1852
Grattan, William, *The Duke of Wellington and the Peninsular Medal*, London, 1845
Grey, 3rd Earl, *Speech of the Rt. Hon. Earl Grey on the second reading of the Militia Bill*, London, 1852
Griffiths, Capt. F. A. *Notes on Military Law*, Woolwich, 1841
The Guards and the Bearskin Caps, London 1854
Guthrie, G. J., *Commentaries on the Surgery of the War in Portugal, Spain, France, and the Netherlands*, London, 1853, 1855
Hardbargain, Henry, *Hints to Subalterns of the British Army*, London, 1843
Harvey, Maj. H. B., *A Visit to the Camp of Beverloo*, London, 1852
Head, Sir Francis, *The Defenceless State of Great Britain*, London, 1850
He would not neglect the defence of the country, London, 1845
Hill, Frederic, *National Force, Economical Defence of the Country from Internal Tumult and Foreign Aggression*, London, 1848
A History of the Sudden and Terrible Invasion of England by the French, in the month of May 1852, London, 1853
Hodge, William Barwick, 'On the mortality arising from military operations',

Journal of the Statistical Society of London, XIX, 1856, p. 219
Hough, Capt. William, *The Practice of Courts-martial, and other Military Courts*, London, 1834
Horse Guards, *Field Exercise and Evolutions of the Army*, London 1824, 1833
  The Infantry Manual, London, 1854
  Instruction of Musketry, London, 1855
  The King's Regulations and Orders for the Army, London, 1837
  The Queen's Regulations and Orders for the Army, London, 1844
  Regulations for Encampments, London, 1853
[Hort, Lt. Col.], The Two Mounted Sentries, *The Horse Guards*, London, 1850
[Hort, R.], *The Days when we had tails on us*, London, 1850
Hort, Lt. Col. [Richard], *The Guards and the Line*, London, 1851
Hughes, Capt. R. M., *The Duties of Judge Advocates*, London, 1845
Jackson, Robert, *A View of the Formation, Discipline and Economy of Armies*, London, 1845
Jervis, Lt. J.-W., *Manual of Field Operations*, London, 1852
Kennaway, C. E., *The War and the Newspapers*, Ottery St. Mary and London, 1856
Kinglake, A. W., *The Invasion of the Crimea*, 8 vols., Edinburgh, 1863-1888
Kinloch, John, *Proposal for the Defence of the Country*, Edinburgh, 1852
Knox, Capt. Charles, *The Defensive Position of England*, London, 1852
Le Couteur, Col. John, *The Rifle*, London, 1855
Lefroy, Capt. J. H. (ed.), *A Handbook for Field Service*, London, 1854
Lendy, A. F., *The Principles of War*, London, 1853
Letter of an Old Field Officer on Military Punishments and Regimental Discipline, London, 1837
Lyster, Capt. F. Torrens, *Manual of Information for Regimental Officers*, London, 1853
McClellan, George B., *Report of the Secretary of War, communicating the report of Captain George B. McClellan, . . . one of the officers sent to the seat of war in Europe in 1855 and 1856*, Washington, 1857
Macfarlane, Charles, *The Camp of 1853*, London, 1853
Macgregor, Capt. Robert S., *A plan for raising a defensive force*, Edinburgh, 1849
Macgregor, W. L., *Practical Observations on the Principal Diseases affecting the health of the European and Native Soldiers in the North-western Provinces of India*, Calcutta, 1843
[McMullen, J.], A late staff sergeant of the 13th Light Infantry, *Camp and Barrack-room*, London, 1846
McMurdo, Maj. Montagu, *Sir Charles Napier's Indian Baggage-corps. Reply to Lieut. Col. Burlton's attack*, London, 1850
Macnamara, Maj. Ulysses, *The British Army*, London, 1839
Malcolmson, John G., *A Letter of the Rt. Hon. Sir Henry Hardinge, K. C. B., M. P., on the effects of solitary confinement, on the health of soldiers, in warm climates*, London, 1837
Malins, William, *A Plan for additional National Defences*, London, 1848
Marshall, Henry, *On the enlisting, discharging and pensioning of soldiers*, Edinburgh, 1839

Bibliography 279

 Hints to young medical officers of the army on the examination of recruits, London, 1828
 Military Miscellany, London, 1846
Martin, Lt., *Guide to the Military Examination*, London, 1851
Maurice [de Sellon], Baron P.-E., *On National Defence in England*, London, 1852
Miles, *War! How best met, or prevented*, Edinburgh, 1846
A Military Tutor, *The Pattern Military Officer*, London, 1855
Mitchell, Lt. Col. J., *Thoughts on Tactics*, London, 1835
Mordecai, Alfred, *Military Commission to Europe, in 1855 and 1856. Report of Major Alfred Mordecai of the Ordnance Department*, Washington, 1860
Napier, Lt. Gen. Sir C. J., *Defects, Civil and Military, of the Indian Government*, London, 1853
 A Letter on the Defence of England, by Corps of Volunteers and Militia, London, 1852
Napier, C. J., *A letter to the Rt. Hon. Sir J. Hobhouse on the Baggage of the Indian Army*, London, 1849
Napier, Maj. Gen. Sir Charles (ed.), *Lights and Shades of Military Life*, 2 vols. London, 1840.
Napier, Maj. Gen. Charles J., *Remarks on Military Law and the Punishment of Flogging*, London, 1837
[Napier, Elers], *Past and Future Emigration; or the Book of the Cape*, London, 1849
Napier, Maj. Gen. Sir William, *Six letters, in vindication of the British Army, exposing the calumnies of the Liverpool Financial Reform Association*, London, 1849
The National Defences, London, 1845
Observations upon the peace establishments of the Army, London, 1822
O'Doodle, Sir Phelim, *The Subaltern's Check-book*, London, 1848
An Officer, *A Few words on the Defence of the Country from Invasion*, London, 1846
 Observations on the Army, London, 1825
An Officer of the Corps, *The Royal Artillery: a few remarks on its deficiency and inefficiency*, London, 1849
An Officer of the Line, *Some Remarks on the Rank, Promotion and Expense of the Establishment of Officers belonging to the Guards*, London, 1849
Ordnance, Board of, *Regulations and Instructions for the Royal Artillery on Matters of Finance, and Points of Discipline connected therewith*, London, 1850
 Standing Orders and Regulations for the Royal Regiment of Artillery at Home and Abroad, London, 1847
 Orders and Regulations for the Guidance of the Corps of the Royal Engineers and Royal Sappers and Miners, London, 1831
Paget, Lord George, *A Letter to Lord John Russell, containing suggestions for raising a reserve force*, London, 1852
Para Bellum, *Brief suggestions on the subject of War and Invasion*, London, 1852
Prendergast, Harris, *The Law relating to Officers in the Army*, London, 1849

Pro Patria, *Suggestions for the formation of a Corps of Volunteer Cavalry*, [London], 1854
[Prosser, Lt. Col.], Z., *A Letter, by authority, on the Royal Military College at Sandhurst*, London, 1848
Raines, Lt. Col. J. R., *A Guide to the Organisation and Training of the Militia, Yeomanry, Infantry, and Volunteer Corps*, London, [1852]
Ranelagh, Viscount, *Observations on the present state of our National Defences*, London, 1845
A Regimental Officer, *A Few Remarks about the British Army*, London, 1857
Remarks on the Education of the Royal Artillery, [possibly by Capt. F. Eardley-Wilmot], Edinburgh, 1848
A Retired Artillery Officer, *The Defence of Our Mercantile Seaports*, London, 1852
Riddell, Capt. C. J. B., *Remarks on the Organization of the British Royal Artillery*, London, 1852
Roberts, Frederic, *Cursory Remarks on Recruiting and Recruits*, London, 1852
On the Development of Military Offences in Camp and Quarters, Chatham, 1853
Rolt, Col. John, *Moral Command*, London, 1842
Routh, Sir R. I., *Observations on Commissariat Field Service and Home Defences*, London, 1852
Rules and Regulations agreed upon between the Quarter Master, Non-commissioned Officers, etc., of His Majesty's Second (or Royal North British) Regiment of Dragoons, for the establishing of a fund by the name of Saint Andrew's Fund for the purpose therein mentioned, Dublin, 1819
Scheme of a Seminary for the Sons of Officers: with Remarks and Suggestions regarding the Diffusion of Military Education throughout the Army, London, [1850].
Shipp, John, *Flogging and its substitute*, London, 1831
Shirley, Lt. Col. Arthur, *Remarks on the Transport of Cavalry and Artillery*, London, 1854
Simmons, Capt. T. F., *Remarks on the Constitution and Practice of Courts Martial*, London, 1843
[Simmons, Lt. T. F.], *Remarks on the Promotion of the Officers of the Corps of Artillery in the British Service, and on the application of that arm in the field*, London, 1819
Smith, John, *A System to Organize and Establish Military Discipline in a Patriotic or Defence Army*, London, 1845
Smyth, Robert Carmichael, *Memorandum on the Necessity of a Secretary of State for our Defence and War Establishments*, London, 1852
Spearman, Capt. J. Morton, *Notes on Military Education*, London, 1853
Standing Orders by Colonel Baumgardt, C.B., for the 2nd or Queen's Royals, Chichester, 1846
Standing Orders for the Second: (or Royal North British) Dragoons, Dublin, 1839
Stocqueler, J. H., *The British Officer*, London, 1851
  Familiar History of the British Army, London, 1871
  The Military Encyclopaedia, London, 1853
  A Personal History of the Horse Guards from 1750 to 1872, London, 1873

Suggestions for the Defence of Great Britain without increased expenditure, London, 1851
Torrens, Col. A. W., *Notes on the French Infantry*, London, 1852
[Torrens, A. W.], A Field Officer, *Six Familiar Lectures, for the use of young military officers*, London, 1851
Walshe, Capt. Anthony, *A Catechism and Handbook on Regimental Standing Orders*, London, 1852
War Office, *Militia Regulations*, London, 1854
  A Collection of Warrants and Regulations, issued to the Army on Matters of Finance, London, 1844
Weale, John, *Letter to the Rt. Hon. Lord John Russell, on the Defence of the Country*, London, 1847
Wood, H., *Observations on Military Education for the British Army*, Brighton, 1847
Woodford, Lt. Gen. Sir Alexander, *General Regulations and Standing Orders for the Garrison of Gibraltar*, Gibraltar, 1839

V. Diaries, memoirs, etc.

Alexander, Sir James E., *L'Acadie*, 2 vols., London, 1849
  Narrative of a Voyage of Observation among the Colonies of Western Africa, in the flag-ship Thalia; and of a campaign in Kaffir-land, on the staff of the Commander-in-Chief, in 1835, 2 vols., London, 1837
  Passages in the Life of a Soldier, 2 vols., London, 1857
Anderson, Lt. Col. Joseph, *Recollections of a Peninsular Veteran*, London, 1913
Anglesey, Marquess of (ed.), *Little Hodge*, London, 1971
  Sergeant Pearman's Memoirs, London, 1968
Astley, Sir John Dugdale, *Fifty Years of My Life*, 2 vols., London, 1894
Baird, J. G. A. (ed.), *Private Letters of the Marquess of Dalhousie*, Edinburgh, 1910
[Bayley, J. A.], *Reminiscences of School and Army Life, 1839 to 1859*, privately printed, 1875
Benson, A. C., and Esher, Viscount, *The Letters of Queen Victoria 1837-1861*, 3 vols., London, 1907.
Bisset, Maj.-Gen. [J.], *Sport and War*, London, 1875
Brialmont, M., and Gleig, the Rev. G. R., *History of the Life of Arthur, Duke of Wellington*, 4 vols., London, 1860
Broughton, Lord, *Recollections of a Long Life*, edited by Lady Dorchester, 6 vols., London, 1910-1911.
Bruce, H. A. (ed.), *Life of General Sir William Napier, K.C.B.*, 2 vols., London, 1864
Bunbury, Thomas, *Reminiscences of a Veteran*, 3 vols., London, 1861
Cathcart, Sir George, *Correspondence of Lieut-General the Hon. Sir George Cathcart, K.C.B., relative to his military operations in Kaffraria*, London, 1856
Chesney, L. and J., *The Life of the late General F. R. Chesney*, London, 1893

Combermere, Mary, Viscountess, *Memoirs and correspondence of Field-Marshal Viscount Combermere*, 2 vols., London, 1866
Cumming, Lt. James S., *A Six Years' Diary*, London, 1847
Dasent, A. I., *John Thadeus Delane, Editor of 'The Times', His Life and Correspondence*, London, 1908
de Ainslie, Gen. [C.], *Life as I have found it*, Edinburgh, 1883
Douglas, Sir George, and Ramsay, Sir George Dalhousie (ed.), *The Panmure Papers*, 2 vols., London, 1908
Douglas, Pte. William, *Soldiering in Sunshine and Storm*, Edinburgh, 1865
Eardley-Wilmot, Mrs. F. M., *Memorials of Fredk. M. Eardley-Wilmot, Maj.-Gen., R.A., and F.R.S.*, London, 1879
Ewart, Lt. Gen. J. A., *The Story of a Soldier's Life*, 2 vols., London, 1881
Fergusson, William, *Notes and Recollections of a Professional Life*, edited by James Fergusson, London, 1846
Ferrar, M. L. (ed.), *Diary of Colour-Serjeant George Calladine, 19th Foot, 1793-1837*, London, 1922
Fullom, S. W., *The Life of General Sir Howard Douglas*, London, 1863
Gleig, G. R., *Personal Reminiscences of the 1st Duke of Wellington*, Edinburgh, 1904
Gooch, G. P. (ed.), *The Later Correspondence of Lord John Russell*, London, 1925
Gordon-Brown, A. (ed.), *The Narrative of Private Buck Adams*, Cape Town, 1941
Hall, J. H. W., *Scenes in a Soldier's Life*, Montreal, 1848
Henderson, R., *The Soldier of Three Queens*, 2 vols., London, 1866
Higginson, Gen. Sir George, *Seventy-one Years of a Guardsman's Life*, London, 1916
Humbley, Capt. W. W. W., *Journal of a Cavalry Officer*, London, 1854
Jagow, Kurt (ed.), *Letters of the Prince Consort 1831-1861*, London, 1938
Kealy, P. H., *General Sir Charles William Pasley*, [Chatham, 1932]
King, Capt. W. R., *Campaigning in Kaffirland*, London, 1853
Knollys, Col. Henry (ed.), *Life of General Sir Hope Grant*, Edinburgh, 1894
Leach, Lt. Col. J., *Rambles along the Styx*, London, 1847
Lefroy, Lady (ed.), *Autobiography of General Sir John Henry Lefroy, C.B., K.C.M.G., F.R.S.*, privately printed, 1895
Lysons, Gen. Sir Daniel, *Early Reminiscences*, London, 1896
McGrigor, Sir James, *The Autobiography and Services of Sir James McGrigor, Bart., late Director-General of the Army Medical Department*, London, 1861
Mackenzie, Lt. Gen. Colin, *Storms and Sunshine of a Soldier's Life*, Edinburgh, 1884
Marshman, John C., *Memoirs of Major-General Sir Henry Havelock, K.C.B.*, London, 1876
Martin, Theodore, *The Life of His Royal Highness the Prince Consort*, London, 1875-6
Martineau, John, *The Life of Henry Pelham, 5th Duke of Newcastle*, London, 1908
Mitra, S. M., *The Life and Letters of Sir John Hall*, London, 1911
Mountain, Mrs. A. S. H. (ed.), *Memoirs and Letters of the late Colonel Armine*

S. H. Mountain, C.B., London, 1858

Munro, Surgeon-Gen. [William], *Records of Service and Campaigning in Many Lands*, 2 vols., London, 1887

Napier, Lt. Col. E. Elers, *Excursions in Southern Africa*, 2 vols., London, 1849

Napier, Col. Elers, *The Linesman*, 3 vols., London, 1856

Napier, Lt. Gen. Sir W., *The Life and Opinions of General Sir Charles James Napier, G.C.B.*, 4 vols., London, 1857

Neill, J.M.B., *Recollections of Four Years' Service in the East with H.M. Fortieth Regiment*, London, 1845

Parker, Charles Stuart, *Life and Letters of Sir James Graham*, 2 vols., London, 1907

Patterson, Maj. John, *Camp and Quarters*, 2 vols., London, 1840

Pinney, Thomas (ed.), *The Letters of Thomas Babington Macaulay*, vol. III, Cambridge, 1976

Rait, Robert S., *The Life and Campaigns of Hugh, 1st Viscount Gough, Field Marshal*, 2 vols., London, 1903

Ramsay, Lt. Col. B. D. W., *Rough Recollections of Military Service and Society*, 2 vols., Edinburgh, 1882

[Reid, Sgt. David], *Memorials of the Life of a Soldier*, Edinburgh, 1864

Robertson, Col. James P., *Personal Adventures and Anecdotes of an Old Officer*, London, 1906

Russell, Rollo (ed.), *Early Correspondence of Lord John Russell 1805-40*, 2 vols., London, 1913

[Ryder, John], A Private Soldier, *Four Years' Service in India*, Leicester, 1853

Sanderson, Charles R., (ed.), *The Arthur Papers*, 3 vols., Toronto, 1957-9.

Shadwell, Lt. Gen., *The Life of Colin Campbell, Lord Clyde*, 2 vols., Edinburgh, 1881

Sidney, Rev. Edwin, *The Life of Lord Hill*, London, 1845

[Smith, Dr.], *The Christian Soldier; being a memorial of the late Lieut.-Colonel Fordyce*, London [? 1855]

Smith, G. C. Moore, *The Life of John Colborne, Field Marshal Lord Seaton*, London, 1903

The Autobiography of Lieutenant-General Sir Harry Smith, London, 1901

[Somerville, A.], *The Autobiography of a Working Man*, London, 1848

Soyer, Alexis, *Soyer's Culinary Campaign*, London, 1857

Stanhope, Philip Henry, fifth Earl, *Notes of Conversations with the Duke of Wellington 1831-1851*, London, 1938

Stanmore, Lord, *Sidney Herbert, Lord Herbert of Lea, A Memoir*, 2 vols., London, 1906

Stuart, Col. W. K., *Reminiscences of a Soldier*, 2 vols., London, 1874

Swinson, Arthur, and Scott, Donald, (ed.), *The Memoirs of Private Waterfield*, London, 1968

Taylor, Sgt. Maj. [William], *Life in the Ranks*, London, 1843

Thackwell, Edward J., *Narrative of the Second Seikh War*, London, 1851

Tulloch, Maj. Gen. Sir A. B., *Recollections of Forty Years' Service*, Edinburgh, 1903

Verner, Col. Willoughby, *The Military Life of H.R.H. George, Duke of*

Cambridge, 2 vols., London, 1905
Von Orlich, Capt. Leopold, *Travels in India, including Scinde and the Punjab*, London, 1845
Walpole, Spencer, *The Life of Lord John Russell*, London, 1889
The War in India, despatches of Hardinge, Gough and Smith, London, 1846
Ward, S. G. P., (ed.), *The Hawley Letters*, London, 1970
Watts, Alaric Alfred, *Alaric Watts, A Narrative of His Life*, 2 vols., London, 1884
Wellington, 2nd Duke of, *Despatches, Correspondence and Memoranda of Field Marshal Arthur, Duke of Wellington, K.G.*, 8 vols., London, 1867-1880
Whittingham, Maj. Gen. Ferdinand (ed.), *A Memoir of The Service of Lieut.-General Sir Samuel Ford Whittingham, K.C.B., K.C.H., G.C.F.*, London, 1868
Wolseley, Field-Marshal Viscount, *The Story of a Soldier's Life*, 2 vols., London, 1903
Wrottesley, Lt. Col. the Hon. George, *Life and Correspondence of Field Marshal Sir John Burgoyne, Bart.*, 2 vols., London, 1873
The Military Opinions of General Sir John Fox Burgoyne, Bart., G.C.B., London, 1859
Wylly, Col. H. C., *The Military Memoirs of Lieut. General Sir Joseph Thackwell*, London, 1908

VI. *Secondary works*

(Regimental histories listed in Arthur S. White, *A Bibliography of Regimental Histories of the British Army* (London, 1965) are not included here, unless cited in the footnotes.)

Anglesey, Marquess of, *A History of the British Cavalry 1816 to 1919*, 2 vols., London, 1973-5
One Leg, London, 1961
Anderson, Olive, *A Liberal State at War*, London, 1967
'Early experiences of manpower problems in an industrial society at war: Great Britain, 1854-56', *Political Science Quarterly*, vol. LXXXII, 1967, pp. 526-545
'The growth of Christian militarism in mid-Victorian Britain', *English Historical Review*, vol. LXXXIV, 1971, pp. 46-72.
Atkins, J. B., *The Life of Sir William Howard Russell*, vol. I, London, 1911
Atkinson, C. T., *Regimental History, The Royal Hampshire Regiment*, vol. I, Glasgow, 1950.
Austin, M., *The Army in Australia 1840-50*, Canberra, 1979
Bartlett, C. J., *Great Britain and Sea Power 1815-1853*, Oxford, 1963
Bartlett, H. Moyse, *Louis Edward Nolan and his influence on the British Cavalry*, London, 1971
Bayley, C. C., *Mercenaries for the Crimea*, Montreal, 1977
Best, G. F. A., 'National education in England, 1800-70', *Cambridge Historical Journal*, vol. XII, 1956, pp. 155-173

Blanco, Richard L., 'Reform and Wellington's post-Waterloo army, 1815-1854', *Military Affairs*, vol. XXIX, 1965, pp. 123-131
Bond, Brian, 'Prelude to the Cardwell reforms 1856-68', *Journal of the Royal United Services Institution*, vol. CVI, 1961, pp. 229-236.
 'Recruiting the Victorian army 1870-92', *Victorian Studies*, vol. V, 1961-2, p. 331
 The Victorian Army and the Staff College, 1854-1914, London, 1972
Bourne, Kenneth, *Palmerston. The early years 1784-1841*, London, 1982
Bourne, Kenneth (ed.), *The Letters of the Third Viscount Palmerston to Laurence and Elizabeth Sulivan 1804-1863*, Camden, 4th series, vol. 23, London, 1979
Bowyer-Bower, T. A., 'The Development of Educational Ideas and Curricula in the Army during the 18th and 19th centuries', Nottingham University, M. Ed. thesis, 1954
Bruce, Anthony, *The Purchase System in the British Army 1660-1871*, London, 1980
Burroughs, Peter, 'The human cost of imperial defence in the early Victorian age', *Victorian Studies*, vol. XXIV, 1980, pp. 7-32
 'The Ordnance Department and colonial defence, 1821-1855', *Journal of Imperial and Commonwealth History*, vol. X, 1982, pp. 125-149
Calkins, W. N., 'A Victorian free trade lobby', *Economic History Review*, 2nd series, vol. XIII, 1960, pp. 90-104
Cantlie, Sir Neil, *A History of the Army Medical Services*, 2 vols., Edinburgh, 1974
Cary, A. D. L., and McCance, Stouppe, *Regimental Records of the Royal Welch Fusiliers*, 2 vols., London, 1923
Caulfield, J. E., *One Hundred Years' History of the 2nd Batt. West India Regiment*, London, 1899
Chaplin, H. D., *The 97th or Earl of Ulster's Regiment 1824-1881*, Maidstone, 1973
Clark, G. Kitson, *Churchmen and the Condition of England, 1832-1885*, London, 1973
 'Statesmen in disguise: reflexions on the history of the neutrality of the civil service', *Historical Journal*, vol. II, 1959, pp. 19-39
Cole, Howard N., *The Story of Aldershot*, Aldershot, 1951
Conacher, J. B., *The Aberdeen Coalition 1852-1855*, Cambridge, 1968
Cowper, L. I. (ed.), *The King's Own*, 2 vols., Oxford, 1939
Cunningham, Hugh, *The Volunteer Force*, London, 1975
Curtiss, John Shelton, *The Russian Army under Nicholas I, 1825-1855*, Durham N. C., 1965
Davidson, H., *History and Services of the 78th Highlanders (Ross-shire Buffs) 1793-1881*, Edinburgh, 1901
Dinwiddy, J. K., 'The early nineteenth century campaign against flogging in the army', *English Historical Review*, vol. XCVII, 1982, pp. 308-331
Drummond, J. C., and Wilbraham, Anne, *The Englishman's Food*, London, 1957
Dunn-Pattison, R. P., *The History of the 91st Argyllshire Highlanders*, Edinburgh, 1910

Forbes, A., *A History of the Army Ordnance Services*, 3 vols., London, 1929
Fortescue, J. W., 'The army', in G. M. Young (ed.), *Early Victorian England 1830-1865*, 2 vols., London, 1934
  The British Army 1783-1802, London, 1905
  A History of the British Army, vols. XI-XIII, London, 1923-1930
  The Last Post, Edinburgh, 1934
  The Royal Army Service Corps, A History of Transport and Supply in the British Army, vol. I, Cambridge, 1930
  A Short Account of Canteens in the British Army, Cambridge, 1928
  Six British Soldiers, London, 1928
Gardyne, C. Greenhill, *The Life of a Regiment*, 2 vols., Edinburgh, 1903
Gash, Norman, *Sir Robert Peel*, London, 1972
Glover, Richard, *Peninsular Preparation*, Cambridge, 1963
Godwin-Austen, A. R., *The Staff and the Staff College*, London, 1927
Gooch, Brison D., *The New Bonapartist Generals in the Crimean War*, The Hague, 1959
Griffith, P. G., 'Military Thought in the French Army 1815-1851', Oxford University D. Phil. thesis, 1975
Guggisberg, F. G., *'The Shop', The Story of the Royal Military Academy*, London, 1900
Hamilton, C. I., 'The Royal Navy, Seapower, and the Screw Ship of the Line, 1845-1860', Cambridge University Ph. D. thesis, 1974
Hanham, H. J., 'Religion and nationality in the mid-Victorian army', in M. R. D. Foot (ed.), *War and Society*, London, 1973
Hardinge, Charles, Viscount, *Rulers of India: Viscount Hardinge*, Oxford, 1891
Harries-Jenkins, Gwyn, *The Army in Victorian Society*, London, 1977
Harris, John, *The Gallant Six Hundred*, London, 1973
Hart, Jenifer, 'Nineteenth century social reform: a Tory interpretation of history', *Past and Present*, no. 31, 1965, pp. 38-53
  'Sir Charles Trevelyan at the Treasury', *English Historical Review*, vol. LXXV, 1960, pp. 92-110.
Hay, George Jackson, *An Epitomized History of the Militia (the 'Constitutional Force')*, London, [1906]
Hearnshaw, F. J. C., *The Centenary History of King's College, London 1828-1928*, London, 1929
Hibbert, Christopher, *The Destruction of Lord Raglan*, London, 1961
Hime, H. W. L., *History of the Royal Regiment of Artillery 1815-1853*, London, 1908
Hobsbawm, E. J., *Labouring Men*, London, 1964
Hobsbawm, E. J., and Hartwell, R. M., 'The standard of living during the industrial revolution: a discussion', *Economic History Review*, 2nd series, vol. XVI, 1963, pp. 119-146
Hogg, O. F. G., *The Royal Arsenal. Its background, origin and subsequent history*, 2 vols., London, 1963
Hopkins, Harry, *The Strange Death of Private White*, London, 1977
Houlding, J. A., *Fit for Service. The Training of the British Army 1715-1795*, Oxford, 1981

Howard, Michael, *Studies in War and Peace*, London, 1970
Hughes, Edward, 'Sir Charles Trevelyan and civil service reform, 1853-5', *English Historical Review*, vol. LXIV, 1949, pp. 53-88, 206-234
Irvine, Dallas D., 'The origin of capital staffs', *Journal of Modern History*, vol. X, 1938, pp. 161-179
Irwin, D. Hastings, *War Medals and Decorations*, London, 1890
Jarvis, A. C. E., 'My predecessors in office', *Journal of the Royal Army Chaplains' Department*, vol. III, 1931, pp. 444-480, 481-520; vol. IV, 1931, pp. 14-77
Journal of the Society for Army Historical Research
Keegan, John, 'Regimental ideology', in Geoffrey Best and Andrew Wheatcroft (ed.), *War, Economy and the Military Mind*, London, 1976
Leask, J. C., and McCance, H. M., *The Regimental Records of the Royal Scots*, Dublin, 1915
Lehmann, Joseph H., *Remember you are an Englishman. A Biography of Sir Harry Smith 1787-1860*, London, 1977
Liddell, R. S., *The Memoirs of the Tenth Royal Hussars*, London, 1891
Linklater, Eric and Andro, *The Black Watch*, London, 1977
Luvaas, Jay, *The Education of an Army*, London, 1965
MacDonagh, Oliver, *Early Victorian Government 1830-1870*, London, 1977.
'The nineteenth-century revolution in government: a reappraisal', *Historical Journal*, vol. I, 1958, pp. 52-67
Mather, F. C., *Public Order in the Age of the Chartists*, Manchester, 1966
Morgan, M. C., *Cheltenham College*, Chalfont St. Giles, 1968
Moorsom, W. S., *Historical Record of the 52nd Regiment (Oxfordshire Light Infantry)*, London, 1860
Morrell, W. P., *British Colonial Policy in the Age of Peel and Russell*, Oxford, 1930
British Colonial Policy in the Mid-Victorian Age, Oxford, 1969
Moyer, R. A., 'The Mfengu self-defence, expansion and the frontier wars', unpublished paper given at conference on the history of the Transkei and Ciskei
Oatts, L. B., *Proud Heritage*, vols. I and II, Edinburgh, 1952-9
Oman, C. W. C., *Wellington's Army 1809-1814*, London, 1912
Parris, Henry, 'Nineteenth century revolution in government: a reappraisal reappraised', *Historical Journal*, vol. III, 1960, pp. 17-37
Perkin, Harold, *The Origins of Modern English Society*, London, 1969
Pollock, J. C., *Way to Glory*, London, 1957
Porter, Whitworth, *History of the Corps of Royal Engineers*, 2 vols., London, 1889
Pycroft, George, *The Origin of the Volunteer Movement of 1852 and History of the First Volunteer Rifle Corps*, London, 1881
Razzell, P. E., 'Social origins of officers in the Indian and British home army 1758-1962', *British Journal of Sociology*, vol. XIV, 1963, pp. 248-260
Roads, C. H., *The British Soldier's Firearm 1850-1864*, London, 1964.
'The History of the Introduction of the Percussion Breech-loading Rifle into British Military Service 1850-70', Cambridge University Ph. D thesis, 1961

Samut-Tagliaferro, A., *History of the Royal Malta Artillery*, vol. I, Malta, 1976
Schofield, R. S., 'Dimensions of illiteracy 1750-1850', *Explorations in Economic History*, summer 1973, p. 437
Scott, J. B., 'The British Soldier on the Eastern Cape Frontier, 1800-1850', University of Port Elizabeth Ph. D. thesis, 1973
Skelley, Alan Ramsay, *The Victorian Army at Home*, London and Montreal, 1977
Smyth, Sir John, *In this Sign Conquer — The Story of the Army Chaplains*, London, 1968
Southgate, Donald, *The Passing of the Whigs 1832-1886*, London, 1962
Spiers, Edward M., *The Army and Society 1815-1914*, London, 1980
Stacey, C. P., *Canada and the British Army, 1846-1871*, London, 1936
Strachan, Hew, 'The early Victorian army and the nineteenth-century revolution in government', *English Historical Review*, vol. XCV, 1980, pp. 782-809
   'The 1855 uniform changes: an example of pre-Crimean reform', *Journal of the Society for Army Historical Research*, vol. LV, 1977, pp. 85-117, 165-174
   'Soldiers, strategy and Sebastopol', *Historical Journal*, vol. XXI, 1978, pp. 303-325
Sutherland, Gillian (ed.), *Studies in the growth of nineteenth-century government*, London, 1972
Sweetman, John, 'The Effects of the Crimean War upon the Administration of the British Army (1852-1856)', London University Ph. D. thesis, 1972
   'Military transport in the Crimean war, 1854-1856', *English Historical Review*, vol. LXXXVIII, 1973, pp. 81-91
Tancred, George, *Historical Record of Medals and Honorary Distinctions*, London, 1891
   War Medal Record, 2 vols., London, 1896-8
Thomas, Donald, *Charge! Hurrah! Hurrah!*, London, 1974
Thomas, Hugh, *The Story of Sandhurst*, London, 1961
Thompson, E. P., *The Making of the English Working Class*, London, 1963
Tunstall, W. C. B., 'Imperial defence, 1815-1870', in *The Cambridge History of the British Empire*, vol. II, Cambridge, 1940
Vale, W. L., *History of the South Staffordshire Regiment*, Aldershot, 1969
Wake, Joan, *The Brudenells of Deene*, London, 1953
Ward, B. R., *The School of Military Engineering, 1812-1909*, Chatham, 1909
Ward, S. G. P., *Faithful*, Edinburgh, 1963
   Wellington's Headquarters, Oxford, 1957
Webb, R. K., 'Literacy among the working classes in nineteenth century Scotland', *Scottish Historical Review*, vol. XXXIII, 1954, pp. 100-114
Wheaton, John, 'The Effect and Impact of the Administrative Reform Movement upon the Army in the mid-Victorian period', Manchester University Ph. D. thesis, 1968
Wheeler, Owen, *The War Office Past and Present*, London, 1914
Whinyates, F. A., *From Coruna to Sevastopol*, London, 1884
White, A. C. T., *The Story of Army Education 1643-1963*, London, 1963
Wilkinson, Nevile, *The Guards' Chapel 1838-1938*, London, 1938

Williams, N. T. St. John, *Tommy Atkins' Children*, London, 1971
Woodham-Smith, Cecil, *The Reason Why*, Harmondsworth, 1958
Worthington, Ian, 'Antecedent education and officer recruitment: the origins and early development of the public school–army relationship', *Military Affairs*, vol. XLI, 1977, pp. 183-9

Index

Aberdeen 51
Aberdeen, Earl of, 3, 38, 42
Adams, F., 131
Adams, H. W., 173
Addington, Charles, 2
Adelaide, Queen, 129
Adjutant General, duties of a department of, 147, 149
Adjutant General at the Horse Guards 7, 8, 14, 17, 26, 35, 39-41, 104, 149, 151, 172, 231, 233, 251; *see also* Brown, Sir George; Cathcart, Sir George; Macdonald, Sir John; Wetherall, G. A.
Adjutant General in the Crimea 173, 237; *see also* Estcourt
Admiralty 197, 199, 231, 248, 250, 253, 262
Afghan War, 1st, 101, 173, 183, 237; *see also* Ghuznee; Jellalabad; Kabul
Africa, West, 180, 185, 188, 245-6
Africa, South, *see* Kaffir Wars; South Africa
agricultural labourers as recruits 53, 57, 111
aides-de-camp, duties of, 146, 147, 152, 174
Airey, Sir Richard, 14, 41, 42, 150, 151, 152, 173, 217, 218, 237
Albert, Prince, 13, 35-6, 38, 40, 43, 120, 157, 164-6, 170-1, 200, 202, 217-18, 220, 254, 259
Albuera, battle of, 13
Aldershot, purchase of, 142, 170-1, 201
Alexander, Sir J. E., 22
Aliwal, battle of, 172
Alma, battle of, 158, 174
Ambala 164
ammunition stores 166-7, 236-7, 260
Anglesey, Marquess of, 13, 18, 35, 73, 118, 157, 172, 198, 256
Anson, Sir George, 33
Antigua 185
Army and Ordnance expenditure, 1849-50 select committee on, 240, 254-8
Army Medical Department 2, 10, 25, 66, 160, 185, 230, 235, 237, 241-6, 258
Arnold, Thomas, 124
Arthur, Sir George, 80, 89
Articles of War 10, 63, 135, 231, 235
artillery 37, 38, 41-3, 87, 124-5, 133-4, 158, 160, 170, 201, 210, 233
Artillery Studies, Department of, 134
artisans as recruits 53
Ashton 61
Australia 64, 180, 184, 186, 187, 190, 194-6, 214, 245
Austria, army, 162, 171, 182, 192

Bagshot 164, 166
Bahamas 185, 188
Balaclava, battle of, 152, 174
Balkan War 173
Ballingall, Sir George, 245
Baptists 65

Index

Barbados 183, 185, 188
barracks 12, 21, 28, 60-3, 68, 88, 93, 171, 185, 232-3, 235-6, 254
battalions, size of, 211-12, 217-18, 219; *see also* regiment
bayonet exercise 14, 27
Belgium, army, 129, 171, 201
Bell, Andrew, 90, 94
Bentham, Maj. J., 26
Benthamism 103, 247, 269
Bentinck, Henry, 172
Bentinck, Lord William, 82
Berbice 180
Beresford, Viscount, 13, 74
Bermuda 183
Beverloo 171
Bisset, Sir John, 238, 240
Blakeney, Sir Edward, 34, 156
Blackwood's Magazine 4
Blomfield, C. J., 87, 97
Board of General Officers 4, 41, 126, 232, 233, 235
Bombay 31, 33, 92, 138, 163-4
Boomplatz, battle of, 244
Booth, William, 59, 240
bounty money 55, 56, 83
Boxer, E. M., 125, 261
Bradford, Sir Thomas, 89
brevet rank 116, 118-21
brigades, formation of, 147, 155, 159-61, 219; *see also* training
Bright, John, 11
Bristol 204
British Army Despatch 24, 32
British Auxiliary Legion 7, 82, 173
British Guiana 190
British Military Library 20
British Soldier 25
Brougham, Lord, 73
Brown, Sir George, 11, 15, 17, 18, 20, 27, 39-41, 56, 62, 94, 119, 137, 151-2, 165, 169, 173, 216, 239, 240
Browne, T. G., 96
Brudenell, James, *see* Cardigan, Earl of
Buddiwal, battle of, 172

Buller, George, 173
Bunbury, Thomas, 147
Burgoyne, Sir John, 27, 62, 121, 125, 137, 157, 172, 181, 190, 198-9, 202, 239
Burma War, 1st, 120, 173
Bury 61
Butler, Sir William, 53-4
Byng, Sir John, *see* Strafford, Earl of

Calladine, George, 34
Cambridge, Adolphus, Duke of, 13
Cambridge, Prince George, Duke of, 7, 27, 32-3, 35, 39-40, 64, 103, 120, 129, 156, 161-2, 165, 168, 169, 172, 174, 217-18, 220
camp of exercise 31, 34, 42, 87, 162-71
Campbell, Colin, 172, 173-4
Campbell, Ensign, 131
Campbell, James, 148, 149
Campbell, Sir John, 173
Canada 12, 13, 25, 56, 58, 67, 72, 113, 150, 183, 186-7, 190-6, 213, 236, 238, 245, 271
Canning, George, 8, 247
canteens 66-7
Cape, *see* South Africa
Cape Corps 30
Cape Mounted Rifles 90, 189-91
Cardigan, Earl of, 7, 34, 74, 116, 174
Cardwell, Edward, 1, 74, 212, 219, 262
Carshalton, preparatory school at, 123, 127
Catholicism 86-8, 93
Cathcart, Charles, Earl, ix, 27, 62, 84, 121, 165
Cathcart, Sir George, ix, 9, 41-2, 146-7, 149, 152, 162, 172, 174, 211, 221, 239, 257, 260
cavalry 54-7, 72, 83, 89, 99, 102, 116, 134, 136, 160, 168, 173-4, 214
Cavalry Depot 214
Ceylon 180, 186-7, 190, 214
Ceylon Rifles 188-9
Chancellor of the Exchequer 199, 230,

236, 240, 257; *see also* Treasury
Channel Islands 197, 199, 203, 206
chapels 62, 88
Chaplain General to the Forces 87; *see also* Gleig
chaplains 86-8, 93-4, 231
Chartists 28, 61, 111, 162, 203, 204, 209
Chatham 27, 84, 91, 93, 132, 134, 138, 156-9, 170, 200, 214, 241
Chatterton, J. C., 63, 101
Cheltenham College 128
Chesney, F. R., 118, 254
Chichester, C. R., 23, 131
Chichester, Sir Charles, 63, 90, 97, 159
children of soldiers 90; *see also* marriage
Chillianwallah, battle of, 172
China 101, 173, 183, 184, 188
Chobham camp 4, 38, 41-2, 127, 164, 166-74, 201
Church of England 93-4
civil power, aid to, 203-4, 212, 213, 268
Claremont, E. S., 149
Clarendon, Earl of, 163
'classification' system 100
Clerke, T. H. Shadwell, 20, 27, 30-1, 131
coast defences, committee on, 197, 199, 200, 233
Cobden, Richard, 11, 110, 209, 268
Cochrane, W. G., 5, 34
Codrington, Sir William, 119, 150, 173-4
Colborne, Sir John, *see* Seaton
Colburn, Henry, 20-2
Coldstream Guards 29
Cole, Sir Lowry, 189
colonial regiments 12, 187-96
colonial self-defence 190-6
Combermere, Viscount, 13, 73-4, 172
Commander-in-Chief, character and status of, 6-9, 11, 13-16, 17-20, 26, 35-43, 74, 87, 96, 122, 129, 149, 181, 231-2, 245, 247-8, 250, 252-6, 261-2, 270; *see also* Hardinge; Hill; Wellington; York
Commissariat 12, 58-9, 160-2, 164, 168, 170, 175, 230-2, 236-40, 243, 245, 246, 248-50, 252, 254, 256-7, 260, 268
company as independent unit 34-5
Conservatives 7, 13
contract system 58-9
Cork 214, 243
Corunna 37
Cotton, Willoughby, 27
Council for National Defence 199, 235, 261-2
courts-martial 80-3, 103, 231
cricket 13, 85
Crimean War 1-4, 27-8, 42-3, 56-7, 64, 88, 99, 119-21, 130, 139, 140, 148-52, 158, 160, 172-5, 218-21, 234, 236-7, 239, 240, 259-62, 267-8, 270-1
Cubitt, Mr, 171

Dakins, W. W., 86-7
Dalbiac, Sir Charles, 26
Dalhousie, Marquess of, 2, 29, 33
Dalhousie, 11th Earl of, *see* Panmure
de Ainslie, C., 27
Delane, J. T., 2, 37
Demerara 58, 61, 180
depots 188, 211-19
Derby, Lord Stanley, Earl of, 9, 36-7, 73, 181, 190, 208, 217, 259
Derinzy, B. R., 34
de Ros, Lord, 74, 151, 173, 239, 260
desertion 12, 57, 67, 70, 81, 83, 89, 103, 182, 191, 193
Devonport 84
diet 12, 30, 57-9, 185, 268
discharge 71-4, 83, 100, 102-3, 187, 195, 196, 205, 216
disease 60-1, 64-5, 68, 184-5, 187, 220, 243, 267
divisions, as formations, 151, 155-6, 159, 160-1, 163-4, 168, 219, 239
Dixon, W. M., 125
Dockyard Battalions 199

Index

Dominica 185
Donkin, Sir Rufane, 27
Douglas, Sir Howard, 27, 62, 71, 73
Douglas, Sir Neil, 99
Dover 170
Drummond, Henry, 3
drunkenness 30, 55, 58, 64-8, 83, 89, 96, 185
Dublin 70, 84, 92, 156, 158, 160, 162, 174, 200, 201, 243
du Bourdieu, Arthur, 52
Dumbreck, David, 246
Dundas, Sir David, 39
Dundas, George, 3

Eardley-Wilmot, F. M., 123, 133-4
East India Company 28-9, 61, 66, 82, 101, 150, 182-4, 192, 205, 214
Edinburgh 151, 162, 201, 214
Edinburgh Review 139
Edinburgh University 243
education of officers 12, 27, 29, 31-2, 42, 91, 99, 111, 122-41; *see also* examinations; promotion, examinations for; Royal Military Academy, Woolwich; Royal Military College, Sandhurst; training, staff
education of other ranks 30-2, 88-97, 99, 130, 139
Ellenborough, Earl of, 16, 37, 259
Ellice, Edward, 259
Ellice, R., 137
Elphinstone, W. G. K., 20, 114, 255
England, as recruiting area, 57, 89
England, Sir Richard, 173
Estcourt, James B., 149-50, 173
Eton College 128
Evans, Sir George de Lacy, 7, 82, 101, 120, 149, 152, 172-3, 221, 230, 243
Everton 162
examinations for first commissions 99, 128-30, 136, 139
examinations for promotion, *see* promotion
Eyre, Sir William, 41, 173

Falkland Islands 196
Felix, Orlando, 40
Fergusson, James, 132, 199
Fergusson, William, 65, 66, 70
Ferozeshah, battle of, 159, 243
field training, *see* training
Filder, William, 240, 260
Firebrace, Col., 20, 21
Fitzclarence, Lord Frederick, 29-33, 39, 63, 90-2, 97, 137-8, 155-6, 160, 163-4
fives 13, 85
Foot Guards 38, 63, 89, 172, 174, 183
Foot Guards, privileges of, 16, 21-2, 24, 26, 119, 126
foreign corps in British pay 56, 221
Foreign Secretary 229
fortifications, study of, 91, 124-5, 127, 129, 130, 132, 136, 137
fortifications, use of, 190, 197-200, 202, 210
France, army, 26, 30, 31, 33, 80, 129, 148-50, 154, 157, 161, 171, 172, 182, 197-8, 201, 267, 269
France, fear of invasion by, *see* home defence
France, navy, 199
Frederick the Great 237

Gambia 196, 245
Gardiner, Sir Robert, 11, 254
George IV 8, 112, 247, 252
Ghuznee, storming of, 101
Gibraltar 58, 185, 190
Gladstone, W. E., 170
Glasgow, as recruiting area, 52, 70
Gleig, G. R., 67, 86-8, 90-4, 96-7, 122, 129, 130, 135, 138, 139, 154
Glenelg, Lord, 10, 188, 250-2
Gold Coast Corps 188
Goldie, T. L., 172
Gomm, Sir William, 27
good conduct, rewards for, 12, 13, 34, 43, 63, 68, 96, 99-102, 193-5
Gordon, Sir J. Willoughby, 11-13, 15, 35, 39, 59, 114, 151, 187, 192, 197, 211-12

Gough, Sir Hugh, Viscount, 13, 18, 147, 172
Graham, Sir James, 140, 190, 197, 204, 206, 248
Grenada 185, 187
Grenadier Guards 54, 166
Grey, Charles, 2nd Earl, 247
Grey, Sir Charles, 12, 43, 70, 100, 120, 193, 214-20
Grey, George, 192
Grey, Henry, Viscount Howick, 3rd Earl, 37-8, 43, 120-1
  as Secretary at War (1835-39), 10-13, 27, 55, 58, 65, 67, 71, 84, 92, 100, 185-6, 188, 192-4, 205, 206, 214, 230-1, 249-54
  as Secretary of State for War and the Colonies (1846-52), 9, 14, 16-17, 69, 71-4, 91, 101, 115, 128-9, 135, 137, 140, 157, 181, 189-91, 194-8, 205, 207, 209-10, 212, 215-17, 219-20, 229, 234, 256, 257-60, 262, 268, 270
Guernsey 28, 206
Guthrie, G. J., 242, 244, 246
Gwalior 101, 165, 181

half-pay 26, 30, 113-15, 118, 203, 204, 209, 241-2
Hall, Sir John, 244
Halliday, Sir Andrew, 58
Hamley, Edward, 4
Hardinge, Arthur, 171
Harding, Sir Henry, Viscount, 36-7, 74, 101, 255, 257
  as Secretary at War (1828-30), 37, 65, 68, 86, 125, 127-8, 242, 249
  as Secretary at War (1841-44), 13, 16, 37, 55, 84, 87, 94, 119, 183, 204, 206, 212, 256-7
  as Governor-General of India (1844-48), 13, 37, 82, 147, 159, 201
  as Master General of the Ordnance (1852), 37, 59, 63, 158, 199, 201, 216, 237, 244, 258
  as Commander-in-Chief (1852-56), 3, 17, 26, 35, 36-43, 52, 59, 93, 120-1, 130, 139, 140, 151, 152, 157-8, 161, 165-7, 169-74, 199, 201, 203, 211, 212, 217-20, 231, 234, 261, 268, 270
Hardy, Henry, 34
Harrow School 128
Hart, H. G., 22, 27, 30
Havelock, Henry, 18, 33, 65, 131
Head, Sir Francis, 199
health, *see* disease; medicine, preventive
Herbert, Sidney, 12, 16, 38, 42, 73, 87, 92, 94-5, 99, 100, 120, 130, 135, 139, 154, 166, 173, 194, 206, 217-21, 231, 240, 243, 259, 261-2
Higginson, George, 35, 166
Highland regiments 51-3, 56, 215
High Wycombe 152
Hill, Lord, 6-8, 10, 12, 13, 37, 39, 56, 65-7, 84-5, 90, 92, 94, 156, 185-6, 192-3, 211, 214, 231, 247, 252
Hobhouse, Sir J. C., 10, 69, 247, 249, 250
Holland, army, 129, 162
home defence 14, 15, 29, 37, 39, 41, 120, 151, 158, 161-2, 164-7, 171, 181, 183, 196-211, 213, 219-20, 229, 234, 237, 239, 240, 268, 270
Home Secretary 9, 61, 170, 199, 229, 231, 236, 243, 253, 259, 260
Honduras 188
Hong Kong 180, 184, 187-8
Hopkins, J. P., 27
Horfield 62
Horse Guards 6-7, 9-11, 14, 18-20, 30, 35, 38-42, 66, 69, 81, 83, 96, 102, 104, 119, 120, 130, 135-7, 146, 151, 172, 180, 191-2, 199, 201, 204, 214-15, 229, 231-2, 235, 245, 247, 251-7, 259-61
Hort, Lt. Col., 18, 25
hospitals, administration of, 243-6
Hounslow 82
Howick, Viscount, *see* Grey, Henry
Hudson's Bay 196
Hume, Joseph, 7, 11, 21, 181, 248, 256, 259, 260

Index 295

Hythe School of Musketry 42, 157-8

imperial defence 12, 37, 180-96, 229, 234, 244, 246, 267-71
India 55-6, 61, 64, 66, 112, 116, 119, 150, 157, 161, 163, 172, 174, 181-4, 186-7, 191, 211, 214, 219-20, 267; see also East India Company
infantry 54-5, 57, 72-3, 89, 96, 99, 102, 110, 117, 134, 156-7, 160, 168, 266
infantry drill 30, 39
infantry, light, 210
Inkerman, battle of, 42, 152, 158, 174
inspections, half-yearly, 80, 83, 134, 180
Inspector of Military Schools 95-6
Inspector General of Cavalry 156, 173
Inspector General of Fortifications 62, 151, 190, 199, 233, 251
inspectorship of infantry proposed 156
invasion, fear of, see home defence
Ionian Islands 180, 183, 185, 190, 220
Ireland, as recruiting area, 51-3, 57, 89
Ireland, as station, 59, 81, 84, 86, 92, 156, 162, 204

Jackson, Robert, 53, 71
Jamaica 58, 183-5, 187, 194, 245
Jarry, François, 153
Jebb, J., 84, 131, 171, 200
Jellalabad, siege of, 65, 101
Jersey 60
Jervis, J. W., 238
Joinville, Prince de, 197
Jomini, A. H., 131, 153
Jones, H. D., 125, 132, 168
Jones, Inigo, 160
Judge Advocate General 231

Kabul 20, 28, 114, 148, 237, 255
Kaffir Wars 9, 41, 173, 184, 191; see also South Africa
Kay-Shuttleworth, James, 94, 97
Keane, Sir John, Lord, 13

Kempt, Sir James, 248-9
Kennaway, C. E., 2
Kennedy, Sir Robert, 237, 240
Kennedy, Gen. Shaw, 27, 32
Kersal Moor 162
King's College, London, 128
Kingscote, Nigel, 3
Knollys, Sir William, 171

Lanark 51
Lancashire 209
Land Transport Corps 28
Langmeade, G. W., 88
Layard, A. H., 3
Layard, B. V., 71, 74
Leach, Jonathan, 26, 39
Lefroy, J. H., 133, 150, 160, 269
Lewis, G. G., 200
libraries 13, 30, 34, 61, 92-3, 95, 138-9, 231
Life Guards 68, 102
limited enlistment 16-17, 69-75, 187, 195, 198, 205, 215, 216, 218, 219
Lindsay, Hon. James, 67
literacy among recruits 53, 89-90; see also education
Liverpool Financial Reform Association 11
Liverpool, Lord, 181
Lloyd, Henry, 131, 153
London, as recruiting area, 52-3, 70
London, as station, 84, 119, 161, 165, 170, 200, 201, 243
Londonderry, Marquess of, 13, 73, 74
Louis Philippe 199
Lovell, Lovell Badcock, 27
Luard, John, 102
Lucan, Earl of, 74, 152, 173-4
Lucas, William, 55

Macaulay, T. B., 13
Macdonald, Sir John, 7, 8-9, 14, 39, 104, 111, 173
Macdonald, John C., 3
MacDougall, Patrick, 153
Mackinnon, Daniel, 84
MacNaughten, Sir William, 255

Maidstone 214
Maitland, Sir Peregrine, 148
Malta 172, 180, 185, 189-90, 200
Manchester 162
manpower 9, 14, 56-7, 87, 99, 180-4, 187, 197-8, 202-3, 210-11, 213, 218, 220-1, 267; see also reserve
manuals, lack of, 31-2, 155, 160
manuals, official, 30, 39, 134, 135, 138, 155, 158-60, 163, 169, 238
manuals, unofficial, 125, 133, 155, 160
Markham, F., 136
Marlborough, Duke of, 7, 91
marriage of soldiers 56, 62-5, 194
Marshall, Henry, 57, 61, 65, 70, 71, 88, 185, 187, 188
Master General of the Ordnance, see Ordnance
Maule, Fox, see Panmure
Maule, Lauderdale, 18, 135, 254
Maurice de Sellon, Baron P. E., 199, 202
Mauritius 180, 186, 187, 190, 214
McGrigor, Sir James, 65, 184-5, 241-4
McMullen, J., 110-11
McMurdo, W. M. G., 28
McNeill, Sir John, 3, 109
medals 19, 24, 30, 99, 101-2, 242, 243
medicine 12, 53-4, 262
medicine, preventive, 58, 60-1, 64-5, 68, 184-8, 241, 244, 246; see also Army Medical Department; disease; hospitals
Melbourne, Viscount, 12, 248, 250-3
messes, officers', 111-12
Miani, battle of, 28, 101, 120
Middlesex Yeomanry 24
military colonies 192-6
Military Magazine 25
Military Review 25
Military Secretary 6, 36, 41, 231, 251; see also Raglan
Military Train 140
militia 9, 14, 24, 29, 56, 57, 87, 114, 170, 190, 192, 198, 202-3, 205-11, 215-19, 232, 260

militia artillery 210
Millbank penitentiary 84
Mitchell, John, 20, 27, 116-17, 269
Monsell, William, 261
Montserrat 185
Moola-Moota river 163
Moore, Sir John, 29, 34, 36, 79, 85, 103, 166
moral education, officers, 123-4, 129
moral education, other ranks, 80, 85, 87
Morning Chronicle 198
Moseley, Henry, 94
Mountain, A. S. H., 33-4, 37, 97, 116
Mudki, battle of, 147
Munster, Earl of, 27
Murray, Sir George, 13, 61, 149, 151, 197, 198, 200, 206, 233
musketry training 41-2, 157, 168
Mutiny Act 10, 80, 83, 84, 135, 231

Napier, Sir Charles, 27-9, 31, 34, 37, 61, 62, 64, 99, 101, 111, 120, 131, 159, 161, 165, 166, 173, 204, 235-7, 254
Napier, Elers, 31
Napier, Sir George, 18
Napier, Sir William, 6, 21, 27-9, 32, 111, 131, 206
Napoleon I 146, 237, 267, 269
Napoleon III 199, 209
Narrien, John, 153
Naval and Military Gazette 19, 21-6, 28-9, 31, 36, 43, 71, 89, 115, 123, 128, 136, 137, 156, 169, 214, 243
Naval and Military Magazine 20
Newcastle, Duke of, 42, 148, 151, 166, 191, 203, 220, 259-62
Newfoundland Veteran Companies 192-3
New South Wales, see Australia
New Zealand 180, 184, 187, 189, 194-6
Nightingale, Florence, 2
Nihill, Daniell, 84
Nolan, L. E., 152, 174
noncommissioned officers 21, 51, 55,

Index

62, 64, 88, 90, 91, 93, 95-8, 100-2, 131
Normal School 94, 95, 97
Normanby, Marquess of, 61
Northumberland 52
Nottingham 67
Nova Scotia 183

officers, retirement of, 113-15, 117, 121
officers, role in reform, 33-5, 103
officers, social origins of, 110-11, 122, 139-41
officers, see also education; half-pay; pay; promotion
Oglander, Henry, 34
O'Halloran, D., 19
Ordnance, Board of, 12, 21, 58-9, 60, 62, 66, 85, 87, 93, 151, 171, 199, 200, 231-5, 237, 245, 248-9, 250-2, 254-7, 260-2
Ordnance, Clerk of the, 233, 261-2
Ordnance, Lieutenant General of the, 261-2
Ordnance, Master General of the, appointments as, 7, 13, 26, 36, 37, 61, 118, 151, 158, 197-8
  role and status of, 9, 123, 201, 232-5, 245, 248-52, 256, 258, 260-1; see also Anglesey, Hardinge, Kempt, Murray, Raglan, Vivian, Wellington
Ordnance Medical Department 257-8
Ordnance Select Committee 233, 235
Ordnance Survey 232
Osborne, Bernal, 110, 255, 256
Osborne, S. G., 3
other ranks, recruiting, 51-7
other ranks, regard for officers, 33, 34, 79-80, 109-10
other ranks, see also desertion; diet; discharge; drunkenness; education; good conduct; marriage; pay; pensions; promotion; punishment; noncommissioned officers

Paget, Sir Edward, 13, 27, 127
Paget, Lord George, 174
Pakington, Sir John, 259-60
Palmerston, Lord, 21, 42, 170, 181, 198, 206-8, 211, 231, 247, 249, 250, 259, 261
Panmure, Fox Maule, Lord, 16-18, 32, 42, 62-3, 69, 72-3, 87, 92, 135, 137-40, 150, 154, 173, 187, 207-8, 210, 216-17, 231, 255-7, 259, 262
Parkhurst 215
Parliament 8, 10, 11, 38, 62, 71-4, 80-2, 101, 103-4, 167, 171, 181, 203, 205, 209, 210, 230, 234, 246-7, 250, 253, 255
Pasley, Sir C. W., 27, 125, 132
paternalism 34, 79-80
pay, officers', 98, 112-13, 213, 241-2; see also half-pay
pay, other ranks', 57-9, 63, 67-8, 70, 83, 98, 100-1, 193
Pay Master General 94, 248
Peel, Frederick, 209
Peel, Sir Robert, 8, 13, 14, 37, 38, 87, 128, 181, 197-8, 200, 202, 205-7
Pembroke 197
Peninsular War 1, 6, 13, 14, 16, 19, 20, 24, 26, 73, 80, 86, 88, 98, 101, 120, 132, 149, 151, 152, 153, 158, 160, 168, 169, 236-7, 239, 241, 243-4, 269
Pennefather, J. L., 173
pensioners, 56, 68-9, 194-5, 203, 206
pensioners, enrolled, 10, 114, 194-6, 204-5, 215, 217
pensioners, in colonies, 187, 193-6
pensions 43, 55, 68-9, 71, 73, 100-2, 186
pensions, deferred, 215-18
Pentonville 84
percussion musket 23
Percy, J. W., 3
Peterloo 204
Philippart, Sir John, 20-2, 24, 29
physical standards for recruits 53-4
Pitt, Fort, 241-3
Plumstead 158

Plymouth 214
Poona 31, 32, 92, 138, 163-4
popularity of army 79-80, 164, 167, 171, 209
Portsmouth 30-3, 84, 91-2, 97, 138, 156, 158, 161, 170, 197, 200, 214
Pottinger, Sir Henry, 189
Presbyterians 86, 88
press 2-3, 37, 41, 271
press, military, 18-27, 30-1, 35, 39, 41, 71, 74, 87, 92, 97, 99, 103-4, 120, 123, 156, 184, 239, 243, 248, 270
Preston 61
Principal Storekeeper 233, 251
prisons 81, 83-5, 102
profession, army viewed as, 124, 129-31, 133, 135, 139, 180, 234, 269
promotion, 1840 commission on, 15-16, 114-15, 117, 118, 120-1, 242
promotion, 1854 commission on, 42, 120-1
promotion, current of, 98, 115, 118-19, 241-2, 258
promotion examinations 17, 24, 134-9, 153
promotion, favouritism in, 18, 29-30, 115-16, 121-2
promotion, from ranks, 21, 31, 97-9, 101, 135, 141
promotion, selective, 120-1, 135, 138
promotion, seniority, 117-18, 122
Prosser, G. W., 127, 155
Provisional Battalion 52, 157, 214-18
Prussia, army, 30, 100, 129, 134, 149, 150, 154, 161-2, 171, 182, 218, 271
punishment 12, 80-5, 103
punishment, corporal, 22, 29, 80-2, 104, 168
punishment, 1836 commission, 12, 67, 71, 81-3, 85, 92, 97-9, 235
Punjab 131; *see also* Sikh Wars
purchase of commissions 23, 24, 27, 110, 116-17, 122, 134, 139
purveyor, medical, 244-5

Quarterly Review 67, 87
Quarter Master General, duties of a department of, 147, 149, 151-2, 153
Quarter Master General, at the Horse Guards, 11, 13, 35, 42, 94, 149, 151, 184, 187, 231, 233, 235, 248, 251; *see also* Gordon
Quarter Master General, in the Crimea, 42, 173, 174, 237, 239, 260; *see also* Airey, de Ros
quartermasters 96, 98

Raglan, Fitzroy Somerset, Lord, as Military Secretary (1827-52), 6-7, 10, 11, 18, 35-6, 39, 111, 122, 216, 239, 240, 258
  not appointed Commander-in-Chief (1852), 35-6, 38, 40, 43
  as Master General of the Ordnance (1852-55), 35-6, 62, 158, 166, 171, 261
  as Commander-in-Chief in the Crimea (1854-55), 2-3, 29, 42, 99, 101, 148, 150, 152, 172-4, 220, 237, 261, 262, 270-1
railways 51, 61, 161, 164, 166, 201-2, 240
recruiting 51-7, 68-71, 74, 79, 182, 215-16, 218
recruiting system 21
recruits' training, *see* training
Reform Bill riots 203-5
regiment, importance of, 34, 56, 67-8, 92, 96, 99-100, 103-4, 134, 159, 180, 216, 219, 244, 258, 269
regiment, local links, 215-18
regiment, organisation of, 196, 211-19
regiments (numbered titles only; others indexed alphabetically)
  1st (King's) Dragoon Guards 41
  1st Foot 52
  2nd Dragoons 85
  2nd Foot 90
  3rd Light Dragoons 109
  4th Foot 90, 184

Index

6th Dragoons 55
7th Hussars 82
7th Royal Fusiliers 30, 31, 90
8th Hussars 174
9th Foot 131, 184
10th Hussars 112
11th Hussars 7, 34
11th Foot 30
12th Foot 97
13th Light Dragoons 54
13th Light Infantry 34, 65, 97
14th Foot 22, 97
18th Foot 173
19th Foot 34
21st Foot 96
23rd Royal Welch Fusiliers 52, 80
26th Foot 34, 51, 97
27th Foot 97
29th Foot 243-4
32nd Foot 54
38th Foot 2, 56
40th Foot 97
42nd Royal Highland Regiment 51, 53, 56
43rd Light Infantry 35, 137
52nd Light Infantry 26, 34, 35, 95
65th Foot 26
67th Foot 90
71st Highland Light Infantry 12, 51, 99-100, 111, 213
72nd Highlanders 51
74th Highlanders 51
77th Foot 24, 32
78th Highlanders 51, 184
79th Highlanders 18, 51, 99, 135, 169, 254
80th Foot 147
81st Foot 63, 90, 97
85th Light Infantry 213
86th Foot 34, 65
91st Foot 86, 196
92nd Highlanders 97, 184
93rd Highlanders 51, 90, 97
95th Foot 159, 167
98th Foot 184
Reid, David, 54

Reid, G. A., 136-7
Reigate 165
reserve army 71, 72, 74, 183, 198, 206, 207, 211, 215-19; *see also* manpower; militia; pensioners; volunteer corps
'respective officers' 232-3
retirement, officers', 21
Richards, A. B., 25
Richmond, Duke of, 247-9, 251, 258
Rifle Brigade 11, 20, 26-7, 35, 65, 70, 89, 119, 173
rifles 18, 41-2, 87, 157-8, 166-7, 254
Ripon, Lord, 16, 159, 165
Roberts, Frederic, 27, 89
Robertson, Frederick, 28, 29, 99, 123
Roebuck, J. A., 3, 6, 7, 103, 111, 238, 245
Rolt, John, 80
Ross, Sir Hew, 121, 134, 261
rotation of battalions 12, 26, 184-7, 195, 211, 213-14, 217-18
Routh, Sir Randolph, 59, 168, 236, 238, 240, 257
Royal African Corps 188
Royal Artillery 9, 22, 28-9, 37, 51, 54, 72, 89, 98, 117-18, 121-2, 125, 132-4, 140, 158, 201, 232, 236, 244, 249, 251, 254, 260, 261, 269
Royal Artillery Institution 25, 133-4
Royal Cambridge Asylum for Soldiers' Widows 64
Royal Canadian Rifles 193-6
Royal Engineers 9, 25, 27, 60, 98, 117-18, 121-2, 125, 132-3, 137, 157, 200, 232, 233, 249, 251, 260, 269
Royal Engineers Establishment, Chatham, 132, 157
Royal Engineers, *Professional Papers of*, 25, 132, 254
Royal Horse Guards 68
Royal Laboratory 261
Royal Malta Fencibles 189
Royal Military Academy, Woolwich, 26, 122-5, 132, 134, 140, 154-5,

232
Royal Military Asylum 10, 94-5
Royal Military Calendar 20
Royal Military College, Sandhurst, 10, 27, 99, 117, 125-30, 154-5, 173, 232
  Senior Department 135, 152-5, 235
Royal Military Magazine 25
Royal Navy 189-90, 197, 199, 205, 232, 257, 269, 270-1
royal prerogative 7, 35, 38, 103-4, 234, 250, 252, 253, 259
Royal Sappers and Miners 54, 64, 72, 91, 98, 127, 132, 167
Royal Staff Corps 151
Royal Waggon Train 11, 28, 238
Russell, Lord John, 8, 35, 36, 73, 84, 149, 165, 190, 191, 193, 195, 198, 202, 206-10, 214, 216, 217, 220, 247-9, 253-4, 259-61
Russell, W. H., 2
Russia, army, 11, 112, 161, 171-3, 182, 192, 267, 270
Ryder, John, 54

St. Helena 180, 183, 186, 192, 193
St. Kitts 187
St. Lucia 180, 185
St. Vincent 185
Salisbury plain 164
Sandhurst, *see* Royal Military College
savings banks 13, 34, 43, 64, 67-8
Scarlett, Sir, J. Y., 174
schoolmasters, training and appointment, 90, 92, 95-6
schools, public, and officer education 127-8, 140
schools, officers', 137-9; *see also* Royal Military Academy; Royal Military College
schools, regimental, 30, 31, 34, 61, 90-2, 94-7, 231
Scinde 13, 28, 65, 101, 173, 181, 184, 237
Scotland, as recruiting area, 51-2, 57, 89
Scotland, as station, 86, 150-1

Scots Fusilier Guards 99, 171
Scovell, Sir George, 126, 152, 153
Scrivener, Frederick, 92, 95, 138
Scutari 2, 3
sea power 189-90, 197-9, 238, 263, 269, 270-1
Seaton, Sir John Colborne, Lord, 34, 39, 41, 71, 73, 74, 125, 131, 166-9, 172, 193, 216, 239, 254, 268
Sebastopol 3, 4, 202, 221, 262, 270-1; *see also* Crimean War
Secretary at War, character and status, 10-13, 37, 38, 42, 87, 126, 199, 231, 233, 245, 247, 249, 252-3, 255-6, 262; *see also* Ellice, Edward; Grey, Henry; Hardinge, Henry; Herbert; Hobhouse; Macaulay; Panmure
Secretary of State for War, creation of office, 252-3, 255-6, 258-62
Secretary of State for War and the Colonies, character and status, 9-10, 15-17, 38, 42, 199, 229, 231, 249, 253, 255-6; *see also* Derby; Glenelg; Grey, Henry; Newcastle; Pakington
Senior, Henry, 26
Seymour, Lord, 259
Shah Shujah 101
Sheerness 197
Shoeburyness 158
Shorncliffe 34, 85, 162
Shrapnel N.S., 25
Sierra Leone 185, 188
Sikh War, 1st, 37, 101, 147, 159, 172, 201,
  2nd, 147, 172, 173
Simmons, J. L. A., 201
Simmons, T. F., 27
Simpson, Sir James, 173, 174
Sleigh, A. W., 24-5, 32
Small Arms Committee 233
Smith, Andrew, 2, 230, 241, 243-5
Smith, Sir Frederic, 91, 132
Smith, Sir Harry, 9, 39, 62, 131, 159-60, 161, 165, 166, 172, 189, 196, 237, 244

Index

Smyth, John, 61
Somerset, Lord Fitzroy, see Raglan
South Africa 9, 14, 41, 70, 72, 148-50, 172-3, 180, 184, 186-7, 189-91, 194-6, 213-14, 239, 244, 254, 260
Spearman, J. M., 127, 154
sport 13, 85
Spottiswoode, Andrew 23
staff 4, 14, 21, 125, 146-52, 174-5
staff appointments for Crimea 172-4
Staff, Chief of, 35-6, 149-50, 173
Staff College 153-5, 171
staff training, see training
Stocqueler, J. H., 24, 26, 28, 31, 103, 129, 159, 167, 232
Stovin, Sir Frederick, 39
Strafford, Sir John Byng, Earl of, 16, 27, 80
supply 231-2, 236-40, 256-7, 260, 262, 267-8; see also Commissariat; transport
supply of medicines 244-5, 268
Surveyor General 233

Taylor, Sir Herbert, 21, 149
temperance societies 66-7
Thackwell, Sir Joseph, 39, 173
Times, The, 2-3, 4, 27, 41, 87, 259
Tobago 180, 185
Torrens, A. W., 80, 161, 165-7, 171-2
towns as source for recruits 53, 57
training, artillery, 158
training, brigade, 28, 31, 41, 159-60, 169
training, field, 17, 31-2, 91, 155-8, 162, 166-8
training, recruits', 213, 214, 216, 218
training, staff, 42, 152-5, 159, 161-3
transport 262, 267-8
transportation, as punishment, 83
transport, land, 28, 29, 201, 236-40; see also Commissariat; railways
transport, sea, 180, 184, 238, 254
transport of sick 244
Treasury 12, 58-9, 67, 85, 88, 93, 95, 101, 133, 185, 230, 233, 234, 236-40, 245, 250, 257, 260

Trevelyan, Sir Charles, 139-40, 238, 240, 256-7
Trinidad 34, 180
Tulloch, A. M., 3, 12, 27, 58, 61, 109, 185-8, 194-5, 215

uniform, cost of, 51, 112-13
uniform, factor in recruiting, 51, 54
uniform, improvements in, 167, 232
United Service Club 23, 25
United Service Gazette 19, 21-4, 26-7, 31, 35, 37, 88, 117, 120, 135, 137-8
United Service Institution 20, 131-2, 155
United Service Journal 20, 22-3, 25-7, 30, 39, 60, 89, 114, 115, 131, 134, 162, 186
United Service Magazine 4, 20-1, 25, 27-8, 31, 37, 71, 99, 101, 117, 127, 199, 229
United States, army, 269
Utilitarianism 103, 247, 269

Van Diemen's Land 180, 196
Vauban's system of fortification 91, 127, 129, 131, 136
Victoria, Queen, 14, 15, 36, 38, 73, 99, 101, 251-2, 259
Vincennes 157
Vittoria, battle of, 158
Vivian, Sir Hussey, Lord, 26, 27, 34, 61, 71, 81, 118, 123, 185-6, 197, 249, 251-2
volunteer corps 25, 29, 203, 207, 209-10
'volunteering' system 55-6, 183-4, 215

Wakefield, E. G., 194
Wales, as recruiting area, 52, 89
Wales, as station, 165
Walpole, Spencer, 208, 210
War Office 10, 12, 21, 39-40, 87, 96, 100, 103, 135, 137, 229, 231, 235, 243, 245-6
War Office, consolidation of, 16-18,

21-2, 42, 199, 246-62
War Office, divided administration of, 235, 240, 246, 268
warrant rank 96
Waterloo, battle of, 1, 19, 73, 101, 149, 269
Watts, A. A., 22-4, 27-8, 88
Webb, Sir John, 258
Weedon 164
Wellington, Duke of, 6-7, 25-6, 68, 80-1, 104, 113, 128, 129, 249-50, 253, 271
   in Peninsular and Waterloo campaigns, 1, 50, 101, 119, 131, 146, 149, 151, 237, 239
   as Master General of the Ordnance (1818-27), 61, 118, 124, 181, 197
   as Commander-in-Chief (1827-28), 8, 247
   as Commander-in-Chief (1842-52), 8, 9, 13-20, 26, 28, 35-6, 37, 39, 40, 72-3, 82, 85, 87, 95, 96, 97, 102, 111, 115, 121-2, 135, 140, 157, 164-5, 167, 181, 187, 190, 191, 195, 197-207, 209, 211, 214-17, 219, 235, 246, 255-8
Wellington and United Services Benevolent Institution 64
Wellington College 128
West India Regiments 98, 115, 187-9, 196
West Indies 58, 61, 119, 183-7, 212, 214, 236, 245
Westminster College 128
Wetherall, G. A., 41, 150
Whigs 7, 8, 11-12, 17, 21, 139, 205, 247, 253, 268
Whittingham, Sir Samford, 27, 148, 161, 183
Wight, Isle of, 215
Wilkinson, Henry, 132
William IV 29, 250-2
Williams, W., 203
Winchester 164
Winchilsea, Lord, 36
Windward and Leeward Islands 58, 183, 185, 188, 245
wives of soldiers, *see* marriage
Wolseley, Garnet, 1, 4, 74
Wood, Sir Charles, 207, 257
Wood, Evelyn, 4
Wood, R. B., 171
Woolwich 157-8; *see also* Royal Military Academy

yeomanry 9, 24, 203-4, 209
York, Duke of, 6, 7, 8, 33, 79, 90, 231, 232, 234, 247, 253
Yorkshire 52, 209

UA
649
.S84
1984

UA 649 .S84 1984
Strachan, Hew.
Wellington's legacy

UA 649 .S84 1984
Strachan, Hew.
Wellington's legacy

$40.00

CANISIUS COLLEGE LIBRARY
BUFFALO, N.Y.